Ultimate Pentesting for Web Applications

Unlock Advanced Web App Security Through Penetration Testing Using Burp Suite, Zap Proxy, Fiddler, Charles Proxy, and Python for Robust Defense

Dr. Rohit Gautam
Dr. Shifa Cyclewala

www.orangeava.com

First published: May 2024

Published by: Orange Education Pvt Ltd, AVA™

Address: 9, Daryaganj, Delhi, 110002, India

275 New North Road Islington Suite 1314 London,

N1 7AA, United Kingdom

ISBN: 978-81-97081-87-3

www.orangeava.com

Dedicated To

My Beloved Parents:

Shri Braj Kishor Gautam

Smt Snehalata Gautam

and

My Siblings

Rahul, Shweta, and Sweety

- Dr. Rohit Gautam

My Beloved Parents for Love and Support and
My Guiding Light My Mother
Mrs. Naseem and My Father Mr. Arif

and

My Sisters
Saba and Saima

- Dr. Shifa Cyclewala

About the Authors

Dr. Rohit Gautam is currently working as CISO and Director at Hacktify Cyber Security. He holds an honorary Ph.D. in cyber security from German University and has been awarded as Cyber Security Samurai of the year award by Bsides Bangalore 2023. He has found various zero days in modern open source and commercial softwares. He is the member of Board of Education of various Universities and the author of best-selling Bug Bounty Course on e-learning platforms. He has been a trainer and speaker at various international conferences, including Gisec Global, California Tech Summit, OWASP, Bsides Bangalore and many more.

He is an active mentor for armed forces and defence personnels and certified instructor for National Security Database.

Dr. Shifa Cyclewala is currently working as CEO and Director at Hacktify Cyber Security. She holds an honorary Ph.D. in cyber security from German University. She has been awarded as a Women Influencer of the Year in Cyber Security by Bsides Bangalore 2023 and Top 20 Women Influencer in Security 2021 by Security Today. She is the member of Board of Education of various Universities and the author of best-selling Bug Bounty Course on various e-learning platforms.

She has been a trainer and speaker at various international conferences, including Gisec Global, California Tech Summit, OWASP, Bsides Bangalore, Wicked6, SIFS and many more. She actively promotes women in cyber security and leads the Mumbai Chapter for World Wide Women in Cyber Security (W3-CS).

About the Technical Reviewers

Ronit Bhatt, a seasoned cybersecurity professional, brings a wealth of expertise from his distinguished four-year career. His proficiency lies in Vulnerability Assessment and Penetration Testing (VAPT), complemented by a proven track record in Red Teaming within the realm of network security.

Throughout his career, Ronit has showcased a meticulous approach to identifying and mitigating security vulnerabilities. He employs advanced methodologies for conducting comprehensive security assessments and delivers actionable insights to fortify organizational defenses. His experience spans various projects, enabling him to navigate diverse environments and tailor security solutions to specific organizational needs.

Ronit's commitment to staying at the forefront of industry advancements ensures that he is well-versed in the latest offensive security techniques. This expertise allows him to simulate realistic threats and guide organizations toward robust cybersecurity postures.

Divesh Sood brings with him a wealth of experience spanning over 9 years in the realms of information security and cyber security. Holding a comprehensive educational background with an M.Sc in Network Technology and an M.Tech in Information Security, Divesh has traversed through diverse industry domains, from communications to insurance and logistics.

His journey has seen him assume pivotal roles, from spearheading research and development initiatives to providing invaluable technical consultancy and support. Currently, as the Founder of The Next Consultants, Divesh is dedicated to empowering national and international clients in fortifying their information security posture. His expertise extends to areas such as Risk Management, Third-Party Management, and ensuring compliance with stringent information security and quality standards.

Acknowledgements

Writing this cybersecurity book was made possible by the unwavering support, encouragement, and guidance of many. My heartfelt gratitude to family, friends, and mentors for their belief in me.

Special thanks to my team members and Mr. Aftab Khan for enriching discussions and invaluable insights. This book is a collective effort, and I'm deeply grateful to all who contributed. Your feedback, discussions, and support have been invaluable.

To everyone who has supported, encouraged, and inspired me along the way, thank you from the bottom of my heart. This book is as much yours as it is mine, and I hope it serves as a valuable resource for navigating the complex cybersecurity landscape.

I am honored to have embarked on this journey with such an incredible support system. Together, we have created something meaningful that will impact the cybersecurity community for years to come.

- Dr. Rohit Gautam

I extend my heartfelt gratitude to my family, friends, and mentors for their unwavering support throughout this journey. Special thanks to Saba Cyclewala for her valuable technical insights.

This book is a collaborative effort, and I'm deeply appreciative of all contributions. Your feedback and encouragement have been invaluable. To everyone who has supported and inspired me, thank you sincerely. This book reflects our collective dedication and passion for cybersecurity. I am honored to have embarked on this journey with such an incredible support system.

- Dr. Shifa Cyclewala

Preface

Welcome to the "*Ultimate Pentesting for Web Applications.*" In this guide, we explore various aspects of cybersecurity, including ethical hacking basics, Linux fundamentals, networking, cryptography, social engineering, reconnaissance, security testing, and authentication bypass techniques. Let's dive deeper into the specifics of what each chapter explores.

Chapter 1. The Basics of Ethical Hacking: Discover the fundamentals of ethical hacking, debunking myths, and laying the groundwork for your journey into cybersecurity.

Chapter 2. Linux Fundamentals: Learn essential Linux skills, from commands to scripting, unlocking the power of open-source technology.

Chapter 3. Networking Fundamentals: Explore the basics of network communication and protocols, empowering you to navigate the digital landscape with ease.

Chapter 4. Cryptography and Steganography: Unravel the secrets of securing information through encryption and steganography techniques.

Chapter 5. Social Engineering Attacks: Understand practical defense strategies against cyber threats, including phishing and identity manipulation.

Chapter 6. Reconnaissance and OSINT: Dive into cybersecurity intelligence, uncovering content discovery and OSINT resources.

Chapter 7. Security Testing and Proxy Tools: Fortify web applications using tools like Burp Suite and Fiddler, with real-world case studies for prevention.

Chapter 8. Cross-Site Scripting: Demystify digital threats like XSS attacks and learn mitigation strategies.

Chapter 9. Broken Access Control: Identify and fortify against web application security vulnerabilities, including privilege escalation.

Chapter 10. Authentication Bypass Techniques: Master strategies to fortify web security against authentication bypass attacks.

Join us on this journey through cybersecurity, where simplicity meets robust defense.

Get a Free eBook

We hope you are enjoying your recently purchased book! Your feedback is incredibly valuable to us, and to all other readers looking for great books.

If you found this book helpful or enjoyable, we would truly appreciate it, if you could take a moment to leave a short review with a 5 star rating on Amazon. It helps us grow, and lets other readers discover our books.

As a thank you, we would love to send you a free digital copy of this book, and a **30%** discount code on your next cart value on our official websites:

www.orangeava.com

www.orangeava.in (For Indian Subcontinent)

☑ **Here's how:**

Leave a review for the book on Amazon.

Take a screenshot of your review, and send an email to **info@orangeava.com** (it can be just the confirmation screen).

Once, we receive your screenshot, we will send you the digital file, within 24 hours.

Thank you so much for your support – it means a lot to us!

Downloading the code bundles and colored images

Please follow the links or scan the QR codes to download the
Code Bundles and Images of the book:

https://github.com/ava-orange-education/Ultimate-Pentesting-for-Web-Applications

The code bundles and images of the book are also hosted on
https://rebrand.ly/4d99e0

In case there's an update to the code, it will be updated on the existing GitHub repository.

Errata

We take immense pride in our work at **Orange Education Pvt Ltd,** and follow best practices to ensure the accuracy of our content to provide an indulging reading experience to our subscribers. Our readers are our mirrors, and we use their inputs to reflect and improve upon human errors, if any, that may have occurred during the publishing processes involved. To let us maintain the quality and help us reach out to any readers who might be having difficulties due to any unforeseen errors, please write to us at :

errata@orangeava.com

Your support, suggestions, and feedback are highly appreciated.

DID YOU KNOW

Did you know that Orange Education Pvt Ltd offers eBook versions of every book published, with PDF and ePub files available? You can upgrade to the eBook version at **www.orangeava.com** and as a print book customer, you are entitled to a discount on the eBook copy. Get in touch with us at: **info@orangeava.com** for more details.

At **www.orangeava.com**, you can also read a collection of free technical articles, sign up for a range of free newsletters, and receive exclusive discounts and offers on AVA™ Books and eBooks.

PIRACY

If you come across any illegal copies of our works in any form on the internet, we would be grateful if you would provide us with the location address or website name. Please contact us at **info@orangeava.com** with a link to the material.

ARE YOU INTERESTED IN AUTHORING WITH US?

If there is a topic that you have expertise in, and you are interested in either writing or contributing to a book, please write to us at **business@orangeava.com**. We are on a journey to help developers and tech professionals to gain insights on the present technological advancements and innovations happening across the globe and build a community that believes Knowledge is best acquired by sharing and learning with others. Please reach out to us to learn what our audience demands and how you can be part of this educational reform. We also welcome ideas from tech experts and help them build learning and development content for their domains.

REVIEWS

Please leave a review. Once you have read and used this book, why not leave a review on the site that you purchased it from? Potential readers can then see and use your unbiased opinion to make purchase decisions. We at Orange Education would love to know what you think about our products, and our authors can learn from your feedback. Thank you!

For more information about Orange Education, please visit **www.orangeava.com**.

Table of Contents

1. The Basics of Ethical Hacking **1**

Introduction 1

Structure 1

Introduction to the World of Ethical Hacking 2

Defining Ethical Hackers 5

Goals of White Hat Hackers 5

Benefits of White Hat Hackers 5

Steps to Become a White Hat Hacker 6

Ethical Hackers' Code 6

Understanding the Ethical Hacker's Role 7

The Need for Ethical Hackers 8

Ethical Hacking as a Dynamic Profession 8

Ethical Hacking Terminologies 9

Dispelling Hacking Myths 10

Ethical Hacking Unmasked 11

Creating Awareness about Ethical Hacking in the Real World 12

Demystifying Hacking 13

The Human Side of Hacking: Understanding Motivations and Psychology 14

Setting Up Your Ethical Hacking Environment 14

Creating a Secure Playground for Ethical Hacking 20

Preparing for the Journey Ahead 21

Resources for Aspiring Ethical Hackers 23

Becoming the Digital Guardian 23

Conclusion 24

2. Linux Fundamentals **25**

Introduction 25

Structure 25

Navigating the Linux World 25

Exploring Linux Distributions: Ubuntu, Kali, CentOS, and Parrot OS 26

Unleashing the Power of Kali Linux: A Hacker's Haven 27

Embarking on the Journey: Installing Kali Linux 28

Essential Linux Commands for Everyday Use 37

Unraveling the Linux Bootstrapping Process 45

`Init` *Systems:* `SysVinit` *versus* `systemd` 46

Mastering File Permissions 48

Understanding Linux File System Hierarchy 52

Bash Scripting Essentials 54

Writing Your First Bash Script 55

Conclusion 58

3. Networking Fundamentals 59

Introduction 59

Structure 59

Basics of Network Communication 60

Importance of Networks in Computing: The Unseen Foundations of the Digital Landscape 60

Decoding IP Addresses 60

IPv4 versus IPv6: Embracing Evolution 61

Understanding the Concept of IPv6 61

Moving to IPv6: A Guide for an Easy Switch 62

Subnetting Simplified: Creating Digital Neighborhoods 63

Decoding the Way Devices Talk in Networks 63

Importance of Ports: Special Tags for Network Chit-Chat 63

Unveiling Common Protocols: The Etiquette of Network Interaction 64

Types of Networks 64

Exploring the Neighborhood: Understanding Local Area Networks (LANs) 64

Home and Small Office Networks: The Everyday LAN Experience 65

LAN Components: The Building Blocks of Local Connectivity 65
LAN Configuration: Establishing Connections and Sharing Resources 66
Bridging Distances: Exploring Wide Area Networks (WANs) and the Internet 66
Connecting Networks Across Distances: The WAN Infrastructure 67
The Internet and Its Infrastructure: A Global Network of Networks 67
Untethered Connectivity: Exploring Wireless Networks and Wi-Fi Essentials 68
Wi-Fi Essentials: Making Wireless Connections Easy 68
Securing Wireless Networks: Protecting Your Digital Horizon 69
Network Topologies 69
Deciphering Network Architectures: Navigating the Kingdom of Network Topologies 70
Unlocking Network Power: Understanding Hybrid Topologies 73
Hybrid Topologies: A Fusion of Network Architectures 74
Essential Networking Commands 75
Pinging: Probing Connectivity with Echo Requests 76
Traceroute: Unveiling the Network Path 77
Checking Network Configuration with ifconfig 78
Deep Dive into Networking Protocols 80
Unveiling the Heart of Networking: Delving into the Transmission Control Protocol (TCP) 80
TCP: Making Sure Your Data Gets There Safely 81
TCP's Mechanism: A Symphony of Error Checking and Acknowledgment 81
Hands-on Example: Basic TCP Connection with Netcat 81
User Datagram Protocol (UDP): Exploring the Swift and Simple Side of Digital Communication in Kali Linux 83
NMAP Demystified 86
Introduction to NMAP – Unraveling the Secrets of Network Discovery in Kali Linux 86

Basic NMAP Commands 87
Practical NMAP Application: Security Auditing 87
Conclusion 90
4. Cryptography and Steganography **91**
Introduction 91
Structure 91
Decrypting Cryptography: Unraveling the Basics 92
Guardians of Data: Unveiling the Significance of Encryption in Cybersecurity 92
Real-Life Examples: How Encryption Safeguards Against Cyber Threats 93
Encryption: A Must-Have Tool in the Digital Age 94
The Art of Securing Information 94
The Hidden Threats: Revealing Dangers to Information Security 95
Cyber Intruders: The Crafty Infiltrators 95
Malware: The Hidden Threat in the Digital Shadows 96
Real-Life Impact of Data Breaches: A Serious Warning 96
Types of Encryption 97
Symmetric Encryption: Sharing a Secret 97
Public-Key Encryption: The Digital Locksmith 98
Digital Envelopes: Sealing Information for Secure Transit 98
Hashing: The Digital Fingerprint 99
Digital Signatures: Sender Verification 99
Symmetric Encryption: Sharing a Secret to Secure Communication 100
The Shared Key Analogy: A Practical Example 100
Asymmetric Encryption: A Digital Lock with Two Unique Keys 101
The Public Key: A Widely Accessible Key 102
The Private Key: A Closely Guarded Secret 102
Establishing a Secure Channel of Communication: A Two-Key Partnership 102

Ensuring Data Integrity with Hash Functions: Digital Fingerprints 104
Cryptographic Ciphers 106
Types of Ciphers: Substitution and Transposition 107
Symmetric and Asymmetric Ciphers: Sharing Secrets and Public Keys 107
Advanced Encryption Standard (AES): The Guardian of Our Digital Secrets 108
Data Encryption Standard (DES): A Legacy of Innovation and Security 108
Unveiling Steganography: The Art of Concealing Information in Plain Sight 109
Beyond Encryption: A Complementary Approach 109
Tools for Cryptography and Steganography 111
Understanding the Role of Cryptographic Tools 111
Exploring Common Cryptographic Tools: A Look at the Toolkit 111
Hands-On with Open-Source Encryption Software 112
Digital Camouflage: Using Steganography Tools to Hide Data in Plain Sight 115
Steganography Tools: A User-Friendly Approach 116
Exploring the Unseen: Unveiling Advanced Cryptographic Concepts 117
Quantum Cryptography: Harnessing Quantum Mechanics to Encrypted Communication 117
Homomorphic Encryption: Performing Computations on Encrypted Data 117
Conclusion 118
5. Social Engineering Attacks 119
Introduction 119
Structure 119
Social Engineering Unmasked: A Practical Guide to Understanding and Defending Against Deceptive Attacks 120

The Significance of Understanding Social Engineering 120
Empowering Readers to Protect Themselves and Their Organizations 120
Unmasking the Deceptive World of Social Engineering 121
Social Engineering Fundamentals 121
Unveiling the Roots of Social Engineering Through History 122
The Psychology Behind Social Engineering 122
Unlocking Social Engineering Tactics 122
Decrypting the Motivations Behind Deceptive Attacks 124
Common Goals of Social Engineering Attacks 125
Social Engineering versus Traditional Cyber Threats 125
The Human Element: The Achilles' Heel of Cybersecurity 125
Unlocking Phishing Tactics 126
Diving into the World of Phishing: A Crafty Hunt for Sensitive Data 126
Email Phishing: The Broad Net Approach 126
Spear Phishing: Precision Strikes 126
Vishing: Phishing by Phone 126
Unveiling the Phishing Puzzle: Understanding the Deceptive Blueprint 127
Defend Yourself Against Phishing: Stay Alert and Informed 127
Red Flags to Identify Phishing Attempts 128
Unmasking Phishing: Real-Life Tales of Deception 128
Shielding Yourself from Phishing Attacks: Navigating the Digital Terrain Safely 129
Real-Life Deceptions 130
Unveiling the Masters of Deception: Case Studies of Notable Social Engineering Attacks 130
ID and Homograph Attacks 131
ID Attacks 132
Impersonation: Entering the Domain of False Identities 132
Delegation: A False Grant of Authority 132

Common ID Attack Techniques 132
Protecting Against ID Attacks: Staying Vigilant and Verifying Identities 133
Homograph Attacks 133
The Illusion of Authenticity: Misdirection through Character Similarity 133
Common Homograph Attack Techniques 133
Defending Against Homograph Attacks: A Guide to Vigilance and Detail 134
The Role of a Social Engineer 135
Professional Roles of Social Engineers 135
Inside the Social Engineer's Mind: Understanding Empathy and Persuasion 136
Essential Skills of a Social Engineer 136
Exploring Social Engineering Tools 136
Working of these Tools 138
Functionalities and Applications 138
Ethical Use of Social Engineering Tools for Educational Purposes 138
Future Trends in Social Engineering 140
Recommendations for Staying Ahead of Evolving Threats 140
Unveiling the AI Menace: Case Studies in Advanced Social Engineering Attacks 141
Conclusion 142
Quiz: Mastering Social Engineering Awareness 142
Reinforcement Tasks 145
6. Reconnaissance and OSINT 146
Introduction 146
Structure 146
Web Reconnaissance Unveiled: A Beginner's Guide to OSINT and Beyond 146
Definition and Importance 147

Unveiling the Importance in Web Application Penetration Testing 147

The Reconnaissance Process 150

Overview of the Intelligence Gathering Lifecycle 150

Unlocking the Importance of Thorough Reconnaissance 151

Real-World Instances 152

Google Dorking: Discover Concealed Information 153

Creating Effective Google Dorks 154

Key Google Dork Operators 155

Hands-on Exercise: Uncovering Hidden Information 158

Ensuring Privacy and Ethical Considerations in Google Dorking 158

Case Studies: Real-world Scenarios Showcasing the Power of Google Dorking 159

Shodan: The Search Engine for Devices 160

Understanding Shodan's Capabilities and Limitations 160

Responsible Shodan Usage 161

Harnessing Shodan: Real-world Case Studies in Penetration Testing 161

Practical Exercises on Finding Devices with Potential Vulnerabilities 162

Asset Discovery: WHOIS, ASN Lookup 166

WHOIS Basics: Understanding WHOIS and Its Role in Reconnaissance 166

Understanding WHOIS 167

Working of WHOIS 167

Role of WHOIS in Reconnaissance 167

Limitations of WHOIS 167

Beyond WHOIS 168

Impact of Privacy Regulations on WHOIS Data Availability 169

Practical Exercises of WHOIS 171

Decoding Autonomous System Numbers (ASNs) for Advanced Asset Discovery 172

Decoding SSL/TLS Certificates: Understanding Their Importance in Reconnaissance....174
Demystifying SSL/TLS Certificates....174
Significance of SSL/TLS Certificates in the World of Reconnaissance....175
Basics of SSL/TLS: Understanding the Encryption Process....175
Recent Changes in SSL/TLS Protocols and Certificate Standards....176
Delving into SSL/TLS Certificate Analysis....177
Content Discovery Basics: Unveiling the Hidden Gems of the Web....179
Importance of Revealing Concealed Directories and Files....179
Techniques for Content Discovery....180
Leveraging Historic Datasets....182
Other OSINT Resources....184
Conclusion....186
7. Security Testing and Proxy Tools....187
Introduction....187
Structure....187
Introduction to Security Testing in Web Applications....188
The Crucial Role of Security Testing Amidst Cyber Challenges....188
Types of Security Testing Tools....189
Selecting Appropriate Security Testing Solutions....190
Optimizing the Use of Security Testing Tools....190
Burp Suite –A Swiss Army Knife for Web App Testing....191
Delving into the Burp Suite Arsenal....191
Unlocking Burp Suite's Potential....192
Proxy Features: Unveiling Burp Suite's Interception Process....192
The Essence of Proxying....192
Unlocking Proxy Potential....193
Spider and Scanner Tools: Unraveling Web Application Vulnerabilities....193
The Spider's Web-Crawling Process....193
The Scanner's Vigilant Vulnerability Detection....193

Intruder and Repeater: Unleashing Advanced Techniques for Web App Security ... 193

Intruder: Your Digital Ninja ... 194

Repeater: Your Precision Marksman ... 194

ZAP Proxy – Open-Source Testing with ZAP ... 199

ZAP Proxy: A Versatile Arsenal for Web Security ... 200

ZAP Proxy's Unparalleled Features ... 200

Unlocking ZAP Proxy's Full Potential ... 200

Installation and Configuration ... 201

Automated Scanning: Unleashing ZAP Proxy's Automation Process ... 203

Automated Scanning Excellence with ZAP Proxy ... 203

Automating Scanning with ZAP ... 204

Fiddler – Unraveling the Mysteries of Web Traffic ... 205

Fiddler's Role in Web Traffic Analysis ... 205

Benefits of Fiddler for Web Traffic Analysis ... 205

Practical Applications of Fiddler ... 206

Installation and Configuration of Fiddler ... 206

Inspecting HTTP/HTTPS Traffic: Unraveling the Web's Digital Conversations ... 208

Charles Proxy – Debugging Web Applications ... 211

Charles Proxy: A Debugging Companion ... 211

Charles Proxy's Debugging Prowess ... 211

Practical Debugging Scenarios ... 211

Installation and Configuration of Charles Proxy ... 213

Integration of Proxy Tools with Web Browsers ... 215

Case Studies: Analyzing Security Breaches and the Role of Proxy Tools in Prevention ... 216

Reporting and Documentation ... 219

Documentation Best Practices ... 221

Conclusion ... 222

8. Cross-Site Scripting **223**
Introduction 223
Structure 223
Understanding Cross-Site Scripting 224
Overview of XSS 224
Impact of XSS 224
Working of XSS: Unraveling the Attack Mechanism 225
Types of XSS: Reflected, Stored, and DOM-based 226
Reflected XSS: The Bait and Switch of Cross-Site Scripting 226
Stored XSS: When Innocence Turns into Information Theft 228
Reflected XSS versus Stored XSS: A Side-by-Side Comparison 230
DOM-based XSS: Unraveling the Digital Puppeteer 232
Understanding Sources and Sinks in DOM-Based XSS 234
Reflected XSS, DOM-based XSS, and Stored XSS: Hands-on 235
Attack Vectors and Payloads 238
Attack Vectors 238
Payloads: Unveiling the Digital Mischief 239
Crafting Payloads: Try It Yourself 240
Payload Balancing 241
Detection of XSS Vulnerabilities 243
Mitigation and Best Practices 244
Input Validation and Sanitization: Fortifying Your Web Defenses 245
Real-world Case Studies of Notable XSS Attacks 246
Conclusion 249
9. Broken Access Control **250**
Introduction 250
Structure 250
Broken Access Control: An Exploitable Vulnerability 250
Broken Access Control: Unveiling the Myths and Misconceptions 252
Insecure Direct Object Reference 253

Detecting IDOR Vulnerabilities: Tools and Techniques 255
Privilege Escalation: Vertical and Horizontal 256
Climbing the Ladder: Understanding Vertical Privilege Escalation 256
Moving Sideways: Unveiling Horizontal Privilege Escalation 258
Access Control Vulnerabilities 260
Implications of Weak Access Controls: Unraveling the Domino Effect 261
Identifying and Exploiting Vulnerabilities 263
Interactive Learning: Exposing the Mysteries of Broken Access Control 263
Ethical Hacking Techniques: Safeguarding by Breaking Safely 265
Secure Access Control Design 267
Case Studies in Access Control Failures 269
Conclusion 271
10. Authentication Bypass Techniques 272
Introduction 272
Structure 272
Unlocking the Web: Mastering Authentication Bypass Techniques 273
The Significance of Authentication Bypass 273
Authentication Bypass Fundamentals 273
Introduction to Common Authentication Mechanisms 274
Recent Advancements and Emerging Trends in Authentication Technology 276
Response Manipulation – Cracking the Code of Authentication 277
Response Manipulation – Bypassing the Gatekeeper with Header Hijinks 278
Status Code Manipulation - Decrypting the Guardian's Signals 281

Status Code Manipulation – Deciphering the Cipher for Unrestricted Entry 283

OTP Bypass Techniques 284

Putting Your Knowledge to the Test: Hands-on Experiments with OTP Bypass Techniques 286

Two-Factor Authentication (2FA) Bypass: Unveiling the Cracks in the Fortress 286

Two-Factor Authentication (2FA) Bypass: Hands-on Training for Security Champions 288

Session Fixation Attacks 289

Hijacking the Session: Real-World Examples and Preventive Measures 291

Understanding Vulnerability: Real-World Examples 291

Credential Reuse Attacks 292

Unmasking the Domino Effect: Practical Demonstrations of Credential Reuse Attacks 294

Captcha Bypass Methods: Cracking the Code 295

Methods for Evading Captcha Controls 295

Advancements in CAPTCHA Technology 296

Safeguarding the Treasure: Minimizing Captcha Bypass Risks 298

Cracking the Code: Hands-on Guide to Bypassing Captchas 298

Cookie Manipulation: Crumbling the Cookie Jar 299

Tampering with the Tokens: Techniques for Exploiting Cookie Manipulation 300

Securing Your Digital Delicacies: Mitigating Risks of Cookie Tampering 300

Unmasking the Sweet Deception: Practical Examples and Countermeasures against Cookie Manipulation 301

Securing Your Digital Treats: Navigating the Cookie Jar Safely 303

Token-Based Authentication Bypass 303

Cracking the System: Exploiting Weaknesses in Token-Based Authentication 304

Safeguarding the Treasure: Addressing Risks in Token-Based Authentication..........304
Breaking the Code: Hands-on Exercises for Token-Based Authentication Bypass..........305
Conclusion..........306
Index..........307

CHAPTER 1
The Basics of Ethical Hacking

Introduction

Welcome to the enthralling journey into **The Basics of Ethical Hacking.** This chapter serves as a gateway to the dynamic world of cybersecurity, introducing you to the fundamental concepts of ethical hacking. We will decipher the role of ethical hackers, unravel the terminologies that surround this field, and debunk common myths associated with hacking. As we delve into creating awareness about ethical hacking in real-world scenarios, our focus will be on demystifying the art of hacking itself. Practical insights await as we guide you through the process of setting up your ethical hacking environment, laying the foundation for the exciting exploration that lies ahead. By the end of this chapter, you will not only have a clear understanding of ethical hacking but also be well-prepared for the enlightening journey that follows.

Structure

In this chapter, we will cover the following topics:

- Introduction to the World of Ethical Hacking
- Defining Ethical Hackers
- Understanding the Ethical Hacker's Role
- Ethical Hacking Terminologies
- Dispelling Hacking Myths
- Creating Awareness about Ethical Hacking in the Real World
- Demystifying Hacking
- Setting Up Your Ethical Hacking Environment
- Preparing for the Journey Ahead

Introduction to the World of Ethical Hacking

Imagine you have a house filled with valuable belongings. To protect your house from intruders, you install locks, alarms, and security cameras. But what if there are hidden weaknesses in your security system that you do not know about?

This is where ethical hackers come in. They are like security experts who come to your house to test your security system and find any hidden weaknesses. They do not try to break into your house to steal your belongings; instead, they want to help you make your house more secure so that bad guys can't get in.

Ethical hackers use special tools to scan your house for vulnerabilities, just like doctors use special machines to scan your body for illnesses. They carefully examine every part of your house, from the locks on the doors to the alarms in the windows, to make sure everything is working properly.

If they find any weaknesses, they will tell you about them so you can fix them. They might also give you advice on how to improve your security overall, such as by installing stronger locks or adding more security cameras.

Ethical hackers are like the good guys in the world of cybersecurity. They work hard to protect people's information and systems from bad guys. They are the ones who help to make the internet a safer place for everyone.

In the world of cybersecurity, ethical hacking serves as a digital guardian, safeguarding systems from malicious attacks. Just as a locksmith uses their skills to test and reinforce the security of locks, ethical hackers employ their expertise to identify vulnerabilities and protect against cyber threats.

For instance, ethical hackers were hired to hack into a family's smart home, revealing potential security flaws and demonstrating the importance of securing IoT devices. Their work involves gaining authorized access to systems to shield them from cybercriminals, a practice known as penetration testing. It is akin to a security audit, but to uncover weaknesses that could be exploited by hackers.

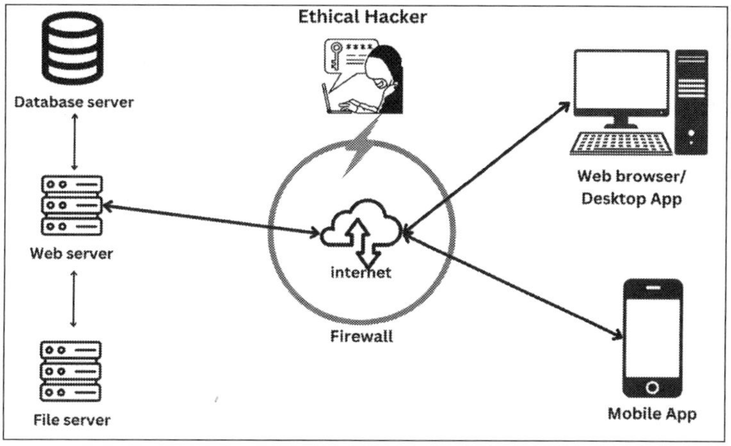

Figure 1.1: *Ethical Hacker in Action*

In the ever-expanding world of technology, cybersecurity has emerged as a top priority. As we rely more on digital platforms for communication, commerce, and the storage of sensitive information, protecting these systems against cyber threats is more important than ever.

Consider an extensive digital landscape, a domain of interconnected networks and systems, each of which represents a critical component of our modern reality. The lifeblood of organizations and individuals flows like an elaborate river system through this terrain.

The digital landscape, like the physical landscape, is vulnerable to cyberattacks conducted by unscrupulous actors attempting to exploit weaknesses for personal gain or to cause harm.

In this volatile context, ethical hackers emerge as the digital world's defenders. They are the skilled navigators of this ever-changing terrain, their expertise honed to identify hidden flaws, test security measures, and protect against potential cyber threats.

The world of cybersecurity is constantly evolving as malicious actors devise new techniques and exploit emerging technologies. Ethical hackers must stay abreast of these advancements, continuously expanding their knowledge and adapting their skills to stay ahead of the curve.

Consider the rise of cloud computing, which stores and processes sensitive data on remote servers. Ethical hackers must become acquainted with the specific security problems provided by cloud settings to ensure that these systems are appropriately safeguarded against cyberattacks.

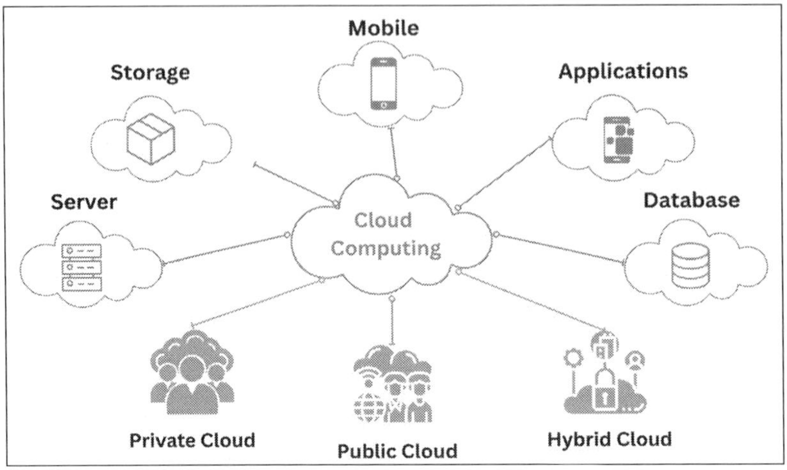

Figure 1.2: *Cloud Computing Model*

Similarly, the growth of mobile devices and the Internet of Things (IoT) has added to the cybersecurity landscape's complexity. Ethical hackers must understand the complexities of these technologies to keep our digital devices and networked networks secure.

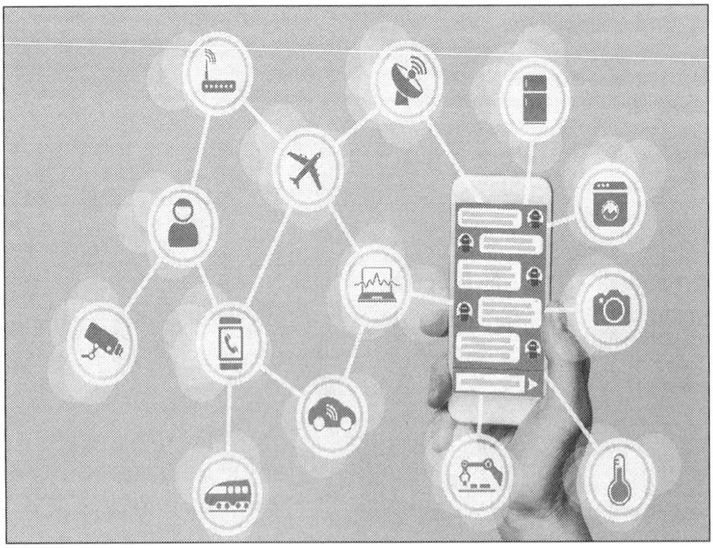

Figure 1.3: *IoT Devices*

The demand for ethical hackers is growing at an exponential rate as organizations across industries seek to fortify their defenses against cyber threats. Ethical hackers are not merely technicians; they are strategic thinkers, problem solvers, and creative minds capable of navigating the complexities of the digital landscape and outsmarting malicious actors. In essence, ethical hackers are the sentinels of the digital space, safeguarding the integrity of our interconnected world.

Defining Ethical Hackers

Ethical hackers, often referred to as white hat hackers, are not motivated by financial gain or malicious intentions. Their driving force is a deep sense of responsibility and a commitment to safeguarding the digital world. They navigate the intricacies of computer systems to uncover hidden vulnerabilities, utilizing a distinctive blend of technical expertise, problem-solving skills, and creativity.

Ethical hackers are crucial in finding and addressing security flaws before they are exploited by cybercriminals. The guiding values of ethical hacking include obtaining legal approval, maintaining accurate documentation, and fostering open communication with companies. By developing a code of conduct, ethical hackers differentiate themselves from cybercriminals, avoid legal troubles, and create trust among enterprises in need of their services.

Goals of White Hat Hackers

White hat hackers are primarily responsible for identifying and repairing flaws in computer systems and networks. This is accomplished by:

- **Penetration testing:** Simulating attempts at hacking to find flaws that attackers may exploit.
- **Vulnerability scanning:** Scan a system for known vulnerabilities using automated tools.
- **Security audits:** Examine the security rules and processes of a system to detect any flaws.

White hat hackers also play a vital role in boosting cybersecurity awareness and educating others on the most recent risks and best practices.

Benefits of White Hat Hackers

White hat hackers provide several benefits to organizations, including:

- **Minimized Risk of Cyberattacks:** Through the identification and resolution of vulnerabilities, white hat hackers contribute to lowering the risk of cyberattacks for organizations.
- **Enhanced Security Posture:** White hat hackers play a crucial role in assisting organizations in enhancing their overall security posture. They provide recommendations to improve security policies, procedures, and technologies.
- **Heightened Peace of Mind:** Organizations gain increased peace of mind by having their systems tested by white hat hackers. This assurance stems from the knowledge that their systems are less susceptible to compromise.

Steps to Become a White Hat Hacker

There are several steps you can take to become a white hat hacker, including:

1. Get an education in computer science or information security.
2. Gain experience in penetration testing, vulnerability scanning, or security audits.
3. Earn certifications in ethical hacking.
4. Join a professional organization for ethical hackers.

Their expertise, specific skills, certifications, and knowledge of infrastructure technology and programming languages are essential in safeguarding the digital world. Ethical hackers are instrumental in preventing data compromise, strengthening security, and enhancing customer trust. Their proactive approach to improving security and their commitment to protecting sensitive data contribute to building trust and confidence in the digital world.

Ethical Hackers' Code

Ethical hackers, like their counterparts in the physical world, adhere to a strict code of conduct, ensuring that their actions remain within the bounds of legality and ethics. This code serves as a moral compass, guiding their activities and ensuring that their skills are employed for the greater good.

The ethical hacker's code is founded upon the following principles:

- ***Consent:*** Ethical hackers obtain explicit permission from the system's owner before conducting any testing. They recognize that systems and networks are not playgrounds and that unauthorized access, even for testing purposes, is a violation of trust and privacy.
- ***Scope:*** Ethical hackers operate within the agreed-upon scope of testing. They respect the boundaries set by system owners, avoiding unauthorized access to sensitive data or systems beyond the agreed-upon scope. This ensures that their testing activities remain focused and relevant to the specific vulnerabilities they are investigating.
- ***Confidentiality:*** Ethical hackers maintain confidentiality regarding any vulnerabilities discovered during testing. They understand that disclosing vulnerabilities before they can be addressed could put systems at risk, and they are committed to responsible disclosure practices.
- ***Non-destructive Testing:*** Ethical hackers avoid causing any damage or disruption to the system during testing. They recognize that their actions should not harm the systems they are assessing, and they take all necessary

precautions to minimize any potential impact.

- ***Transparency:*** Ethical hackers communicate openly and honestly with system owners throughout the testing process. They provide regular updates on their findings, and they are always willing to answer questions and address concerns.
- ***Legal Compliance:*** Ethical hackers operate within the confines of the law. They are aware of and abide by relevant laws and regulations, ensuring that their activities remain legal and ethical.
- ***Respect for Privacy:*** Ethical hackers respect the privacy of individuals and organizations. They avoid collecting or accessing personal information that is not relevant to the testing process, and they handle all sensitive data with the utmost care and discretion.
- ***Continuous Learning:*** Ethical hackers recognize that the cybersecurity landscape is constantly evolving, and they are committed to continuous learning. They stay abreast of emerging threats and vulnerabilities, and they regularly update their skills and knowledge to remain effective in their role.

Through upholding this code, ethical hackers showcase their allegiance to ethical standards and their unwavering commitment to safeguarding the digital domain. They transcend being merely skilled technicians; they embody responsible professionals who grasp the significance of trust, transparency, and integrity.

Fundamentally, the ethical hacker's code stands as a guiding light for ethical conduct in the continually evolving world of cybersecurity. It serves as a compass for ethical hackers as they navigate the intricacies of the digital landscape, ensuring that their actions are motivated by a higher purpose –the protection of the integrity of our interconnected world and the preservation of the valuable assets it holds.

Understanding the Ethical Hacker's Role

Imagine a world where castles are digital and the treasure is sensitive information–this is where the ethical hacker steps in. Their mission is not to plunder but to fortify these digital castles against potential invaders. Let us unfold the layers of their role.

- ***Unveiling Vulnerabilities:*** Ethical hackers function as cyber detectives, diligently scouring computer systems, networks, and applications for vulnerabilities. They embody the digital Sherlock Holmes, meticulously scrutinizing every aspect to unearth potential weak points before they can be exploited by malicious actors.
- ***Simulating Cyber Threats:*** In a simulated cyber battleground, ethical hackers mimic the tactics of real attackers. They use their expertise to launch controlled cyberattacks, testing the defenses of systems and identifying areas that need reinforcement.

- ***Penetration Testing:*** A key aspect of the ethical hacker's role is penetration testing, commonly known as pen testing. It is akin to stress-testing a bridge to ensure it can withstand heavy loads. Ethical hackers conduct simulated attacks to evaluate the robustness of digital systems, uncovering vulnerabilities and suggesting strategies for improvement.
- ***Ethical Hacking Principles:*** Ethical hackers follow a set of principles that guide their actions. Integrity, responsibility, and respect for privacy serve as their guiding principles. Their objective extends beyond merely identifying vulnerabilities; they aim to address them ethically, enhancing the resilience of systems without jeopardizing user privacy or compromising data integrity.
- ***Staying One Step Ahead:*** In the ever-evolving landscape of cybersecurity, ethical hackers must be a step ahead of potential adversaries. They continuously update their skills, adapt to new technologies, and anticipate emerging threats to effectively safeguard digital assets.
- ***Educating and Empowering:*** Beyond finding vulnerabilities, ethical hackers play a crucial role in educating organizations and individuals. They share insights gained from their experiences, helping others understand the importance of cybersecurity and empowering them to take proactive measures.

The Need for Ethical Hackers

As organizations increasingly rely on technology for their operations, ethical hackers act as guardians, ensuring the resilience and integrity of digital infrastructures. Their ethical and responsible approach distinguishes them from malicious hackers, as they leverage their skills to protect rather than exploit. By continuously assessing and enhancing cybersecurity measures, ethical hackers contribute to the overall safety of sensitive data, financial assets, and the privacy of individuals.

In essence, the need for ethical hackers stems from the constant and evolving nature of cyber threats. Their proactive efforts serve as a first line of defense, mitigating risks, and fostering a secure digital environment for businesses and individuals alike. As we navigate the complexities of the digital age, ethical hackers stand as crucial allies in the ongoing battle against cyber threats.

Ethical Hacking as a Dynamic Profession

The dynamic nature of ethical hacking lies in its continuous adaptation to evolving cyber threats. Ethical hackers are tasked with not only understanding current attack methodologies but also anticipating future trends. This requires a commitment to ongoing learning, staying updated on the latest technologies, and gaining insights into emerging cyber threats.

Moreover, ethical hacking is a profession that values creativity and out-of-the-box thinking. As cyber threats become more sophisticated, ethical hackers need to employ innovative strategies to identify and counter potential vulnerabilities. The profession thrives on problem-solving and the ability to anticipate the strategies of malicious hackers.

Ethical hacking is not merely a job; it is a mindset–a commitment to securing digital ecosystems ethically and responsibly. Professionals in this field act as digital guardians, ensuring the safety of critical information, sensitive data, and the privacy of individuals.

Ethical Hacking Terminologies

- ***Vulnerabilities - Weaknesses in the Armor***

  Definition: Vulnerabilities are like chinks in the armor of a computer system. They are weaknesses that naughty actors could exploit to gain unauthorized access, disrupt operations, or steal data.
  Example: Think of a vulnerability as an unlocked door in your house. Ethical hackers find and fix these unlocked doors to keep your digital space safe.

- ***Exploits - Using Weaknesses for Mischief***

  Definition: Exploits are like magic spells hackers use to take advantage of vulnerabilities. They are pieces of code or techniques that turn weaknesses into opportunities for unauthorized access or mischief.
  Example: If a vulnerability is like an open door, an exploit is a spell that allows a mischievous character to slip through unnoticed.

- ***Penetration Testing - Ethical Hacking Practice***

  Definition: Penetration testing, also known as pen testing, is akin to a cybersecurity practice session. Ethical hackers engage in simulated cyberattacks to discover and rectify vulnerabilities before malicious actors can exploit them.
  Example: Picture a sports team honing their skills to face opponents. Ethical hackers engage in similar practice sessions to keep your digital 'team' in peak condition against potential cyber adversaries.

- ***Vulnerability Scanning - Cybersecurity Check-Up***

  Definition: Vulnerability scanning is comparable to a routine health check-up for your computer systems. It autonomously detects and categorizes vulnerabilities, keeping you a step ahead of potential cyber threats.
  Example: Like a doctor utilizes tools to assess your health, vulnerability scanners employ specialized tools to evaluate your digital systems for weaknesses.

- ***Risk Assessment - Cybersecurity Crystal Ball***

  Definition: Risk assessment is like gazing into a cybersecurity crystal ball. It is the process of predicting and evaluating potential cyber threats and vulnerabilities to prioritize security efforts.

  Example: Before going on a journey, you check the weather forecast. Similarly, organizations assess cybersecurity risks to prepare for potential storms.

- ***Patch Management - Updating Digital Armor***

  Definition: Patch management is like updating the armor of your digital castle. It is the process of applying security patches to fix vulnerabilities in software and operating systems.
  Example: Just as you update your phone's apps for new features and security, patch management ensures your digital tools stay strong against cyber threats.

- ***Firewalls - Digital Bouncers***

  Definition: Firewalls serve as the digital bouncers at the entrance of your network party. They oversee and manage incoming and outgoing traffic, permitting only trusted guests to enter.
  Example: Imagine a bouncer meticulously inspecting IDs at a club entrance. Similarly, firewalls scrutinize digital IDs to determine who gains entry and who remains outside.

- ***Intrusion Detection Systems (IDS) - Digital Alarm Systems***

  Definition: Intrusion Detection Systems are like digital alarm systems for your network. They continuously scan for suspicious activity and alert you when something does not seem right.
  Example: If someone tries to break into your house, the alarm system notifies you. IDS does the same for your digital space.

- ***Intrusion Prevention Systems (IPS) - Digital Security Guards***

  Definition: Intrusion Prevention Systems act like digital security guards. They not only detect suspicious activity but actively block or mitigate cyberattacks to prevent harm.
  Example: If an alarm goes off and a security guard stops an intruder, that is similar to what IPS does in the digital world.

- ***Encryption - Digital Secret Code***

  Definition: Encryption is like speaking a secret code. It converts data into a scrambled format that only those with the correct decoder can understand.
  Example: Imagine sending a letter written in a secret language that only you and the recipient understand. Encryption ensures your digital messages stay private.

Dispelling Hacking Myths

Welcome to the myth-busting kingdom of hacking. Let us unravel common misconceptions and bring clarity to the fascinating world of cybersecurity.

1. **Myth: All hackers are criminals**

   Reality: Not all hackers wear black hats. There are ethical hackers, the white hats, who use their skills for good. They work to strengthen digital defenses, uncover vulnerabilities, and protect against cyber threats.

2. **Myth: Hacking is always malicious**

   Reality: Hacking itself is neutral; it is the intent that matters. Ethical hacking exists, where experts use their skills to identify and fix vulnerabilities. It is a positive force in the ongoing battle to secure digital landscapes.

3. **Myth: Ethical hacking is just a cover-up for cybercrime**

   Reality: Ethical hacking is a legitimate and crucial cybersecurity practice. Organizations hire ethical hackers to fortify their digital infrastructure. It is about defense, not deception.

4. **Myth: Only highly skilled professionals can be ethical hackers**

   Reality: While expertise is valuable, ethical hacking is also accessible to dedicated learners. Training programs and certifications exist to help individuals develop the skills needed to contribute positively to cybersecurity.

5. **Myth: Hacking is always illegal**

   Reality: Unlawful access and malicious activities are illegal, but ethical hacking is legal and often essential for maintaining a strong security posture. Legal frameworks and agreements govern ethical hacking practices.

6. **Myth: Cybersecurity is only an issue for big corporations**

   Reality: Small businesses and individuals are also vulnerable. Cyber threats target anyone with a digital presence. Ethical hacking is valuable for organizations of all sizes to protect against potential attacks.

Ethical Hacking Unmasked

Now, let us unveil the truth about ethical hacking and its positive impact on cybersecurity.

- ***Fortifying Digital Defenses***

  Ethical hacking is a preventative measure against cyber risks. Ethical hackers improve businesses' overall cybersecurity posture by detecting and addressing vulnerabilities before they may be exploited.

- ***Identifying Weaknesses Before Cybercriminals***

  Ethical hackers operate as digital detectives, identifying flaws that criminal actors may exploit. They prevent attackers from getting an advantage by proactively identifying and resolving these flaws.

- ***Ethical Hacking as a Learning Tool***

  Ethical hacking is more than simply a job for cybersecurity experts; it is a lifelong learning process. It hones skills, keeps people informed about emerging threats, and fosters a proactive mindset in the face of evolving cyber challenges.

- ***Proactive Cybersecurity Measures***

  Ethical hacking extends past reactive tactics. It fosters a proactive cybersecurity culture in which firms continually analyze and improve their security procedures to remain ahead of possible attacks.

- ***Ethical Hackers as Cyber Guardians***

  Ethical hackers are the digital sphere's defenders. They aim to safeguard and empower people and organizations so that they may traverse the digital world with confidence, knowing that their digital assets are in skilled hands.

- ***A Noble Contribution to a Safer Digital World***

  Ethical hacking is, in essence, a noble contribution to a safer digital environment. It debunks misunderstandings about hacking while stressing its beneficial influence on cybersecurity. As you read on, you will learn more about the critical role ethical hackers play in protecting our linked digital lives.

Creating Awareness about Ethical Hacking in the Real World

Ethical hacking, often shrouded in mystery and misconceptions, plays a critical role in safeguarding our digital world. Far from being a malicious endeavor, ethical hacking is a force for good, a proactive approach to identifying and addressing vulnerabilities before they can be exploited by cybercriminals.

- ***Securing the Financial Sector***

  In the financial sector, where vast sums of money and sensitive data flow, ethical hackers are indispensable allies. They probe the systems of banks, investment firms, and payment processors, uncovering hidden weaknesses that could lead to financial fraud or data breaches. Their efforts have prevented countless cyberattacks, protected financial stability, and safeguarded the hard-earned savings of individuals and businesses.

- ***Protecting Critical Infrastructure***

  Our contemporary society heavily depends on crucial infrastructure, encompassing power grids, transportation networks, healthcare systems, and governmental agencies. Ethical hackers assume a pivotal role in securing these vital systems, actively identifying and addressing potential vulnerabilities that might otherwise disrupt essential services and pose widespread harm. Their efforts have contributed to averting power outages, preserving communication channels, and even preventing physical damage to critical infrastructure components.

- ***Safeguarding the Internet of Things (IoT)***

  The increased use of Internet of Things (IoT) devices, which range from smart household appliances to industrial sensors, has introduced a new layer of complexity to the cybersecurity arena. Ethical hackers are leading the effort in safeguarding these networked gadgets, exposing hidden flaws, and preventing their inclusion in large botnets or targeted assaults. Their actions are critical in protecting consumers against privacy breaches and companies from operational interruptions caused by hacked IoT devices.

- ***Promoting Cybersecurity Awareness and Education***

  Ethical hackers go beyond identifying and fixing vulnerabilities; they also play an important role in raising awareness and teaching others about cybersecurity best practices. They enable individuals and businesses to defend themselves against cyber dangers by delivering seminars, attending conferences, and developing instructional materials. Their efforts have helped to foster a culture of cybersecurity awareness, making the digital world a safer place for everyone.

These real-world examples demonstrate the huge influence of ethical hacking on securing our digital lives and the crucial systems that support modern civilization. We can celebrate ethical hackers' unrelenting dedication to creating a better and more secure digital world for everybody by acknowledging their good contributions.

Demystifying Hacking

Movies have long portrayed hacking as a glamorous, adrenaline-fueled activity where lone hackers swiftly penetrate high-security systems with a few strokes of the keyboard. While this dramatized depiction may be entertaining, it bears little resemblance to the reality of ethical hacking, a methodical, rigorous, and often tedious process that demands patience, expertise, and a deep understanding of computer systems and networks.

In the real world, ethical hacking is far from the flashy, action-packed portrayal often seen on television and in movies. It involves meticulous research, careful analysis, and a structured approach to identifying and exploiting vulnerabilities. Ethical hackers must possess a comprehensive knowledge of programming languages, operating systems, network protocols, and security tools, enabling them to navigate the complexities of modern computer systems and uncover hidden weaknesses.

Hackers are frequently portrayed in movies as socially awkward, reclusive individuals with malicious intent. In contrast, ethical hackers come from diverse backgrounds and motivations, driven by a genuine desire to protect and strengthen cybersecurity. They are often employed by organizations to conduct penetration testing, vulnerability scanning, and security audits, and they work with management and technical teams to address vulnerabilities and enhance security measures.

The Human Side of Hacking: Understanding Motivations and Psychology

The world of hacking is not just about technical expertise; it also involves a deep understanding of human behavior and psychology. Ethical hackers must be able to think like malicious actors, anticipating their tactics and techniques to effectively identify and address potential threats.

One of the key motivations for ethical hackers is the challenge and intellectual stimulation that the field provides. The ever-evolving nature of cybersecurity presents a constant stream of new puzzles to solve and new techniques to master, keeping ethical hackers engaged and constantly learning.

Another driving force for ethical hackers is the desire to make a positive impact on the world. They recognize the importance of cybersecurity in protecting sensitive data, critical infrastructure, and the digital lives of individuals and organizations. Their efforts help to safeguard our online world and prevent cyber attacks that can cause significant harm.

Ethical hackers also find satisfaction in the collaborative nature of their work. They often work in teams, sharing knowledge, exchanging ideas, and collaborating to tackle complex cybersecurity challenges. This sense of camaraderie and shared purpose fosters a strong sense of community among ethical hackers.

In conclusion, ethical hacking is far from the Hollywood stereotype of lone hackers with malicious intent. It is a multifaceted field that demands a combination of technical expertise, analytical thinking, and an understanding of human behavior. Ethical hackers are driven by a desire to protect and strengthen cybersecurity, working collaboratively to address emerging threats and safeguard our digital world.

Setting Up Your Ethical Hacking Environment

Welcome to the digital space, where ethical hacking takes center stage. To embark on this exciting journey, you need to have the right tools in your arsenal. Let us explore the essential components of your digital toolkit.

- **NMAP (*Network Mapper*):** Think of NMAP as your digital compass. It helps you navigate and map networks, providing valuable insights into connected devices, open ports, and potential vulnerabilities. This is a must-have for any ethical hacker.

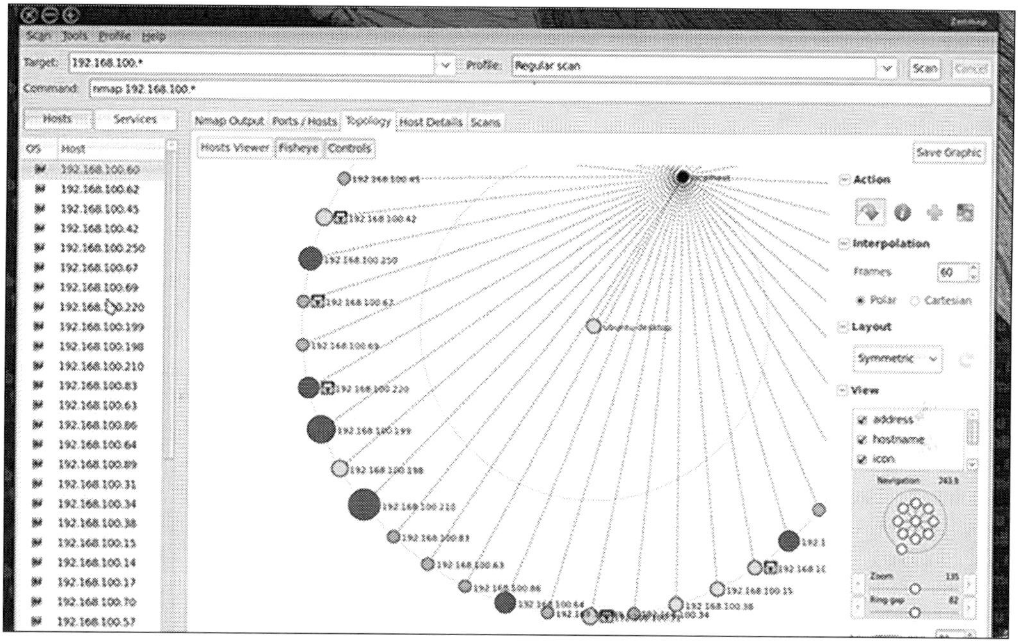

Figure 1.4: *NMAP Interface*

- ***Wireshark:*** Consider Wireshark for your digital microscope. It allows you to dissect and analyze network traffic. With Wireshark, you can uncover hidden patterns, detect anomalies, and identify potential security threats.

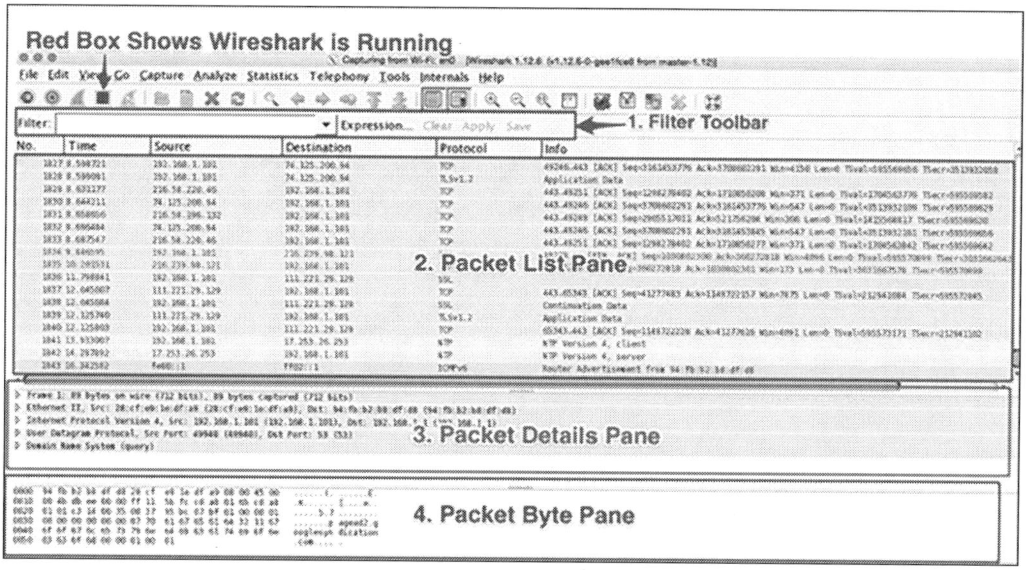

Figure 1.5: *Wireshark Interface*

- ***Metasploit Framework:*** Metasploit functions as a virtual Swiss Army knife. It is a robust framework for creating, testing, and executing exploits. Metasploit allows you to mimic cyber-attacks to better understand and defend against them.

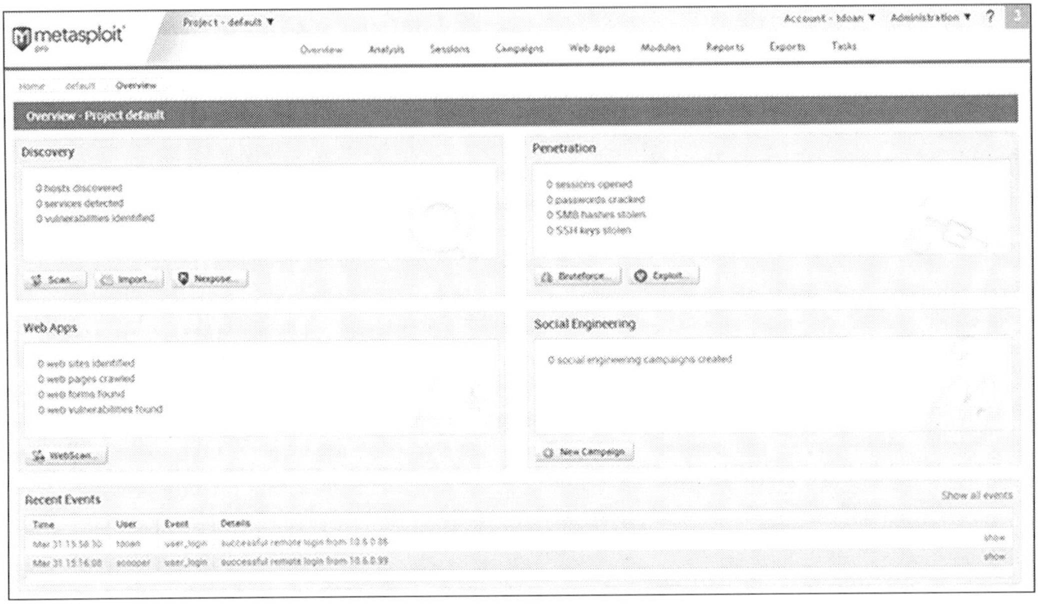

Figure 1.6: *Metasploit Interface*

- ***Burp Suite:*** Burp Suite is your web application security digital detective kit. It assists you in identifying and repairing vulnerabilities in web applications. Burp Suite is a must-have tool for ethical hackers, from scanning to crawling.

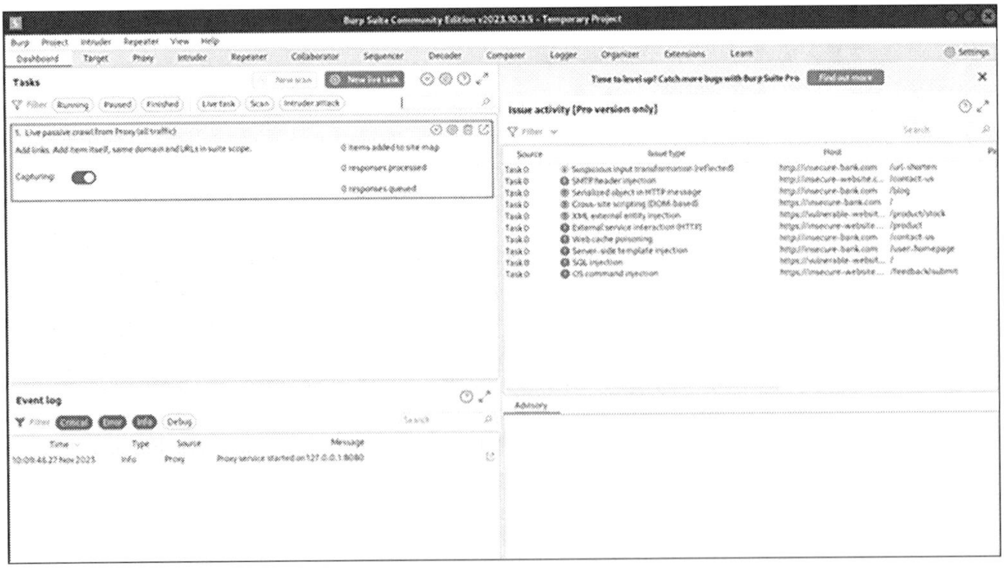

Figure 1.7: *Burpsuite Interface*

- ***Aircrack-ng:*** Aircrack-ng is the go-to tool for ethical hackers exploring wireless network security. It aids in analyzing Wi-Fi network security, finding flaws, and guaranteeing strong encryption standards.

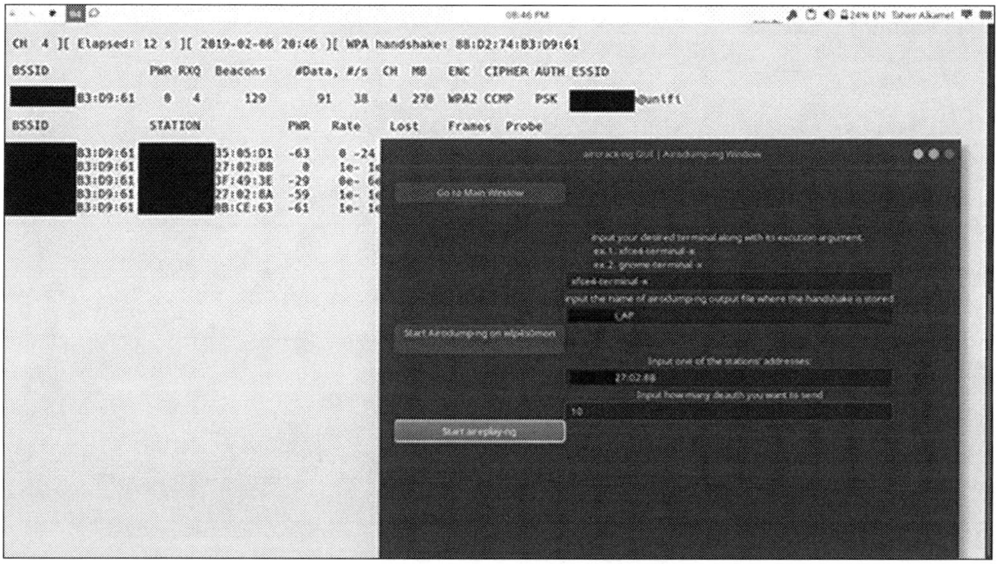

Figure 1.8: *Aircrack-ng Interface*

- ***John the Ripper:*** Consider John the Ripper as your digital lock pick. It is a password-cracking tool that ethical hackers use to test the strength of passwords and strengthen security against unauthorized access.

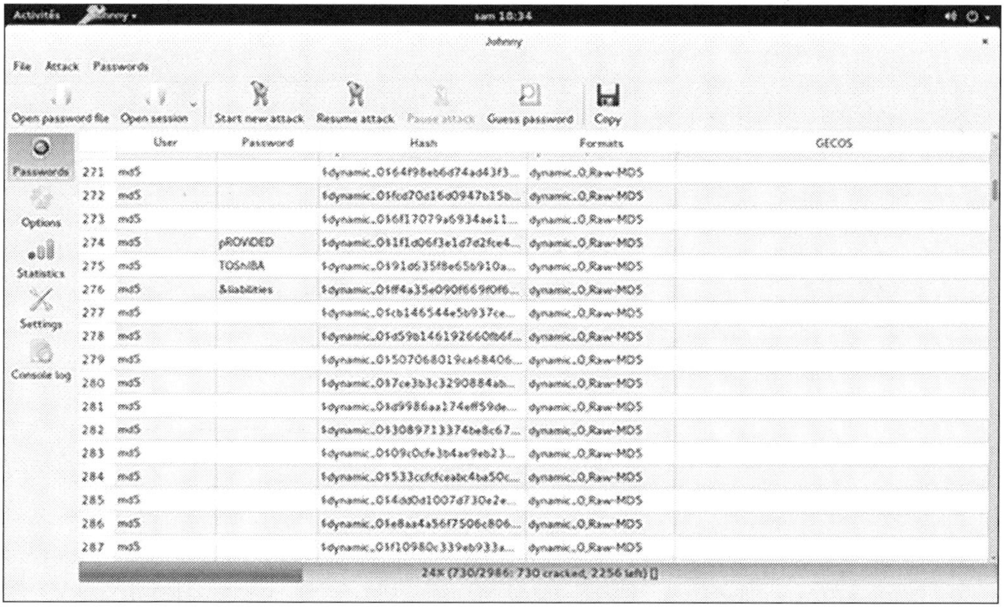

Figure 1.9: *John the Ripper Interface*

- **OWASP ZAP (Zed Attack Proxy):** In the world of web application security, OWASP ZAP is a treasure trove. It helps identify vulnerabilities in web applications and acts as a proactive shield against potential cyber threats.

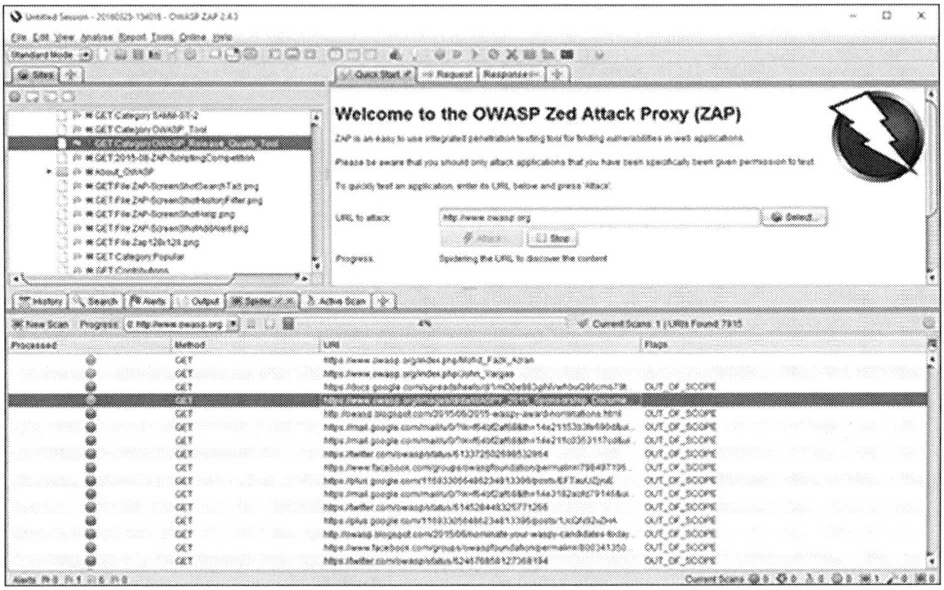

Figure 1.10: OWASP ZAP *Interface*

- ***Hashcat:*** Hashcat is your digital puzzle solver. It is a versatile password-cracking tool that supports various algorithms. Ethical hackers use Hashcat to test password strength and enhance security measures.

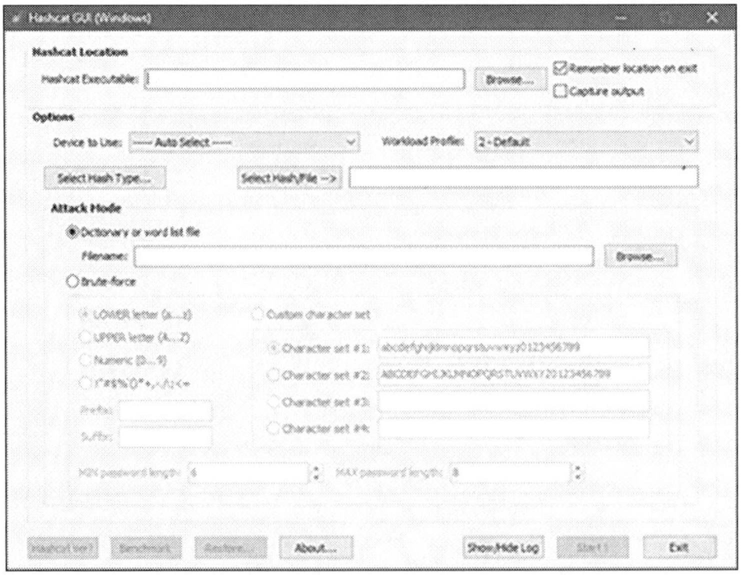

Figure 1.11: *Hashcat Interface*

- ***Snort:*** Imagine Snort as your digital security guard. It is an open-source intrusion detection system that helps detect and prevent network intrusions, providing an extra layer of defense in your ethical hacking endeavors.

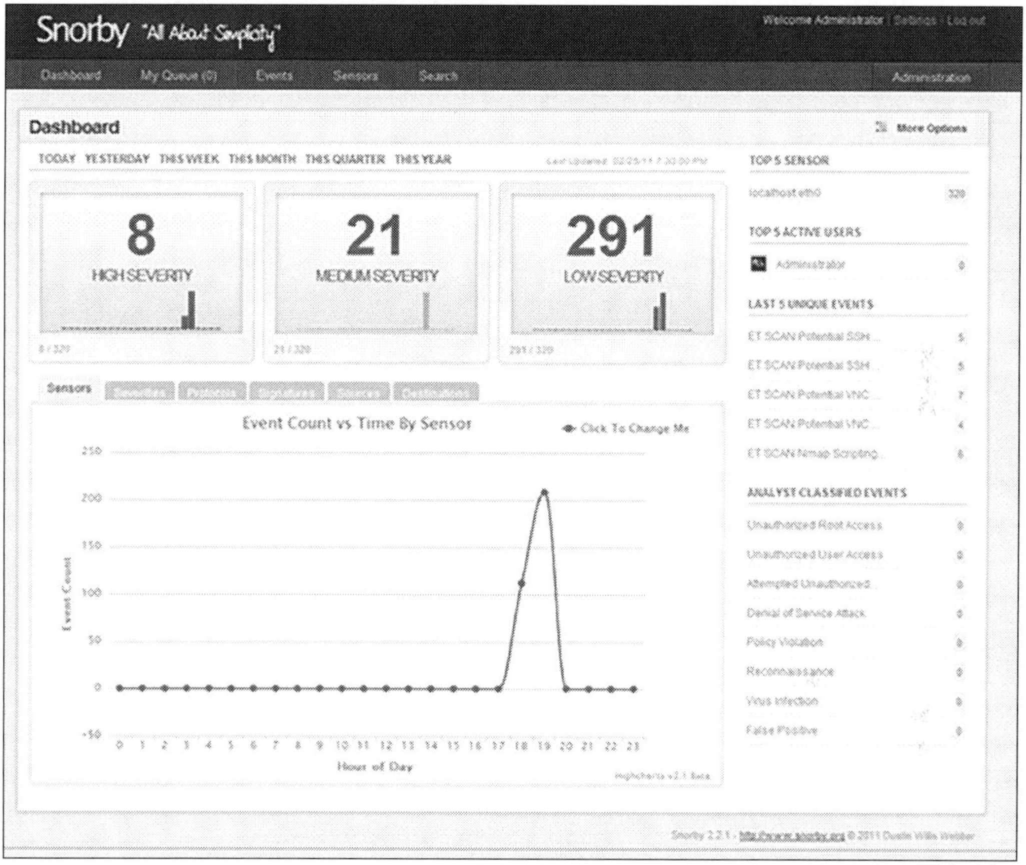

Figure 1.12: *Snort Interface*

- ***Hydra:*** Hydra is your digital multi-tool for brute-force attacks. It supports various protocols and services, making it invaluable for ethical hackers assessing the strength of authentication mechanisms.

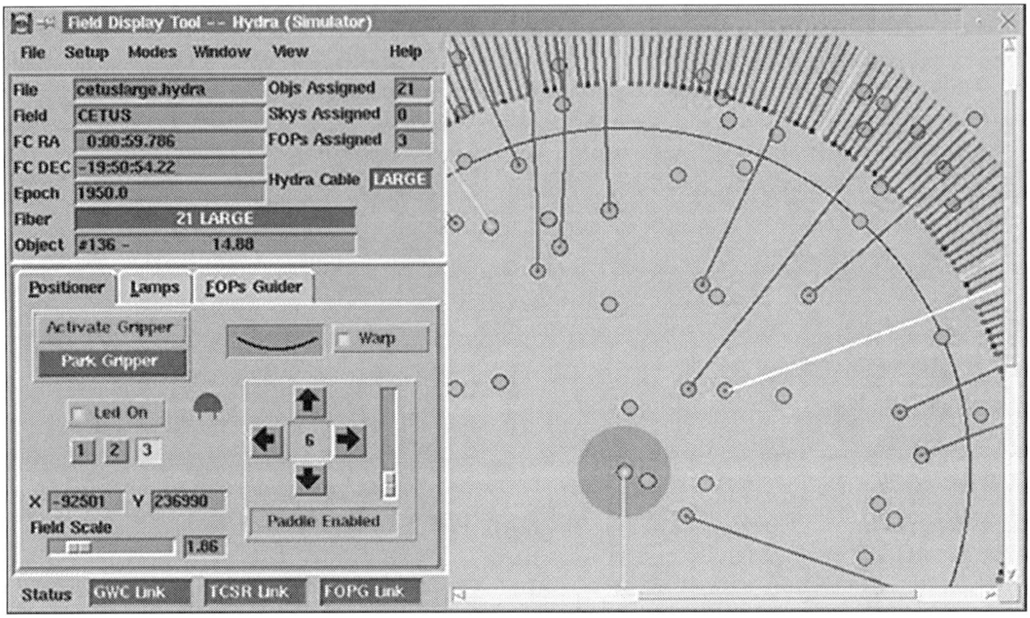

Figure 1.13: *Hydra Simulator Interface*

Your digital toolkit is your key to ethical hacking success. As you explore the chapters ahead, you will learn how to wield these tools effectively, turning your curiosity into expertise in the ever-evolving landscape of cybersecurity.

Creating a Secure Playground for Ethical Hacking

Now that you have your digital toolkit, it is time to set up a secure playground for your ethical hacking experiments. Follow this step-by-step guide to ensure a safe and controlled environment.

1. ***Virtualization Software:*** Start by installing virtualization software like VMware or VirtualBox. These tools allow you to create isolated virtual machines (VMs) where you can conduct your ethical hacking experiments without affecting your main operating system.

2. ***Operating System for Ethical Hacking:*** Select an operating system specifically designed for ethical hacking, such as Kali Linux or Parrot Security OS. These OS distributions come pre-loaded with a plethora of hacking tools, saving you time on installations.

3. ***Network Configuration:*** Set up a virtual network within your virtualization software. This enables you to create multiple VMs that can communicate with each other, simulating a real-world network environment.

4. ***Snapshots:*** Before conducting any experiments, take snapshots of your virtual machines. Snapshots allow you to revert to a previous state if anything goes awry during your ethical hacking endeavors.

5. ***Isolation:*** Ensure that your ethical hacking environment is isolated from your regular home or work network. This prevents any accidental interference with other devices and ensures a controlled testing environment.

6. ***Backup:*** Back up any important data on your main system before diving into ethical hacking activities. While the goal is to create a secure environment, it is always wise to have a safety net in case of unforeseen circumstances.

7. ***Educational Resources:*** Arm yourself with educational resources and guides specific to ethical hacking. Having reference materials on hand will enhance your learning experience and provide guidance as you navigate your secure playground.

8. ***Responsible Practices:*** In your hacking experiments, use responsible and ethical procedures. Keep your virtual environment lawful and approved, and avoid any acts that may compromise real-world systems.

9. ***Continuous Learning:*** Ethical hacking is a never-ending learning process. Keep abreast with the most recent tools, methods, and ethical hacking strategies. To broaden your expertise, join online communities, participate in fora, and interact with other ethical hackers.

10. ***Ethical Guidelines:*** Finally, in your ethical hacking attempts, follow ethical principles. The idea is to improve cybersecurity rather than compromise it. Approach your experiments with a feeling of responsibility and a desire to have a positive impact on the field.

Preparing for the Journey Ahead

Welcome to the dynamic and ever-evolving world of ethical hacking. As you embark on this journey, it is essential to embrace the learning curve that comes with mastering the art of ethical hacking. Here is how you can build a mindset for continuous learning:

- ***Curiosity as Your Guide:*** Curiosity is the fuel that propels ethical hackers forward. Approach every challenge with a curious mindset, eager to understand the intricacies of systems, the nuances of vulnerabilities, and the solutions that fortify digital defenses.
- ***Learn from Challenges:*** Challenges are not hindrances in the world of ethical hacking, but rather stepping stones. Each challenge provides an opportunity to learn new things and improve your skills. Accept problems as opportunities to improve your skillset and deepen your understanding of cybersecurity.

- ***Networking and Collaboration:*** Ethical hacking thrives on community collaboration. Establish connections with fellow ethical hackers, participate in fora, and actively engage in discussions. Networking not only broadens your understanding but also exposes you to a variety of perspectives and problem-solving approaches.
- ***Stay Informed:*** The cybersecurity landscape undergoes constant evolution. Stay abreast of the latest trends, emerging threats, and cutting-edge technologies. Follow trustworthy blogs, subscribe to cybersecurity newsletters, and engage in webinars to ensure your knowledge remains current and up-to-date.
- ***Experiment and Apply Knowledge***: Theory is valuable, but practical experience is indispensable. Set up your virtual lab, experiment with tools and techniques, and apply your knowledge to real-world scenarios. Hands-on experience enhances your understanding and builds confidence in your abilities.
- ***Accept Failure as a Stepping Stone:*** In ethical hacking, not every attempt will be a success, and that is perfectly normal. Accept failure as a part of the learning process. Analyze what went wrong, iterate on your approach, and use each setback as a stepping stone toward improvement.
- ***Seek Mentorship***: Mentorship can significantly accelerate your learning journey. Seek guidance from experienced ethical hackers, either through formal mentorship programs or informal connections. Learning from someone with practical experience provides valuable insights and shortcuts in your learning curve.
- ***Continuous Training:*** Invest in continuous training through workshops, online courses, and certifications. The field of ethical hacking offers a multitude of learning resources. Stay enrolled in courses that cover both foundational and advanced topics to ensure a well-rounded skill set.
- ***Celebrate Milestones:*** Recognize and take pride in your accomplishments throughout your journey. Whether it is conquering a challenging exercise, obtaining a certification, or securing a virtual environment, each milestone serves as evidence of your advancement in the world of ethical hacking.
- ***Adaptability is Key:*** The field of ethical hacking is dynamic, marked by the continuous emergence of new challenges and threats. Develop adaptability as a fundamental skill, being prepared to pivot, acquire new tools and techniques, and adjust your strategies to navigate the ever-evolving cybersecurity landscape.

Keep in mind that the ethical hacking journey is not a sprint but a marathon. Embrace the learning curve with enthusiasm, recognizing that each lesson learnt brings you one step closer to becoming a proficient ethical hacker.

Resources for Aspiring Ethical Hackers

Now, let us explore a curated list of books, courses, and online platforms that will serve as invaluable resources on your journey to becoming an ethical hacker:

Online Platforms:

- **TryHackMe:** An online platform that offers a variety of cybersecurity courses as well as hands-on labs.
- **HackTheBox:** A platform that provides virtual machines for practicing ethical hacking.
- **HackerOne:** A bug bounty platform that recognizes ethical hackers for discovering and reporting vulnerabilities.

Certifications:

- **CEH (Certified Ethical Hacker):** Offered by EC-Council, this certification validates your skills in ethical hacking.
- **OSCP (Offensive Security Certified Professional):** A certification that requires passing a 24-hour hands-on exam, proving practical skills in penetration testing.
- **CompTIA Security+:** A foundational certification covering various aspects of IT security, including ethical hacking.

Keep in mind that this list serves as a foundation. Delve into these resources, uncover your specific areas of interest, and customize your learning journey accordingly. The field of ethical hacking is expansive, and ongoing learning is the essential factor for staying ahead in this ever-evolving field. Best of luck on your journey!

Becoming the Digital Guardian

As you conclude this chapter and prepare to venture into the broader sphere of ethical hacking, remember that you are not just acquiring skills– you are becoming a digital guardian. The role of an ethical hacker is more than a profession; it is a commitment to safeguarding the digital world. Here is a final encouragement:

1. ***A Noble Calling:*** Ethical hacking is not just about breaking into systems; it is about building a safer digital world. Your skills are a force for good, protecting individuals, organizations, and the integrity of the online space.
2. ***Positive Impact:*** Your journey as an ethical hacker contributes to strengthening cybersecurity postures, protecting sensitive data, and promoting a culture of awareness. Every action you take has a positive impact on the digital community.

3. ***Continuous Contribution:*** Embrace the responsibility that comes with your newfound knowledge. Whether you aspire to protect your organization, pursue a career in cybersecurity, or simply satisfy your curiosity, your journey as an ethical hacker is a continuous contribution to the evolving landscape of digital security.

4. ***Guardianship of the Digital Kingdom:*** As a digital guardian, you hold the keys to fortifying digital fortresses. Your commitment to ethics, continuous learning, and responsible practices sets you apart as a defender of the interconnected world.

5. ***Unlocking the Secrets:*** Accept the adventure, reveal the secrets, and bravely enter the world of ethical hacking. Your commitment to becoming a professional ethical hacker will not only affect your future but will also help to create a safer and more secure digital world for years to come.

Conclusion

As we conclude this chapter on the basics of ethical hacking, you have embarked on a thrilling journey into the realm of ethical hacking. We have outlined the meaning of ethical hacking, delved into the ethical hacker's role, explained key terminologies, dispelled common myths and showcased the real-world impact of ethical hacking. By demystifying hacking, you have gained valuable insights into its responsible and positive applications.

Kudos on taking those initial steps toward becoming an ethical hacker. Your curiosity and dedication to learning are truly praiseworthy. In the upcoming chapter, we will delve into the foundational concepts of Linux, a vital groundwork for ethical hacking. Get prepared to enrich your skills and understanding in the cybersecurity domain. The excitement continues!

CHAPTER 2
Linux Fundamentals

Introduction

Building on the ethical hacking basics learned in the previous chapter, we dive into **Linux Fundamentals**. This chapter equips you with essential skills, from mastering Linux commands and understanding file permissions to navigating the file system and delving into Bash scripting. We will explore the heart of open source and discover how contributions shape the future of technology. Whether you are a novice or an enthusiast, unlock the keys to open-source mastery in this concise exploration of Linux fundamentals.

So, join us on this adventure through time and technology. Let us explore how Linux, with its humble beginnings, has become a beacon of open-source excellence, forever altering the course of the computing landscape. Get ready to unlock the doors to a world where collaboration knows no bounds and where the penguin reigns supreme—the Linux world awaits!

Structure

In this chapter, we will cover the following topics:

- Navigating the Linux World
- Unleashing the Power of Kali Linux
- Essential Linux Commands for Everyday Use
- Unraveling the Linux Bootstrapping Process
- Mastering File Permissions
- Understanding Linux File System Hierarchy
- Bash Scripting Essentials

Navigating the Linux World

Linux, often heralded as the penguin-powered marvel of the tech world, has an origin story as compelling as its capabilities. Our adventure begins with Linus Torvalds, a computer science student from Finland, who sparked a revolution in the world of operating systems.

Picture the early '90s, when proprietary operating systems dominated the landscape. Against this backdrop, Linus, driven by a desire to create something collaborative and free, unveiled the first version of Linux in 1991. Little did he know that this collaborative experiment would evolve into a global force, a testament to the power of open-source development.

As we delve deeper into Linux's history, we uncover the spirit of collaboration that defines its core. The open-source community, a diverse and passionate collective, played a pivotal role in shaping Linux into the robust and versatile system we know today.

Linux's journey is not just a technological tale but a narrative that disrupts the status quo. Its impact resonates across industries, from powering servers and embedded systems to being the foundation for Android devices. The story of Linux is a celebration of community, innovation, and the boundless possibilities that arise when minds collaborate in the open.

Linux is in a constant state of evolution, propelled by the collaborative efforts of the open-source community and the dynamic demands of the ever-evolving technological terrain. With the rising significance of artificial intelligence, cloud computing, and edge computing, Linux stands ready to assume an increasingly pivotal role in influencing the trajectory of computing in the times ahead.

Exploring Linux Distributions: Ubuntu, Kali, CentOS, and Parrot OS

Welcome to the vibrant domain of navigating the Linux world. In this segment, we are set to explore the diverse and exciting landscape of Linux distributions, where a multitude of options cater to various preferences and purposes. Linux is not a one-size-fits-all proposition. Instead, it offers a dazzling array of distributions, each tailored to specific needs and preferences. Let us embark on a journey through some notable names in the Linux universe: Ubuntu, Kali, CentOS, and Parrot OS.

- **Ubuntu: The User-Friendly Maverick**

  Imagine a Linux distribution that is not only powerful but also user-friendly. Enter Ubuntu, a maverick in the Linux world. Known for its ease of use, extensive community support, and regular updates, Ubuntu has become a go-to choice for those stepping into the Linux universe. Whether you are a desktop user or diving into server management, Ubuntu welcomes all with open arms.

- **Kali: Unleash the Potential of Ethical Hacking**

  For individuals fascinated by the fields of ethical hacking and cybersecurity, Kali Linux serves as a guiding light. Crafted specifically for penetration testing and digital forensics, Kali arrives equipped with an arsenal of tools tailored for security professionals. Join the community of ethical hackers and security aficionados who leverage the capabilities of Kali Linux to investigate vulnerabilities, conduct penetration tests, and fortify digital safeguards.

- **CentOS: Stability for Servers**

  In the sphere of server environments, CentOS takes center stage. Renowned for its stability and reliability, CentOS is a popular choice for servers powering critical operations. As a downstream version of Red Hat Enterprise Linux (RHEL), CentOS offers a robust platform without the associated costs, making it ideal for businesses and organizations seeking a stable server environment.

- **Parrot OS: A Secure Haven**

  Step into the world of security-focused Linux distributions with Parrot OS. Crafted with cybersecurity in mind, Parrot OS is a favorite among penetration testers and security professionals. Packed with tools for anonymity, digital forensics, and ethical hacking, Parrot OS empowers users to navigate the cybersecurity landscape with confidence.

Choosing the right Linux distribution is akin to finding the perfect tool for the job. Whether you are drawn to user-friendly interfaces, ethical hacking pursuits, server stability, or cybersecurity endeavors, Linux distributions cater to diverse needs. So, join us as we unravel the distinct features, use cases, and vibrant communities behind Ubuntu, Kali, CentOS, and Parrot OS. Your Linux adventure awaits!

Unleashing the Power of Kali Linux: A Hacker's Haven

Welcome to the thrilling field of Kali Linux, the cybersecurity warrior among Linux distributions. In our exploration of the Linux world, Kali stands out as a formidable ally for those delving into the intricacies of ethical hacking and digital defense.

What makes Kali Linux special?

Kali Linux is not your average penguin. It is tailored for the bold, the curious, and the cybersecurity enthusiasts. Here is why hackers and security professionals prefer Kali:

1. **Arsenal of Cybersecurity Tools**

   - ***Pros:*** Kali comes pre-loaded with a vast array of cybersecurity tools. From penetration testing to digital forensics, Kali's toolkit is a treasure trove for those safeguarding the digital frontier.
   - ***Cons:*** The abundance of tools can be overwhelming for beginners. However, fear not; we will guide you through the purpose and application of each tool.

2. **Ethical Hacking Friendly**
   - ***Pros:*** Kali Linux is designed with ethical hacking in mind. Its tools and functionalities are geared towards identifying and fixing vulnerabilities, making it an ideal choice for cybersecurity enthusiasts.
   - ***Cons:*** While Kali is excellent for ethical hacking, using it without proper knowledge and permission can lead to legal and ethical issues. Our practical sessions will emphasize responsible and ethical use.
3. **Regular Updates and Community Support**
   - ***Pros:*** Kali Linux is continually updated to stay ahead in the cybersecurity game. Additionally, it boasts a vibrant community where users share knowledge and experiences.
   - ***Cons:*** Updates may require a stable internet connection, and the sheer volume of community resources might be daunting. But worry not—we are here to guide you through the updates and community engagement.

Embarking on the Journey: Installing Kali Linux

Step into the dynamic kingdom of Kali Linux, an operating system meticulously crafted for ethical hacking and penetration testing. This all-encompassing guide is your companion through the sequential steps of installing Kali Linux in VirtualBox, a widely embraced virtualization software enabling the concurrent operation of multiple operating systems on your computer.

Step 1: Download the Kali Linux ISO Image

Before embarking on this journey, you will need to download the Kali Linux ISO image. Head over to the official Kali Linux website and navigate to the Downloads section. Choose the appropriate ISO image for your system architecture (32-bit or 64-bit).

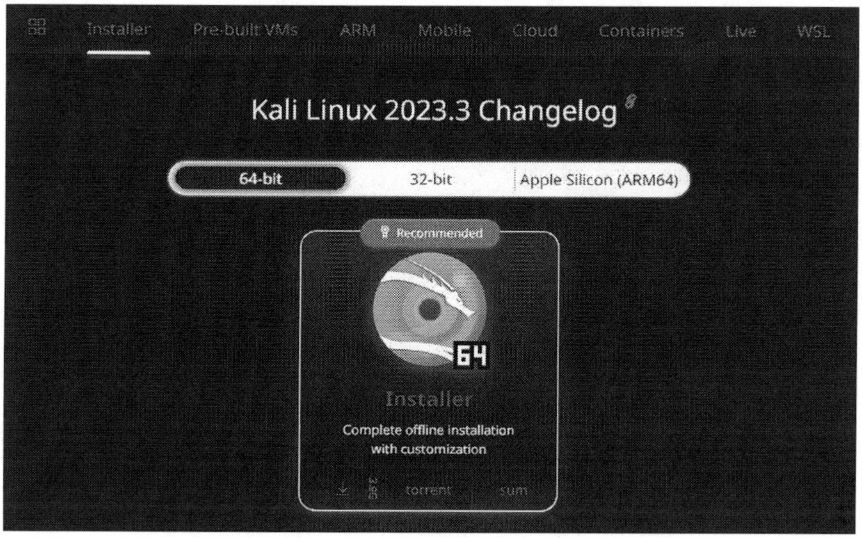

Figure 2.1: *Downloading Kali Linux Installer*

Step 2: Install VirtualBox

If you haven't already, install VirtualBox on your computer. It is available for Windows, macOS, and Linux operating systems. You can download VirtualBox from its official website.

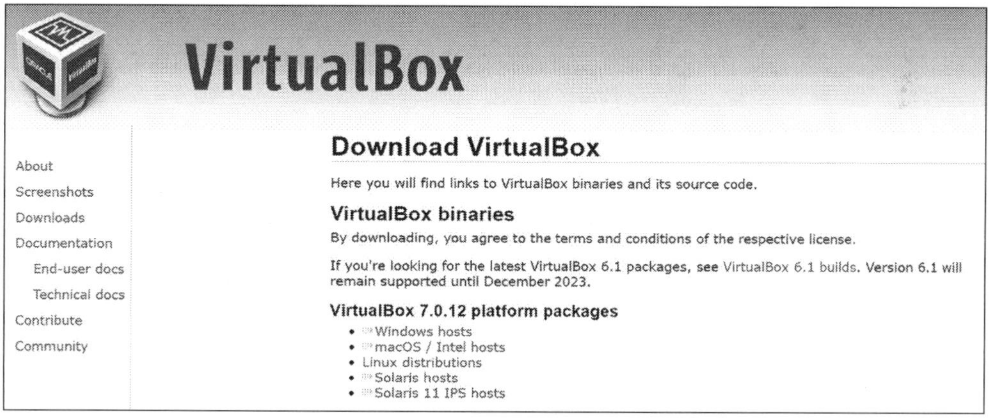

Figure 2.2: *Downloading Oracle VirtualBox*

Step 3: Create a New Virtual Machine

Launch VirtualBox and click the **`New`** button. Select **`Linux`** as the operating system type and **`Debian (64-bit)`** as the version. Click **`Next`** to proceed.

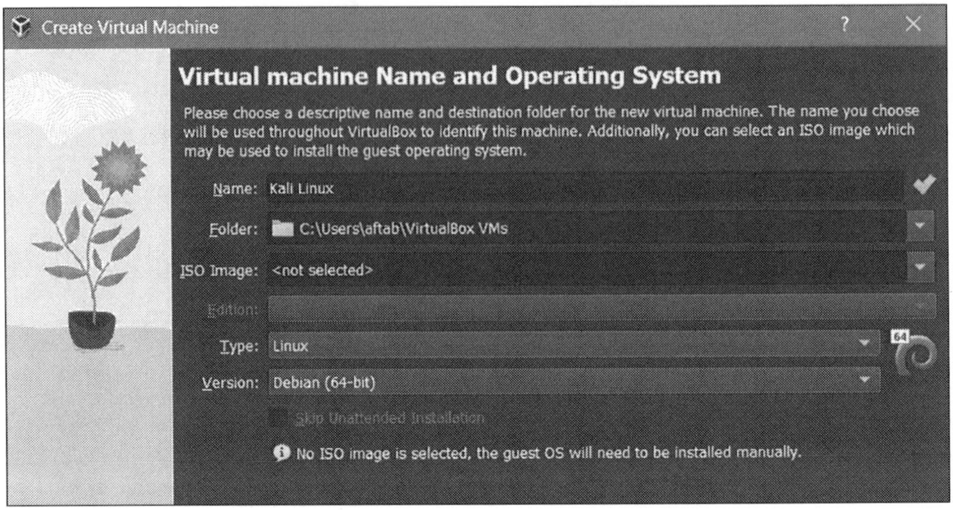

Figure 2.3: *Creating a New Virtual Machine*

Step 4: Allocate RAM and Storage

Specify the amount of RAM you want to allocate to your Kali Linux virtual machine. A minimum of 2GB is recommended, but 4GB or more is preferred for optimal performance. Next, select the storage file type and choose a suitable location on your hard drive for the virtual disk. Allocate at least 20GB of storage space.

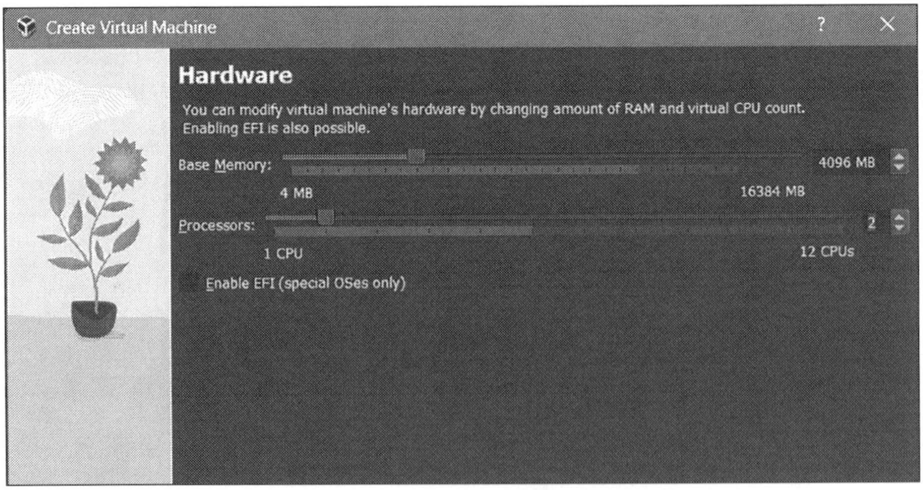

Figure 2.4: *Allocating RAM and Processors*

Step 5: Attach the Kali Linux ISO Image

Click the `Browse` button next to the CD/DVD drive and select the downloaded Kali Linux ISO image. Ensure that the `Enable CD/DVD Autoconnect` option is checked. Click `Create` to finalize the virtual machine configuration.

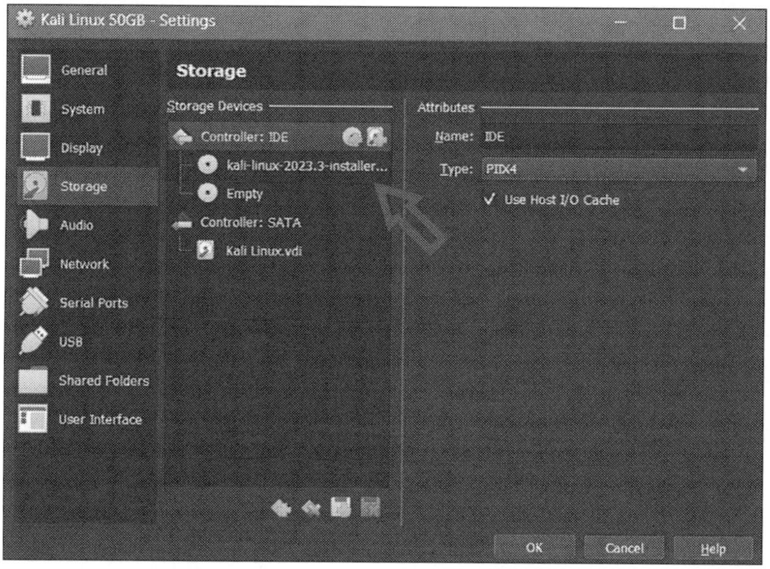

Figure 2.5: *Adding the Kali Linux ISO File*

Step 6: Start the Kali Linux Virtual Machine

Select the newly created Kali Linux virtual machine and click the **`Start`** button. The virtual machine will boot from the Kali Linux ISO image, initiating the installation process.

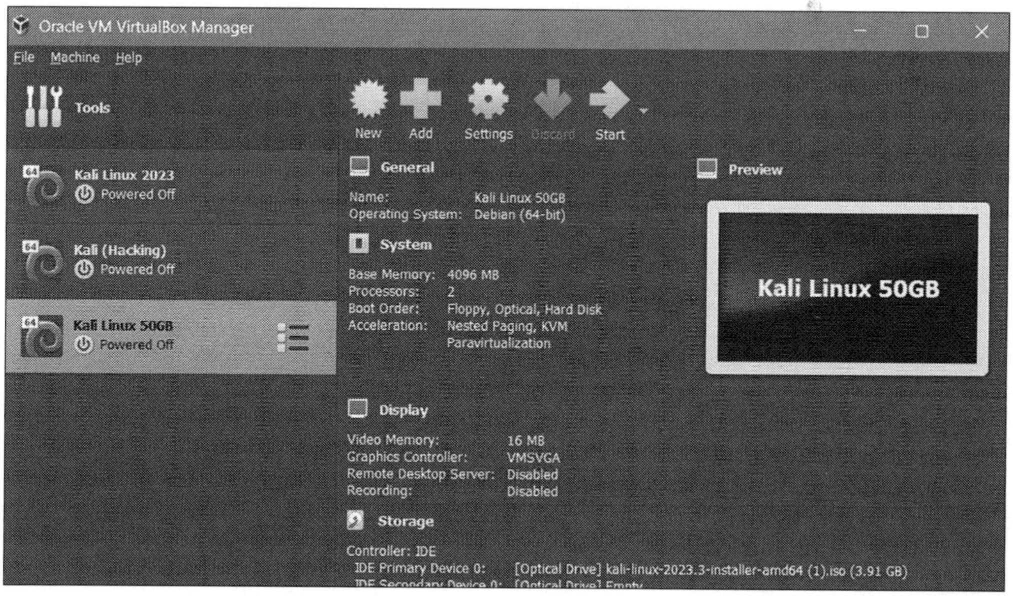

Figure 2.6: *Press the Start Button*

Step 7: Choose the Installation Language

When prompted, select your preferred language for the installation process. Click **`Continue`** to proceed.

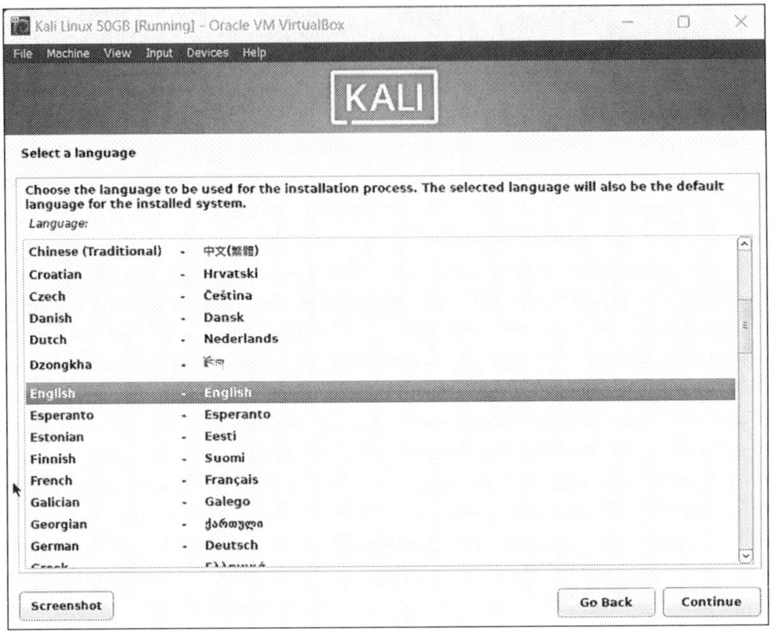

Figure 2.7: *Choose the Installation Language*

Step 8: Select Keyboard Layout

Choose the keyboard layout that matches your physical keyboard. Click **`Continue`** to move forward.

Step 9: Configure the Network

Select the network connection method for your virtual machine. If you are using a wired connection, ensure it is properly connected. For Wi-Fi, choose your network and enter the password.

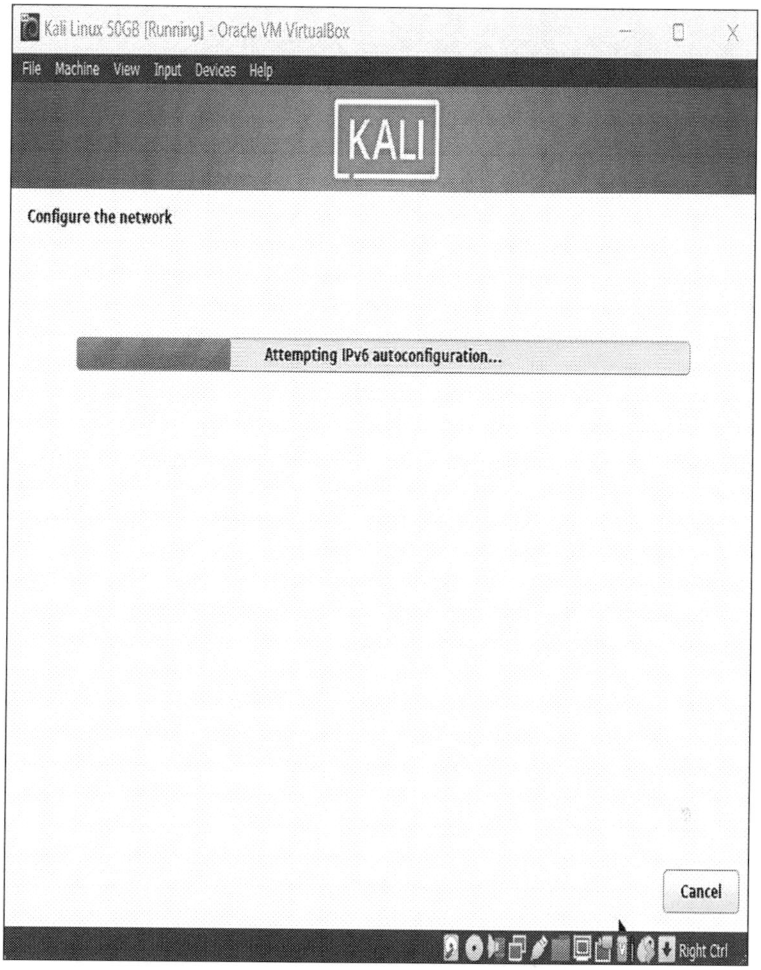

Figure 2.8: *Configure the Network*

Step 10: Establishing Hostname and Domain Name

Assign a distinctive hostname to your Kali Linux virtual machine, leaving the domain name blank if not applicable.

Step 11: Securing Root Access

Define a robust password for the root user, the paramount administrative account for Kali Linux. Ensure the password is intricate and resistant to unauthorized access.

Step 12: Tailoring User Accounts

As an additional security measure, consider creating a standard user account for daily activities. This not only enhances security but also facilitates seamless transitions between administrative tasks under the root user and routine activities with the regular user account.

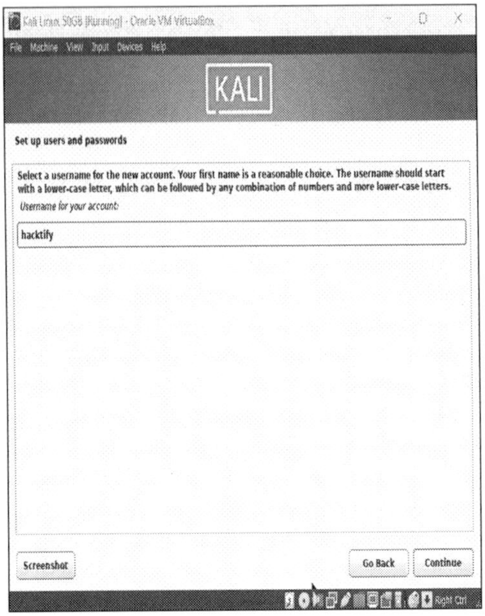

Figure 2.9: *Create Username and Password*

Step 13: Disk Partitioning

Opt for the preferred disk partitioning method for your virtual hard drive. For those new to the process, the guided partitioning option is advisable, automating the creation of essential partitions for Kali Linux.

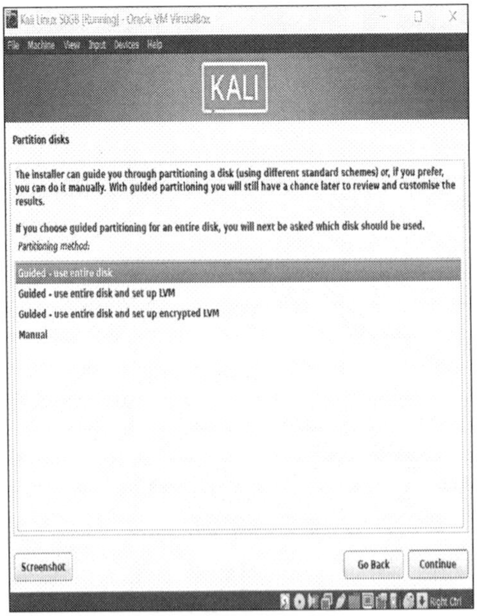

Figure 2.10: *Partitioning the Disks*

Step 14: Commence Installation

Initiate the installation process by clicking `Install Now`. This action triggers the transfer of Kali Linux files to your virtual hard drive while configuring the system settings.

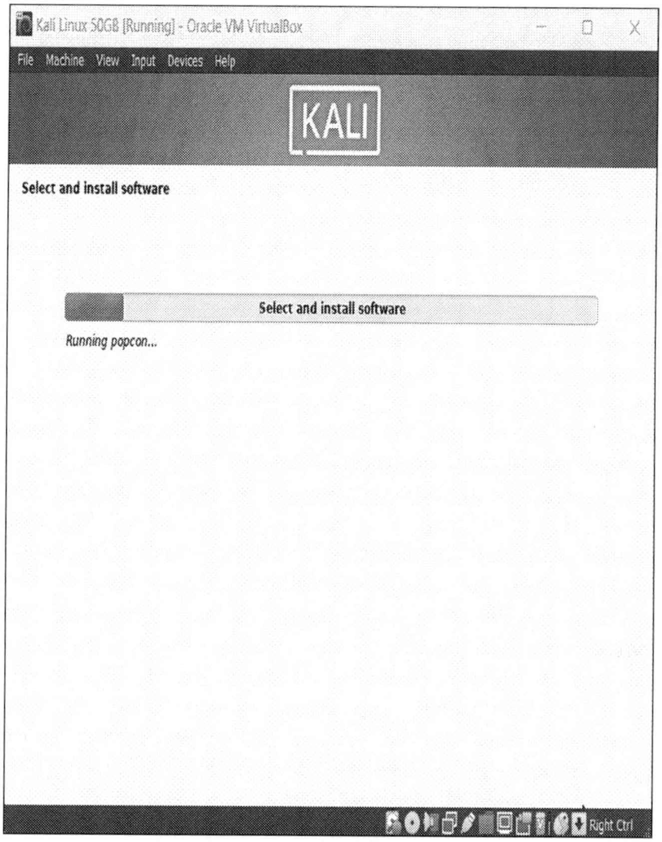

Figure 2.11: *Begin the Installation Process*

Step 15: Tailoring the Installation

For those seeking a personalized touch, there is an option to customize the installation. This involves selecting additional packages or desktop environments according to your preferences. However, beginners may find the default settings to be optimal for a seamless experience.

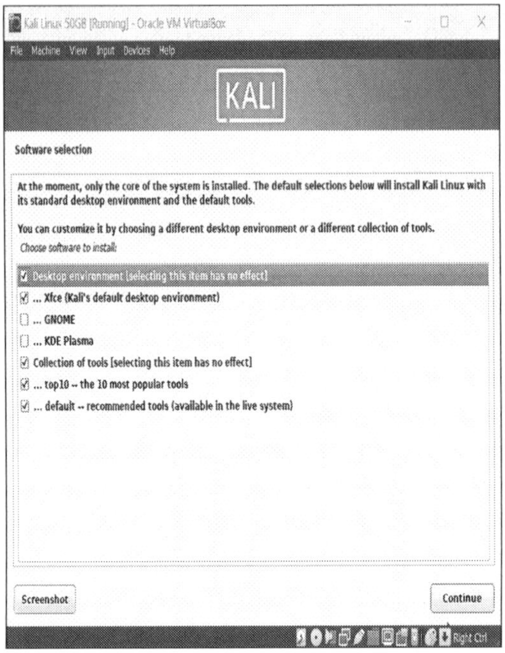

Figure 2.12: *Personalizing the Installation*

Step 16: Installation Complete

Upon completion of the installation, a prompt will instruct you to eject the Kali Linux ISO image from the virtual CD/DVD drive. Simply click `Continue` to move forward.

Figure 2.13: *Installation Complete*

Step 17: Reboot and Access

Allow the virtual machine to reboot, and you will find yourself at the Kali Linux login screen. Input the root user password established earlier and press `Enter`.

Congratulations! Your installation of Kali Linux in VirtualBox is triumphant. Now, within the secure environment of your virtual machine, you are poised to delve into the expansive world of ethical hacking and cybersecurity.

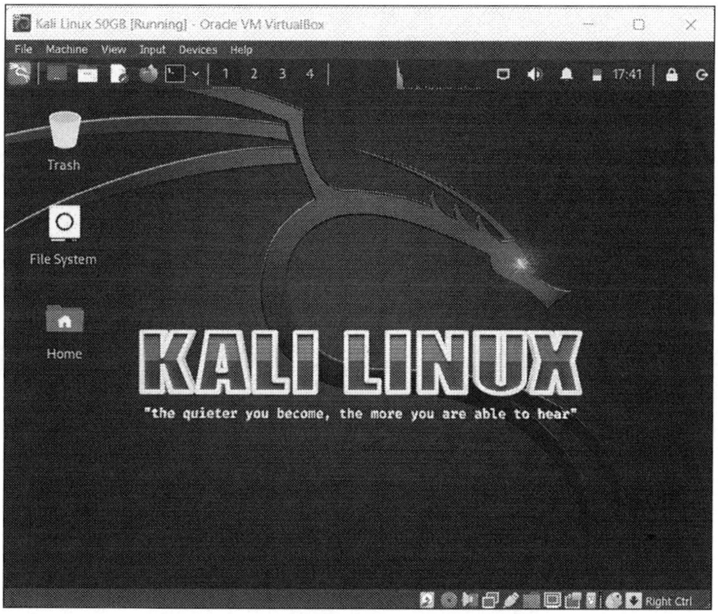

Figure 2.14: *Kali Linux Home Screen*

Essential Linux Commands for Everyday Use

Here is a compilation of 20 crucial commands that form the backbone of everyday Linux usage:

1. `cd`: Change directory. Shifts the current working directory to the specified location.

Figure 2.15: *cd Command*

2. **`ls`**: List directory contents. Provides an overview of files and directories in the present working directory.

Figure 2.16: *ls Command*

3. **`mkdir`**: Create a directory. Establishes a new directory bearing the given name.

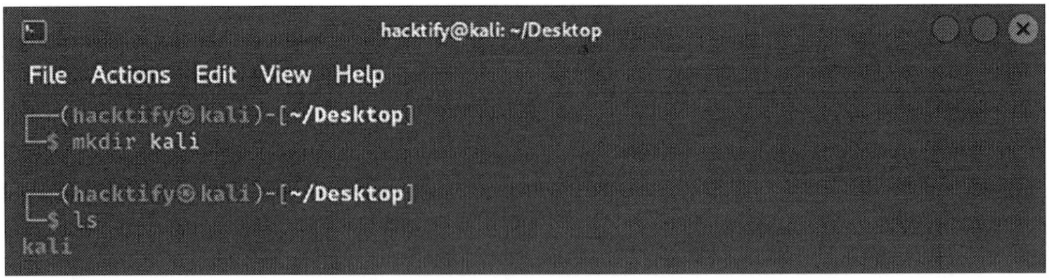

Figure 2.17: *mkdir Command*

4. **`rmdir`**: Remove directory. Erases an empty directory identified by the specified name.

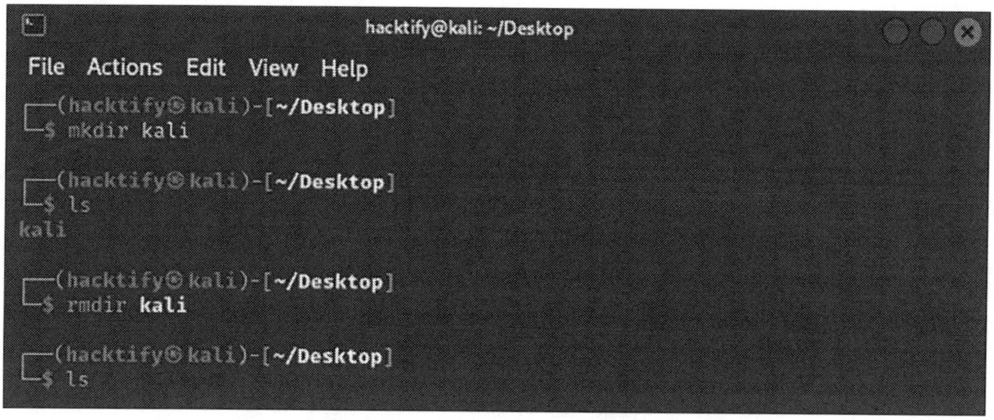

Figure 2.18: *rmdir Command*

5. **mv**: Move or rename files or directories. Transfers or gives a new name to a file or directory.

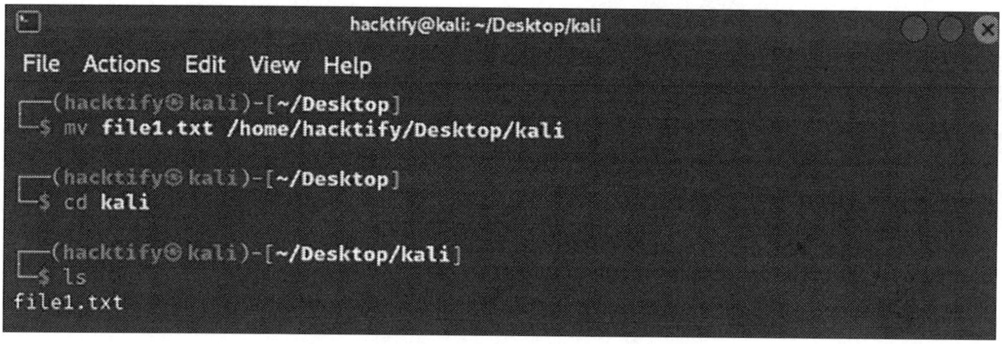

Figure 2.19: *mv Command*

6. **cp**: Copy files or directories. Duplicates a file or directory to a designated location.

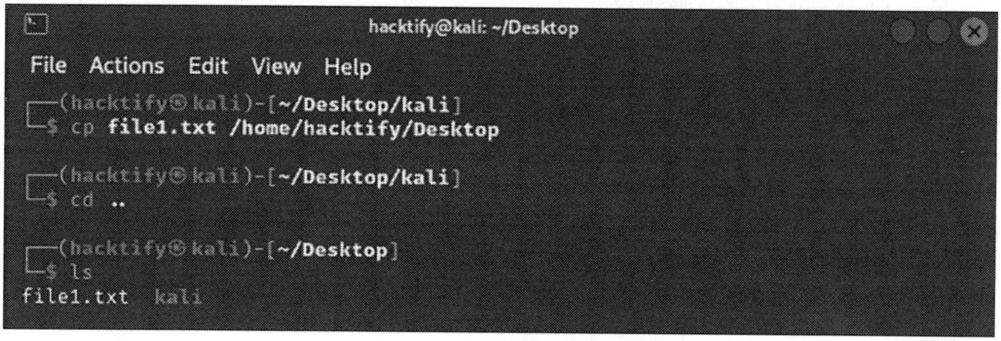

Figure 2.20: *cp Command*

7. **rm**: Remove files or directories. Deletes a file or directory from the system.

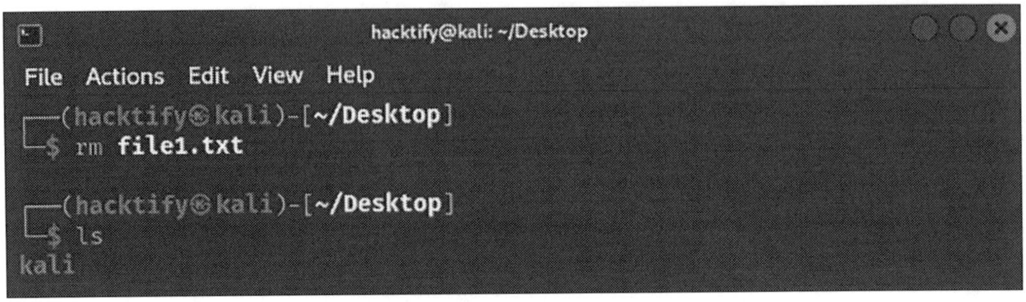

Figure 2.21: *rm Command*

8. **touch:** Create empty files. Generates empty files associated with the given name.

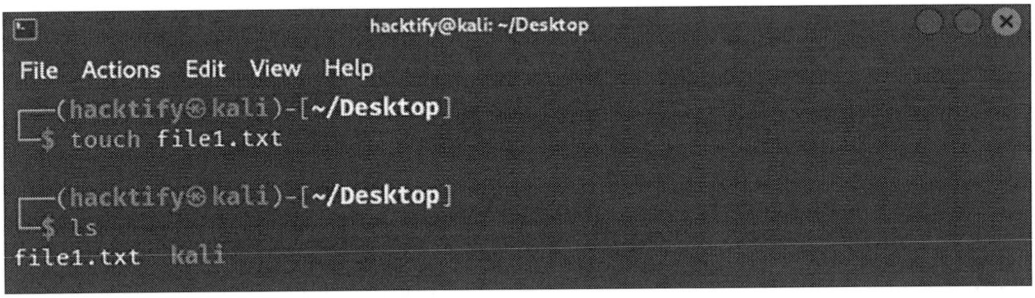

Figure 2.22: *touch Command*

9. **clear**: Clear the terminal screen. Wipes the content of the terminal window for a fresh start.

Figure 2.23: *clear Command*

10. **grep**: Search for text patterns. Scours files for a specified text pattern or expression.

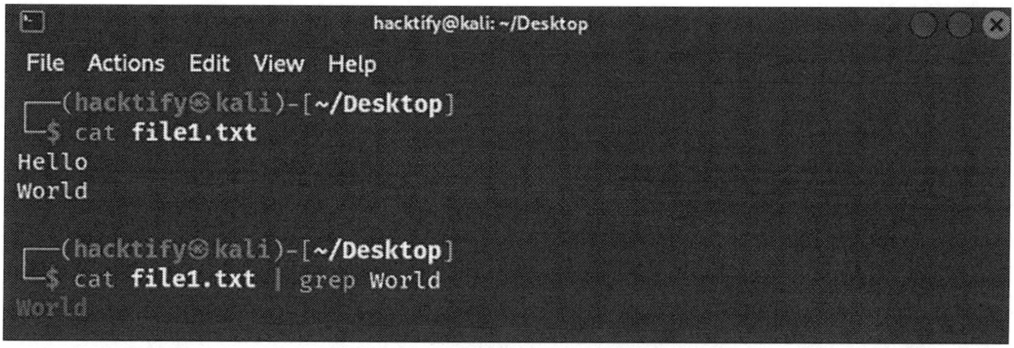

Figure 2.24: *grep Command*

11. **sudo**: Execute commands with administrative privileges. Enables the execution of commands with elevated rights.

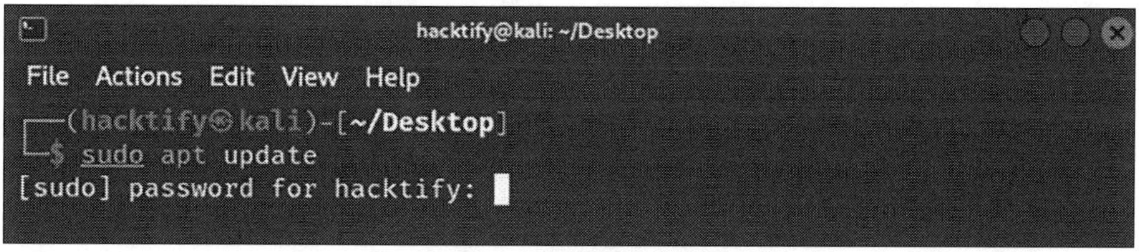

Figure 2.25: *sudo Command*

12. **pwd**: Print the working directory. Exhibits the complete path of the current working directory.

Figure 2.26: *pwd Command*

13. **ps**: List running processes. Presents a roster of presently active processes on the system.

Figure 2.27: *ps Command*

14. **`top`**: Monitor CPU usage. Exhibits information regarding the ongoing CPU usage of processes.

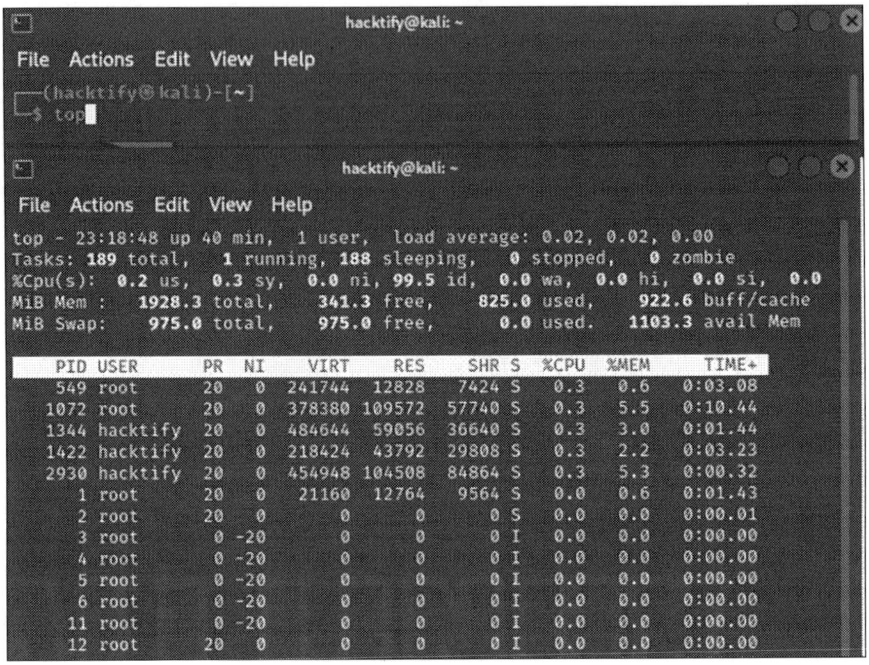

Figure 2.28: *top Command*

15. **`help`**: Get command help. Furnishes assistance and information for the specified command.

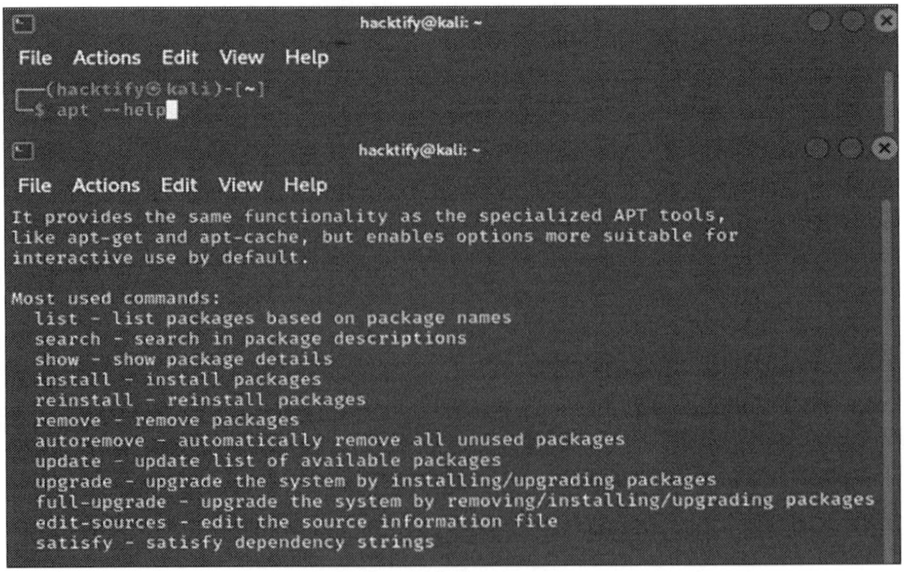

Figure 2.29: *help command*

16. **`cat`**: Display file contents. Reveals the content of a specified file.

Figure 2.30: *cat Command*

17. **`man`**: Access manual pages. Offers comprehensive documentation for Linux commands.

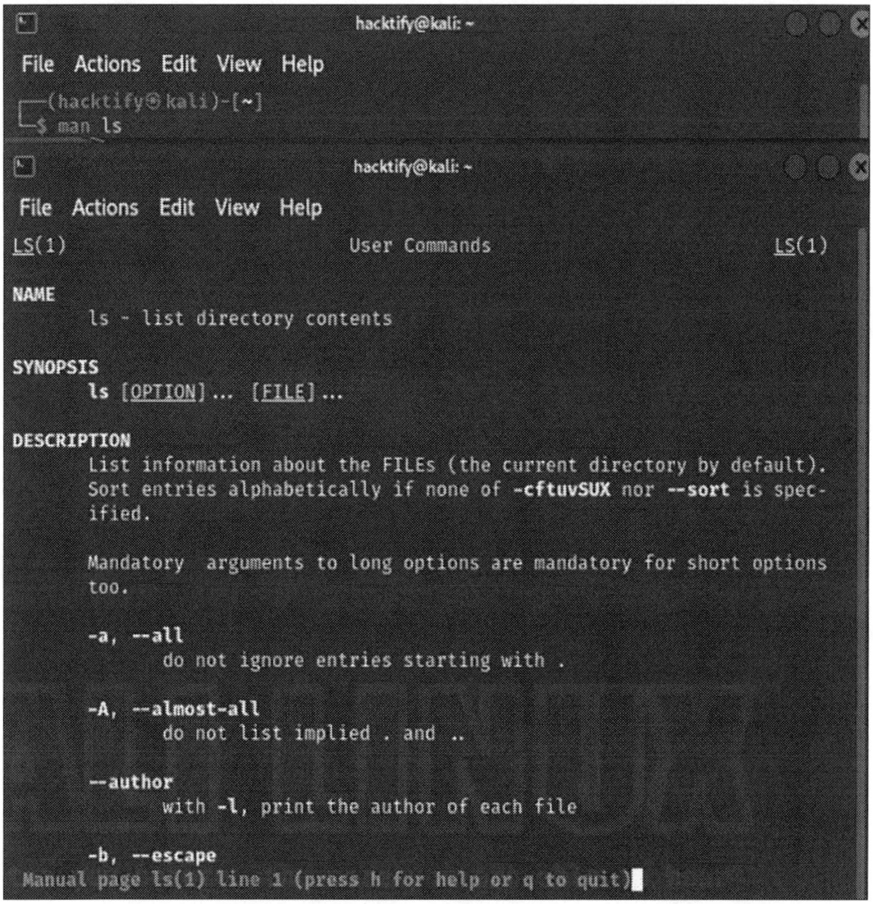

Figure 2.31: *man Command*

18. **`nano`**: Edit text files. Unveils a text editor for the modification of file contents.

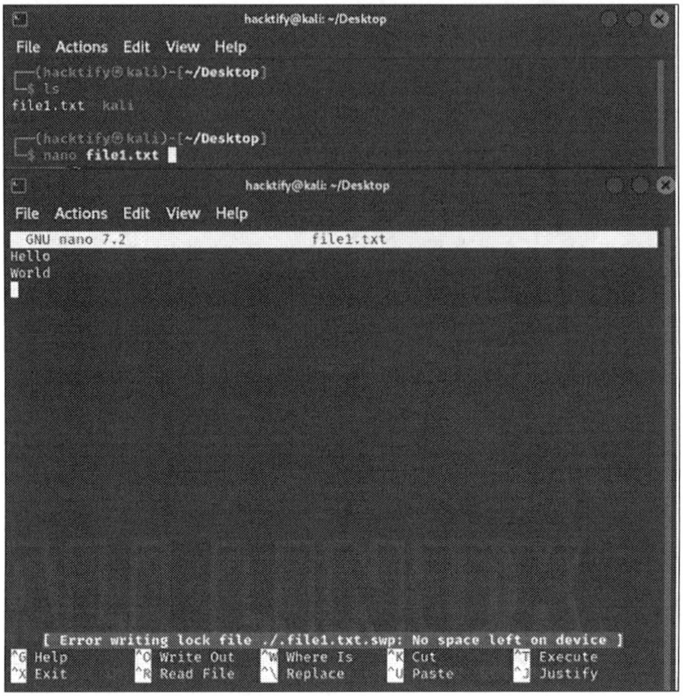

Figure 2.32: *nano Command*

19. **`chmod`:** Change file permissions. Adjusts the access permissions for files and directories.

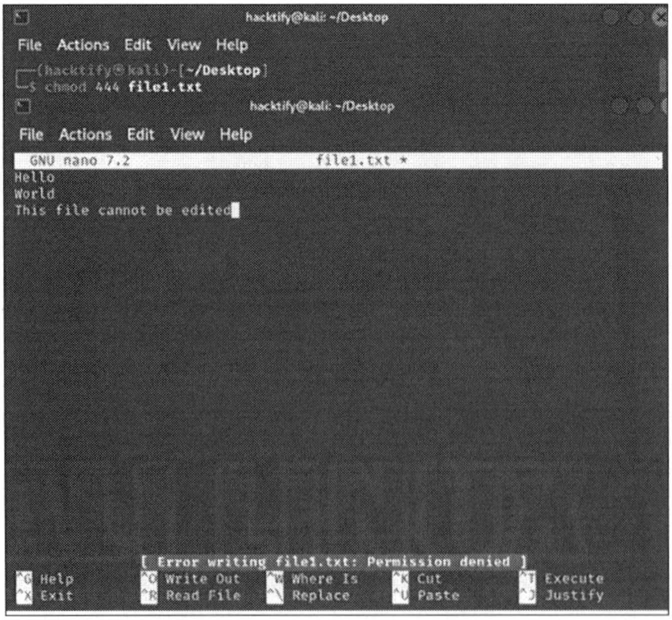

Figure 2.33: *chmod Command*

20. **chown**: Change file ownership. Transfers ownership of files or directories to a specified user or group.

Figure 2.34: *chown Command*

This repertoire of commands serves as a foundational toolkit for navigating and managing the Linux environment efficiently.

Unraveling the Linux Bootstrapping Process

Welcome to the foundational steps of the Linux domain, where the journey begins with the intricacies of bootstrapping the system. In this section, we will demystify the BIOS, delve into the sector of bootloaders, and unveil how Linux leaps to life during the boot process.

Step 1: Unraveling BIOS

- ***Understanding* BIOS:**
  - BIOS, or Basic Input/Output System, assumes a pivotal role in system initiation. It serves as the code orchestrating the awakening of your hardware, setting the startup sequence into motion.

Step 2: Spotlight on GRUB (Grand Unified Bootloader)

- ***Introducing* GRUB:**
  - GRUB takes the spotlight as the bootloader, acting as the sentinel in the Linux startup performance. Functioning as the gatekeeper, it ensures the seamless loading of the Linux kernel into memory, orchestrating a smooth transition from hardware initiation to the enchantment of the Linux OS.

Step 3: GRUB in Action

- ***Loading the Kernel*:**
  - Witness the graceful handoff as GRUB loads the Linux kernel. This crucial step marks the transition from the hardware-focused BIOS to the software-driven Linux environment.

Step 4: The Kernel Awakening

- ***Kernel Initialization*:**
    - As the kernel awakens, it sets the stage for the entire Linux operating system. It initializes critical system components and prepares the environment for user interaction.

By understanding these initial steps, you are not just witnessing the boot process—you are also gaining insight into the orchestration that transforms your computer into a Linux-powered machine. Curiosity piqued? Stay tuned as we navigate deeper into the intricate layers of Linux in the chapters that follow.

Init Systems: SysVinit versus systemd

Let us explore the differences between **SysVinit** and **systemd**, two pivotal Linux initialization systems. We will gain insights into their evolution, functionalities, and ongoing debates, whether you are familiar with the traditional **SysVinit** or curious about the modern **systemd** approach.

- **The Evolution of Init Systems**

  The Linux operating system has undergone a significant evolution in its approach to initializing and managing system services. Traditionally, **SysVinit**, an **init** system based on scripts, served as the backbone for starting and stopping services during the boot process. However, with the emergence of **systemd**, a more modern and versatile **init** system, the landscape has shifted.

- **The Drawbacks of SysVinit**

  SysVinit, while reliable and widely used, presented several limitations. Its reliance on scripts made it complex to manage dependencies between services, often leading to startup delays and potential conflicts. Moreover, **SysVinit's** configuration was static, requiring manual edits to scripts, which could be time-consuming and error-prone.

- **The Rise of systemd**

  systemd emerged as a response to these shortcomings, offering a more dynamic and flexible approach to init system management. Its architecture, based on a collection of systemd units, provides a structured and organized way to manage services, dependencies, and system resources.

- **The Benefits of systemd**

  systemd offers several advantages over **SysVinit**, which are as follows:

    - **Dependency management**: **systemd** automatically handles service dependencies, ensuring that services start and stop in the correct order.

  - **Parallel startup**: **`systemd`** can start multiple services in parallel, reducing boot times.
  - **Journaling**: **`systemd`** maintains a detailed log of system events, providing valuable insights into service failures and troubleshooting.
  - **Resource management**: **`systemd`** actively monitors and manages system resources, ensuring efficient utilization of CPU, memory, and disk space.

- **Managing Services with `SysVinit`**

  To manage services with **`SysVinit`**, administrators would typically use scripts or command-line tools such as **`/etc/init.d/`** or **`chkconfig`**. These tools allowed for starting, stopping, and disabling services.

- **Administering Services using `systemd`**

In the field of **`systemd`**, the administration of services, targets, and mount points revolves around **`systemd`** units. Admins can wield the **`systemctl`** command, appending the service name and an action like start, stop, or status, to oversee and control these elements.

- **Practical Scenarios: SysVinit versus systemd**

  Consider a scenario where you need to restart the Apache web server.

  With **`SysVinit`**, you would use the command:

  `sudo /etc/init.d/apache2 restart`

Figure 2.35: *SysVinit Command in Action*

  With **`systemd`**, you would use the command:

  `sudo systemctl restart apache2`

Figure 2.36: *systemd Command in Action*

Both commands achieve the same outcome, but **`systemd`**'s syntax is more concise and consistent across different services.

In another scenario, you might need to check the status of the MySQL database service. With **SysVinit**, you would use the command:

```
sudo service mysql status
```

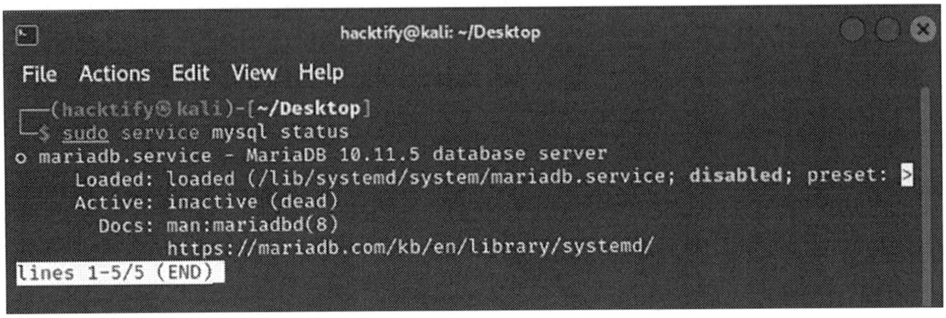

Figure 2.37: *SysVinit Command in Action*

With **systemd**, you would use the command:

```
sudo systemctl status mysql
```

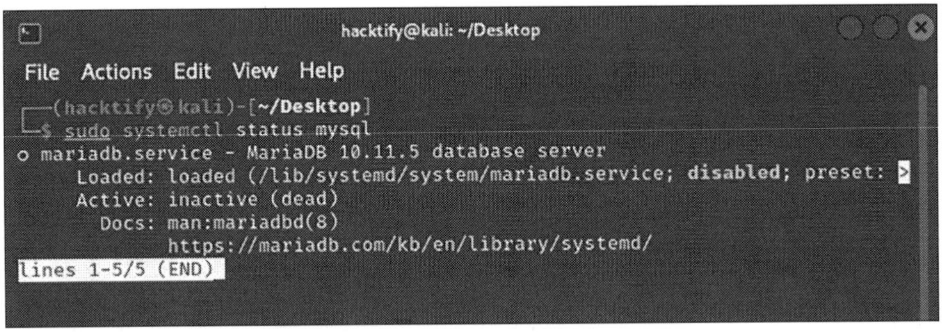

Figure 2.38: *systemd Command in Action*

Again, both commands provide service status information, but **systemd**'s output is more detailed and organized.

- **Closing Thoughts: Embracing Versatility**

  The shift from **SysVinit** to **systemd** signifies a progression in Linux **init** systems, embracing enhanced versatility, efficiency, and user-centric design.

Mastering File Permissions

Get ready to understand and control who can access what in Kali Linux! In this section, we will explore file permissions in a simple way. We will learn how to keep your files safe and control who gets to see them. Whether you are securing important stuff or are just curious, this section will give you the skills you need for a strong cybersecurity foundation in Kali Linux.

- **Understanding Permissions: Owner, Group, and Others**

  In the intricate world of Linux, file permissions play a crucial role in safeguarding your data and maintaining system integrity. These permissions determine who can access, modify, or execute files and directories, ensuring that sensitive information remains protected while allowing authorized users to perform their tasks effectively.

- **The Trio of Permissions: Owner, Group, and Others**

  In the Linux file permission framework, three pivotal categories–owner, group, and others–dictate user classes and their corresponding access levels to files or directories.

  - **Owner**: Singularly representing the user who crafted the file or directory, the owner enjoys the utmost privileges, conventionally marked by the 'u' in permission strings. This includes read, write, and execute permissions.
  - **Group**: Constituting a cluster of users linked to the file or directory, the group holds a predefined level of access, typically denoted by the 'g' in permission strings. Members can read and write but might lack execution permissions.
  - **Others**: Encompassing all users beyond the owner and group, the 'others' category, indicated by 'o' in permission strings, experiences the most constrained access. By default, others lack read, write, or execute permissions for files or directories.

- **Permission Representations: Symbolic and Octal Modes**

  File permissions find expression through two distinct representations: symbolic mode and octal mode.

  - **Symbolic Mode**: Employing the letters `'r'` (read), `'w'` (write), and `'x'` (execute), the symbolic mode delineates permissions for the owner, group, and others. For instance, `'rwxr-xr-x'` signifies read, write, and execute permissions for the owner, read and execute permissions for the group, and solely read permission for others.
  - **Octal Mode**: Octal mode employs a three-digit octal number to denote permissions. Each digit signifies the permission level for the owner, group, and others. For instance, the octal number `'755'` aligns with the symbolic mode `'rwxr-xr-x'`.

- **Real-World Examples: Illustrating Permission Concepts**

  To solidify the understanding of file permissions, consider these real-world examples:

  - **Sensitive Documents**: A company's confidential documents should have permissions set to `'rw-------'` (600), allowing only the owner (the company's file manager) to read and write the documents.

- **Shared Project Files**: A group of developers working on a project might set permissions for their shared files to **‘rwxr-xr-x’** (755), allowing them to read, write, and execute the files while restricting access to outsiders.
- **Publicly Accessible Files**: A website's public HTML files might have permissions set to **‘r--r--r--’** (777), allowing everyone to read the files but preventing unauthorized modifications.

- **Permission Management Tools: Changing and Monitoring Access**

  Linux provides several tools for overseeing file permissions, with the **‘chmod’** and **‘chown’** commands taking the lead. **‘Chmod’** empowers you to adjust the permissions of a file or directory, while **‘chown’** facilitates the alteration of ownership for a file or directory.

- **Conclusion: The Cornerstone of Data Security**

  Proficiency in comprehending and managing file permissions stands as a pivotal factor in upholding data security and integrity within the Linux space. By meticulously regulating access, modifications, and executions of files and directories, you establish a robust defense mechanism, safeguarding critical information and fortifying your system against unwarranted breaches.

In the domain of Linux, mastering file permissions is a pivotal skill, and several commands facilitate a nuanced comprehension of this aspect:

- **ls -l**: This command serves as a window into the contents of a directory, revealing a detailed, long-format listing that includes the permissions associated with each file or directory.

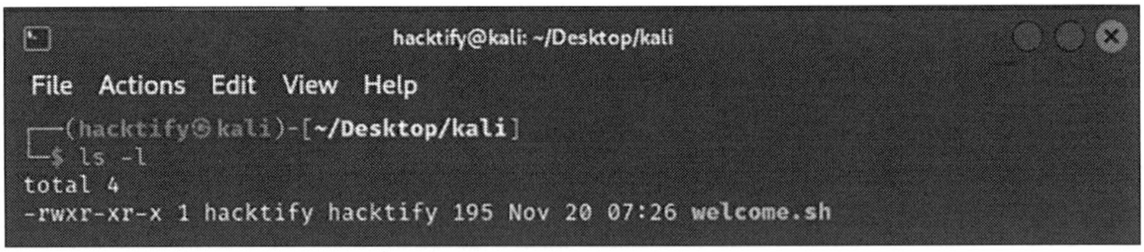

Figure 2.39: *ls -l Command*

- **chmod**: A cornerstone command for manipulating permissions, **‘chmod’** empowers users to modify the permissions of a file or directory. The syntax follows:

```
chmod [options] <permissions> <file or directory>
```

Essential options for the **‘chmod’** command include:

- **u**: Adjusts permissions for the owner of the file or directory.
- **g**: Modifies permissions for the group associated with the file or directory.
- **o**: Alters permissions for other users.

- **a**: Changes permissions universally for all users.
- **+**: Adds specified permissions.
- **-**: Removes specified permissions.

Understanding and wielding these commands are fundamental steps toward unraveling the intricacies of file permissions in Linux, empowering users to fine-tune access control with precision and clarity.

Here are some examples of how to use the **chmod** command:

- To make a file executable for all users:

Figure 2.40: *chmod Command to Make a File Executable*

- To make a directory readable and writable for all users:

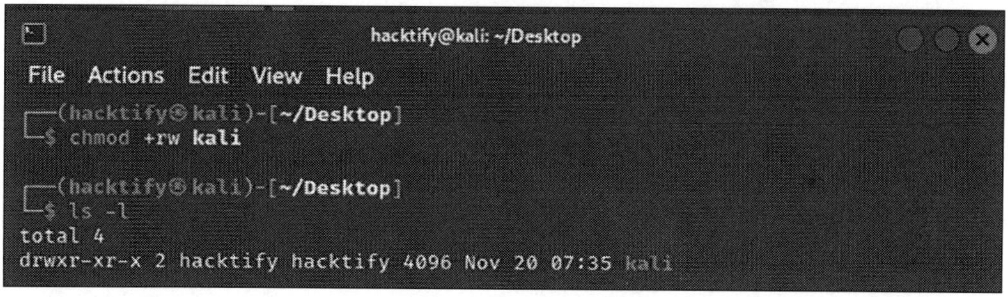

Figure 2.41: *chmod Command to Make a Directory Readable and Writable for All Users*

- To remove write permissions for the group of a file:

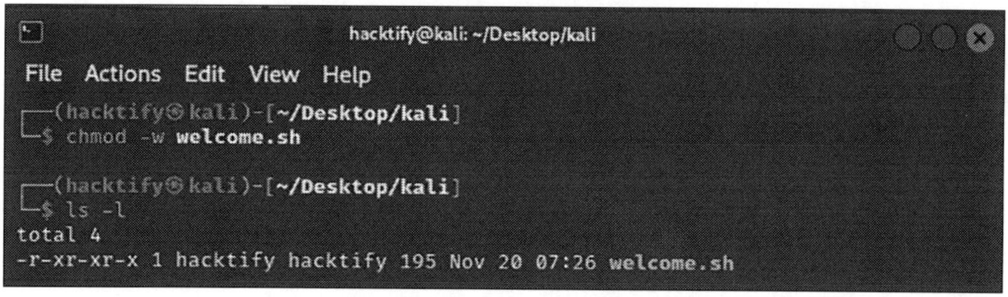

Figure 2.42: *chmod Command to Remove Write Permission for the Group*

chown: This command changes the ownership of a file or directory. The syntax is as follows:

```
chown [options] <owner>:<group> <file or directory>
```

Here are some common options for the **chown** command:

- **R**: Recursively changes the ownership of all files and directories in a directory tree.
- **u**: Changes the owner of the file or directory to the specified user.
- **g**: Changes the group of the file or directory to the specified group.

Here is an example of how to use the **chown** command to change the owner of a file to the user **'root'**:

- **sudo**: The **'sudo'** command is instrumental for executing commands with superuser privileges (root). The syntax is as follows:

```
sudo <command>
```

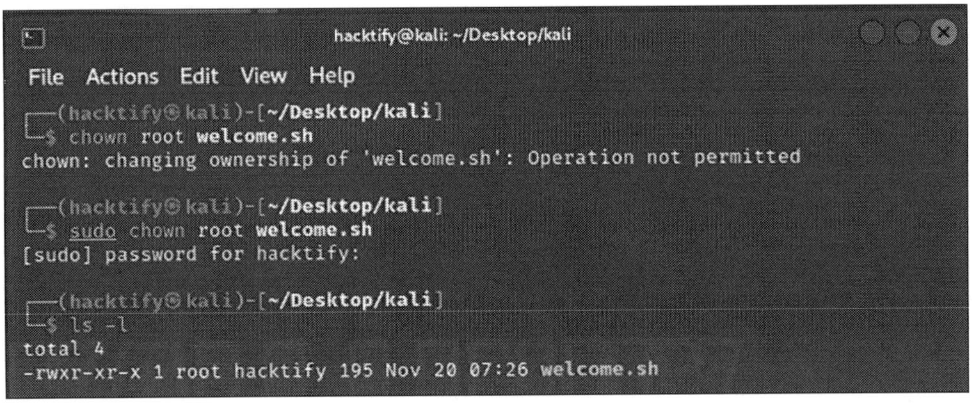

Figure 2.43: *chown Command in Action*

By assimilating these options and commands, users can navigate the intricacies of file ownership in Linux with precision, and elevate their understanding of permission management.

Understanding Linux File System Hierarchy

The Linux file system hierarchy, also known as the FHS (Filesystem Hierarchy Standard), is a standardized layout for organizing files and directories in Linux-based operating systems. This structured approach ensures consistency, simplifies file management, and promotes ease of use across various Linux distributions.

- **The Root Directory – The Foundation of the Hierarchy**

  The root directory, denoted by **'/'**, serves as the starting point of the entire file system hierarchy. It encompasses all other directories and files, forming the foundation upon which the Linux system is built.

- **Key Directories and their Roles**

The Linux file system encompasses crucial directories at its root, each serving a distinct purpose in data organization and storage:

  - **/bin**: This directory hosts executable programs universally utilized by all users, such as **'ls'** for listing directory contents or **'cp'** for copying files.
  - **/etc**: Centralizing configuration files for system-wide applications and services, this directory contains settings governing network connections, user accounts, and diverse system parameters.
  - **/home**: Functioning as the hub for user-specific files and directories, **/home** houses individual subdirectories for users to store personal documents, configuration files, and other data.
  - **/lib**: Containing indispensable library files vital for executable program functionality, these libraries facilitate common operations like input/output or memory management.
  - **/media**: Operating as a mount point for removable storage devices like USB drives, **/media** enables access to their contents through subdirectories.
  - **/mnt**: Acting as a versatile mount point for temporarily mounted file systems, **/mnt** accommodates diverse file systems, from network shares to local partitions.
  - **/opt**: Dedicated to optional software packages separate from the core OS, **/opt** empowers users to install and manage additional software without impacting system files.
  - **/proc:** A virtual directory offering access to system-related information, **/proc** provides details on processes, hardware configurations, and kernel statistics for administrators and developers.
  - **/root:** As the home directory for the root user, **/root** stores configuration files and personal data exclusive to the root user, who holds complete administrative control.
  - **/sbin**: Hosting executables essential for system administrators, **/sbin** comprises programs crucial for system maintenance and administrative tasks, often requiring elevated privileges.
  - **/srv**: Reserved for data related to network services, **/srv** is a designated repository for files associated with web servers, mail servers, or FTP servers.
  - **/sys:** A virtual directory enabling access to system device information and configuration settings, **/sys** facilitates direct interaction with hardware devices.

- `/tmp`: Serving as a temporary storage location for files generated by applications, `/tmp` is periodically cleared to reclaim disk space.
- `/usr`: Housing user-specific programs and data, `/usr` includes applications, libraries, and documentation about user-installed software.
- `/var`: Holding variable data that changes over time, `/var` stores dynamic data like log files, cache files, and spool directories for printing or email services.

Comprehending these key directories provides a foundational grasp of the Linux file system hierarchy. Armed with knowledge about where different file types are stored, users can navigate the system, manage files, and troubleshoot issues with enhanced proficiency.

Bash Scripting Essentials

In the intricate world of Linux, the shell serves as the pivotal gateway to the operating system, providing users with a crucial interface to interact with the system and execute commands. Amidst the array of available shells, Bash (Bourne-Again Shell) takes precedence, emerging as the default shell for the majority of Linux distributions.

- ***The Shell – A Portal to Linux:*** Functioning as a command interpreter, the shell adeptly translates user-input commands into executable instructions comprehensible to the operating system. It operates as a mediator between users and the system, facilitating control over diverse facets of the operating system. This spans tasks from manipulating files and directories to launching applications and configuring intricate system settings.
- ***Bash – The Pervasive Shell of Linux:*** With its origins rooted in the original Bourne shell crafted by Stephen Bourne in 1977, Bash, the Bourne-Again Shell, has undergone substantial evolution. Today, it stands as the preeminent shell for Linux systems, wielding a potent and adaptable command language tailored to meet the needs of both fledgling users and seasoned system administrators.
- ***Unveiling the Significance of Bash in Linux:*** The pervasive influence of Bash in the Linux landscape is underpinned by a myriad of advantages, including:
    - ***User-friendliness:*** Bash unfolds a user-friendly interface, extending accessibility to users across various skill levels.
    - ***Versatility:*** With an extensive command language, Bash empowers users to navigate tasks ranging from fundamental file management to intricate system administration.
    - ***Powerful scripting capabilities:*** Bash's scripting support enables users to automate repetitive tasks and craft intricate workflows seamlessly.

- ◦ ***Wide availability:*** Pre-installed on the majority of Linux distributions, Bash ensures seamless compatibility across diverse systems.
- ***A Journey to Bash Mastery – Elevating Your Linux Journey:*** A command over Bash bestows users with the prowess to unlock the full potential of their Linux systems. Through adept mastery of Bash commands, users can:
  - ***Efficiently manage files and directories:*** Seamlessly execute tasks such as copying, moving, deleting, and organizing files with finesse.
  - ***Launch applications:*** Effortlessly execute programs and applications directly from the command line.
  - ***Configure system settings:*** Navigate and modify system settings while adeptly managing user accounts.
  - ***Automate tasks:*** Harness the potential of scripting to automate repetitive tasks, streamlining workflows for heightened efficiency.
  - ***Troubleshoot system issues:*** Navigate and resolve system problems using diagnostic tools and specialized commands.

Embracing Bash as your portal to the Linux universe unlocks a kingdom of power and adaptability. Through dedication and practice, proficiency in Bash transforms you into a capable navigator of the Linux environment, fostering confidence and efficiency.

In the expansive domain of Linux, the shell serves as the conduit to the operating system, providing a user-friendly interface for executing commands and engaging with the system. Bash (Bourne-Again Shell), standing as a stalwart among Linux shells, claims its position as the default choice for a myriad of Linux distributions.

Writing Your First Bash Script

Scripting in Bash provides a powerful means of automating tasks, enhancing productivity, and extending the functionality of your Linux system. Embark on your scripting journey by crafting your first Bash script, a simple yet meaningful program that displays a personalized welcome message.

1. The Shebang Line – Setting the Stage

Every Bash script begins with a special line, known as the shebang line, which informs the system about the interpreter to use for executing the script. The standard shebang line for Bash scripts is:

```
#!/bin/bash
```

This line instructs the system to invoke the Bash interpreter when the script is executed.

2. Script Structure – The Anatomy of a Bash Script

A Bash script essentially consists of a series of commands, each representing an instruction to be executed. These commands are typically arranged in a logical sequence to accomplish a specific task.

3. Crafting Your Initial Script – A Personalized Greeting

Embark on script creation with a simple yet impactful welcome message:

```
#!/bin/bash
# Ask for the user’s name
echo “Hello! What’s your name?”
# Read user input
read username
# Display a customized welcome message
echo “Welcome, $username! We’re glad to have you.”
```

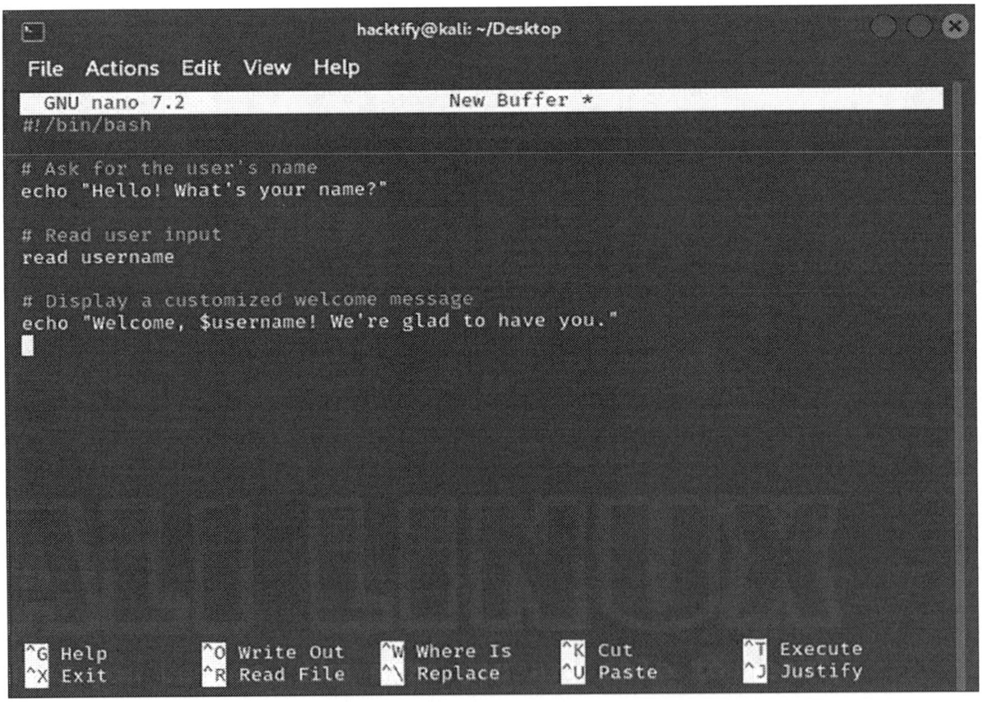

Figure 2.44: *Writing the Bash Script*

Save this code as '**welcome.sh**' (http://welcome.sh/) in your preferred directory.

Grant executable permissions using the **`‘chmod’`** command:

```
chmod +x welcome.sh
```

Execute the script by entering its name in the terminal:

```
./welcome.sh
```

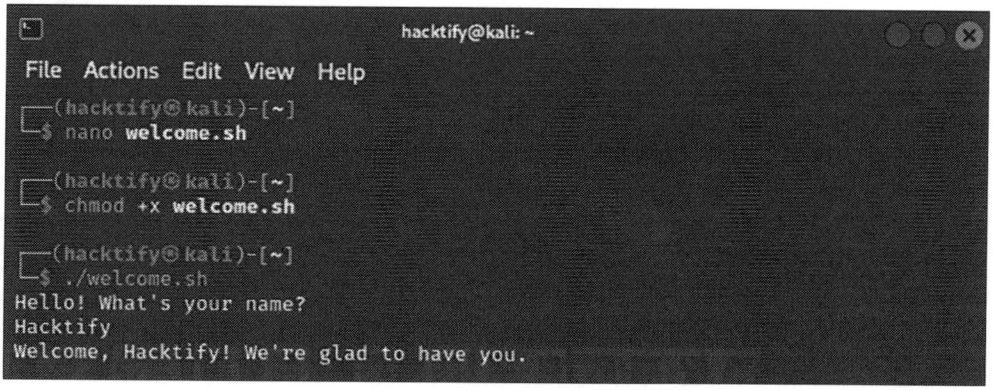

Figure 2.45: *Executing the Bash Script*

The script unfolds a personalized welcome, extending a warm greeting personalized with your username.

4. Script Execution: Bringing Your Code to Life

When you execute a Bash script, the interpreter reads the script line by line, interpreting and executing each command sequentially. This process continues until the end of the script or until an error occurs.

5. Unveiling Crucial Syntax: The Foundation of Bash

In the field of Bash scripting, essential syntax elements serve as the bedrock for command definition, execution flow control, and variable handling. Here are the pivotal syntax components:

a. **Comments:** Marked with a **'#'** symbol, comments are non-executable lines crafted to elucidate the purpose of specific code segments.

b. **Variables:** These containers hold data, are recognized by names commencing with a letter or underscore, and are assigned values via the **'='** operator.

c. **Echo Command:** The **'echo'** command acts as a messenger, showcasing text or variable values within the terminal.

d. **Control Flow Statements:** Steering the command sequence, these statements include **'if'** for conditional execution and **'for'** loops for iterative tasks.

Mastering these syntax elements empowers Bash scripters to wield the language effectively, paving the way for efficient and robust script creation.

Conclusion

Congratulations on completing the exploration of Linux fundamentals, where we delved into the heart of open-source mastery. From navigating the Linux world and unleashing the power of Kali Linux to mastering essential commands and understanding file permissions, you have gained practical skills that form the foundation of your Linux journey. The unraveling of the Linux bootstrapping process and exploring the Linux file system hierarchy provided insights into the inner workings of this powerful operating system. Bash scripting essentials opened the door to automation, making tasks more efficient. As you conclude this chapter, equipped with newfound knowledge, get ready to apply these skills in the exciting world of cybersecurity.

In the upcoming chapter, we will dive into fundamental networking concepts, expanding your understanding of how systems communicate. Keep up the great work, and let us continue this learning adventure!

CHAPTER 3
Networking Fundamentals

Introduction

Embark on a captivating journey into the heart of networking with our comprehensive chapter on **Networking Fundamentals**. Building upon the Linux Fundamentals discussed earlier, this chapter serves as a gateway to understanding the backbone of our interconnected world. Explore the basics of network communication, unravel the intricacies of various network types, and grasp the significance of network topologies. Delve into essential networking commands, empowering yourself with the ability to navigate the digital landscape effortlessly. Take a deep dive into networking protocols, unlocking the secrets of how devices communicate. To add a touch of mystique, unravel the enigma of NMAP, a powerful network scanning tool.

Whether you are a novice or an enthusiast, this chapter promises to demystify the complexities of networking, ensuring that every reader gains a solid foundation in this ever-evolving world.

Structure

In this chapter, we will cover the following topics:

- Basics of Network Communication
- Types of Networks
- Network Topologies
- Essential Networking Commands
- Deep Dive into Networking Protocols
- NMAP Demystified

Basics of Network Communication

Welcome to the captivating world of networks, where devices converse, information flows freely, and the digital landscape unfolds before us. In this introductory chapter, we will embark on a journey to comprehend the fundamentals of network communication, laying the groundwork for your mastery of networking concepts.

Network communication, the essence of modern technology, refers to the process by which devices exchange information over a network. It is akin to a lively conversation between individuals, where data packets, the building blocks of information, serve as the words and phrases that convey meaning.

Imagine a world without networks; our devices would be isolated islands, unable to share data or collaborate. Networks have revolutionized our lives, enabling seamless communication, global collaboration, and access to a vast repository of knowledge.

Importance of Networks in Computing: The Unseen Foundations of the Digital Landscape

Networks have emerged as the silent weavers binding the digital fabric of our contemporary world, assuming a central role in diverse facets of computing:

- ***Business Evolution:*** Networks serve as the operational backbone for businesses, fostering seamless communication, collaborative file sharing, and centralized data management. This dynamic connectivity propels productivity and sparks innovation within organizational ecosystems.
- ***Global Interconnectivity:*** Networks obliterate geographical barriers, providing a conduit for individuals to connect with friends and family across the globe. They facilitate participation in online communities and grant access to a wealth of global resources, fostering a sense of interconnectedness on a planetary scale.
- ***Smart Technological Advancements:*** Networks form the foundational infrastructure for smart technologies, enabling interconnected devices to communicate and exchange data. This connectivity lays the groundwork for the Internet of Things (IoT), where everyday objects become part of a vast network, seamlessly interacting to enhance efficiency and convenience.

By delving into the fundamentals of network communication, you embark on a journey to comprehend the transformative force wielded by networks in our daily existence.

Decoding IP Addresses

In the expansive domain of networking, IP addresses serve as the linchpin for seamless communication between devices, resembling the digital postal codes that meticulously guide data packets to their intended destinations. This exploration aims to demystify the fundamentals of IP addresses, laying the foundation for your odyssey into the sphere of networking.

IPv4 versus IPv6: Embracing Evolution

Envision each device within a network as a distinct residence and an IP address as its exclusive identifier. Historically, IPv4 functioned as the standard, akin to a neighborhood with finite addresses. However, with the burgeoning digital landscape, the need for more addresses arose, culminating in the advent of IPv6.

IPv4, the traditional 32-bit addressing system, employs a sequence of four sets of numbers separated by dots (for example, 192.168.1.1). While effective, the escalating number of connected devices necessitated additional unique addresses, catalyzing the transition to IPv6.

IPv6, the contemporary 128-bit successor, mirrors a vast metropolis, providing an abundance of unique addresses to accommodate our ever-expanding digital footprint. It adopts a hexadecimal format, offering an extensive array of possibilities, exemplified by addresses like 2001:0db8:85a3:0000:0000:8a2e:0370:7334.

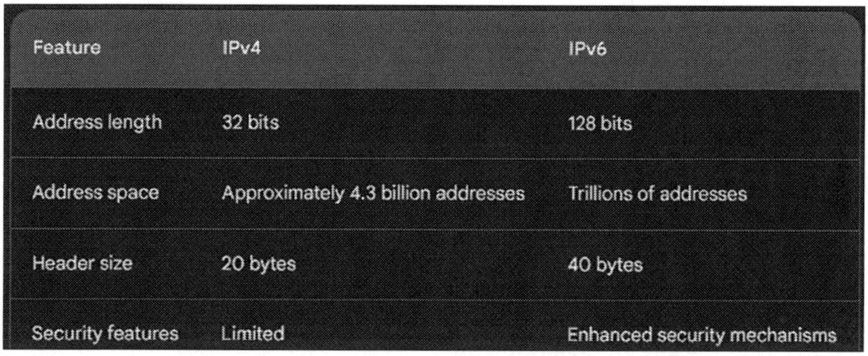

Feature	IPv4	IPv6
Address length	32 bits	128 bits
Address space	Approximately 4.3 billion addresses	Trillions of addresses
Header size	20 bytes	40 bytes
Security features	Limited	Enhanced security mechanisms

Figure 3.1: *IPv4 versus IPv6*

Understanding the Concept of IPv6

The online world is evolving rapidly as the demand for connectivity surges, leading to a depletion of IPv4 addresses. To address this challenge, IPv6 emerges as the next-generation solution, offering a significantly larger pool of IP addresses. This section delves into the workings of IPv6, the transition process, and optimal utilization strategies.

IPv6 is like a superhero in the digital world, offering lots of addresses, stronger security, and quicker traffic routing. It solves the problem of running out of addresses with IPv4. Transitioning to IPv6 happens gradually, allowing for the easy addition of devices and networks that use IPv6 alongside the old ones. However, integrating IPv6 into existing IPv4 setups requires careful planning and setup.

In simple terms, IPv6 is the cool, new way of keeping everyone connected online without running out of space.

Moving to IPv6: A Guide for an Easy Switch

Switching to IPv6 might sound complicated, but with the right plan, it can be smooth and trouble-free. Here are some ways to make the transition easy:

- ***Dual-stack setup***: Run both IPv4 and IPv6 at the same time. This way, devices can talk to each other using both types of addresses without any problems.
- ***Tunneling tricks***: Tunneling encapsulates IPv6 packets within IPv4 packets, enabling the transmission of IPv6 messages through IPv4 networks. This process is akin to placing an IPv6 letter inside an IPv4 envelope, allowing it to travel seamlessly across IPv4 infrastructure.
- **NAT64 *Translation (Network Address Translation for IPv6)***: Think of this as a language translator. It turns IPv4 talk into IPv6 talk, making sure devices that use the old way can still chat with the new ones.

IPv6 Best Practices: Ensuring a Successful Migration

To ensure a successful IPv6 migration, several best practices should be followed, including:

- ***Conduct a thorough network assessment***: Conduct a comprehensive network assessment to identify IPv4-only and IPv6-capable devices and infrastructure components.
- ***Define migration goals and objectives***: Specify the scope of the migration and include exact goals to ensure effective execution. Setting specific, quantifiable objectives for the IPv6 migration that are in line with more general commercial or technical goals is crucial. This tactical approach improves the effectiveness of the migration procedure, enabling better progress tracking and evaluation.
- ***Develop a comprehensive migration plan***: Outline the steps involved in the migration process, including timelines, resource allocation, and risk mitigation strategies.
- ***Educate and train network administrators***: Provide training to network administrators on IPv6 concepts, configuration, and troubleshooting techniques.
- ***Monitor and optimize performance***: Continuously monitor network performance and optimize IPv6 routing and configuration to ensure seamless operation.

The transition to IPv6 is a crucial step towards ensuring a sustainable and scalable internet infrastructure that can support the ever-growing demands of the digital world. By understanding IPv6 implementation strategies, best practices, and the benefits it offers, you will be well-equipped to navigate this transformative journey and contribute to the future of connectivity.

Subnetting Simplified: Creating Digital Neighborhoods

Subnetting is like dividing a large neighborhood into smaller blocks. In networking, it involves breaking down a large network into smaller, more manageable parts. Each part, known as a subnet, contains a group of devices that can communicate directly with each other without going through a router. This division helps in organizing and managing network traffic efficiently.

Subnetting offers several benefits. Firstly, it helps in optimizing network performance by reducing unnecessary traffic. By grouping devices that frequently communicate with each other into the same subnet, data can be sent directly, saving bandwidth and improving response times. Secondly, subnetting enhances network security by creating logical boundaries. Devices within the same subnet can communicate freely, but communication between devices in different subnets requires routing, adding an extra layer of security.

Finally, subnetting simplifies network management. It allows administrators to apply different network policies and configurations to specific subnets based on their requirements, making it easier to troubleshoot and maintain the network infrastructure.

Decoding the Way Devices Talk in Networks

In the complex world of networking, devices chat with each other using a fancy language ruled by protocols and ports. These crucial elements make sure information flows smoothly, making sure data gets right where it needs to go. Let us dive into the secrets of ports and protocols to understand how they shape the digital world.

Importance of Ports: Special Tags for Network Chit-Chat

Think of a busy city with each building having a special address. This way, mail carriers can deliver packages right where they need to go. Ports work the same way for devices talking on a network. They are like special tags that help devices know what kind of data or app they are dealing with.

Every port has a unique number, and it ranges from 0 to 65535. When a device sends data, it includes the port number of the device it is talking to. This ensures the information reaches the right app or service on the other end.

Unveiling Common Protocols: The Etiquette of Network Interaction

Protocols, likened to the etiquette governing a conversation, delineate the guidelines for how devices exchange data. They meticulously define the format, structure, and sequence of data packets, ensuring seamless communication between devices, irrespective of their variations in hardware or software.

Among the plethora of protocols, two stalwarts, TCP (Transmission Control Protocol) and UDP (User Datagram Protocol), stand out as the linchpins of networking. Each protocol serves a unique function:

- **TCP:** Positioned as a stalwart in reliability, TCP guarantees the flawless delivery of data packets to their designated destinations, maintaining the correct order and mitigating errors. It operates akin to a meticulous postal service, conscientiously ensuring the safe delivery of every letter and package.
- **UDP:** In stark contrast, UDP prioritizes speed over unwavering reliability. It willingly foregoes error checking and packet ordering to expedite data transmission. Picture UDP as a swift courier service, emphasizing rapid delivery even if there is a minimal chance of a misplaced item.

Understanding the Protocol and Port Combination

The combination of a protocol and a port creates a unique identifier for a specific network service. For instance, the combination of TCP and port 80 is associated with web browsing, allowing devices to connect to web servers and access websites.

Ports and protocols are the fundamental building blocks of network communication, enabling devices to exchange information seamlessly.

Types of Networks

Embark on a swift journey through vital network domains. From the intimacy of Local Area Networks (LANs) to the expansive reach of Wide Area Networks (WANs), we will explore components, configurations, and the backbone of the Internet. Delve into the essentials of Wireless Networks, grasp Wi-Fi intricacies, and learn the art of securing these connections. In this concise section, simplicity meets connectivity–welcome to the core of networking.

Exploring the Neighborhood: Understanding Local Area Networks (LANs)

Venturing into the world of networking, we encounter Local Area Networks (LANs), the foundation upon which our digital neighborhoods are built. LANs connect devices within a confined area, such as a home, office, or school, enabling seamless communication and resource sharing. Embark on a journey to grasp the intricacies of LANs, from their components to their configurations, and gain insights into their role in shaping our digital interactions.

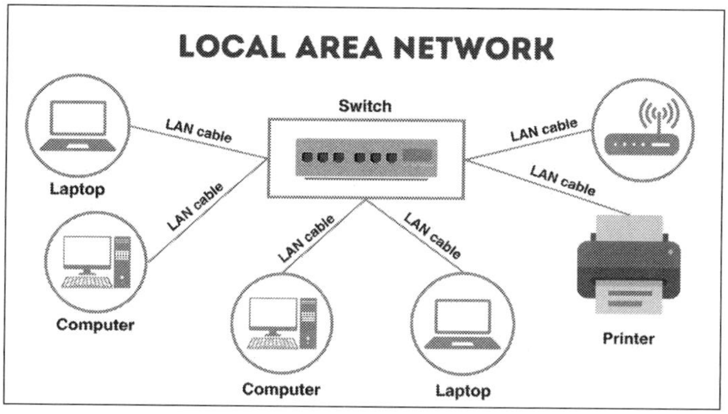

Figure 3.2: *Local Area Network* (LAN)

Home and Small Office Networks: The Everyday LAN Experience

LANs are not confined to large corporate environments; they also play a crucial role in our homes and small offices. Home LANs connect our personal devices, such as computers, smartphones, and tablets, allowing us to share files, stream multimedia content, and access internet resources. Similarly, small office LANs facilitate collaboration among employees, enabling them to share files, access central databases, and communicate efficiently.

LAN Components: The Building Blocks of Local Connectivity

To establish a functional LAN, several essential components come together:

- ***Network Interface Cards (NICs):*** NICs act as the communication gateways for devices, enabling them to connect to the network. Imagine NICs as network adapters, providing the physical connection to the network.
- ***Network Cables:*** Network cables, the physical conduits for data transmission, come in various types, including Ethernet and fiber-optic cables. These cables serve as the roads and highways upon which data travels through the network.
- ***Switches and Hubs:*** Switches and hubs, the traffic control centers of a LAN, connect multiple devices and facilitate data exchange. Switches are more intelligent, directing data to specific destinations, while hubs broadcast data to all connected devices.

- ***Wireless Access Points (APs):*** Wireless APs eliminate the need for physical cabling, allowing devices to connect to the network via Wi-Fi. Think of APs as invisible towers, broadcasting network signals throughout the area.

LAN Configuration: Establishing Connections and Sharing Resources

Configuring a LAN involves assigning IP addresses to devices, enabling them to identify and communicate with each other. Routers, the network traffic managers, connect LANs to the internet and other networks, while firewalls protect LANs from unauthorized access.

In addition to device connectivity, LANs facilitate resource sharing. File servers provide centralized storage for shared files, while print servers manage shared printers, eliminating the need for individual printers at each workstation.

LANs, the cornerstone of local connectivity, provide a foundation for seamless communication and resource sharing within homes, offices, and other confined areas. Understanding the components, configurations, and applications of LANs empowers you to navigate your digital neighborhood with confidence and expertise, maximizing the benefits of local networking in your daily life.

Bridging Distances: Exploring Wide Area Networks (WANs) and the Internet

As we venture beyond the confines of local area networks, we enter the horizon of Wide Area Networks (WANs), the bridges that connect networks across vast geographical distances. WANs enable us to communicate and share resources with individuals and organizations worldwide, blurring the boundaries of location and time. Embark on a journey to comprehend the intricacies of WANs, from their technologies to their applications, and gain insights into their role in shaping our interconnected digital world.

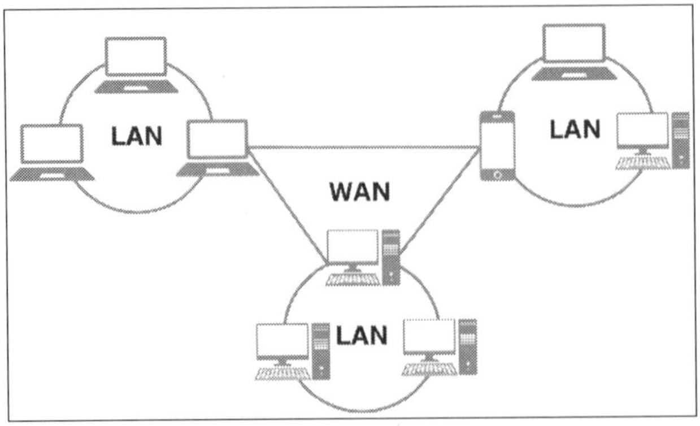

Figure 3.3: *Wide Area Network (WAN)*

Connecting Networks Across Distances: The WAN Infrastructure

WANs employ various technologies to connect networks over long distances, including:

- ***Leased Lines:*** Leased lines provide dedicated, high-speed connections between two points, ensuring consistent and reliable data transmission. Think of leased lines as private highways, exclusively reserved for your data traffic.
- ***Telephone Lines:*** Traditional telephone lines can be used for WAN connections, but their bandwidth limitations make them less suitable for data-intensive applications. Imagine using a narrow country road for heavy truck traffic, resulting in congestion and delays.
- ***Satellite Links:*** Satellite links provide connectivity in remote regions where terrestrial infrastructure is limited. However, satellite signals are susceptible to latency, making them less ideal for real-time applications. Think of satellite links as bridges over vast oceans, connecting remote islands to the mainland.
- ***Microwave Links:*** Microwave links transmit data using radio waves over short distances. They are often used to connect buildings or towers within a campus or metropolitan area. Picture microwave links as high-speed communication beams, connecting neighboring buildings like laser pointers.

The Internet and Its Infrastructure: A Global Network of Networks

The internet, the pinnacle of WAN technology, is a vast network of interconnected networks that spans the globe. It enables individuals and organizations to communicate, share information, and access resources without geographical barriers.

The internet's infrastructure comprises:

- ***Internet Service Providers (ISPs):*** ISPs provide internet access to individuals and organizations, connecting them to the global network. Think of ISPs as gatekeepers of the internet, granting access to the vast digital space.
- ***Internet Exchange Points (IXPs):*** IXPs facilitate the exchange of internet traffic between ISPs, optimizing data routing and reducing latency. Imagine IXPs as traffic junctions on an internet highway, directing data packets efficiently.
- ***Backbone Networks:*** Backbone networks, the core of the internet infrastructure, carry the bulk of internet traffic, connecting major cities and countries. Picture backbone networks as the main arteries of the internet, transporting data across vast distances.

WANs have revolutionized the way we communicate, collaborate, and access information, making the world a smaller, more interconnected place. The internet, built upon the foundation of WAN technologies, serves as a global platform for innovation, education, and commerce.

Untethered Connectivity: Exploring Wireless Networks and Wi-Fi Essentials

In the ever-evolving world of networking, wireless technology has emerged as a transformative force, liberating us from the constraints of physical cables and ushering in an era of untethered connectivity. Wireless networks, the cornerstone of this revolution, have permeated our homes, offices, and public spaces, enabling seamless communication and resource sharing without the hassle of tangled wires. Embark on a journey to comprehend the fundamentals of wireless networks, unravel the mysteries of Wi-Fi, and discover strategies to secure your wireless connections.

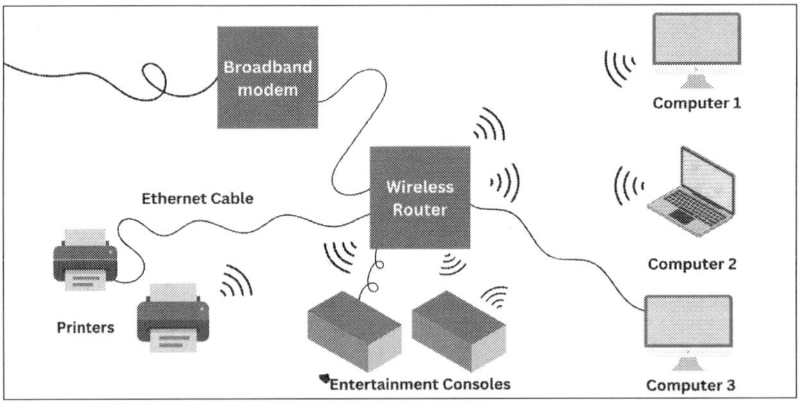

***Figure 3.4**: Wi-Fi Network*

Wi-Fi Essentials: Making Wireless Connections Easy

Wi-Fi, the go-to wireless tech, is like magic for wireless connections. It uses radio waves to send data between devices, letting them hop online and share stuff without any pesky cables.

Here are the important parts of a Wi-Fi setup:

- ***Wireless Access Points (APs):*** APs are like the central wizards of Wi-Fi. They send out magic signals (radio waves) that let devices connect. Picture them as invisible towers spreading Wi-Fi all around a building.
- ***Wireless Network Interface Cards (NICs):*** These are like the radios inside your devices. They are the things that make your gadgets talk to Wi-Fi. Just like your car radio tunes into stations, these NICs tune into Wi-Fi signals.

- ***Routing Protocols:*** These are like traffic managers for Wi-Fi. They make sure the data traveling through the air reaches where it is supposed to go. Think of them as the guides that keep things moving smoothly.

Securing Wireless Networks: Protecting Your Digital Horizon

While wireless networks offer convenience and flexibility, they also introduce security vulnerabilities. To safeguard your wireless connections, consider these essential steps:

- ***Strong Passwords:*** Employ strong and unique passwords for your Wi-Fi network and APs, making it difficult for unauthorized access. Think of passwords as the gatekeepers of your wireless domain, preventing intruders from entering.
- ***Encryption:*** Enable encryption protocols, such as WPA2, to scramble data transmissions, ensuring that sensitive information remains protected. Imagine encryption as a secret code, making your data unreadable to eavesdroppers.
- ***Firewalls:*** Implement firewalls on connected devices to filter incoming and outgoing traffic, blocking potential threats. Picture firewalls as watchful sentinels, protecting your network from malicious intrusions.
- ***Regular Updates:*** Regularly update your wireless devices, APs, and routers with the latest security patches to address vulnerabilities and prevent exploits. Think of updates as armor, strengthening your network's defenses against evolving threats.

Wireless networks have transformed our digital landscape, enabling seamless connectivity and mobility. By understanding the principles of Wi-Fi and implementing robust security measures, you can harness the power of wireless technology to connect, collaborate, and thrive in an increasingly wireless world.

Network Topologies

Dive into the intricate world of network structures in this section, where we decode the language of Star, Bus, Ring, and Mesh Topologies. Visualize the very backbone of connectivity as we explore the pros and cons of each topology. Witness the synergy of Hybrid Topologies, where efficiency takes center stage through strategic combinations. We will not only demystify these network structures but also unveil their real-world applications. Join us in this brief exploration, where the threads of connectivity weave into the tapestry of network topologies. Welcome to the visual symphony of efficient networking!

Deciphering Network Architectures: Navigating the Kingdom of Network Topologies

In the big world of networking, think of devices as dancers and the lines connecting them as the dance floor. This dance floor, or network topology, decides how the dancers (devices) talk to each other, making sure they do it smoothly. It is like a choreographer, determining how the dance (data flow) happens and how well the performance (network) works.

Let us take a journey to understand these dances, known as network topologies. We will explore what makes each dance special, how it helps the performance (the network) get better, and what challenges it might face. It is like peeling back the layers of a dance routine to see what makes it unique. So, come along as we dive into the world of network topologies, where we will uncover what makes each dance move tick and why it matters in the grand performance of our digital world.

- ***Star Topology*: A Centralized Hub**

  Imagine a network where all devices connect to a central hub, like branches reaching out to a tree trunk. This arrangement is known as a star topology. The hub acts as the central intermediary, receiving data from all connected devices and retransmitting it to the intended recipient.

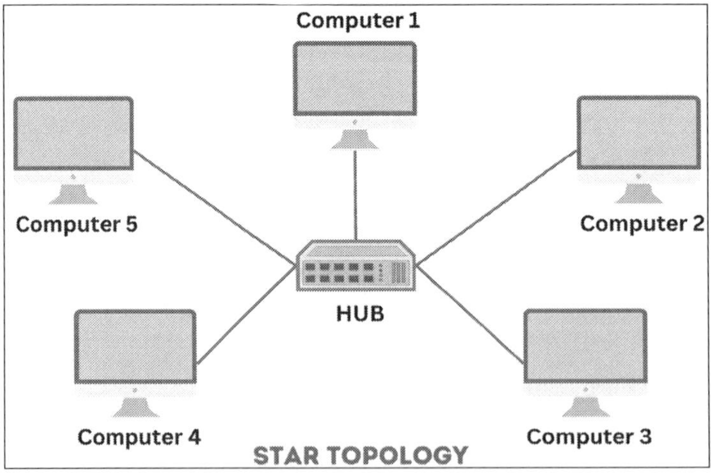

Figure 3.5: *Star Topology*

Advantages of Star Topology:

- ***Easy Setup and Management***: Simple to install and configure, making it suitable for small and medium-sized networks.
    - ***Scalability***: Easy to add or remove devices, allowing for network expansion as needed.

- ○ ***Fault Isolation:*** If a device fails, it does not affect the entire network, making troubleshooting easier.

Disadvantages of Star Topology:

- ○ ***Centralized Dependency:*** The network relies heavily on the central hub, and its failure can bring down the entire network.
- ○ ***Performance Bottleneck:*** The hub can become a bottleneck if data traffic is high, affecting network performance.

- ***Bus Topology: A Linear Network***

Imagine a network where devices are connected to a single cable, like beads strung on a thread. This arrangement is known as a bus topology. Data travels in both directions along the cable, and all devices receive the same data, making it suitable for simple networks where data sharing is not a priority.

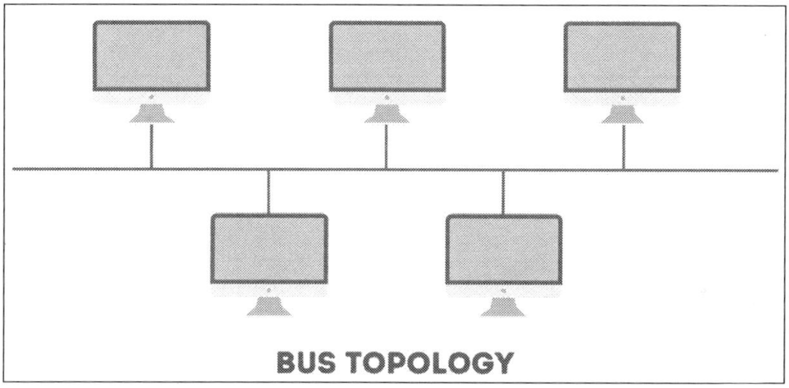

Figure 3.6: *Bus Topology*

Advantages of Bus Topology:

- ○ ***Low Cost:*** Requires minimal cabling, making it a cost-effective solution for small networks.
- ○ ***Easy Installation:*** Simple to install and maintain, with no complex routing or configuration.

Disadvantages of Bus Topology:

- ○ ***Single Point of Failure:*** If the main cable breaks, the entire network goes down.
- ○ ***Signal Degradation:*** As the network grows, signal quality can deteriorate, affecting data transmission.
- ○ ***Collision-Based Access:*** Devices must contend for access to the cable, leading to collisions and data loss in high-traffic situations.

- ***Ring Topology*: A Circular Loop**

  Envision a network where devices are connected circularly, forming a loop. Data travels in one direction around the ring, passing through each device until it reaches its intended destination.

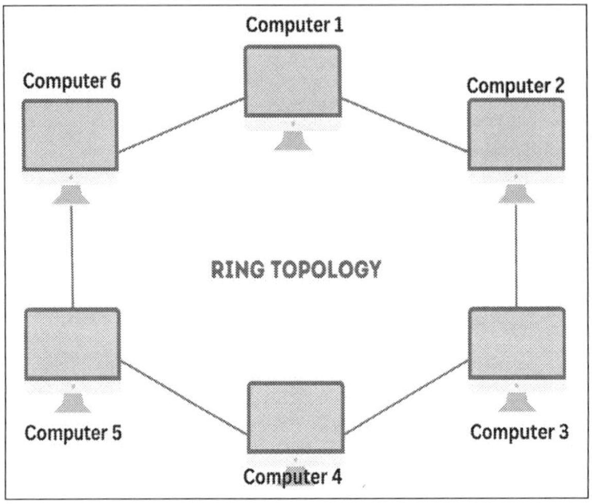

***Figure* 3.7:** *Ring Topology*

Advantages of Ring Topology:

- ***Reduced Collisions*:** Devices receive data tokens, preventing collisions and ensuring orderly data transmission.
- ***Deterministic Data Flow*:** Data travels in a predictable path, providing consistent performance.

Disadvantages of Ring Topology:

- ***Single Point of Failure*:** If a device or cable fails, the entire ring becomes inoperable.
- ***Difficult Troubleshooting*:** Troubleshooting issues can be challenging due to the interconnected nature of the ring.

- ***Mesh Topology*: A Web of Connections**

  Imagine a network where devices are connected to multiple other devices, forming a web-like structure. Data can travel along multiple paths, ensuring redundancy and resilience.

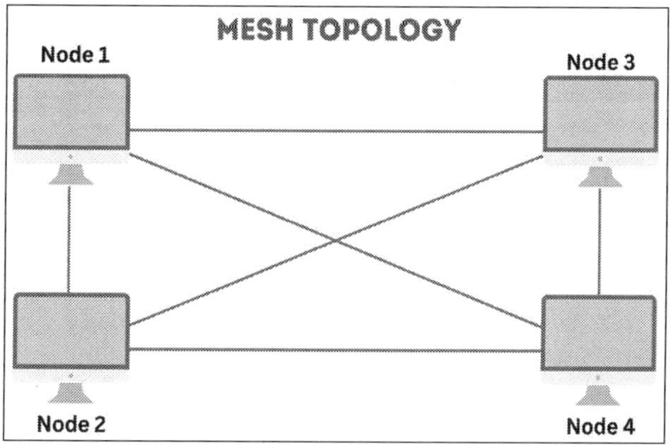

Figure 3.8: *Mesh Topology*

Advantages of Mesh Topology:

- ***Fault Tolerance:*** If a device or cable fails, other paths can still carry data, minimizing network downtime.
- ***Scalability:*** Easily expandable by adding more devices, making it suitable for large and complex networks.
- ***Robustness:*** Provides high availability and resilience against failures.

Disadvantages of Mesh Topology:

- ***Complexity:*** More complex to configure and manage compared to other topologies.
- ***Higher Cost:*** Requires more cabling and network devices, increasing the overall cost.

Think of network topologies as blueprints for building a strong and efficient network. They decide how your devices connect and communicate, influencing how well your network performs, grows, and handles challenges. By understanding what each type of topology is good at and where it might face challenges, you become a smart architect, and are able to design networks that fit your needs perfectly. As you learn more about networking, you will see how these basics are the secret sauce behind the technology that powers our digital world.

Unlocking Network Power: Understanding Hybrid Topologies

In the world of networking, variety is key. It is a bit like how different flavors come together to make a delicious dish. Similarly, in networking, different network topologies can team up to create something special. By blending the strengths of various topologies, we can build hybrid networks that suit specific needs and work well. Let us take a trip to explore these mixed-up topologies, figuring out what makes them great and seeing how they are used in the real world. It is like discovering a secret recipe for network success!

Hybrid Topologies: A Fusion of Network Architectures

Imagine a network that combines the centralized control of a star topology with the resilience of a mesh topology. This is the essence of a hybrid topology, where multiple network architectures are seamlessly integrated to create a network that is more versatile and adaptable than any single topology alone.

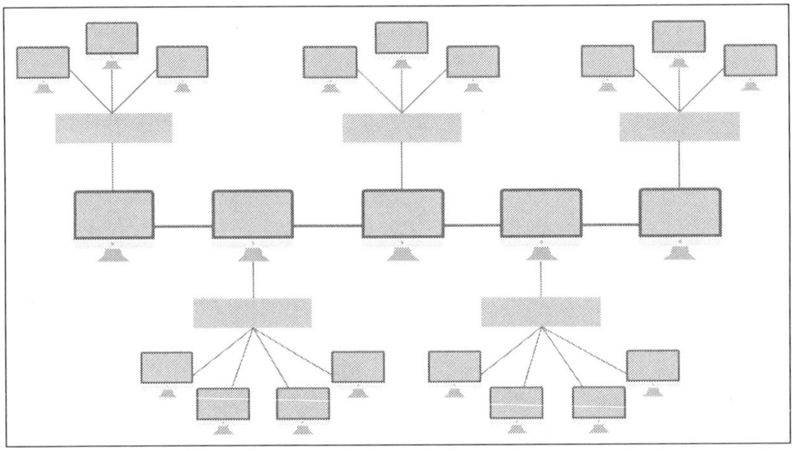

Figure 3.9: *Hybrid Topology*

By leveraging the strengths of different topologies, hybrid networks offer several advantages:

- ***Increased Flexibility:*** Hybrid networks can be customized to meet specific requirements, providing the flexibility to accommodate diverse networking needs.
- ***Enhanced Fault Tolerance:*** The redundancy inherent in hybrid topologies ensures that network operations continue even if individual components fail.
- ***Improved Performance:*** By distributing data traffic across multiple paths, hybrid networks can handle high-bandwidth applications efficiently.

Examples of Hybrid Topologies:

- **Star-Bus Hybrid:**
    - ***Description***: Combines the simplicity of a star with the cost-effectiveness of a bus.
    - ***Application***: Ideal for larger networks where centralized control is needed, but cost efficiency is also a priority.

- ***Mesh-Ring Hybrid:***
    - ***Description***: Integrates the redundancy of mesh with the resilience of a ring.
    - ***Application***: Suitable for critical applications where both redundancy and continuous communication are essential.
- ***Star-Mesh Hybrid:***
    - ***Description***: Merges the centralized control of a star with the robustness of a mesh.
    - ***Application***: Effective for networks where certain devices require constant communication while others demand redundancy.

Real-world Applications: Harnessing Hybrid Network Power

Hybrid topologies are not just theoretical constructs; they are widely used in various real-world scenarios:

- ***Corporate Networks:*** Large organizations often employ hybrid topologies to connect their extensive networks, ensuring efficient communication and data sharing across multiple departments and locations.
- ***Wireless Networks:*** Combining star and mesh topologies can extend Wi-Fi coverage and provide seamless connectivity in large buildings or outdoor areas.
- ***Industrial Networks:*** Hybrid topologies are crucial in industrial control systems, ensuring reliable communication between sensors, actuators, and controllers in critical manufacturing environments.

Hybrid topologies represent a testament to the ingenuity of network engineers, who have devised ways to combine the strengths of different architectures to create networks that are more versatile, resilient, and efficient. By understanding the principles of hybrid topologies, you are empowered to tailor networks to specific requirements, ensuring that your network infrastructure supports your organization's goals and objectives. As you navigate the ever-evolving world of networking, remember that hybrid topologies offer a powerful tool for unleashing the true potential of interconnected systems.

Essential Networking Commands

The CLI offers a rich arsenal of commands specifically designed for network management and troubleshooting. Here are a few essential commands to get you started:

- **`Ping`:** Checks connectivity to a host by sending data packets and measuring their response time.

- **`Traceroute`:** Traces the path taken by data packets as they travel from your device to a remote destination.
- **`Netstat`:** Displays detailed information about network connections, including active sockets, routing tables, and interface statistics.
- **`Nslookup`:** Translates hostnames into IP addresses and vice versa, a crucial tool for resolving domain names.
- **`ipconfig/ifconfig`:** Provides information about network interfaces, including IP addresses, subnet masks, and MAC addresses.

Pinging: Probing Connectivity with Echo Requests

Imagine a network as a vast network of interconnected roads and highways. Just as we use radar to detect the presence of objects, the ping command serves as a network radar, sending echo requests to remote devices to check their connectivity. When a response is received, the command indicates that the device is accessible and the network connection is functional.

Syntax: `ping <destination_IP_address>`

`ping`:

- **Checking connectivity to a website:**

  `ping google.com`

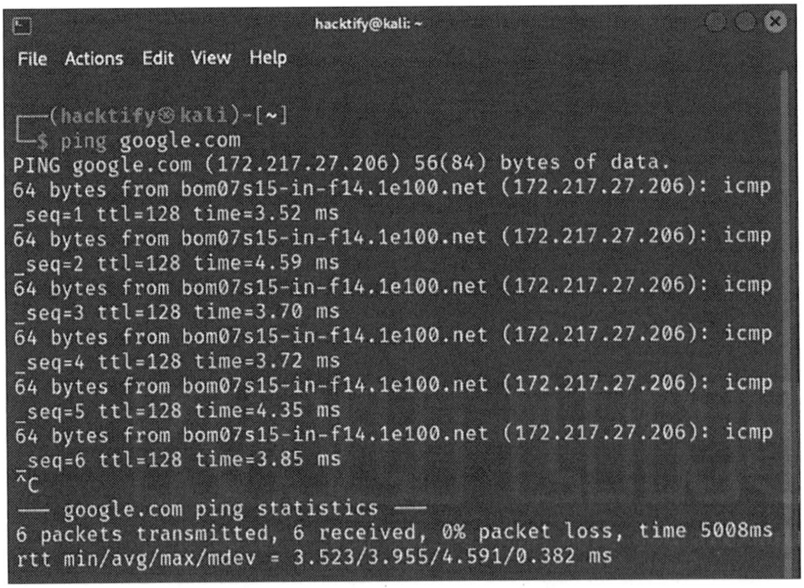

Figure 3.10: *Ping Command 1*

- **Pinging multiple hosts at once:**

  `ping google.com yahoo.com 8.8.8.8`

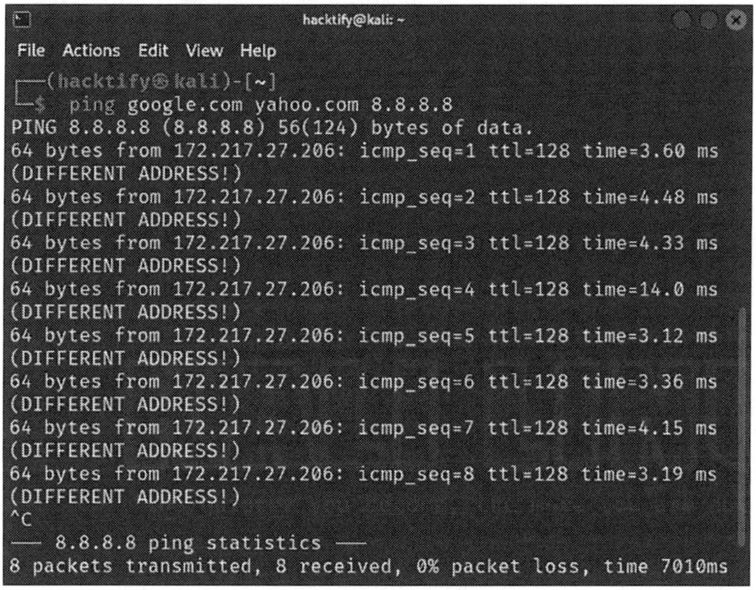

Figure 3.11: *Ping Command 2*

Traceroute: Unveiling the Network Path

As data travels across a network, it traverses a series of interconnected routers, each guiding it closer to its destination. The traceroute command acts as a network map, revealing the path taken by data packets as they journey through the digital sphere. It displays the IP addresses of each router along the way, providing valuable insights into network routing and potential bottlenecks.

Syntax: `traceroute <destination_IP_address>`

`traceroute`:

- **Tracing the path to a website:**

  `traceroute google.com`

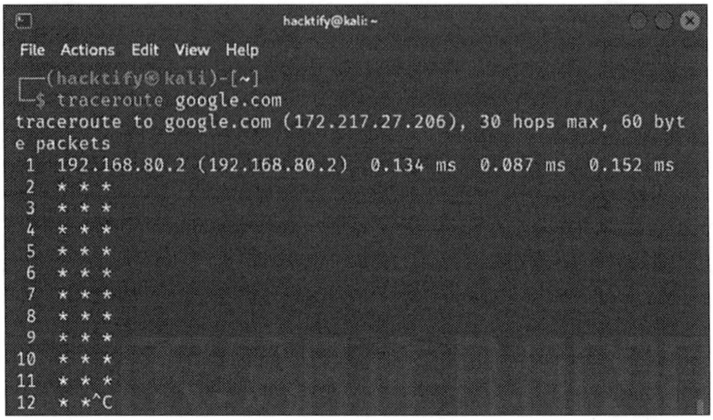

Figure 3.12: *Traceroute Command*

Checking Network Configuration with ifconfig

Just as a ship's captain relies on navigational instruments to steer the vessel, network administrators utilize the **`ifconfig`** command to monitor and configure network interfaces. This versatile tool displays detailed information about network adapters, including their IP addresses, subnet masks, MAC addresses, and transmission speeds.

Syntax: **`ifconfig`**

Output: A comprehensive overview of network interface configurations

- **Displaying information about all network interfaces (Linux):**

  `ifconfig`

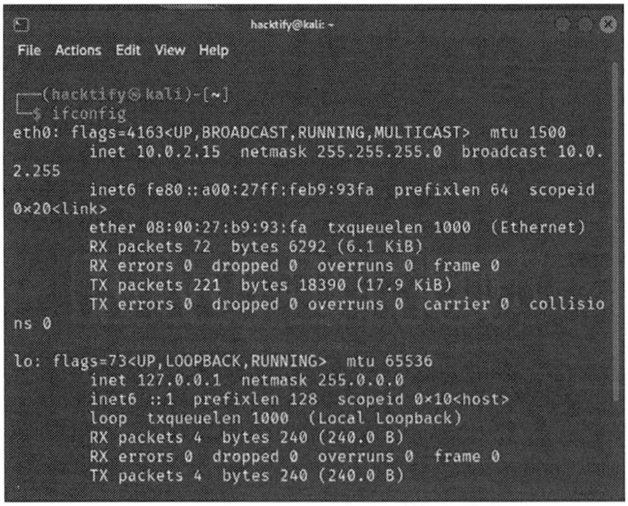

Figure 3.13: *ifconfig Command*

`netstat:`

- **Listing all active TCP connections:**

  `netstat -ant`

***Figure 3.14**: netstat Command 1*

- **Listing all active UDP connections:**

  `netstat -aun`

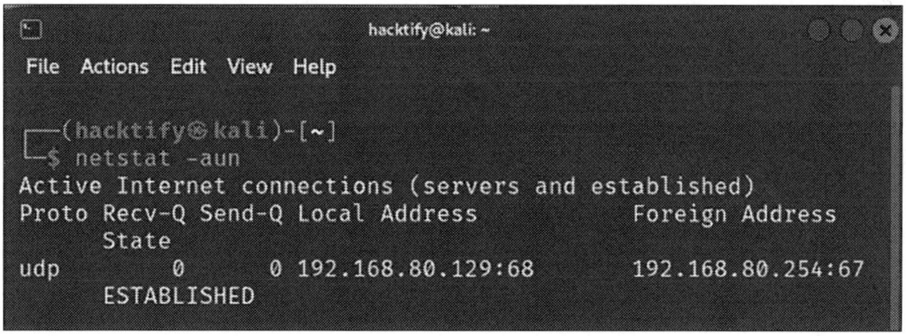

***Figure 3.15**: netstat Command 2*

`nslookup:`

- **Translating a hostname to an IP address:**

  `nslookup google.com`

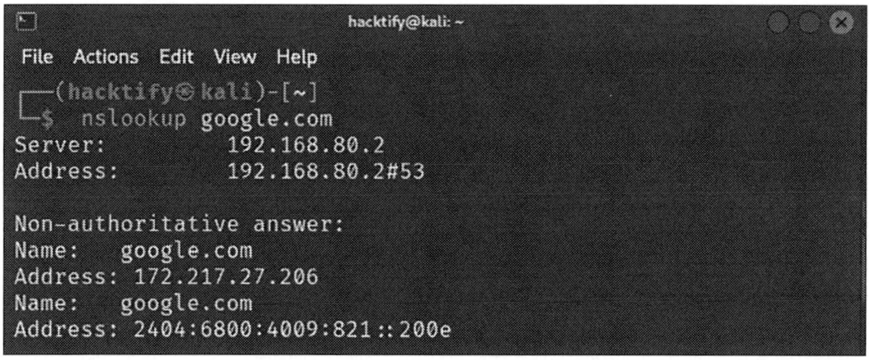

***Figure 3.16**: nslookup Command 1*

- **Translating an IP address to a hostname:**

  `nslookup 8.8.8.8`

Figure 3.17: *nslookup Command 2*

The command-line interface, often perceived as daunting, holds immense power and versatility for network enthusiasts and IT professionals alike. By mastering the basics of the Linux terminal and understanding essential networking commands, you can interact directly with network devices, troubleshoot issues, and optimize network performance. As you delve deeper into networking, the CLI will serve as an invaluable tool, empowering you to navigate the intricacies of network management and configuration with confidence and expertise.

The **`ping`**, **`traceroute`**, and **`ifconfig`** commands represent a cornerstone of networking expertise in Kali Linux. By mastering these essential tools, you gain the ability to probe network connectivity, troubleshoot routing issues, and monitor network interface configurations, laying the foundation for a deeper understanding of network management and optimization. As you venture further into the world of networking, these commands will serve as invaluable companions, empowering you to navigate the intricacies of network operations with confidence and proficiency.

Deep Dive into Networking Protocols

Delve into the intricate world of networking protocols. Uncover the inner workings of the Transmission Control Protocol (TCP), understand its fundamental operations, and gain practical insights through hands-on examples of TCP communication. Navigate further into the sphere of User Datagram Protocol (UDP), unraveling its unique characteristics and discovering real-world use cases. Join us on this illuminating journey where complex protocols become comprehensible, empowering you with practical knowledge for a deeper understanding of network communication.

Unveiling the Heart of Networking: Delving into the Transmission Control Protocol (TCP)

In the field of networking, the Transmission Control Protocol (TCP) stands as the backbone of reliable data transmission, ensuring that information flows seamlessly across networks without errors or loss. Unlike its UDP counterpart, which prioritizes speed over reliability, TCP employs a sophisticated mechanism of error checking, sequencing, and acknowledgment to guarantee the integrity of data packets. Embark on a journey to decipher the intricacies of TCP, understand its workings, and explore its practical applications in the digital world.

TCP: Making Sure Your Data Gets There Safely

Think of TCP like a superhero courier, making sure your packages get to the right place. It is a bit like a busy delivery service in a big city. Before sending any package, the superhero courier checks everything, keeps records, and makes sure the package reaches its destination without any mistakes. TCP works the same way–it creates a special connection between two devices before sending any data. This way, it guarantees that your data arrives safely and in the right order, just like your important packages.

TCP's Mechanism: A Symphony of Error Checking and Acknowledgment

TCP's reliability stems from a carefully orchestrated sequence of events:

- ***Handshake:*** Before data transmission, TCP establishes a connection between the sending and receiving devices, exchanging information about their capabilities and agreeing on parameters for the communication.
- ***Sequencing:*** Each data packet is assigned a sequence number, ensuring that packets are received in the correct order, preventing garbled messages or lost data.
- ***Error Checking:*** Each data packet is accompanied by a checksum, a mathematical calculation that verifies the integrity of the data. If the checksum at the receiving end does not match the original checksum, the packet is discarded, and a request for retransmission is sent.
- ***Acknowledgment:*** Upon receiving a data packet, the receiving device sends an acknowledgment, informing the sender that the packet was received intact. If an acknowledgment is not received within a specified time frame, the sender retransmits the packet.

Hands-on Example: Basic TCP Connection with Netcat

Let us go over a quick hands-on example of TCP communication with Kali Linux. In this example, we will use the netcat (nc) command to connect two terminals using a basic TCP connection.

1. **Open two terminals:** In Kali Linux, launch two separate terminals. This can be accomplished by hitting *Ctrl + Alt + T* or by selecting the terminal icon from the desktop environment.

2. **Set up a listener (server):** Set up a listener in one terminal with the `nc` command. This terminal will operate as the server while it waits for a connection.

```
nc -lvp 4444
```

`l`: Listen mode is used to receive incoming connections.

`v`: Show extra information about the relationship by being more verbose.

`p 4444`: Enter the port number (any accessible port will do).

Figure 3.18: *Setting up a Listener*

3. **Initiate a connection (client):** On the other terminal, initiate a connection to the listener using the same nc command.

```
nc 127.0.0.1 4444
```

`127.0.0.1`: The IP address of the localhost.

`4444`: The port number to connect to.

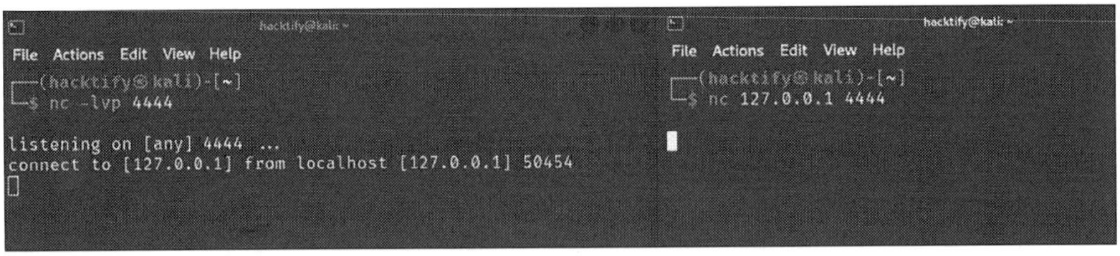

Figure 3.19: *Initiating a TCP Connection*

4. **Communicate between terminals**: Once the connection is established, you can start typing in one terminal, and the text will appear in the other. It is a simple back-and-forth communication.

Example:

In the client terminal, type: **`Hello, this is a demo of TCP`**

You will see the message appear on the server terminal.

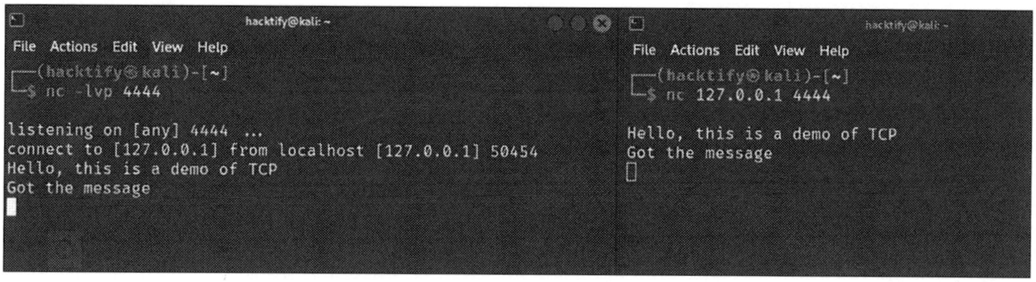

Figure 3.20: *Communicating between Terminals*

5. **Terminate the connection**: To terminate the connection, you can simply close one of the terminals or use the *Ctrl* + C keyboard shortcut in both terminals.

TCP, often overshadowed by flashier protocols, stands as the unsung hero of network communication, ensuring that our digital interactions are reliable, secure, and error-free.

User Datagram Protocol (UDP): Exploring the Swift and Simple Side of Digital Communication in Kali Linux

In the intricate dance of networking, protocols take center stage, each with its unique rhythm and purpose. In this section, we will shine a spotlight on the User Datagram Protocol (UDP), unraveling its characteristics and exploring the scenarios where its swift and simple nature makes it the star of digital communication. Guided by Kali Linux, let us demystify UDP and discover the magic it brings to the networking symphony.

Imagine UDP as the speedster of digital communication, opting for simplicity and speed over the meticulous precision of its counterpart, Transmission Control Protocol (TCP). Let us delve into the key characteristics that define UDP's swift and uncomplicated nature.

Key Characteristics of UDP:

- ***Connectionless:***
  - ***Description:*** UDP is like a postcard; it does not establish a dedicated connection before sending data. It shoots messages into the digital wind, hoping they reach their destination.
  - ***Analogy:*** Sending a message on a paper airplane—quick and direct, but no guarantee it will arrive.
- ***No Handshaking:***
  - ***Description:*** Unlike TCP's elaborate handshake, UDP skips the introductions. It sends data without prior negotiation, assuming it will be received.

  - ***Analogy:*** Dropping a note in a friend's mailbox without ringing the doorbell for confirmation.
- ***Unreliable Delivery:***
  - ***Description:*** UDP does not obsess over ensuring every message arrives intact. It shoots messages off and hopes for the best. If a message is lost, there is no automatic retransmission.
  - ***Analogy:*** Shouting a quick message across a busy street–some may hear, some may not.
- ***Low Overhead:***
  - ***Description:*** With no need for complex handshakes and error-checking mechanisms, UDP operates with minimal overhead. This makes it a lightweight choice for certain scenarios.
  - ***Analogy:*** Sending a brief message on a small postcard instead of a formal letter.

Use Cases for UDP: Where Swiftness Takes Center Stage

Now, let us explore the real-world scenarios where the swift and simple nature of UDP shines, making it the preferred choice for certain types of digital communication.

Use Case 1: Real-time Communication–VoIP and Streaming:

- ***Scenario***: Voice over Internet Protocol (VoIP) calls and streaming services often rely on UDP. Real-time communication values speed and the occasional loss of a packet is acceptable.
- ***Analogy***: Making a phone call, you want to hear the person on the other end in real time, and missing a word here or there is tolerable.

Use Case 2: Online Gaming:

- ***Scenario***: Online gaming thrives on low-latency communication. UDP's quick, connectionless nature is ideal for transmitting game data where immediate response is crucial.
- ***Analogy***: Playing a fast-paced game, you want your actions to be reflected instantly in the virtual world.

Use Case 3: DNS Queries:

- ***Scenario***: Domain Name System (DNS) queries, where a device asks a DNS server to resolve a domain name into an IP address, often use UDP. The lightweight nature of UDP suits these quick and frequent queries.
- ***Analogy***: Asking someone nearby for directions–a quick question with a brief response.

Hands-on Example: Using UDP with Netcat (nc) in Kali Linux:

1. **Open a Terminal in Kali Linux**

2. **Initiate a UDP Server**: Start a UDP server using the `nc` (netcat) command.

```
nc -ulvp 4444
```

`u`: Use UDP

`l`: Listen mode

`v`: Be verbose

`p 4444`: Specify the port number

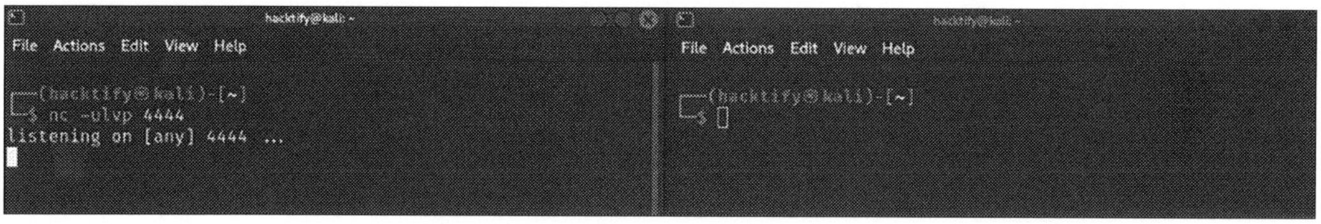

Figure 3.21: *Initiating a UDP Server*

3. **Send a UDP Message:** Open another terminal and send a UDP message to the server.

```
nc -u 127.0.0.1 4444
```

Observe the message appearing on the server terminal.

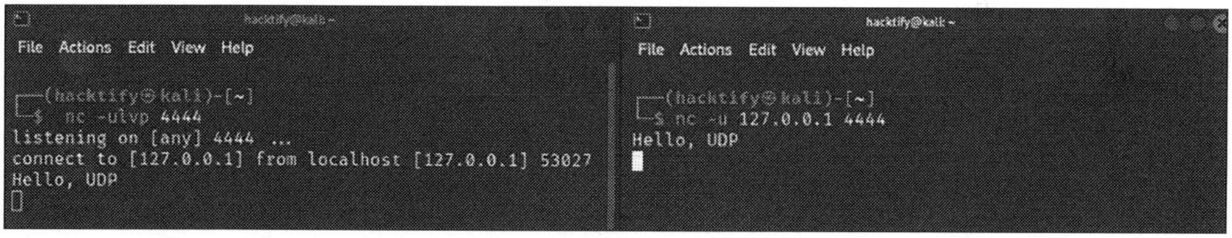

Figure 3.22: *Sending a UDP Message*

4. **Terminate the Server:** Terminate the server by pressing *Ctrl* + C in the terminal where the server is running.

This hands-on example showcases the simplicity and speed of UDP using Kali Linux. The nc command allows you to quickly set up a UDP server and send messages without the overhead of a dedicated connection.

Real-world Application: The Swift Messenger in Cybersecurity

In cybersecurity, UDP's speed and simplicity find applications in scenarios where immediate communication is essential, such as real-time monitoring, gaming, or certain types of network scanning. In conclusion, User Datagram Protocol (UDP) is the swift messenger of the networking world, favoring speed and simplicity in specific scenarios.

NMAP Demystified

Dive into this topic as we demystify NMAP (Network Mapper), a potent networking tool. We will understand its significance, discover basic commands, and explore scanning techniques for effective network exploration. We will also decode NMAP output, learning to analyze and apply this knowledge to practical applications like network discovery and security auditing. You will be able to elevate your networking skills with NMAP's powerful capabilities and uncover the essentials for effective network management in a concise exploration of NMAP's intricacies.

Introduction to NMAP – Unraveling the Secrets of Network Discovery in Kali Linux

In the labyrinth of networking, tools like NMAP emerge as the compass guiding enthusiasts through the twists and turns of digital landscapes. In this section, we will embark on a journey into the heart of NMAP, demystifying its purpose, unraveling its capabilities, and understanding why this tool is a beacon for network explorers. Guided by Kali Linux, let us delve into the world of NMAP and discover the secrets it holds for networking mastery.

Imagine NMAP as a digital explorer's Swiss army knife, equipped with versatile tools for mapping out the terrain of networks. NMAP, short for Network Mapper, is a powerful and flexible open-source tool designed for network discovery and security auditing. Its primary purpose is to probe networks, identify devices, and gather information about their characteristics, services, and potential vulnerabilities.

Key Aspects of NMAP:

- ***Network Discovery:***
  - ***Description:*** NMAP excels at discovering devices on a network, unveiling their IP addresses, MAC addresses, and open ports.
  - ***Analogy:*** Think of NMAP as a virtual scout, mapping out the devices in your digital neighborhood.
- ***Service Enumeration:***
  - ***Description:*** NMAP identifies the services running on devices, providing details about the software, versions, and configurations.
  - ***Analogy:*** It is like peeking into the storefronts of devices to see what services they are offering.
- ***OS Fingerprinting:***
  - ***Description:*** NMAP can attempt to determine the operating system of a target based on subtle differences in how it responds to certain probes.

  - ***Analogy:*** Imagine NMAP as a detective, examining clues to deduce the type of operating system a device is running.
- ***Port Scanning:***
  - ***Description:*** NMAP's arsenal includes various port scanning techniques to identify open ports on devices, revealing potential entry points.
  - ***Analogy:*** It is like checking doors and windows to see which ones are open in a digital house.

Basic NMAP Commands

NMAP offers a comprehensive range of commands for scanning networks and gathering information about their hosts and services. Here are some of the most commonly used basic NMAP commands:

- **`nmap <target_IP_address>`:** This command performs a basic scan of the specified target IP address, identifying active hosts and open ports.
- **`nmap -sS <target_IP_address>`:** This command performs a TCP SYN scan, a stealthier scan that is less likely to be detected by network intrusion detection systems (IDS).
- **`nmap -sU <target_IP_address>`:** This command performs a UDP scan, identifying open UDP ports on the target host.
- **`nmap -T4 <target_IP_address>`:** This command specifies the scan timing, using aggressive timing for faster scans.
- **`nmap -A <target_IP_address>`:** This command performs an aggressive scan, enabling all scanning techniques and increasing verbosity.

Practical NMAP Application: Security Auditing

Scenario: You want to ensure that your digital premises are secure and free from potential threats.

Steps in Kali Linux:

1. **Conduct an Aggressive Scan for Comprehensive Information:**

```
nmap -A [target]
```

Description: This aggressive scan includes various probing techniques such as version detection, OS detection, script scanning, and more, providing a comprehensive security audit.

Result: Detailed information about the target, including open ports, services, version details, and a potentially identified operating system.

```
hacktify@kali: ~
File  Actions  Edit  View  Help
┌──(hacktify㉿kali)-[~]
└─$ nmap -A 8.8.8.8
Starting Nmap 7.94SVN ( https://nmap.org ) at 2023-11-21 23:4
1 IST
Nmap scan report for dns.google (8.8.8.8)
Host is up (0.013s latency).
Not shown: 998 filtered tcp ports (no-response)
PORT    STATE SERVICE    VERSION
53/tcp  open  tcpwrapped
443/tcp open  ssl/https  HTTP server (unknown)
| http-server-header:
|   HTTP server (unknown)
|_  scaffolding on HTTPServer2
|_ssl-date: TLS randomness does not represent time
| fingerprint-strings:
|   HTTPOptions:
|     HTTP/1.0 302 Found
|     X-Content-Type-Options: nosniff
|     Location: https://dns.google/
|     Date: Tue, 21 Nov 2023 18:12:45 GMT
|     Content-Type: text/html; charset=UTF-8
|     Server: HTTP server (unknown)
|     Content-Length: 216
|     X-XSS-Protection: 0
|     X-Frame-Options: SAMEORIGIN
|     Alt-Svc: h3=":443"; ma=2592000,h3-29=":443"; ma=2592000
|     <HTML><HEAD><meta http-equiv="content-type" content="te
xt/html;charset=utf-8">
|     <TITLE>302 Moved</TITLE></HEAD><BODY>
|     <H1>302 Moved</H1>
|     document has moved
|     HREF="https://dns.google/">here</A>.
|_    </BODY></HTML>
| ssl-cert: Subject: commonName=dns.google
```

Figure 3.23: *Conducting an Aggressive Scan*

2. **Focus on Open Ports and Services:**

```
nmap -p [specific-ports] -sV [target]
```

Description: Narrow down the scan to specific ports of interest to assess the security posture of services running on those ports.

Result: Detailed insights into the version and configuration of services on the specified ports.

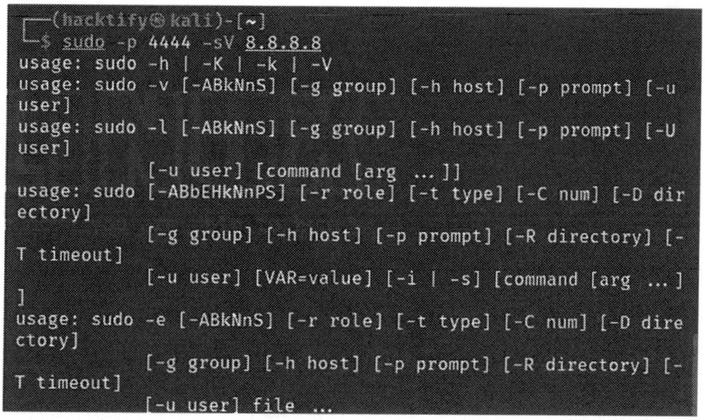

Figure 3.24: *Focusing on Open Ports and Services*

3. **Analyzing NMAP Output:**

Once you have executed your NMAP commands, the output becomes a narrative, telling the story of your network. Let us explore how to decode and interpret the language of NMAP output in Kali Linux.

- **Identifying Vulnerabilities:**
  - ***Output Example:*** 23/tcp open telnet
  - ***Description:*** An open Telnet port could be a potential security risk. Telnet is known for transmitting data in plain text.
  - ***Action:*** Consider securing or disabling Telnet services.
- **Spotting Outdated Software:**
  - ***Output Example:*** 21/tcp open ftp vsftpd 2.0.8 or later
  - ***Description:*** An FTP service running an outdated version may have known vulnerabilities.
  - ***Action:*** Plan an update or consider more secure alternatives.
- **Detecting Unusual Services:**
  - ***Output Example:*** 445/tcp open microsoft-ds
  - ***Description:*** The presence of Microsoft-DS (SMB) might indicate Windows file sharing. It's crucial to secure this service.
  - ***Action:*** Ensure proper access controls and monitoring for SMB services.

In cybersecurity, NMAP is a vital tool for ethical hackers and security professionals. It allows them to assess the security posture of networks, identify potential vulnerabilities, and make informed decisions to enhance the overall cybersecurity strategy.

Conclusion

As we draw the curtain on the chapter **Networking Fundamentals**, congratulations on unraveling the intricate dance of network fundamentals. From grasping the basics of network communication to exploring diverse types and topologies, you have laid a sturdy foundation for understanding the interconnected web of cyberspace. Essential networking commands became your tools, and a deep dive into protocols was a plunge into the veins of digital communication. The enigma of NMAP was demystified, revealing its secrets for robust security testing.

Kudos on mastering these critical elements. Your newfound knowledge of networking sets the stage for robust cybersecurity exploration. In the next chapter, prepare for a fascinating dive into the world of Cryptography and Steganography. These cryptographic arts are more than just locks and keys; they are the guardians of digital secrets. May your journey continue to be enlightening and your cybersecurity endeavors be fortified by this foundational knowledge.

CHAPTER 4
Cryptography and Steganography

Introduction

Welcome to the captivating world of **Cryptography and Steganography**, where secrets are unveiled and information is safeguarded through the ingenious use of encryption. Building on our exploration of Networking Fundamentals in the previous chapter, this section serves as a gateway to understanding the hidden layers that fortify the digital landscape.

In this chapter, we embark on a journey to demystify the art of securing information, exploring the intricacies of cryptographic ciphers, and decrypting the secrets they hold. Discover the types of encryption that form the backbone of digital security and delve into the unseen space of steganography, where messages hide in plain sight. We will guide you through tools essential for cryptography and steganography, offering practical insights into securing data. Get ready to unravel the secrets, enhance your cybersecurity knowledge, and equip yourself with the tools to navigate the unseen in the world of technology.

Structure

In this chapter, we will cover the following topics:

- Decrypting Cryptography
- The Art of Securing Information
- Types of Encryption
- Cryptographic Ciphers
- Unveiling Steganography
- Tools for Cryptography and Steganography
- Exploring the Unseen: Unveiling Advanced Cryptographic Concepts

Decrypting Cryptography: Unraveling the Basics

In an era of unprecedented connectivity, where information flows like a ceaseless river through the digital veins of the world, the need to safeguard sensitive data has never been more paramount. Cryptography emerges as a guardian angel in this intricate tapestry of information exchange, shielding our secrets from prying eyes and ensuring that our digital lives remain secure.

At its core, cryptography is the ingenious art of transforming ordinary information, known as plaintext, into an unreadable form called ciphertext. This process, akin to speaking a secret language, ensures that only authorized individuals can decipher the hidden message. Imagine sending a coded note to a friend, where the words are replaced with symbols or patterns that only you and the recipient understand—that is essentially what cryptography does with digital data.

In today's interconnected world, where data has become a prized commodity, the threat of cyberattacks looms large. Hackers, driven by malicious motives, tirelessly scour the digital landscape, seeking vulnerabilities to exploit and steal valuable information. This is where cryptography steps in, acting as an impenetrable fortress against these cyber threats.

In essence, cryptography has become an indispensable tool in today's digital world, safeguarding our privacy, protecting our financial information, and ensuring the security of our online communications. By understanding its fundamental purpose and appreciating its everyday applications, we can empower ourselves to navigate the digital landscape with greater confidence and security. Encryption is the invisible guardian of our digital lives, ensuring that our secrets remain hidden and our information remains safe in the ever-evolving digital space.

Guardians of Data: Unveiling the Significance of Encryption in Cybersecurity

In the vast expanse of the digital world, where information flows like an endless stream, safeguarding sensitive data is paramount. Encryption emerges as a stalwart sentinel, shielding our precious information from prying eyes and ensuring that our digital lives remain secure. This intricate art of transforming ordinary information into an unreadable form, known as ciphertext, is the cornerstone of cybersecurity.

Imagine a world without locks or passwords, where anyone could access your home, office, or even your personal belongings. This is precisely the scenario we would face in the digital space without encryption. Just as a physical lock secures your possessions, encryption serves as an invisible shield, safeguarding your sensitive data from unauthorized parties. Imagine a medieval castle protected by thick walls and watchful guards; encryption constructs a similar fortress around our digital valuables.

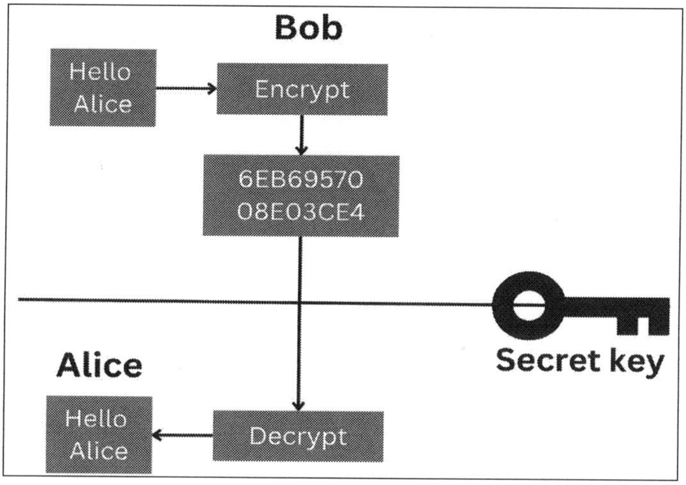

Figure 4.1: *Working of Encryption*

Real-Life Examples: How Encryption Safeguards Against Cyber Threats

Encryption is more than just a concept; it has proven its value in protecting our digital lives in various real-world scenarios. Let us explore instances where encryption has effectively countered cyber threats:

- ***Online Banking Security:*** When you make an online transaction, like purchasing something or managing your finances, your sensitive information, such as credit card details, travels through the vast internet. Without encryption, this data would be exposed to unauthorized eyes, making you vulnerable to fraud and identity theft. Encryption scrambles this data, making it unreadable to those who should not see it. It is akin to a bank vault securing your physical valuables; encryption secures your financial transactions.
- ***Email Confidentiality:*** Sending confidential information via email, such as business plans or personal details, requires confidence that only the intended recipient can read it. Encryption protects the content from unauthorized access, preventing malicious actors from intercepting and exploiting your sensitive information. Think of it like a secure courier service, ensuring that only the right person receives your package.
- ***Messaging App Privacy:*** Popular messaging apps like WhatsApp and Signal facilitate easy communication. However, without encryption, these conversations could be intercepted by hackers, compromising your privacy. Encryption ensures your private messages stay private, stopping unauthorized

individuals from snooping on your communications. It is like having a private conversation in a crowded café.

- ***Securing Cloud Storage:*** Storing sensitive files on cloud services means trusting them with valuable information. Encryption acts as a vigilant guardian, protecting your data from unauthorized access even if the cloud provider faces a security breach. Picture it as having a secure locker in a bank where only you have the key to access your belongings.
- ***Website Data Protection:*** When you visit websites handling sensitive information, like online shopping or banking portals, you want assurance that your data is secure. Encryption guarantees the safety of the data you exchange, preventing hackers from intercepting and stealing your credit card details or other personal information.

Encryption: A Must-Have Tool in the Digital Age

Encryption has become an indispensable tool in a world increasingly reliant on digital technologies. It safeguards our financial information and ensures the security of our online communications. We empower ourselves to navigate the digital landscape with greater confidence and security by understanding its significance and recognizing its everyday applications. Encryption is a fundamental safeguard for our digital lives, not just a technical concept.

Encryption protects our digital assets from malicious actors in the same way that a medieval castle protects its inhabitants from invaders. Encryption is a critical tool in today's digital age, ensuring the privacy and security of our online communications, financial transactions, and stored data. We can empower ourselves to navigate the digital landscape with greater confidence and security by understanding its significance and recognizing its everyday applications. Let encryption be the invisible shield that protects our digital lives.

The Art of Securing Information

In today's interconnected world, where information is the lifeblood of modern society, information security has emerged as a top priority. The digital age has provided numerous benefits, but it has also introduced unprecedented challenges in the field of information security. Individuals and businesses are increasingly relying on digital platforms to communicate, store data, and conduct transactions, so protecting sensitive information has never been more important.

The digital age has changed how we live, work, and interact, but it has also created new opportunities for cyberattacks and data breaches. With its interconnected networks and massive data repositories, the internet provides fertile ground for malicious actors to exploit vulnerabilities and steal sensitive information.

Unique Challenges of the Digital Era:

- ***Increased Reliance on Digital Platforms:*** Our lives are increasingly intertwined with digital platforms, from social media to online banking, making us more susceptible to cyberattacks.
- ***Data Proliferation:*** The exponential growth of data generated and stored digitally has created a treasure trove for cybercriminals to exploit.
- ***Evolving Threats and Attack Methods:*** Hackers are constantly devising new and sophisticated methods to infiltrate systems and exploit vulnerabilities, keeping cybersecurity professionals on their toes.

Personal Implications of Information Security Breaches:

- ***Financial Loss:*** Data breaches can lead to identity theft, financial fraud, and loss of sensitive financial information.
- ***Reputational Damage:*** Information breaches can damage personal reputations and erode trust in individuals and businesses.
- ***Privacy Violations:*** Exposing personal information can lead to privacy violations, unwanted attention, and emotional distress.

Professional Implications of Information Security Breaches:

- ***Financial Losses:*** Businesses can suffer financial losses due to data breaches, including legal fees, remediation costs, and loss of customer trust.
- ***Regulatory Compliance:*** Data breaches can lead to regulatory penalties and non-compliance issues.
- ***Damage to Brand Reputation:*** Breaches can tarnish a company's reputation, leading to the loss of customers and business opportunities.

The Hidden Threats: Revealing Dangers to Information Security

In the expansive digital landscape, where information flows incessantly, securing our sensitive data is crucial. Yet, amidst the convenience and connectivity of the digital age, unseen threats hide in the shadows, constantly endangering our information security. These threats manifest in various forms, from malicious actors aiming to steal or exploit data to sophisticated malware crafted to infiltrate and disrupt systems.

Cyber Intruders: The Crafty Infiltrators

Picture a skilled thief capable of bypassing security measures to gain access to your home or office. In the digital world, hackers operate similarly, utilizing technical expertise and cunning strategies to breach networks, pilfer sensitive information, or hold systems hostage. Motivated by financial gain, espionage, or simply the thrill of the challenge, hackers present a substantial threat to individuals, businesses, and governments alike.

Malware: The Hidden Threat in the Digital Shadows

Malware, a contraction of malicious software, is a broad term covering various types of software crafted to harm or disrupt computer systems. Unlike hackers who actively target specific systems, malware often spreads discreetly through emails, infected websites, or downloaded files. Once installed, malware can pilfer data, encrypt files for ransom, or even seize control of entire systems, resulting in substantial damage and financial losses.

Common Varieties of Malware:

- ***Viruses*:** Programs that replicate themselves, infect files, and spread to other computers.
- ***Trojans*:** Camouflaged as legitimate software, Trojans enable hackers to remotely access infected systems.
- ***Worms*:** Self-propagating programs that swiftly spread across networks, frequently exploiting vulnerabilities in software or operating systems.
- ***Ransomware*:** Malware that encrypts files and demands payment in exchange for the decryption key.

Real-Life Impact of Data Breaches: A Serious Warning

Data breaches, unauthorized access, and the exposure of sensitive information are not just abstract concepts in the digital age; they are a harsh reality. Data breaches can have far-reaching and devastating consequences, affecting individuals, businesses, and entire industries.

Examples of Data Breach and Their Consequences:

- ***Yahoo Data Breach* (2013–2014):** Over 3 billion user accounts were compromised, exposing personal information such as email addresses and passwords.
- ***Equifax Data Breach* (2017):** The credit reporting agency exposed over 147 million Americans' personal information, including Social Security numbers and driver's license numbers.
- ***Marriott Data Breach* (2018):** The hotel chain suffered a massive data breach that exposed passport numbers, credit card information, and travel itineraries for over 500 million guests.

These incidents highlight the seriousness of data breaches, which frequently result in identity theft, financial fraud, reputational harm, and legal ramifications for affected organizations.

The Importance of Strong Security Measures in the Digital Age

The frequency of cyber threats, as well as the consequences of data breaches, underline the critical need for robust security measures. Individuals, corporations, and governments must take a proactive approach to information security, putting in place comprehensive strategies to protect sensitive data and reduce risks.

Key Security Practices:

- ***Encryption:*** Protect sensitive information by jumbling it into a code that only the right key can unlock, ensuring its secrecy.
- ***Access Controls:*** Limit entry to sensitive data and systems, allowing only authorized individuals and keeping out unauthorized users.
- ***Regular Security Checks:*** Consistently test and check systems for vulnerabilities, fixing them before attackers can take advantage.
- ***Employee Training:*** Educate employees on cybersecurity basics, covering password habits, safe online conduct, and how to recognize and avoid phishing attempts.
- ***Response Plans for Incidents:*** Create and put into action plans for dealing with data breaches or cyberattacks, minimizing harm, and swiftly restoring normal operations.

Types of Encryption

Dive into the domain of encryption with Types of Encryption. Uncover the simplicity of symmetric encryption, akin to sharing a secret key, and explore its applications and trade-offs. Transition to asymmetric encryption, where the digital lock and key ensure secure communication. Lastly, grasp the importance of hash functions, likened to digital fingerprints, in maintaining data integrity. Join us to demystify encryption methods and enhance your grasp of data security.

Symmetric Encryption: Sharing a Secret

Think of sending a coded email to a friend as sharing a secret password to lock and unlock a virtual mailbox. Only you and your friend know the password, so only you and your friend can access the email contents. This type of coding is commonly used in secure messaging apps and file encryption software.

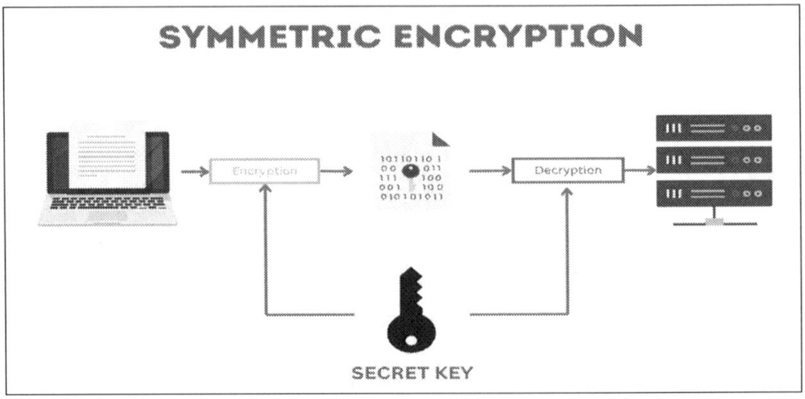

Figure 4.2: *Symmetric Encryption*

Public-Key Encryption: The Digital Locksmith

Public-key encryption is like a digital locksmith creating a unique pair of keys for each person–a public key and a private key. The public key, like a name tag, can be shared with anyone, while the private key, like a house key, must be kept secret. To send a coded email using public-key encryption, you would use the recipient's public key to lock the message. Only the recipient, with their private key, can unlock and read the message. This type of coding is widely used in web browsers for secure online transactions and communication.

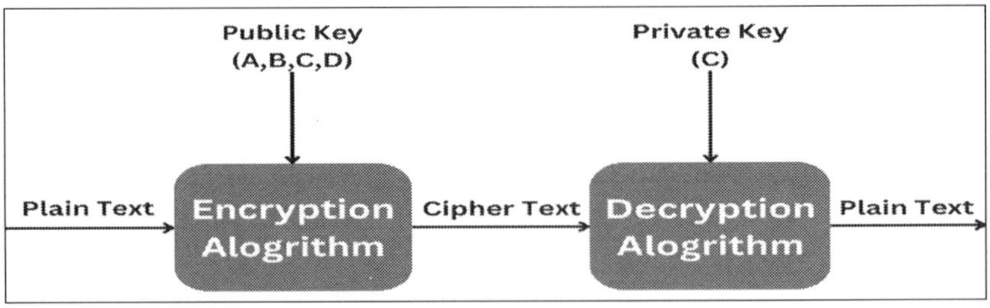

Figure 4.3: *Public-Key Encryption*

Digital Envelopes: Sealing Information for Secure Transit

Imagine sending a package of private documents and using a tamper-proof envelope to seal it. Digital envelopes work similarly, using coding to seal and protect information during transmission. When you send a coded email, the email client wraps the message in a digital envelope, making sure that only the intended recipient can open it. It is like sealing the package with a unique lock and key that only the recipient possesses.

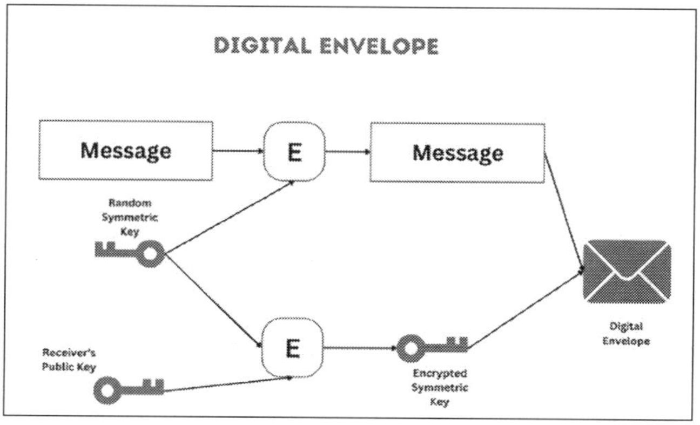

Figure 4.4: *Digital Envelope*

Hashing: The Digital Fingerprint

Imagine comparing two fingerprints to ensure they belong to the same person. Hashing functions work similarly in the digital field. They generate a unique digital fingerprint, known as a hash value, for a given piece of data. This hash value serves as a reference point to verify the integrity of the data. For example, when you download a software update, the download site provides a hash value for the update file. You can generate your hash value for the downloaded file and compare it to the provided hash value. If the two values match, it confirms that the file has not been tampered with during transit.

Figure 4.5: *Hashing Algorithm*

Digital Signatures: Sender Verification

Consider signing a contract to prove your identity and establish an agreement. Digital signatures work similarly in the digital world, employing cryptography to authenticate the sender of a message or document. When you digitally sign an email, your email client creates a digital signature, which is a unique identifier linked to your private key. The recipient can validate your signature using your public key, ensuring that the message came from you and was not altered. This is analogous to signing a contract with your unique signature, making it difficult for someone else to forge your signature.

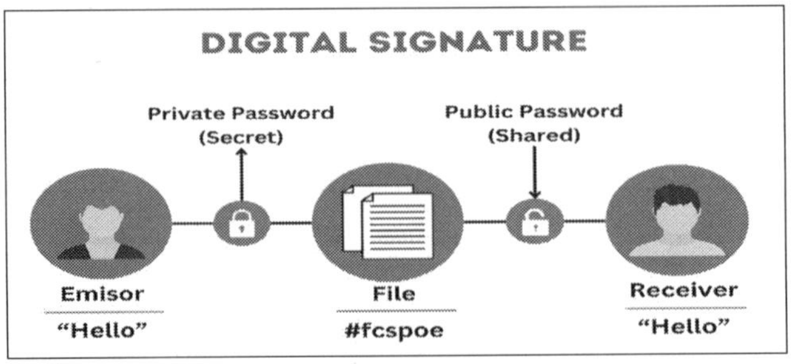

Figure 4.6: *Digital Signature*

Cryptography, with its intricate algorithms and powerful techniques, serves as the cornerstone of modern cybersecurity. It protects our privacy, safeguards our financial information, and ensures the security of our online communications. By understanding these fundamental concepts and appreciating their everyday applications, we can navigate the digital landscape with greater confidence and security.

Symmetric Encryption: Sharing a Secret to Secure Communication

Imagine that you and your best friend want to exchange secret messages without anyone else being able to read them. You agree on a special code, known as a shared secret key, that only you two know. When you write a message, you use this shared key to scramble it into an unreadable form, known as ciphertext. Your friend, using the same shared key, can unscramble the ciphertext back into the original message.

The Shared Key Analogy: A Practical Example

Consider a locked box with a single key. Only you possess this key, and only you can open the box and access its contents. Symmetric encryption operates similarly. Both the sender and the receiver of an encrypted message use the same secret key to encrypt and decrypt the information, ensuring that only authorized parties can access it.

Figure 4.7: *Symmetric Encryption*

Advantages of Symmetric Encryption:

- ***Simplicity:*** Symmetric encryption is relatively simple to implement and use, making it a popular choice for everyday applications.
- ***Efficiency:*** Symmetric encryption algorithms are generally faster than public-key encryption algorithms, allowing for efficient data transfer.

Limitations of Symmetric Encryption:

- ***Key Management:*** The shared secret key must be securely distributed to all authorized parties, and its confidentiality must be maintained. If the key is compromised, all encrypted messages using that key can be decrypted and read by unauthorized individuals.

Here is an everyday scenario for symmetric encryption:

Securing Wi-Fi with WPA2 Encryption:

- **WPA2:** WPA2 is a widely used way to keep Wi-Fi networks safe. It works like a secret code for the information going between devices and the Wi-Fi router, making sure that sensitive data is not accessed by unauthorized users.

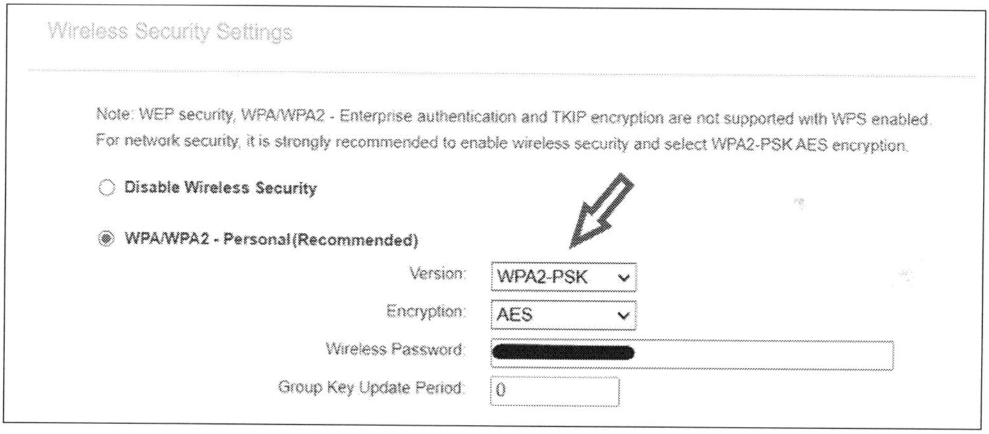

Figure 4.8: *Securing Wi-Fi with WPA2 Encryption*

Symmetric encryption, with its shared secret key concept, provides a simple and efficient method for securing communication and protecting sensitive data. While key management can be a challenge, the benefits of symmetric encryption make it a widely used and valuable tool in modern cybersecurity.

Asymmetric Encryption: A Digital Lock with Two Unique Keys

Imagine a special lock that requires two unique keys to open it: a public key, known to everyone, and a private key, known only to you. This is the essence of asymmetric encryption, also known as public-key encryption. Unlike symmetric encryption, which uses a shared secret key, asymmetric encryption employs two distinct keys, each playing a crucial role in ensuring secure communication.

The Public Key: A Widely Accessible Key

Think of the public key as a readily available key that anyone can use to lock a door. Just as you can share the address of your house without compromising your security, the public key can be freely distributed without compromising the private key.

The Private Key: A Closely Guarded Secret

Envision the private key as a closely guarded secret, like the actual key to your house. Just as you would never share your house key with others, the private key must remain confidential and only known to the intended recipient.

Figure 4.9: *Asymmetric Encryption*

Establishing a Secure Channel of Communication: A Two-Key Partnership

The magic of asymmetric encryption lies in the interplay between the public and private keys. When you want to send an encrypted message, you use the recipient's public key to lock the message. Only the recipient, using their corresponding private key, can unlock the message.

A Practical Example: Secure Email Communication

Consider sending an encrypted email to a friend. You would use your friend's public key to lock the email, ensuring that only your friend with their private key could read it. This is like sending a letter with a special lock that only your friend can open with their unique key.

Asymmetric Encryption Benefits:

- ***Secure Key Distribution:*** The public key can be freely shared without jeopardizing the private key's security.

- ***Digital Authentication:*** Public keys can be used to verify an individual's or entity's identity, ensuring secure communication with trusted parties.

Asymmetric Encryption Limitations

- ***Overhead in Computing:*** Because asymmetric encryption algorithms are slower than symmetric encryption algorithms, they are less efficient for large data transfers.
- ***Key Administration:*** The private key must be carefully guarded and kept private. If the corresponding public key is compromised, unauthorized individuals can decrypt all messages encrypted with it.

Here is an everyday scenario for asymmetric encryption:

Secure Email Communication:

- ***TLS/SSL:*** TLS/SSL (Transport Layer Security/Secure Sockets Layer) protocols are widely used to secure email communication. These protocols utilize asymmetric encryption to establish secure channels between email servers and clients, ensuring that emails are protected from interception and tampering.

Hands-on Example:

1. Open your webmail client or email app.
2. Compose a new email message.
3. Observe that the recipient's email address is preceded by **"`https`"** and has a padlock icon in the address bar. This indicates that the email connection is encrypted using TLS or SSL.

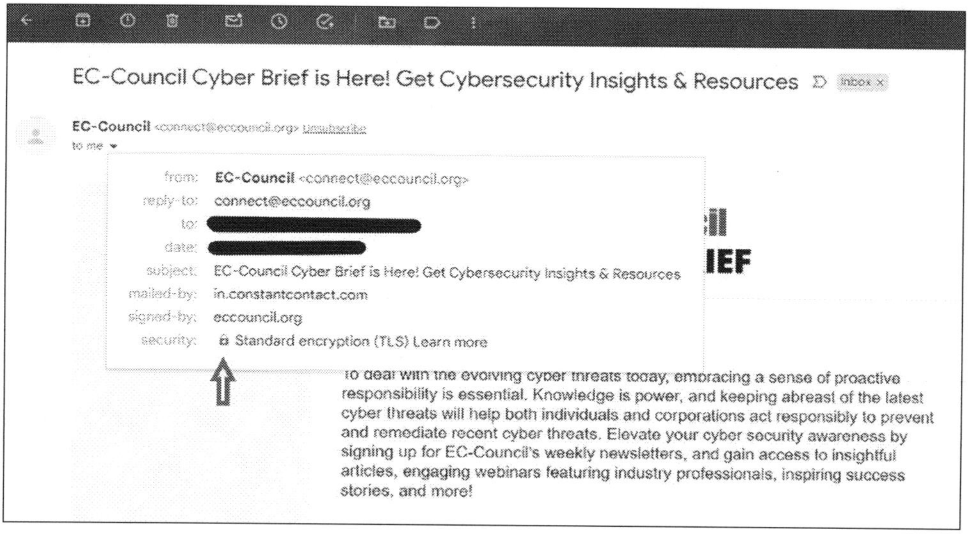

Figure 4.10: *Secure Email Communication*

Asymmetric encryption, with its unique pair of public and private keys, provides a robust and versatile method for secure communication and digital authentication.

Ensuring Data Integrity with Hash Functions: Digital Fingerprints

In the world of digital information, keeping data intact is crucial. Like a fingerprint uniquely identifies a person, a hash function creates a special digital fingerprint for a piece of data. This fingerprint, called a hash value, acts as a point of reference to confirm that the data has not been altered during its journey or while stored.

Imagine you have a digital document, maybe a legal contract or a financial report. Your goal is to make sure this document stays the same, even if someone tries to change it. A hash function works like a digital fingerprint for this document. It produces a unique hash value that you can use to check the document's integrity.

Using Hash Functions: Spotting Tampering

Let us say you are downloading a software update from the internet. You want to be sure that the file you get is real and hasn't been messed with by hackers. The software company provides a hash value for the update file on its website. You can create your hash value for the downloaded file and compare it to the one they gave. If the two values match, it means the file hasn't been tampered with during the download.

Common Hash Functions:

- **MD5 (*Message-Digest Algorithm* 5):** This hash function is known for its speed and simplicity, and it is used widely.
- **SHA-1 (*Secure Hash Algorithm* 1):** Although older, it is still used in some applications.
- **SHA-256 (*Secure Hash Algorithm* 256):** A more secure and widely used hash function compared to its predecessors.

How Hash Functions are Used:

- ***Verifying Data Integrity*:** Hash functions are applied to check if downloaded files, software updates, and data on disks or sent-over networks are intact.
- ***Creating Digital Signatures*:** Hash functions play a role in making digital signatures, which authenticate the sender of a message or document.
- ***Storing Passwords Safely*:** Passwords are securely stored using hash functions, making it challenging for hackers to uncover passwords in plain text.

Here is an everyday scenario for hash functions:

1. Downloading Software Updates:

- **Windows Updates**: When you download and install software updates from Microsoft, hash values are used to verify the integrity of the update files. Before installing an update, Windows generates a hash value for the downloaded file and compares it to the hash value provided by Microsoft. If the two values match, it confirms that the file has not been tampered with and is safe to install.

Step-by-step Guide:

1. On your Windows computer, launch the "`Settings`" application.
2. Locate and select the "`Update & Security`" option.
3. Click the "`Check for updates`" button.
4. Windows will download and install any available updates.
5. You will notice that Windows verifies the integrity of each update using hash values before installing it.

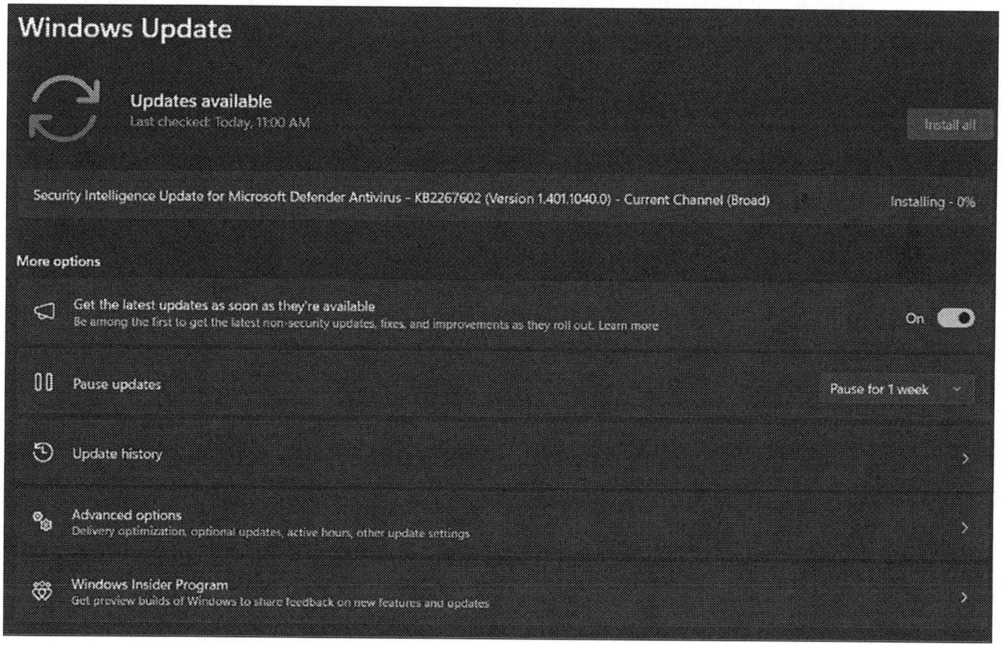

Figure 4.11: *Windows Updates*

2. Password Storage and Authentication:

- ***For Online Accounts:*** When you sign up for a website or an online service, your password gets stored using a hash function. This means that your password is not saved in plain text, making it tough for hackers to retrieve it even if they somehow access the site's database. When you log in, your entered password is hashed, and this hash is compared to the stored hash value. If they match, it confirms you have entered the correct password.

Practical Example:

1. Sign up for a new account on a website or online service.
2. Notice that your password is not saved in plain text but in hashed form.
3. Log in by entering your password and submitting it.
4. The website will hash your password and check it against the stored hash value. If they match, you will successfully log in.

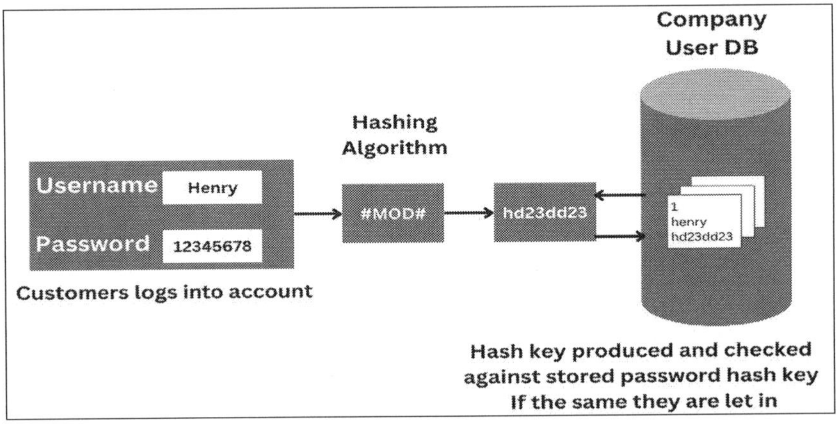

Figure 4.12: *Password Storage and Authentication*

Hash functions, with their ability to generate unique digital fingerprints for data, play a crucial role in maintaining data integrity and ensuring the security of digital information. By verifying hash values, we can detect tampering, protect against data corruption, and safeguard the authenticity of sensitive information.

Cryptographic Ciphers

In the domain of cryptography, ciphers are like secret codes or jumbled messages that transform ordinary information into an unreadable form. Just as a detective deciphers a cryptic message, cryptographic algorithms employ sophisticated techniques to scramble and unscramble data, ensuring its confidentiality and integrity.

Imagine a simple puzzle with pieces that fit together in a specific order to reveal a complete picture. Now, consider scrambling those puzzle pieces, making it impossible to reassemble the picture without the correct arrangement. Ciphers operate similarly, rearranging data in a way that only authorized parties can decipher.

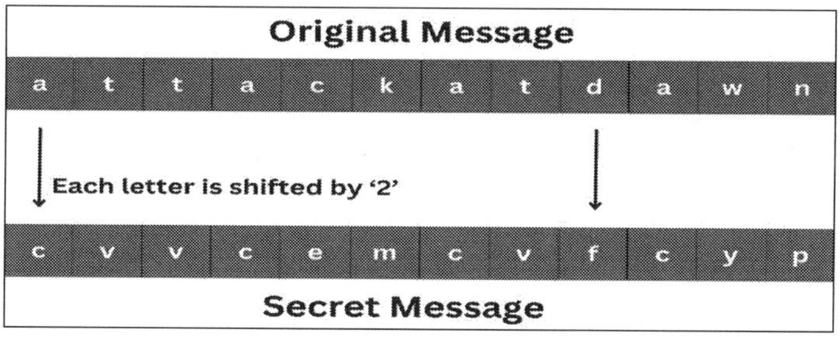

Figure 4.13: *Cipher Technique*

Types of Ciphers: Substitution and Transposition

There are two sorts of ciphers: substitution ciphers and transposition ciphers.

- Substitution ciphers substitute particular characters or symbols with different ones, basically swapping one set of symbols for another. Consider replacing the alphabet with a secret code in which each letter is represented by a distinct symbol.
- Transposition ciphers modify the arrangement of characters or symbols within a message, basically shuffling the jigsaw pieces. Consider rearranging the letters of a word without affecting the individual letters.

Symmetric and Asymmetric Ciphers: Sharing Secrets and Public Keys

Ciphers can also be classified as symmetric or asymmetric. Symmetric ciphers, like shared secret passwords, use the same key for both encryption and decryption. Asymmetric ciphers, like a pair of public and private keys, rely on two distinct keys, one for encryption and the other for decryption.

Real-World Applications of Ciphers:

- ***Secure Online Transactions:*** When you shop online and enter your credit card information, ciphers are used to encrypt the data, protecting it from interception by hackers.
- ***Encrypted Email Communication:*** When you send an encrypted email, ciphers transform the message into an unreadable form, ensuring that only the intended recipient can read it.
- ***Data Storage Security:*** When you store sensitive data on your computer or a cloud storage service, ciphers safeguard the data from unauthorized access.

Ciphers, the foundation of cryptographic systems, are critical to protecting our digital data. Ciphers protect our sensitive data from prying eyes by changing it into unreadable forms, protecting the secrecy, integrity, and authenticity of our online activities. Understanding the underlying concepts of ciphers allows us to navigate the digital field with better confidence and security.

Advanced Encryption Standard (AES): The Guardian of Our Digital Secrets

Imagine a powerful lock that can secure your most valuable possessions—a lock that is resistant to even the most determined attempts to break in. AES, the Advanced Encryption Standard, is like that lock in the digital sphere, safeguarding our sensitive information with its robust encryption algorithms.

AES is a symmetric-key cipher, meaning it uses the same key for both encryption and decryption. This key, known as the secret key, must be kept confidential, ensuring that only authorized parties can access the encrypted data. AES is widely used in various applications, including secure online communication, file encryption, and the storage of sensitive data.

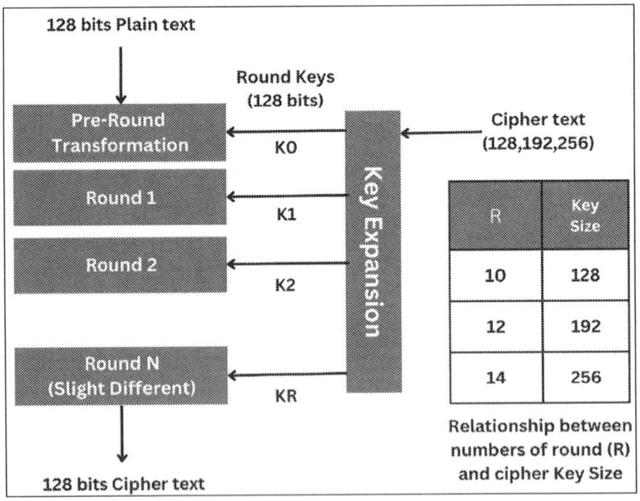

Figure 4.14: AES Algorithm

Data Encryption Standard (DES): A Legacy of Innovation and Security

Imagine an encryption method that stood strong for over two decades, transforming how we safeguard our digital data. That is DES or Data Encryption Standard—an algorithm that became the industry standard for encryption.

DES, a symmetric-key cipher, uses a mix of substitution and transposition ciphers to scramble data. While newer algorithms like AES have surpassed DES in power, its historical significance and impact on modern cryptography are undeniable.

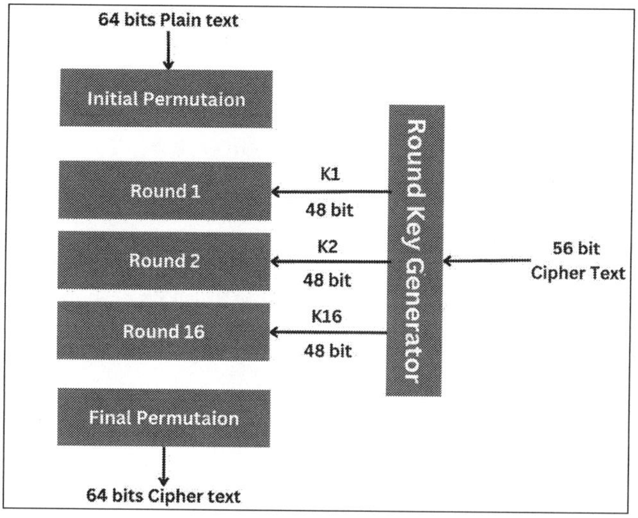

Figure 4.15: *DES Algorithm*

Unveiling Steganography: The Art of Concealing Information in Plain Sight

In the sphere of information security, encryption has long been the cornerstone of safeguarding data. However, there is another, more elusive technique known as steganography, which takes a different approach to protecting sensitive information.

Imagine sending a secret message hidden within an ordinary image or audio file. This is the essence of steganography, the art of concealing information within seemingly innocuous objects. Unlike encryption, which scrambles data into an unreadable form, steganography hides the message itself, making its existence undetectable to the untrained eye.

Beyond Encryption: A Complementary Approach

While encryption ensures that data remains confidential even if intercepted, steganography adds an extra layer of protection by concealing the very presence of a message. This makes it a valuable tool in situations where encryption alone may not be sufficient, such as evading censorship or hiding sensitive information from targeted searches.

Common Steganography Techniques:

- ***Image Steganography***: Hiding data within the least significant bits (LSB) of an image, altering the color values imperceptibly to the human eye.
- ***Audio Steganography***: Embedding data within the audio spectrum of a sound file and modifying the frequencies in a way that doesn't affect the perceived sound.
- ***Text Steganography***: Concealing data within text files using techniques like line-shift coding or whitespace embedding.

Real-World Applications of Steganography:

- ***Digital Watermarking***: Embedding copyright information or ownership marks within digital media to protect intellectual property.
- ***Covert Communication***: Exchanging secret messages between individuals or organizations without raising suspicion.
- ***Forensic Analysis***: Hiding evidence or clues within digital artifacts for later retrieval and analysis.

Image Steganography: Concealing Data in Plain-Sight Images

- ***Copyright Protection***: Digital artists and photographers often embed copyright information or ownership marks within their images using steganography techniques. This watermarking serves as a hidden identifier, making it difficult for others to claim ownership or distribute the copyrighted work without authorization.

Audio Steganography: Hiding Messages in Sound Files

- ***Covert Communication***: Secret messages can be concealed within audio files using steganography techniques, allowing for discreet communication between individuals or organizations.

Text Steganography: Hidden Messages Within Plain Text

- ***Data Embedding***: Data can be embedded within text files using steganography techniques, allowing for the transmission of hidden information without raising suspicion.

These examples illustrate how steganography can be seamlessly integrated into everyday digital interactions, providing an additional layer of protection for sensitive information and enabling discreet communication in various contexts. Steganography, with its ability to conceal information in plain sight, provides a unique approach to data protection.

Tools for Cryptography and Steganography

In today's interconnected world, where sensitive information flows freely across digital channels, cryptography plays a crucial role in safeguarding our data and protecting our privacy. Cryptographic tools, the digital instruments that implement these encryption techniques, have become indispensable allies in the battle against unauthorized access and data breaches.

Understanding the Role of Cryptographic Tools

Imagine a world without encryption, where every message you send, every password you enter, and every financial transaction you make is exposed to the prying eyes of cybercriminals. This is the reality we would face without the powerful protection provided by cryptographic tools.

These tools, ranging from software programs to hardware devices, act as guardians of our digital privacy, employing sophisticated algorithms to transform our data into unreadable forms, ensuring that only authorized parties can access and decipher it. Whether it is protecting the confidentiality of our emails, securing our online transactions, or safeguarding sensitive corporate information, cryptographic tools stand as the sentinels of our digital lives.

Exploring Common Cryptographic Tools: A Look at the Toolkit

Numerous cryptographic tools are at our disposal, each with distinct capabilities and applications. Let us delve into a few of the most popular and user-friendly options:

- ***OpenSSL:*** This open-source cryptography library is widely employed for various cryptographic tasks like encryption, decryption, and digital signatures. Developers and security professionals favor it due to its versatility and robust security features.
- ***GPG (GNU Privacy Guard):*** As a free and open-source implementation of the PGP (Pretty Good Privacy) protocol, GPG stands out for its user-friendly interface and potent encryption capabilities. Users can employ it for encrypting and decrypting emails, signing digital messages, and managing encryption keys.
- ***Cryptool:*** Positioned as a user-friendly cryptographic software suite, Cryptool provides a graphical interface for a range of cryptographic operations, including encryption, decryption, hashing, and digital signatures.

These tools offer just a glimpse of the diverse range of cryptographic software available.

Hands-On with Open-Source Encryption Software

In today's data-driven world, where sensitive information is constantly exchanged through digital channels, safeguarding our privacy and protecting our data have become paramount. Encryption software, the digital guardians of our digital lives, empowers us to encrypt our data, transforming it into an unreadable form and ensuring that only authorized parties can access and decipher it.

Practice Encryption and Decryption using GPG

Step 1: Download and Install GPG on Your System

If you have not already done so, follow these procedures based on your operating system:

```
sudo apt-get update
sudo apt-get install gnupg
```

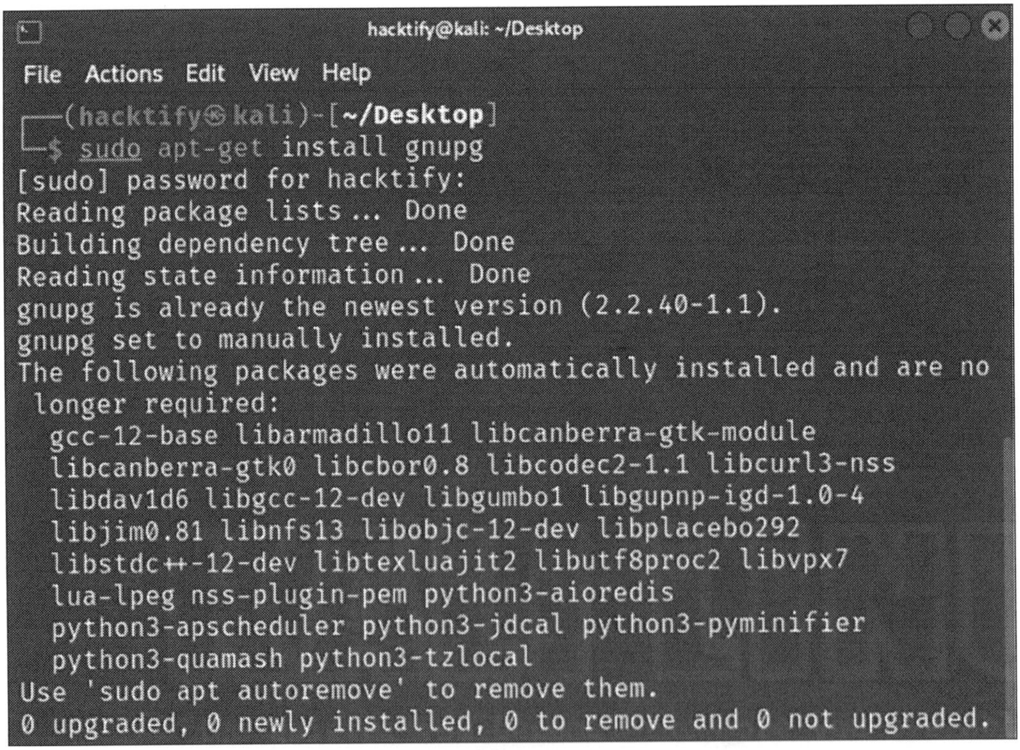

Figure 4.16: *Installing gnupg*

For Windows: Download the GPG installer from the official GPG4Win website: GPG4Win Download (https://www.gpg4win.org/download.html)

Step 2: Make Your GPG Key Pair

Run the following command in a terminal or command prompt:

```
gpg --full-generate-key
```

Enter your name, email address, and establish a password as directed. This pass provides an additional degree of protection for your key.

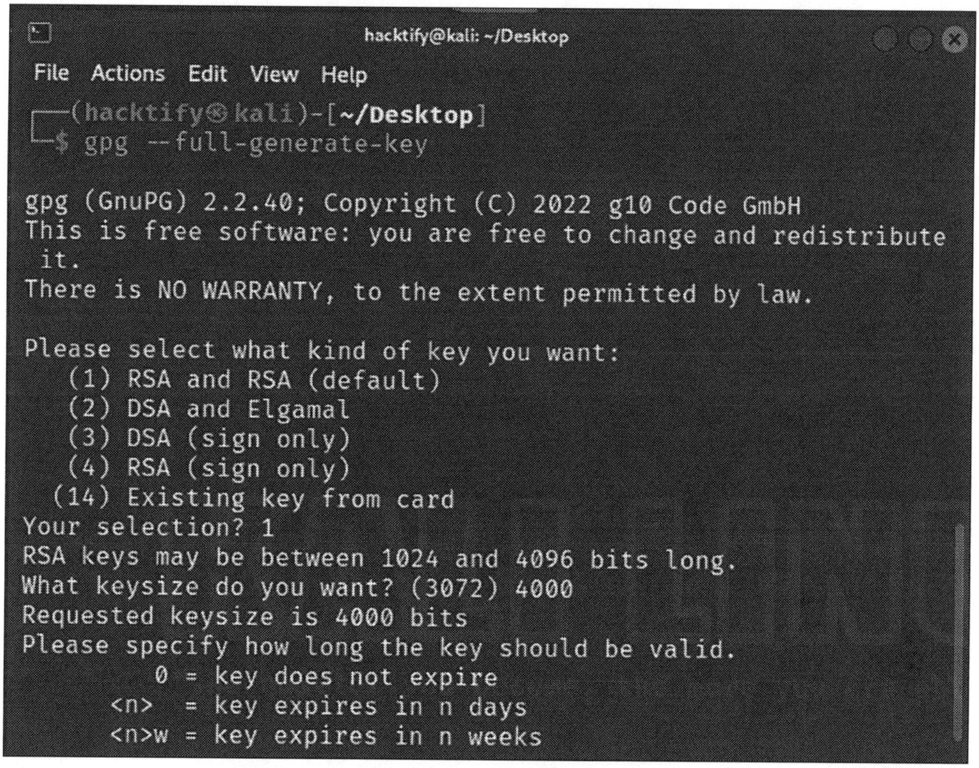

Figure 4.17: *Making gpg Key Pair*

Step 3: Message Encryption

1. Open a text editor and compose a brief message.
2. Save the message to a text file called **`message.txt`**.

Figure 4.18: *Creating a Message*

3. To encrypt the message, open a terminal or command prompt and type the following command:

```
gpg -e -r recipient@example.com message.txt
```

Replace **recipient@example.com** with the email address associated with the recipient's GPG key.

4. GPG will generate an encrypted version of the message, which is usually titled **message.txt.gpg**.

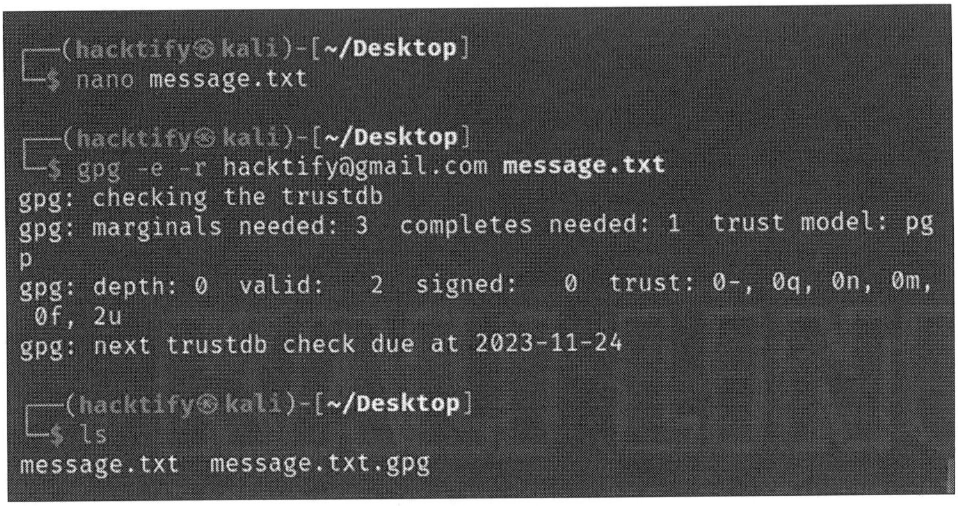

Figure 4.19: *Encrypting the Message*

Step 4: Message Decryption

1. Send the receiver the encrypted file (**message.txt.gpg**).

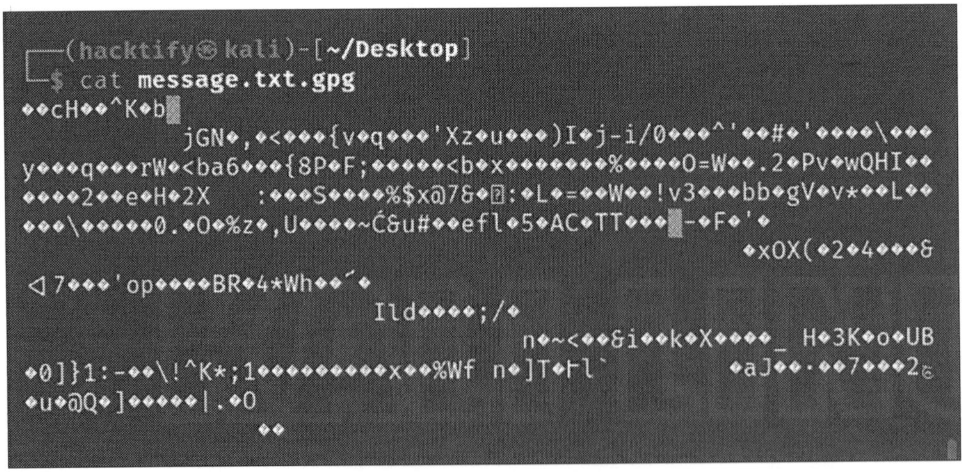

Figure 4.20: *Encrypted Message*

2. The receiver should launch a terminal or perform the following command:

```
gpg -d message.txt.gpg
```

The receiver will be asked for their passcode.

3. Once the file has been decrypted, GPG will display the original message on the screen.

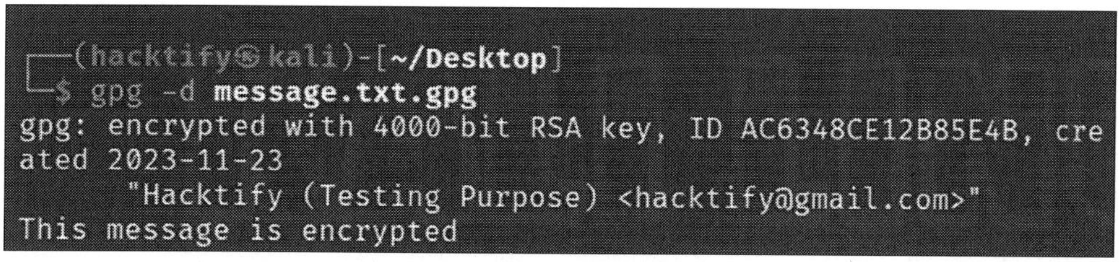

Figure 4.21: *Decrypted Message*

This hands-on exercise demonstrates how to use open-source encryption software, notably GPG, to secure and decode data.

Cryptool: Exploring Cryptographic Concepts

- ***Understanding Hashing Functions:*** Use Cryptool to visualize and experiment with cryptographic hash functions, such as MD5 and SHA-256. These functions generate unique fingerprints for digital files, ensuring data integrity and detecting tampering.

TRY IT YOURSELF

1. Launch Cryptool and select the hashing function option.
2. Choose a hashing algorithm, such as MD5 or SHA-256.
3. Select a digital file and calculate its hash value.
4. Verify the hash value of the file to ensure its integrity and prevent unauthorized modifications.

Cryptographic technologies, the unsung heroes of the digital world, are critical to protecting our privacy and sensitive information. From encrypting emails to safeguarding online transactions, these technologies give us the confidence to navigate the digital environment while keeping our data safe from illegal access and bad intent.

Digital Camouflage: Using Steganography Tools to Hide Data in Plain Sight

In the world of cybersecurity, where information is the currency of power, the art of data concealment has progressed beyond standard encryption. Steganography, the process of concealing secret messages within seemingly benign items, has emerged as an effective solution for protecting sensitive data.

Consider hiding a confidential document beneath an image or a hidden message within an audio clip. These are just a few examples of how steganography technologies allow us to conceal data in plain sight, making it nearly undetected to the untrained eye.

Steganography Tools: A User-Friendly Approach

The sector of steganography is no longer confined to specialized software or complex algorithms. Several user-friendly steganography tools have emerged, making this powerful technique accessible to a wider audience. Let us explore two popular options:

Steghide:

Steghide is a widely used steganography tool that allows users to embed data within various file formats, including images, audio files, and text documents. Its intuitive interface makes it easy to hide and extract secret messages, providing a user-friendly approach to data concealment.

OpenStego:

OpenStego is another popular steganography tool that offers similar functionalities to Steghide. Its open-source nature ensures transparency and security, making it a preferred choice for those seeking a reliable and trustworthy tool for data concealment.

Tool Showcase: Putting Steganography into Practice

To illustrate the capabilities of steganography tools, let us consider a practical scenario:

Imagine you need to transmit a confidential document to a colleague without raising suspicion. Using a steganography tool like Steghide, you can embed the document within an image file, such as a photograph or a company logo. The image will appear unchanged to the naked eye, yet it will carry a hidden message within its digital structure.

Once the recipient receives the image, they can use the same steganography tool to extract the hidden document, allowing them to access the confidential information securely. This demonstrates the practical applications of steganography tools in safeguarding sensitive data and enabling discreet communication.

Steganography technologies have transformed the approach to safeguarding sensitive information and communicating discreetly by concealing data within ordinary digital items. Once limited to specialized applications, these technologies have evolved to become more user-friendly and accessible. Now, individuals and organizations can harness the potential of steganography in the dynamic digital landscape.

Exploring the Unseen: Unveiling Advanced Cryptographic Concepts

In the ever-evolving space of cybersecurity, the quest for impenetrable communication and secure data protection has led to the development of sophisticated cryptographic techniques that transcend traditional encryption methods. Let us delve into two advanced cryptographic concepts that promise to revolutionize the way we safeguard our information in the digital age.

Quantum Cryptography: Harnessing Quantum Mechanics to Encrypted Communication

Imagine a world where the principles of quantum mechanics, the science that governs the behavior of matter at the atomic and subatomic levels, are harnessed to create unbreakable communication channels. This is the promise of quantum cryptography, a revolutionary approach to data encryption that leverages the inherent properties of quantum particles to guarantee the confidentiality and integrity of information.

At the heart of quantum cryptography lies the concept of quantum entanglement, a phenomenon where two or more quantum particles become inextricably linked, sharing the same fate even when separated by vast distances. This entanglement allows for the creation of secure cryptographic keys that are impossible to forge or intercept, rendering any attempt to eavesdrop on encrypted communication futile.

While quantum cryptography is still in its early stages of development, its potential impact on cybersecurity is immense. It holds the promise of safeguarding sensitive information in sectors ranging from financial transactions to national security communications, ensuring that our most valuable data remains protected from unauthorized access.

Homomorphic Encryption: Performing Computations on Encrypted Data

In today's data-driven world, the ability to perform computations on vast amounts of information is crucial for businesses and organizations. However, this often involves storing and processing sensitive data in the cloud, raising concerns about privacy and security.

Homomorphic encryption, a groundbreaking cryptographic technique, addresses this challenge by enabling computations to be performed on encrypted data without decrypting it. This means that data can be stored and processed in the cloud while maintaining its confidentiality, allowing for secure data analysis and collaboration without compromising privacy.

Imagine a scenario where a cloud-based service provider needs to analyze encrypted medical data to identify patterns and trends without revealing individual patient information. Homomorphic encryption makes this possible, allowing the service provider to perform computations on the encrypted data while preserving the privacy of each patient's medical records.

The implications of homomorphic encryption extend far beyond the cloud computing sphere. It has the potential to revolutionize industries like healthcare, finance, and government, enabling secure data sharing and analysis while safeguarding sensitive information.

Quantum cryptography and homomorphic encryption represent the cutting edge of cryptographic research, pushing the boundaries of what is possible in securing our digital information. Quantum cryptography's ability to harness the power of quantum mechanics to create unbreakable communication links holds immense promise for safeguarding sensitive data in the future. Homomorphic encryption, on the other hand, addresses the challenge of performing computations on encrypted data without compromising privacy, opening up new avenues for secure data analysis and collaboration in the cloud. As these advanced cryptographic concepts mature and find practical applications, they are poised to revolutionize the way we protect our information in an increasingly interconnected and data-driven world.

Conclusion

Our journey through cryptography and steganography has unveiled the intricate world of securing information. From decrypting the essence of cryptography to exploring the artistry of cryptographic ciphers and unveiling the secrets of steganography, you have embarked on a fascinating exploration of digital concealment and protection.

Congratulations on navigating these complex concepts! In our next chapter, prepare to delve into the sphere of social engineering attacks, where we unravel the tactics employed to manipulate human behavior and breach security. Get ready for an eye-opening experience as we continue to demystify the intricate landscape of cybersecurity.

Chapter 5
Social Engineering Attacks

Introduction

Step into the world of **Social Engineering Attacks**. Building on our recent exploration of cryptography and steganography, this chapter is your guide to practical defense strategies against the ever-evolving landscape of cyber threats. Dive into the psychology of manipulation, starting from fundamental principles and progressing to advanced phishing techniques like email and spear phishing. Real-life examples underscore the impact, while illuminating discussions on ID and homograph attacks expose the nuances of identity manipulation. Discover the pivotal role and tools of a social engineer, challenge your understanding with a phishing links quiz, and grasp the significance of awareness training. Stay ahead by catching a glimpse of future trends in this dynamic field.

Structure

In this chapter, we will cover the following topics:

- Social Engineering Unmasked
- Social Engineering Fundamentals
- Unlocking Phishing Tactics: Email, Spear, Vishing, and More
- Real-Life Deceptions
- ID and Homograph Attacks
- The Role of a Social Engineer
- Exploring Social Engineering Tools
- Future Trends in Social Engineering
- Quiz: Mastering Phishing Link Detection

Social Engineering Unmasked: A Practical Guide to Understanding and Defending Against Deceptive Attacks

In the ever-evolving field of cybersecurity, social engineering has emerged as a formidable threat, exploiting human psychology and vulnerabilities to gain unauthorized access to sensitive information and systems. Unlike traditional hacking methods that target computer systems directly, social engineering attacks target the human element, manipulating individuals into making mistakes or revealing confidential data.

The prevalence of social engineering attacks is undeniable. In March 2023, Verizon's 2023 Data Breach Investigations Report (DBIR) revealed a worrying incident where data on over 7 million users, including contact information and device details, was exposed on a hacker forum. While the data was not unencrypted, this incident highlights the continued threat of social engineering, as it likely originated from an outside vendor's vulnerability exploited by attackers. This underscores the importance of robust vendor security measures and increased vigilance against social engineering tactics within the supply chain.

This chapter aims to empower readers to become guardians of their digital security. It delves into the intricate world of social engineering, unraveling the techniques employed by attackers and providing practical strategies to recognize, resist, and defend against these insidious assaults.

The Significance of Understanding Social Engineering

In today's interconnected world, where personal and corporate information is often stored digitally, understanding social engineering is no longer a mere option; it is an imperative. For individuals, comprehending these tactics can safeguard their financial information, protect their privacy, and prevent reputational damage.

For organizations, comprehending social engineering is essential to safeguarding sensitive data, maintaining business continuity, and upholding customer trust. A breach caused by social engineering can lead to substantial financial losses, damage brand reputation, and erode customer confidence.

Empowering Readers to Protect Themselves and Their Organizations

This chapter is designed to equip readers with the knowledge and skills necessary to combat social engineering attacks. It provides a comprehensive overview of the various techniques employed by attackers, including phishing, pretexting, baiting, quid pro quo, and tailgating.

Through real-world examples and practical exercises, readers will gain insights into how attackers exploit human vulnerabilities and learn to identify red flags that may signal an impending social engineering attack. The chapter also provides actionable strategies to protect personal and organizational information, including password management, safe online practices, and secure communication protocols.

Unmasking the Deceptive World of Social Engineering

This chapter is not merely an academic treatise; it is a practical guide to navigate the treacherous landscape of social engineering. It empowers readers to become active participants in their own cybersecurity, fostering a culture of vigilance and resilience against deceptive attacks.

Psychological Foundations of Social Engineering Tactics

- ***Reciprocity Principle:*** Exploiting the human tendency to respond positively to a favor, social engineers use enticing baits to create an obligation for reciprocation, often leading to divulging sensitive information.
- ***Authority Exploitation:*** Leveraging the natural inclination to follow figures of authority, social engineers impersonate trusted entities, establishing a false sense of trust and compliance.
- ***Fear of Missing Out (FOMO):*** Creating a sense of urgency, social engineers prey on the fear of missing opportunities, triggering quick and often impulsive responses from individuals.

As we embark on this journey together, let us unravel the tactics of social engineering, demystify the art of deception, and emerge on the other side with a heightened awareness that will fortify our digital defenses. Welcome to a world where knowledge is your strongest armor and awareness is your most potent weapon.

Social Engineering Fundamentals

In the sphere of cybersecurity, social engineering stands as a formidable adversary, employing cunning tactics to breach security parameters and compromise sensitive information. Unlike conventional hacking techniques that target computer systems directly, social engineering attacks exploit the very essence of human interaction, manipulating individuals into making critical mistakes or divulging confidential data.

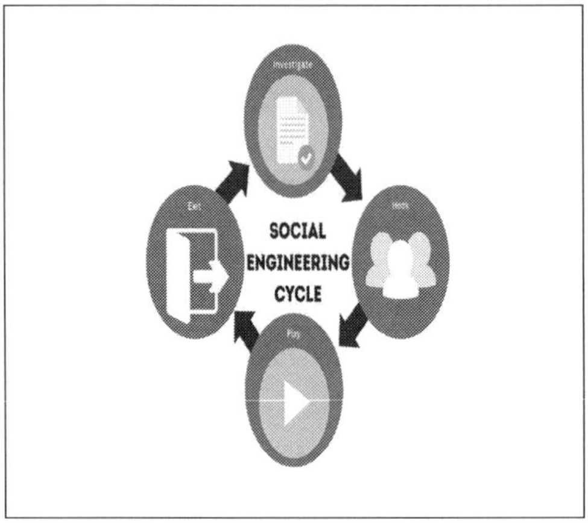

Figure 5.1: *Social Engineering Cycle*

Unveiling the Roots of Social Engineering Through History

The notion of social engineering is far from novel; its roots extend deep into the annals of history, reaching back to ancient civilizations. In old times, the art of deception and manipulation was wielded as a potent tool for attaining political and military objectives. As epochs unfolded, these strata underwent metamorphosis, seamlessly adapting to the ever-evolving technological landscape. In the modern digital era, they have found new avenues of exploitation, showcasing the enduring and adaptive nature of social engineering strategies.

The Psychology Behind Social Engineering

Ever wondered why you clicked that email link you shouldn't have? Social engineering leverages the quirks of human psychology, making us susceptible to manipulation. It taps into our trust, curiosity, and desire to be helpful. Picture a cyber trickster as a master puppeteer, pulling the strings of your emotions.

One key element is the principle of reciprocity–the innate human urge to return a favor. Social engineers exploit this by providing a small concession, like a seemingly harmless link or request, to invoke a sense of indebtedness. Understanding these psychological triggers is like putting on a mental shield. It empowers us to recognize when someone is trying to play with our minds, ensuring we stay one step ahead of the digital puppet show.

Unlocking Social Engineering Tactics

Social engineers deploy an array of techniques strategically tailored to exploit human vulnerabilities. Here are some of the most common tactics:

- ***Phishing:*** Picture this–fraudulent emails or texts cunningly disguised as trustworthy messages, often from familiar sources. Clicking enticing links or attachments in these messages may lead to malware infections or the exposure of sensitive information.

Figure 5.2: *Phishing*

- ***Pretexting:*** It is a charade! Social engineers craft false personas or scenarios to earn your trust and extract confidential information. Whether posing as tech support, financial institutions, or even acquaintances, they aim to manipulate you into revealing sensitive data.

Figure 5.3: *Pretexting*

- ***Baiting:*** Ever seen a tempting item or stumbled upon an intriguing situation? Social engineers leave traps, such as infected USB drives or deceptive pop-up windows posing as security updates, to lure you into revealing sensitive information or compromising security.

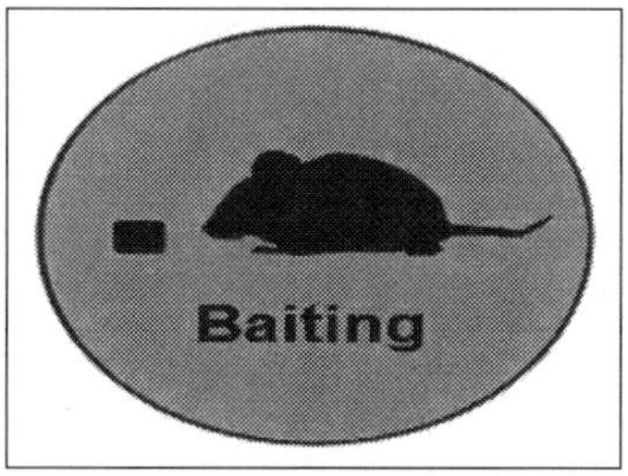

Figure 5.4: *Baiting*

- ***Quid Pro Quo***: A tempting offer awaits! In exchange for your sensitive information or actions, social engineers promise rewards, discounts, or exclusive content. Be cautious, as this could lead to divulging confidential data or unwittingly installing malicious software.

Figure 5.5: *Quid Pro Quo*

- ***Tailgating***: Sneaky infiltration! Social engineers gain physical access to restricted areas or systems by tailing authorized individuals. Pretending to be employees, contractors, or even delivery personnel, they aim to slip through entry points and access secure facilities or networks.

Figure 5.6: *Tailgating*

These methods, often employed in combination, have a remarkable ability to exploit human weaknesses and undermine security. Taking proactive measures to shield oneself and one's organization from these deceitful assaults involves grasping the psychology behind social engineering and being able to identify the typical tactics employed by attackers.

Decrypting the Motivations Behind Deceptive Attacks

Social engineering attacks are not merely random acts of mischief; they are driven by specific goals and objectives that often align with the attacker's motivations.

Understanding these motivations is crucial for anticipating and preventing social engineering attacks.

Common Goals of Social Engineering Attacks

The primary goals of social engineering attacks can be broadly categorized into three main areas:

- ***Financial Gain:*** Social engineers often target individuals and organizations with the intention of stealing financial information, such as credit card numbers, bank account details, or passwords. This information can then be used to make fraudulent transactions, drain accounts, or establish fake identities.
- ***Data Theft:*** Sensitive information, such as personal data, trade secrets, or confidential business documents, is a valuable commodity for social engineers. They may steal this data to sell it on the black market, use it for blackmail or extortion, or gain a competitive advantage.
- ***Access and Control:*** Social engineers may seek to gain unauthorized access to computer systems, networks, or physical facilities. This access can be used to install malware, disrupt operations, or steal sensitive information.

Social Engineering versus Traditional Cyber Threats

Social engineering attacks differ from traditional cyber threats in several key aspects:

- ***Human Factor:*** Social engineering attacks exploit human vulnerabilities, while traditional cyber threats target computer systems or networks directly.
- ***Stealth and Deception:*** Social engineering attacks rely on deception and manipulation to trick individuals into revealing information or performing actions, while traditional cyber threats often involve brute force or technological vulnerabilities.
- ***Wide Attack Surface:*** Social engineering attacks can target anyone, regardless of their technical expertise. This makes the potential attack surface much broader than traditional cyber threats, which often focus on specific systems or software.

The Human Element: The Achilles' Heel of Cybersecurity

Social engineering attacks highlight the critical role of the human element in cybersecurity. While organizations invest heavily in firewalls, encryption, and other technical security measures, these defenses can be circumvented by exploiting human vulnerabilities.

Understanding the goals and uniqueness of social engineering is like learning the playbook of a sly trickster. By knowing their objectives and recognizing how they differ from other cyber threats, we not only strengthen our defenses but also gain a clearer picture of the distinct challenges posed by these digital manipulators. Welcome to the world where awareness becomes your armor against the wiles of social engineering.

Unlocking Phishing Tactics

Dive into the kingdom of cyber deception with unlocking phishing tactics– email, spear, vishing, and more. This guide unveils the secrets behind email phishing, spear phishing, and vishing, arming you with knowledge to fortify your digital defenses. Get ready to stay one step ahead in the ever-evolving world of phishing threats.

Diving into the World of Phishing: A Crafty Hunt for Sensitive Data

Phishing, a widespread trick in the world of cybersecurity, revolves around enticing unsuspecting individuals to share confidential details or take actions that jeopardize their security. Using deceitful emails, text messages, or phone calls, phishers pose as trustworthy entities, manipulating human trust and curiosity to deceive their targets.

Email Phishing: The Broad Net Approach

Email phishing stands out as the most common phishing technique, employing mass-email campaigns to cast a broad net for potential victims. These emails often mirror authentic messages from banks, online stores, or social media platforms, containing urgent requests to update account details, confirm transactions, or verify passwords.

Spear Phishing: Precision Strikes

Spear phishing, a more refined breed of phishing, involves carefully crafted emails tailored to specific individuals or organizations. Attackers delve into research on their targets, gathering personal information from social media, company websites, or leaked data. This personalized touch makes spear phishing attacks more convincing, significantly upping their success rate.

Vishing: Phishing by Phone

Vishing, or voice phishing, exploits the power of phone calls to deceive individuals. Attackers pose as customer service representatives, technical support personnel, or even law enforcement officials, using manipulative tactics to convince their targets to reveal sensitive information or perform actions that compromise security.

Unveiling the Phishing Puzzle: Understanding the Deceptive Blueprint

Phishing attacks typically unfold in a familiar sequence:

- ***First Contact:*** The attacker initiates contact using email, text messages, or phone calls, often adopting urgent or alarming language to grab attention.
- ***Building Trust:*** Posing as a legitimate entity, the attacker leverages logos, branding, and familiar language to establish a false sense of trust.
- ***Urgency Unleashed:*** A crucial step involves creating a heightened sense of urgency, pressuring the target to react hastily, and leaving little room for careful consideration.
- ***Information Plea:*** The attacker, now in a position of trust, requests sensitive information like passwords, credit card details, or account credentials.
- ***Bait Harvesting:*** Once the target unwittingly provides the requested information, the attacker achieves their objective and vanishes from the scene.

Defend Yourself Against Phishing: Stay Alert and Informed

To shield yourself from phishing attacks, stick to these crucial guidelines:

- ***Approach Unsolicited Messages with Caution:*** Treat emails, texts, or calls asking for sensitive details or urgent actions skeptically.
- ***Check Sender Authenticity:*** Scrutinize the sender's email, phone number, or website for any signs of errors or irregularities.
- ***Hover before you click:*** Before clicking any links, hover over them to uncover the actual destination URL. Steer clear of links from unfamiliar or suspicious sources.
- ***Guard Your Credentials:*** Refrain from sharing sensitive information like passwords or credit card details via email, text, or phone calls.
- ***Deploy Security Software:*** To protect your device from potential phishing assaults, use antivirus and anti-malware software.
- ***Stay Updated:*** Keep abreast of the latest phishing tactics and scams through trusted cybersecurity sources.

By recognizing the warning signs of phishing attacks and adopting a vigilant approach, you can effectively shield yourself from these sly attempts to snatch your valuable information. Stay savvy, stay secure!

Red Flags to Identify Phishing Attempts

Imagine you are the detective of your own digital world, and phishing attempts are the cunning criminals trying to pull off a heist. Here are the telltale signs and the red flags that should make your cybersecurity senses tingle:

- ***Generic Greetings:*** If an email starts with a generic "`Dear Customer`" instead of your name, beware. Legitimate entities usually know who you are.
- ***Misspelled URLs:*** Hover over links before clicking. If the URL looks like it has been on a spelling adventure (like "`yourbankk.com`"), it is probably a trap.
- ***Urgency Overload:*** Phishers love making you panic. If the email insists you act urgently, take a deep breath. It is a classic ploy to cloud your judgment.
- ***Unsolicited Attachments:*** Think twice before opening attachments, especially if the email is unexpected. Attachments can be the Trojan horse of phishing attacks.
- ***Check the Sender's Email Address:*** A common trick is using an email address that looks similar to a legitimate one. For example, "`yourbankofficial@gmail.com`" instead of "`yourbank.com`".
- ***Too Good to Be True:*** If an email promises you a lottery win or an unbelievable deal, skepticism is your best friend. Phishers play on our desire for good fortune.

Unmasking Phishing: Real-Life Tales of Deception

Now, let us unravel the narratives where the bait was taken, and the web of phishing successfully ensnared its victims:

- ***Marriott Data Breach (2023):*** Hackers crafted sophisticated phishing emails targeting Marriott hotel staff, tricking them into revealing login credentials. This breach exposed the personal information of over 5.2 million guests, highlighting the vulnerability of even sophisticated companies to well-executed social engineering attacks.
- ***Colonial Pipeline Ransomware Attack (2021):*** Though not directly a classic phishing case, the attack involved a social engineering element. Hackers reportedly gained initial access to Colonial Pipeline's system through a compromised password obtained through a phishing attack on an employee. This incident underscores how seemingly minor social engineering victories can trigger devastating consequences.
- ***Amazon Gift Card Scam (2023):*** This ongoing scam utilizes fake text messages mimicking Amazon notifications informing recipients of "unclaimed gift cards." Clicking the included link leads to a phishing website designed to steal login credentials and credit card information. This example showcases

the continuous adaptation of phishing tactics to exploit popular brands and consumer expectations.

- ***Crypto Trading Platform Hacks (2023-2024):*** Several high-profile hacks of crypto trading platforms like FTX and Crypto.com involved phishing attacks targeting employees. These targeted efforts aimed at gaining access to internal systems and manipulating cryptocurrency transactions. This emphasizes the increasing focus of social engineers on high-value targets within the crypto market.
- ***Deepfake Social Engineering:*** Emerging trends involve using deepfake technology to create fake video calls or voice recordings impersonating trusted individuals. These attacks aim to bypass traditional phishing methods and target victims with personalized deception. This highlights the need for continued vigilance and skepticism toward even seemingly genuine digital interactions.

These chronicles underscore the profound impact of phishing attacks, weaving tales of financial losses, identity theft, and reputational harm for both individuals and organizations alike.

Shielding Yourself from Phishing Attacks: Navigating the Digital Terrain Safely

To keep phishing threats at bay, follow these straightforward guidelines:

- ***Confirm the Sender's Legitimacy:*** Always double-check the sender's email, phone number, or website for any oddities or typos. Legitimate entities stick to official domains and contact details.
- ***Hover before You Click:*** Before plunging into links, hover over them to unveil the actual destination URL. Steer clear of links from unknown or dubious sources, even if they seem legit.
- ***Guard Your Secrets:*** Never spill sensitive information—passwords, credit card details, or personal data—via email, texts, or calls unless you are absolutely sure of the recipient's authenticity.
- ***Forge Fortresses with Strong Passwords:*** Craft robust, unique passwords for all your online haunts. Dodge the obvious choices like birthdays or common words.
- ***Double Up with Two-Factor Authentication (2FA):*** Increase the security of your accounts by enabling 2FA whenever feasible. This additional layer necessitates a second verification mechanism, such as a code given to your phone, in addition to your password.
- ***Stay in the Know:*** Stay in the loop on the latest phishing maneuvers and scams through reliable cybersecurity sources. This savvy awareness helps you spot new tricks and dodge the ever-evolving tactics of phishing.

By embracing these protective steps and keeping a watchful eye, you can significantly slash the risk of succumbing to phishing attacks and secure your precious information. Stay smart, stay secure!

Real-Life Deceptions

Explore the fascinating world of real-life deceptions in the field of social engineering. Delve into gripping narratives that unveil the tactics and consequences of social engineers who exploit human vulnerabilities. Brace yourself for captivating stories that bring to light the impactful and often surprising aspects of cyber manipulation.

Unveiling the Masters of Deception: Case Studies of Notable Social Engineering Attacks

The space of social engineering is rife with cunning tactics and audacious schemes as attackers exploit human vulnerabilities to achieve their malicious goals. By examining real-life social engineering attacks, we can glean valuable insights into the methods employed by these deceptive adversaries and learn crucial lessons to safeguard ourselves and our organizations from such threats.

Case Study 1: The Spear Phishing Attack on Ubiquiti Networks

In 2016, Ubiquiti Networks, a manufacturer of networking equipment, fell victim to a sophisticated spear-phishing attack that resulted in the theft of millions of dollars. The attackers meticulously crafted emails that appeared to be from a legitimate supplier, requesting payments to be made to their bank accounts. Ubiquiti employees, believing the emails to be genuine, authorized the payments, unknowingly transferring funds to the attackers.

- ***Tactics Employed:*** Following are the tactics employed:
  - ***Spear-phishing:*** The attackers targeted specific individuals within Ubiquiti Networks, using personalized information to enhance the credibility of their emails.
  - ***Social Proof:*** The emails were designed to mimic legitimate communications from a trusted supplier, utilizing logos, branding, and familiar language to instill trust.
  - ***Urgency:*** The emails created a sense of urgency, pressuring employees to act quickly without proper verification.

Case Study 2: The Whaling Attack on Energean Oil

In 2019, Energean Oil, an Israeli oil and gas company, fell prey to a sophisticated whaling attack, a type of social engineering that targets high-level executives. The attackers posed as representatives of a trusted financial institution, convincing Energean's CEO to authorize a wire transfer of $11 million.

- ***Tactics Employed:*** Following are the tactics employed:
  - ***Whaling:*** The attackers targeted Energean's CEO, a high-value individual with the authority to approve large financial transactions.
  - ***Social Proof:*** The attackers employed social engineering techniques to establish trust, using familiar names, company references, and fabricated financial documents.
  - ***Exploitation of Trust:*** The attackers exploited the CEO's trust in his colleagues, forging emails from trusted individuals within the company to reinforce their requests.

Case Study 3: The Watering Hole Attack on Saudi Aramco

In 2012, Saudi Aramco, the world's largest oil company, became the victim of a watering hole attack, a type of social engineering that targets specific websites frequented by the intended victims. The attackers compromised a website popular among Saudi Aramco employees, injecting malware that infected their computers when they visited the site.

- ***Tactics Employed:*** Following are the tactics employed:
  - ***Watering Hole Attack:*** The attackers identified and compromised a website frequented by Saudi Aramco employees, making it a target-rich environment.
  - ***Malware Injection:*** The attackers injected malicious code into the compromised website, which infected the computers of unsuspecting employees when they visited the site.
  - ***Exploitation of Vulnerabilities:*** The attackers exploited vulnerabilities in the employees' software to gain access to their systems and steal sensitive information.

These case studies provide a glimpse into the cunning tactics and deceptive methods employed by social engineers. By understanding the techniques used in these real-world attacks, we can better equip ourselves and our organizations to recognize and defend against these sophisticated threats. Vigilance, education, and the implementation of robust security measures are essential to safeguarding our valuable information.

ID and Homograph Attacks

Dive into the intriguing sphere of social engineering as we unravel the clandestine tactics of ID and homograph attacks. In this exploration, discover how cyber adversaries manipulate identities and exploit visual deceptions to compromise security. Uncover the subtle yet powerful methods employed in these attacks, shedding light on the nuanced world of online manipulation and identity theft.

ID Attacks

In the field of social engineering, ID attacks involve impersonation and delegation tactics to gain unauthorized access to sensitive information or systems. Attackers masquerade as trusted individuals or entities, exploiting human trust and authority to deceive their targets.

Impersonation: Entering the Domain of False Identities

In the world of cybersecurity, impersonation attacks unfold when a perpetrator dons the guise of a genuine person or organization to deceive their target into divulging sensitive details or undertaking actions that imperil security. These attackers might employ pilfered identities, fabricate counterfeit profiles, or even resort to deepfakes to convincingly mimic real individuals.

Delegation: A False Grant of Authority

Delegation attacks involve the attacker manipulating their target into delegating authority, such as granting access to sensitive information or systems, under false pretenses. Attackers may pose as IT support personnel, security officials, or even colleagues, using urgency or fabricated scenarios to convince their targets to bypass security protocols.

Common ID Attack Techniques

ID attackers often employ a combination of techniques to deceive their targets:

- ***Social Proof***: Attackers use logos, branding, and familiar language to establish credibility and make their impersonation seem authentic.
- ***Urgency and Fear***: Attackers create a sense of urgency or fear, pressuring their targets to act quickly without critical thinking.
- ***Exploitation of Trust***: Attackers exploit existing trust relationships or authority figures to gain their targets' compliance.
- ***Fake Documentation***: Attackers may use forged documents, credentials, or websites to reinforce their impersonation.

Protecting Against ID Attacks: Staying Vigilant and Verifying Identities

To safeguard yourself against ID attacks, follow these essential guidelines:

- ***Verify Identities Thoroughly:*** Always verify the identity of individuals or organizations requesting sensitive information or access, especially those contacting you unsolicited.
- ***Question Unusual Requests:*** Be wary of unusual requests or demands, especially those involving financial transactions or system access.
- ***Confirm Communication Channels:*** Verify the authenticity of communication channels, such as email addresses, phone numbers, or websites, before engaging in sensitive conversations.
- ***Protect Sensitive Information:*** Never share sensitive information, such as passwords or personal details, with unknown individuals or organizations.
- ***Report Suspicious Activity:*** If you encounter suspicious activity or suspect an ID attack, report it immediately to the appropriate authorities.

By adopting these protective measures and maintaining a vigilant mindset, you can effectively defend yourself against ID attacks and safeguard your valuable information from impersonators and unauthorized access.

Homograph Attacks

In the domain of cybersecurity, homograph attacks, also known as typosquatting attacks, exploit the visual similarity of characters to deceive unsuspecting individuals into visiting malicious websites. Attackers register domain names that closely resemble legitimate website addresses, often substituting visually similar characters such as **`'a'`** for `'α'` or `'l'` for `'1'`.

The Illusion of Authenticity: Misdirection through Character Similarity

When a user types a legitimate website address into their browser, they may inadvertently enter the attacker's homograph domain instead. This can happen due to typos, auto-correction errors, or simply the difficulty of distinguishing between visually similar characters. Once the user lands on the attacker's website, they may be presented with fake login pages, phishing forms, or malware disguised as genuine content.

Common Homograph Attack Techniques

Attackers employ various techniques to execute homograph attacks:

- ***Character Substitution:*** Attackers substitute visually similar characters, such as 'o' for '0' or 's' for '$', in domain names.
- ***IDN Misrepresentation:*** Attackers register domain names using Internationalized Domain Names (IDNs), which allow the use of non-Latin characters. These characters may closely resemble Latin characters, making them difficult to be distinguished.
- ***Typosquatting:*** Attackers register domain names with common typos or misspellings of legitimate website addresses.
- ***URL Shorteners:*** Attackers use URL shorteners to disguise malicious homograph domain names, making them less suspicious when shared through email or social media.

Defending Against Homograph Attacks: A Guide to Vigilance and Detail

Defending against homograph attacks requires staying aware of the latest technological advancements. Here are some cutting-edge defense mechanisms:

- **Advanced URL Inspection Tools:** Employ state-of-the-art URL inspection tools that leverage machine learning algorithms to analyze web addresses for potential homograph elements. These tools can detect subtle variations and anomalies in URLs, providing users with warnings about potential threats.
- **Browser-Based Protections:** Modern web browsers are integrating enhanced security features specifically designed to combat homograph attacks. These features include real-time URL analysis, comparing characters across different scripts, and alerting users when visiting potentially deceptive websites.
- **AI-Powered Email Filtering:** Implement advanced email filtering systems powered by artificial intelligence. These systems can scrutinize incoming emails for signs of homograph attacks, flagging or blocking suspicious messages before they reach the recipient's inbox.
- **User Education and Awareness:** Promote user education and awareness programs to familiarize individuals with the risks of homograph attacks. Training users to scrutinize URLs, especially in emails and messages, can be an effective line of defense.
- **Constant Security Updates:** Regularly update security protocols and software to ensure protection against evolving homograph attack techniques. Security updates often include patches and improvements designed to counter new threats as they emerge.
- **Collaboration with Domain Registrars:** Foster collaboration between cybersecurity experts and domain registrars to identify and mitigate potential

homograph threats at the domain registration level. This proactive approach can prevent malicious actors from exploiting deceptive domain registrations.

- **Community Reporting:** Establish mechanisms for the community to report suspicious URLs and instances of homograph attacks. This collective vigilance can contribute to a dynamic threat intelligence network, allowing for rapid identification and response to emerging homograph threats.

By combining these advanced defense mechanisms, individuals and organizations can significantly bolster their resilience against homograph attacks in the ever-evolving landscape of cybersecurity.

The Role of a Social Engineer

Social engineering, while often associated with malicious intent, has evolved into a legitimate professional field, encompassing individuals who employ their understanding of human behavior and communication to achieve positive outcomes. These social engineers, whether working in cybersecurity, marketing, or other fields, utilize their skills to influence, persuade, and motivate individuals to achieve specific goals.

Professional Roles of Social Engineers

Social engineers find employment in various industries, each with its own unique focus and objectives:

- ***Cybersecurity:*** Social engineers play a crucial role in penetration testing and security assessments, identifying vulnerabilities in human behavior that could be exploited by attackers. They design and execute social engineering tests to evaluate employee awareness, assess the effectiveness of security policies, and identify potential loopholes.
- ***Marketing:*** Social engineers in marketing utilize their understanding of human psychology and persuasion techniques to create effective marketing campaigns, develop compelling brand messaging, and influence consumer behavior. They may conduct market research, analyze customer data, and design targeted marketing strategies to promote products, services, or brands.
- ***Training and Development:*** Social engineers in training and development facilitate workshops, seminars, and training programs to educate individuals on social engineering techniques and enhance their awareness of deception tactics. They may develop training materials, deliver presentations, and conduct role-playing exercises to help individuals recognize and defend against social engineering attacks.
- ***Sales and Negotiation:*** Social engineers in sales and negotiation utilize their understanding of human behavior and communication to build rapport with

clients, identify their needs, and persuade them to make purchasing decisions. They may conduct client consultations, negotiate contracts, and handle customer interactions to achieve sales objectives.

Inside the Social Engineer's Mind: Understanding Empathy and Persuasion

Successful social engineers possess a distinctive mix of skills coupled with a profound insight into human behavior. They exude empathy, forming genuine connections with individuals on a personal level, and cultivating trust and rapport that becomes a conduit for persuasion. Their prowess extends to effective communication, enabling them to craft messages finely tuned to the specific needs and motivations of their targets.

Essential Skills of a Social Engineer

Here are some of the essential skills of a social engineer:

- ***Empathy***: The knack for grasping and sharing others' feelings, forging a connection that builds trust.
- ***Communication:*** Adeptness in both verbal and non-verbal communication to deliver messages persuasively and adapt to diverse communication styles.
- ***Influence***: The skill to shape others' thoughts, emotions, or actions through persuasion and social proof.
- ***Observation:*** Sharp observation skills to collect information about individuals and their surroundings, pinpointing potential vulnerabilities or cues.
- ***Critical Thinking***: The ability to scrutinize situations, assess information, and make informed judgments based on gathered insights.
- ***Ethical Awareness***: A strong ethical compass to ensure that social engineering skills are wielded responsibly and directed towards positive purposes.

Social engineers, when employed ethically and responsibly, can be a powerful force for positive change. They can enhance cybersecurity, promote effective marketing campaigns, facilitate effective training, and drive successful sales negotiations. By understanding the mindset and skills of social engineers, we can better appreciate the diverse applications of this field and the potential benefits it brings to various industries and society as a whole.

Exploring Social Engineering Tools

Exploring the domain of social engineering tools reveals a dynamic landscape with constantly evolving technologies. Here are some of the latest tools being employed in social engineering:

- ***Shellphish:*** Shellphish is a powerful and popular open-source tool designed for phishing and social engineering attacks. It provides a range of phishing templates, making it accessible for attackers to create convincing fake login pages.

- **SET (*Social-Engineer Toolkit*):** Developed by TrustedSec, SET is an open-source framework that includes multiple attack vectors for social engineering campaigns. It covers a broad spectrum, from credential harvesting to creating malicious files for exploitation.

- ***Evilginx2:*** Evilginx2 is a sophisticated man-in-the-middle attack framework specifically tailored for phishing login credentials. It is designed to bypass two-factor authentication mechanisms, making it a potent tool for attackers.

- ***Gophish:*** Gophish is an open-source phishing toolkit that enables security professionals and penetration testers to create and execute phishing campaigns. It provides a user-friendly interface and detailed analytics to assess campaign effectiveness.

- **BeEF (*Browser Exploitation Framework*):** BeEF is an extensive penetration testing tool that focuses on exploiting web browser vulnerabilities. It allows attackers to control and manipulate browsers, making it valuable for social engineering attacks.

- ***Social Mapper*:** Social Mapper is a tool designed for automated social media profiling during social engineering engagements. It identifies and associates social media accounts with a target, providing attackers with valuable information for personalized attacks.

- ***CredSniper*:** CredSniper is a phishing framework that simplifies the process of capturing login credentials. It supports various attack scenarios, including credential harvesting through landing pages and rogue OAuth applications.

- ***MailSniper*:** MailSniper is a penetration testing tool focused on the Microsoft Exchange environment. It facilitates reconnaissance and exploitation of email-related vulnerabilities, enabling attackers to gather valuable information for social engineering attacks.

It is crucial to note that while these tools are mentioned here for educational purposes, their use for malicious intent is illegal and unethical. The awareness of these tools is essential for cybersecurity professionals to better defend against social engineering threats.

Working of these Tools

These tools typically function by automating tasks, generating malicious content, and exploiting vulnerabilities in communication protocols. They may utilize web scraping techniques to gather information from online sources, create fake login pages to capture user credentials, or generate realistic phishing emails that appear to be from legitimate organizations.

Functionalities and Applications

These tools offer a range of functionalities that aid social engineers in carrying out their deceptive schemes:

- ***Email Crafting***: Tools like SET provide templates and modules for creating personalized and convincing phishing emails that can bypass spam filters and deceive targets.
- ***Website Cloning***: These tools allow social engineers to create fake website clones that mimic legitimate websites, tricking users into revealing sensitive information.
- ***Social Media Manipulation:*** Social engineering tools can be used to automate social media interactions, spread misinformation, and manipulate online conversations to influence target audiences.
- ***Vulnerability Exploitation:*** Some tools exploit vulnerabilities in communication protocols, such as SIP (Session Initiation Protocol), to intercept and manipulate voice calls for vishing attacks.

The availability of these tools underscores the importance of vigilance and awareness in the face of social engineering threats. By understanding the capabilities of these tools and adopting protective measures, individuals and organizations can effectively safeguard themselves from deceptive attacks and protect their valuable information.

Ethical Use of Social Engineering Tools for Educational Purposes

Imagine social engineering tools as double-edged swords—potent instruments that can cut through deception but, when wielded responsibly, serve as shields for education. Let us explore the ethical considerations surrounding the use of tools like Shellfish and the Social-Engineer Toolkit (SET) in the field of cybersecurity education:

- **Digital Simulations as Learning Tools:**
  - ***Overview:*** Just as pilots use flight simulators to enhance their skills, ethical hackers and cybersecurity professionals can use social engineering tools

in controlled environments for educational purposes. It is like a virtual training ground where learners can sharpen their defense mechanisms.

  - ***Hands-On Experience:*** Ethical use involves creating simulated scenarios where individuals can experience and recognize social engineering attacks firsthand. This hands-on approach helps bridge the gap between theoretical knowledge and practical skills.

- **Controlled Environments for Skill Development:**
  - ***Labs and Training Platforms:*** Ethical educators use dedicated labs and training platforms to ensure that the use of social engineering tools is contained within a controlled environment. This minimizes the risk of unintended consequences.
  - ***Supervised Learning:*** Like a driving instructor overseeing a learner behind the wheel, ethical use involves supervision. In educational settings, mentors guide learners through the use of these tools, emphasizing responsible and legal practices.
- **Developing Defensive Strategies:**
  - ***Understanding the Adversary:*** Educational use of social engineering tools allows individuals to understand the tactics employed by adversaries. By experiencing simulated attacks, learners gain insights into the methods used against them, enhancing their ability to develop robust defenses.
  - ***Creating Cyber Awareness:*** Ethical use contributes to a culture of cyber awareness. By exposing individuals to potential threats in a controlled setting, educators empower them to recognize and resist social engineering attacks in real-world scenarios.
- **Adhering to Ethical Guidelines:**
  - ***Established Standards:*** Ethical educators adhere to established standards and guidelines when using social engineering tools. These standards emphasize responsible and legal use, ensuring that educational activities align with ethical principles.
  - ***Respecting Privacy:*** Ethical considerations include respecting the privacy and consent of individuals participating in educational simulations. Clear communication and informed consent are fundamental aspects of ethical educational practices.

Understanding the ethical use of social engineering tools in education is like unlocking the potential for positive transformation. By approaching these tools as educational instruments, we empower individuals to become guardians of cybersecurity, equipped with the knowledge and skills to unmask and defend against deceptive attacks. Welcome to the classroom, where ethical education becomes the key to fortifying the digital world against the ever-evolving landscape of social engineering threats.

Future Trends in Social Engineering

Social engineering, already a formidable threat, is poised to evolve further with the integration of artificial intelligence (AI) into its arsenal. As AI capabilities advance, social engineers will likely employ AI-powered tools to personalize attacks, automate deceptive tactics, and enhance their ability to manipulate human behavior.

AI in Social Engineering: Amplifying Deception

AI can play a significant role in social engineering by enabling attackers to:

- ***Craft Personalized Messages:*** AI algorithms can analyze vast amounts of personal data to create highly tailored social engineering messages that resonate with individual targets.
- ***Automate Deceptive Tactics:*** AI can automate tasks such as phishing email generation, website cloning, and vishing campaigns, increasing the volume and sophistication of social engineering attacks.
- ***Manipulate Human Behavior:*** AI can be used to study human psychology and develop advanced techniques for manipulating emotions, exploiting cognitive biases, and influencing decision-making.

Recommendations for Staying Ahead of Evolving Threats

To stay ahead of the evolving social engineering landscape, individuals and organizations should adopt proactive measures:

- ***Continuous Awareness:*** Maintain ongoing awareness of the latest social engineering trends and techniques, including those involving AI-powered tools.
- ***Critical Thinking:*** Cultivate critical thinking skills to question the authenticity of communications, verify information sources, and avoid acting impulsively.
- ***Protective Measures:*** Implement strong cybersecurity practices, such as multi-factor authentication, secure passwords, and data encryption, to minimize potential vulnerabilities.
- ***Reporting Culture:*** Foster an open and supportive culture where employees feel comfortable reporting suspicious activity or potential social engineering attempts.
- ***AI-Powered Defense:*** Explore the potential of AI-powered security solutions to detect and mitigate social engineering attacks, complementing traditional cybersecurity measures.

Unveiling the AI Menace: Case Studies in Advanced Social Engineering Attacks

Let us dive into the sphere of advanced social engineering with "Unveiling the AI Menace." We will explore gripping case studies where artificial intelligence becomes a formidable tool in orchestrating deceptive cyber attacks. We will also discover the sinister potential of AI-driven strategies and the evolving landscape of social engineering threats.

Case Study 1: AI-Enhanced Voice Phishing Exploits

Back in 2019, fraudsters harnessed the power of AI to replicate the voice of a CEO from a UK-based energy company, cunningly persuading him to transfer a significant sum of money. The AI tool demonstrated an extraordinary ability to mirror the CEO's voice, capturing nuances like his German accent and speech pattern. This instance underscores the alarming potential of AI in orchestrating convincingly deceptive voice phishing attacks.

Case Study 2: AI-Generated Phishing Emails

AI algorithms are being used to generate phishing emails that are becoming increasingly difficult to distinguish from legitimate emails. These AI-generated emails can be tailored to the specific interests and demographics of the target, making them more likely to be opened and clicked on. This case demonstrates the ability of AI to create targeted and personalized social engineering attacks.

Case Study 3: AI-Generated Deepfakes

Artificial Intelligence is now actively employed to craft deepfakes—videos or audio recordings altered to portray individuals saying or doing things they never actually did. These deepfakes present a concerning tool for social engineering, enabling the creation of fabricated news stories or impersonations for the purpose of acquiring sensitive information. This case vividly showcases how AI can be harnessed for profoundly deceptive and manipulative social engineering schemes.

Case Study 4: AI-Enhanced Social Media Influence

Utilizing AI algorithms to scrutinize and control social media discussions, disseminate misinformation, and shape public sentiment has become a stark reality. Social engineers leverage AI to pinpoint and focus on influential figures, magnify their messages, and generate a bandwagon effect capable of steering public opinion. This instance accentuates the worrisome potential of AI for orchestrating extensive social engineering campaigns.

Case Study 5: AI-Powered Social Engineering Tools: The Unseen Hands Behind Deceptive Attacks

In the horizon of cybersecurity, AI-automated social engineering tools have emerged as covert architects of deception. These tools, readily available, can streamline nefarious tasks like crafting phishing emails, replicating websites, and fabricating fake social media personas. Their existence not only simplifies the execution of social engineering attacks but also enables a surge in the number of potential targets. This case vividly illustrates how AI effortlessly automates and scales social engineering assaults.

As these case studies exemplify, the sophistication of AI-powered social engineering attacks is on the rise. With the continuous evolution of AI capabilities, social engineers are poised to unleash even more cunning and effective techniques. This underscores the urgency for individuals and organizations to stay abreast of the latest AI-driven social engineering threats and proactively fortify their defenses.

Conclusion

As we conclude the journey through the captivating world of social engineering attacks, we have unraveled the intricate web of manipulation and deceit. From fundamental insights into social engineering to exposing the tactics of phishing, spear phishing, and vishing, each topic has fortified your understanding of this ever-evolving threat landscape. Real-life deceptions, identity and homograph attacks, the role of a social engineer, and an exploration of tools have unveiled the multifaceted nature of these attacks. The quiz has honed your skills in spotting phishing links, and a glimpse into future trends has equipped you to stay ahead in the cybersecurity game.

Congratulations on navigating this crucial chapter! Brace yourself for the next adventure as we delve into the intricacies of Reconnaissance and OSINT in the upcoming chapter.

Quiz: Mastering Social Engineering Awareness

Welcome to the Social Engineering Awareness Quiz, designed to enhance your understanding of deceptive tactics in the cyber world. In this scenario-based quiz, you will navigate through common situations where social engineering attacks lurk. Choose the most appropriate response from the provided options. Let us elevate your awareness to fortify your digital defenses.

Instructions: Carefully read each question and respond to it to the best of your ability. The quiz will furnish detailed explanations for the correct answers, aiding you in grasping the key indicators of phishing links. Let us sharpen those detection skills!

Question 1: Phishing Precision

Consider the following scenario: you receive an email from your bank inviting you to check recent transactions by clicking a link. While the email looks to be genuine, you notice a slight typo in the sender's address. What should your next step be?

A. Click the link to make sure your account is secure.

B. Ignore the email; it was most likely an honest mistake.

C. Contact your email provider and mark the email as spam.

D. Respond to the email, asking for clarity.

Question 2: Suspicious Social Media Outreach

You get a connection request on a professional networking platform from someone claiming to be a high-profile executive in your industry. They express interest in collaboration and request access to confidential business documents. How do you respond?

A. Accept the connection and share the requested documents.

B. Decline the connection without further investigation.

C. Verify the person's identity through a video call.

D. Share only non-sensitive information initially.

Question 3: Urgency in Action

An urgent email arrives from your company's IT department, stating that your account is compromised, and immediate action is needed. The email provides a link to reset your password. What's the best course of action?

A. Click the link and swiftly reset your password.

B. Forward the email to your colleagues for advice.

C. Ignore the email; it is likely a technical glitch.

D. Contact the IT department through a known number or email.

Question 4: Colleague's Curious Request

A colleague emails you a link to a new document-sharing platform, claiming it is for an urgent project. The platform requires your login credentials. What should you do?

A. Click the link and enter your credentials promptly.

B. Verify the legitimacy of the request with your colleague.

C. Ignore the email; it seems like a phishing attempt.

D. Report the email to your IT security team.

Question 5: Tempting Email Offer

You receive an unsolicited email offering a substantial discount on a popular online shopping site. The email contains a link to claim your discount. How do you handle this?

A. Click the link and enjoy the discount offer.

B. Forward the email to friends and family.

C. Report the email to the online shopping site.

D. Delete the email without clicking the link.

Answers and Explanations:

Question 1: Phishing Precision

Correct Answer*: C. *Report the email as spam to your email provider.

Explanation: Phishing emails often use subtle tactics like misspelled sender addresses to deceive recipients. Instead of clicking the link, report the email as spam to your email provider. They can verify its legitimacy and take necessary actions to protect other users.

Question 2: Suspicious Social Media Outreach

Correct Answer*: C. *Verify the person's identity through a video call.

Explanation: It is crucial to verify the identity of unfamiliar connections, especially when they request access to sensitive information. Opt for a video call or other means to confirm their authenticity before sharing any confidential documents.

Question 3: Urgency in Action

Correct Answer*: D. *Contact the IT department through a known number or email.

Explanation: Urgent emails claiming compromised accounts often aim to provoke hasty actions. Instead of clicking the provided link, independently verify the situation by contacting the IT department through a known and trusted communication channel.

Question 4: Colleague's Curious Request

Correct Answer*: B. *Verify the legitimacy of the request with your colleague.

Explanation: Always confirm the authenticity of unexpected requests, even if they seem to come from colleagues. Contact your colleague through a separate, trusted channel to ensure the legitimacy of the document-sharing platform.

Question 5: Tempting Email Offer

Correct Answer*: D. *Delete the email without clicking the link.

Explanation: Unsolicited emails offering significant discounts may be phishing attempts. Avoid clicking on unknown links and delete such emails. If you are interested in the offer, visit the online shopping site directly through your browser.

Congratulations on completing the Social Engineering Awareness Quiz! Your thoughtful responses demonstrate a heightened awareness of potential social engineering threats. Stay vigilant and continue to refine your skills in recognizing and mitigating deceptive tactics in the digital landscape. Well done!

Reinforcement Tasks

Engage in targeted exercises to reinforce your understanding and fortify your defenses against deceptive tactics.:

- ***Hover over Links*:** Practice hovering over links before clicking to unveil the actual destination URL. This helps spot suspicious links that might lead to phishing websites.
- ***Inspect Domain Names*:** Scrutinize domain names meticulously for typos, misspellings, or unusual subdomains. Even minor variations could signal a phishing attempt.
- ***Verify Senders*:** Always double-check the sender's email address before interacting with links or opening attachments. Watch out for suspicious or unfamiliar email addresses.
- ***Watch for Urgency and Fear Tactics*:** Be wary of emails that create urgency or use fear-based tactics to rush you into quick action. These tactics are common in phishing attempts.
- ***Guard Sensitive Information*:** Never share sensitive information, like passwords or credit card details, through email or on uncertain websites.

By adhering to these guidelines and participating in these hands-on exercises, you can significantly boost your ability to spot phishing links and protect yourself from the crafty strategies of social engineering attacks. Keep in mind that vigilance and critical thinking are your best allies in the battle against phishing.

CHAPTER 6
Reconnaissance and OSINT

Introduction

Dive into the sphere of cybersecurity intelligence with **Reconnaissance and OSINT**. From unraveling the art of Google Dorking to mastering Shodan's power and employing techniques like WHOIS and SSL certificate analysis, this chapter is a comprehensive guide. Readers will explore content discovery through fuzzing and brute force, leverage historic datasets strategically, and discover additional OSINT resources. Building on the social engineering discussions in the previous chapter, this segment equips readers to adeptly navigate the cybersecurity landscape, ensuring robust defense against evolving threats.

Structure

In this chapter, we will cover the following topics:

- Web Reconnaissance Unveiled
- Google Dorking: Discover Concealed Information
- Shodan: The Search Engine for Devices
- Asset Discovery: WHOIS, ASN Lookup
- Decoding SSL/TLS Certificates
- Content Discovery Basics
- Leveraging Historic Datasets
- Other OSINT Resources

Web Reconnaissance Unveiled: A Beginner's Guide to OSINT and Beyond

Reconnaissance, in the context of cybersecurity, is like detective work before a mission.

Imagine you are about to enter a mysterious castle, and before charging in, you would want to know everything possible about it. That is what reconnaissance is all about in the digital world. It is the careful art of gathering information before diving into the nitty-gritty of testing web applications.

Definition and Importance

In the space of cybersecurity, reconnaissance refers to the systematic and methodical gathering of information about a target, typically an organization, system, or individual, before launching an attack or conducting a security assessment. It is a crucial phase of any cybersecurity operation, providing valuable insights into the target's vulnerabilities, defenses, and potential attack vectors.

Reconnaissance plays a critical role in various cybersecurity scenarios, including:

- ***Penetration Testing:*** Reconnaissance is the foundation of web application penetration testing, enabling testers to identify potential entry points, gather intelligence about the target's infrastructure and applications, and plan their attack strategy.
- ***Threat Intelligence Gathering:*** Cybersecurity professionals gather threat intelligence through reconnaissance to understand the evolving tactics, techniques, and procedures (TTPs) employed by threat actors, enabling them to proactively protect their organizations from potential attacks.
- ***Risk Assessment:*** Reconnaissance is an integral part of risk assessment, providing the necessary information to identify, analyze, and prioritize security risks effectively.

Unveiling the Importance in Web Application Penetration Testing

In web application penetration testing, reconnaissance takes the lead as the initial step, setting the foundation for subsequent testing phases. It involves gathering crucial information about the target web application, such as its domain name, IP address, subdomains, employed technologies, and potential vulnerabilities. This information is vital for testers to identify potential attack routes and shape their testing strategy effectively.

Reconnaissance techniques commonly used in web application penetration testing include:

- ***Passive DNS Analysis:*** Gathering information about the target's DNS records, including A records, MX records, and CNAME records, to identify potential subdomains and associated servers.

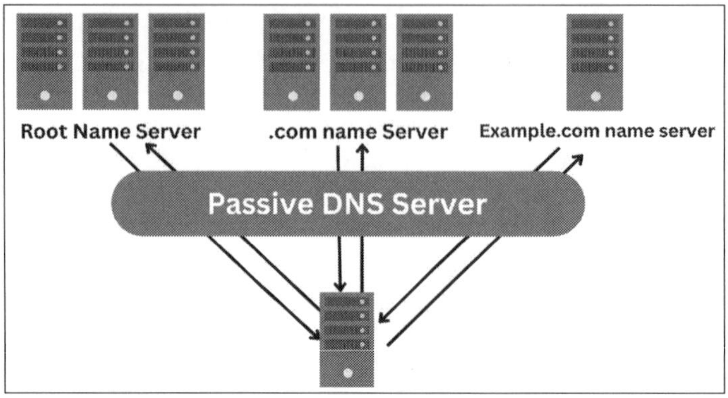

Figure 6.1: *Passive DNS Analysis*

- ***Website Fingerprinting***: Utilizing tools like Wappalyzer or BuiltWith to identify the technologies used on the target website, such as the web server, programming languages, and content management systems (CMS).

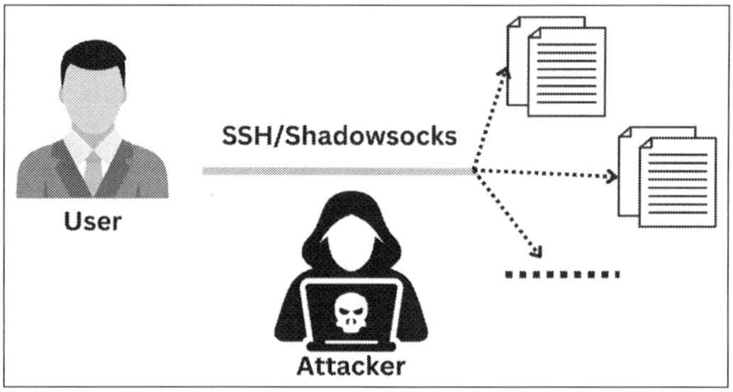

Figure 6.2: *Website Fingerprinting*

- ***Social Engineering***: Gathering information about the target organization or individuals through social media, public records, and online forums to identify potential attack vectors or social engineering opportunities.

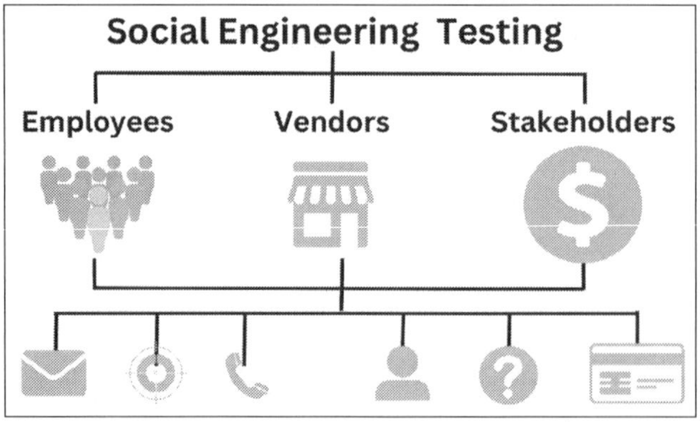

Figure 6.3: *Social Engineering Testing*

- ***Port Scanning***: Identifying open ports on the target system to determine which services are running and potentially vulnerable to attacks.

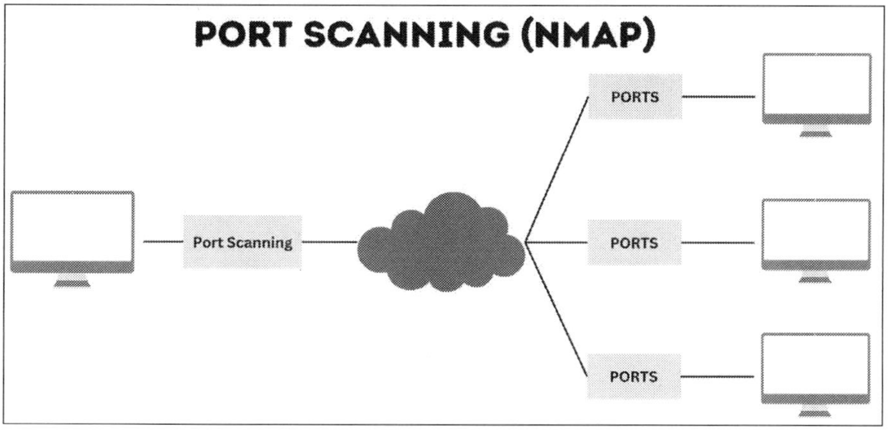

Figure 6.4: *Port Scanning*

- ***Network Traffic Analysis:*** Monitoring network traffic to identify patterns, potential vulnerabilities, and sensitive data transmission.

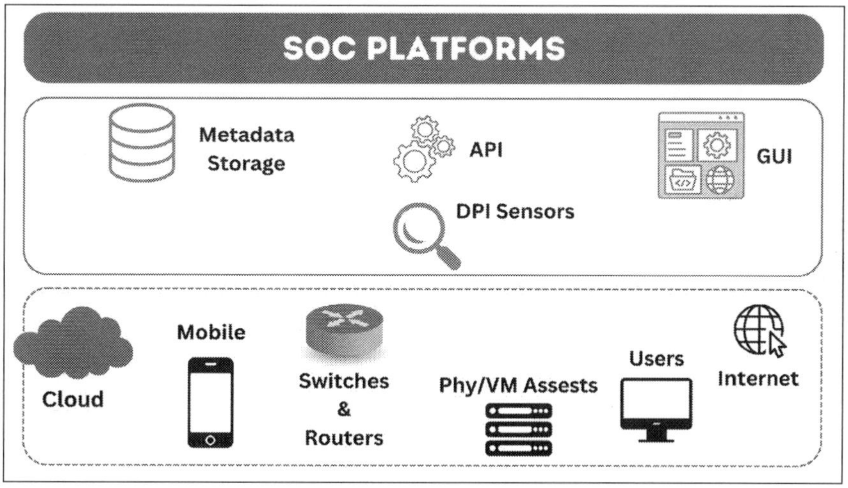

Figure 6.5: *Network Traffic Analysis*

By effectively conducting reconnaissance, penetration testers gain a comprehensive understanding of the target web application, enabling them to identify and exploit vulnerabilities effectively.

In simpler terms, reconnaissance is like having a map before going on an adventure; it helps you navigate the digital landscape and ensures you are ready for whatever challenges lie ahead. So, in our journey through web reconnaissance, understanding this crucial first step sets the stage for a successful and secure web application testing adventure.

The Reconnaissance Process

Reconnaissance, also known as information gathering, is a systematic and methodical approach to collecting information about a target, typically an organization, system, or individual. This process involves various steps, each designed to gather specific types of information and build a comprehensive understanding of the target.

- ***Defining the Scope and Objectives:*** Before embarking on reconnaissance, it is crucial to clearly define the scope and objectives of the exercise. This includes identifying the specific target, determining the type of information needed, and establishing the depth of information required.
- ***Gathering Passive Information:*** Passive information gathering involves collecting data without actively interacting with the target. This includes techniques such as:
    - ***Open-Source Intelligence (OSINT):*** Utilizing publicly available information sources like websites, social media, news articles, and public records to gather information about the target.
    - ***DNS Records Analysis:*** Examining the target's DNS records to identify subdomains, associated servers, and potential attack vectors.
    - ***WHOIS Records Analysis:*** Analyzing WHOIS records to gather information about the target's domain registration, including the owner's contact details.
- ***Active Information Gathering:*** Active information gathering involves directly interacting with the target to gather data. This includes techniques such as:
    - ***Port Scanning:*** Scanning the target system to identify open ports, which may indicate vulnerable services or applications.
    - ***Network Traffic Analysis:*** Monitoring network traffic to identify patterns, potential vulnerabilities, and sensitive data transmission.
    - ***Social Engineering:*** Utilizing social media, email, or phone calls to gather information from individuals associated with the target.
- ***Data Analysis and Reporting:*** Once sufficient information has been gathered, it is essential to analyze and interpret the data to identify patterns, vulnerabilities, and potential attack vectors. The findings should be documented in a comprehensive report that clearly presents the key takeaways and actionable insights.

Overview of the Intelligence Gathering Lifecycle

The reconnaissance process is part of a broader intelligence-gathering lifecycle, which involves the following steps:

- ***Identification:*** This is where you put on your detective hat. You identify the target, be it a website, a network, or an application. It is like knowing which island you are about to explore.
- ***Enumeration:*** Now that you have found your island, it is time to count the trees, rocks, and maybe even the hidden treasures. In the digital world, this means figuring out what services and devices are present.
- ***Footprinting:*** Just as explorers leave footprints, digital entities leave traces. Footprinting involves collecting information about the target's infrastructure, domain names, and IP addresses. It is like following a trail of breadcrumbs in the online world.
- ***Mapping:*** With the collected data, you create a digital map. You connect the dots, understanding how different elements are related. It is like drawing a map of the terrain you are exploring.
- ***Scanning:*** Now, it is time to scan for vulnerabilities. Think of it as checking for weak spots in the fortress before storming it. This phase helps identify potential entry points.
- ***Analysis:*** Finally, you analyze all the gathered data. It is like piecing together a puzzle–making sense of the information to understand the target's strengths, weaknesses, and potential vulnerabilities.

Unlocking the Importance of Thorough Reconnaissance

Thorough reconnaissance holds the key for several crucial reasons:

- ***Understanding Risks:*** It gives us a full picture of a target's vulnerabilities, empowering effective risk assessment and prioritization.
- ***Spotting Weaknesses:*** By pinpointing potential attack paths and vulnerabilities, it helps uncover areas that might be exploited by cyber threats.
- ***Crafting Cybersecurity Plans:*** It lays the groundwork for tailoring a cybersecurity strategy that precisely tackles the risks and vulnerabilities revealed during reconnaissance.
- ***Staying a Step Ahead:*** Thorough reconnaissance is not just about knowing the risks; it is about taking proactive measures to reduce these risks and shield against possible attacks.
- ***Effective Incident Response:*** In the unfortunate event of a security breach, the information gathered during reconnaissance becomes a valuable resource for a swift and effective incident response.

In essence, the reconnaissance process is your digital compass, guiding you through the vast online landscape. In the world of cybersecurity, it is the essential first step that separates a successful mission from a perilous one.

Real-World Instances

Reconnaissance assumes a pivotal role across diverse cybersecurity scenarios, furnishing indispensable insights for robust defense against cyber threats. Let us explore actual instances where adept reconnaissance had a profound impact:

Example 1: The Stuxnet Offensive

In the Stuxnet offensive, an exceptionally sophisticated cyber maneuver directed at Iran's nuclear program, reconnaissance techniques played a pivotal role in pinpointing and exploiting vulnerabilities in Siemens industrial control systems (ICS) managing uranium enrichment centrifuges. By merging passive and active reconnaissance tactics, the assailants gleaned profound insights into the target's infrastructure, vulnerabilities, and communication protocols. This informed the creation of tailored malware, disrupting the centrifuges and putting a dent in Iran's nuclear aspirations.

Example 2: The Marriott Data Breach

In 2018, Marriott International faced a massive data breach that laid bare the personal details of more than 500 million guests. The breach occurred because attackers exploited a weakness in a third-party reservation software that Marriott used. Before executing this breach, the attackers engaged in extensive reconnaissance, diligently hunting for vulnerabilities. They dug into Marriott's network structure, unraveling its layout, and deciphered the company's security defenses. This reconnaissance was not just information gathering; it was the key that unlocked the door, letting the attackers slip past security controls and gain unauthorized access to Marriott's systems. It is a stark reminder of how reconnaissance can be the silent architect of a major cybersecurity incident.

Example 3: The SolarWinds Supply Chain Attack

The SolarWinds supply chain attack, a wide-scale cyber espionage operation, involved compromising the SolarWinds Orion network monitoring software, which is used by thousands of organizations worldwide. The attackers gained access to the SolarWinds source code through reconnaissance techniques, enabling them to insert malicious code that was distributed to SolarWinds customers. This malicious code allowed the attackers to steal sensitive data and spy on their targets.

Example 4: The 2016 Democratic National Committee (DNC) Hack

Back in 2016, the Democratic National Committee (DNC), a political entity in the United States, fell victim to a highly sophisticated cyberattack. This breach led to the theft of sensitive data, including emails, documents, and strategic plans. The attackers, believed to be linked to the Russian government, embarked on a thorough reconnaissance. Their mission is to uncover details about the DNC's network structure, security protocols, and personnel. This reconnaissance was not just information gathering; it was the strategic groundwork that allowed them to pinpoint vulnerabilities and meticulously plan their attack. This real-life event underscores how strategic reconnaissance can be the precursor to a significant cybersecurity breach.

Example 5: The 2020 Colonial Pipeline Ransomware Incident

In 2020, the Colonial Pipeline, a prominent gasoline pipeline operator in the United States, fell victim to a ransomware assault that disrupted fuel distribution along the East Coast. The assailants exploited a vulnerability in a Virtual Private Network (VPN) appliance to infiltrate Colonial Pipeline's systems. Prior to the attack, thorough reconnaissance was conducted to pinpoint this vulnerability and gain insights into the critical infrastructure of the Colonial Pipeline.

Google Dorking: Discover Concealed Information

Google Dorking, sometimes called Google hacking, is a method that employs advanced search operators in Google to reveal internet information that might not be easily accessible through typical search queries. This technique uses Google's search algorithms to find particular text strings within search results. Despite the term "hacking," it is crucial to note that Google Dorking is entirely legal and is frequently employed by security experts to uncover potential vulnerabilities in their systems. It is a tool for legitimate exploration, not a means for illicit activities.

Google Dorking's significance lies in its ability to bypass typical search engine indexing and filtering mechanisms, revealing information that may not be intentionally disclosed. This includes:

- ***Identifying misconfigured websites:*** Google Dorking can uncover websites that have left sensitive information, such as passwords, credit card details, or internal documents, inadvertently exposed.
- ***Locating vulnerable web applications:*** Google Dorking can help identify websites that are running outdated or vulnerable software, potentially exposing them to exploitation.
- ***Gathering competitive intelligence:*** Google Dorking can be used to gather information about competitors' websites, products, and marketing strategies.
- ***Uncovering social engineering opportunities:*** Google Dorking can help identify personal information about individuals, such as email addresses, social media profiles, and professional affiliations, which can be used for social engineering attacks.
- ***Finding Hidden Directories:*** Just like finding a hidden treasure chest in a maze, Google Dorking helps you discover directories and files that are not linked to a website but might contain valuable information.

- ***Locating Vulnerable Devices:*** It is like having a radar for devices that might be susceptible to cyberattacks. Google Dorking allows you to find devices, like cameras or servers, that might not be adequately protected.
- ***Exploring Website Structures:*** Think of it as having X-ray vision for websites. Google Dorking lets you understand the structure of a website, helping you see how information is organized.
- ***Uncovering Login Pages:*** Imagine having a map to secret doors. Google Dorking can lead you to login pages that are not typically visible, giving you insights into potentially vulnerable areas.

Creating Effective Google Dorks

Google Dorking relies on leveraging distinct search operators and keywords to uncover concealed information on the internet. By comprehending and skillfully combining these operators, you can devise potent Google Dorks that deliver valuable insights.

Google Dorking is essentially about crafting specific search queries (dorks) to reveal sensitive information that may be publicly accessible. GHDB serves as a comprehensive repository of such dorks, making it an invaluable resource for beginners.

- **Understanding GHDB:**
    - GHDB is a curated collection of Google dorks, maintained by the information security community.
    - It categorizes dorks based on their potential to reveal sensitive information, such as login credentials, vulnerabilities, or exposed devices.

Practical Beginner's Guide:

- **Exploring GHDB:**
    - Start by visiting the GHDB repository and familiarize yourself with the available categories and dorks.
    - Begin with simple queries, like site-specific searches or filetype-based queries, to understand the basics.
- **Crafting Basic Dorks:**
    - Use GHDB as a reference to create basic dorks. For example, a dork like **site:example.com** helps focus the search on a specific domain.
- **Understanding Operators:**
    - GHDB provides insights into various operators like **inurl**, **intitle**, and filetype. Learn how these operators refine searches for specific information.

- **Avoiding Unethical Practices:**
  - Emphasize the ethical use of Google Dorking. GHDB promotes responsible practices, and beginners should avoid using dorks for any malicious intent.

Key Google Dork Operators

Google Dorks utilizes diverse search operators to fine-tune search queries and pinpoint particular information. Here are some widely used operators:

- **`intitle`**: Seeks specific keywords within the title of a webpage. For instance, **`intitle:"index of"`** might disclose websites with directory listing enabled.

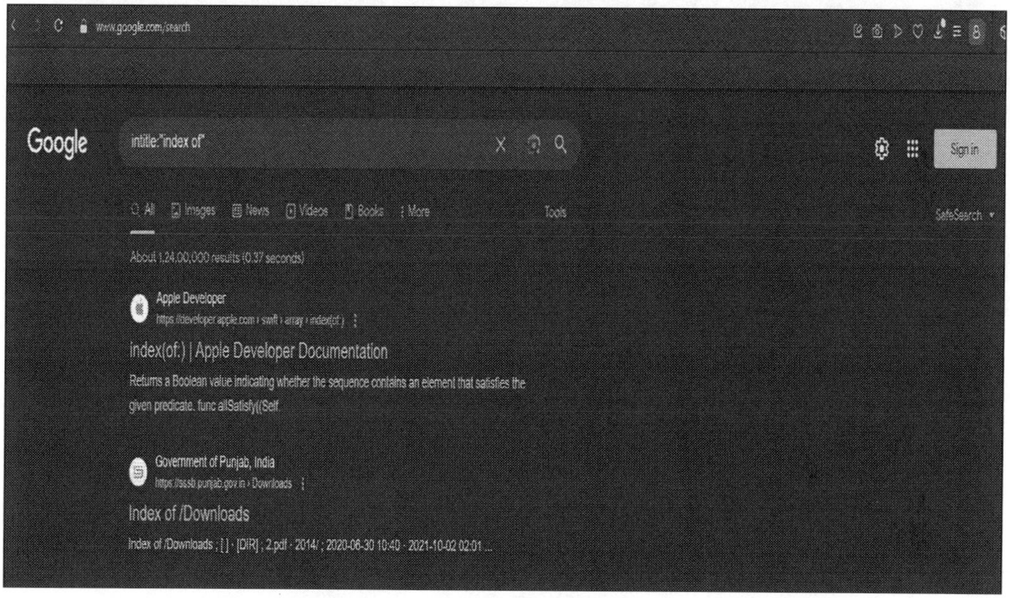

***Figure 6.6**: intitle Command Search Result*

- **`inurl`**: Locates specific keywords within the URL of a webpage. For example, **`inurl:login`** might identify pages with **`'login'`** in the URL.

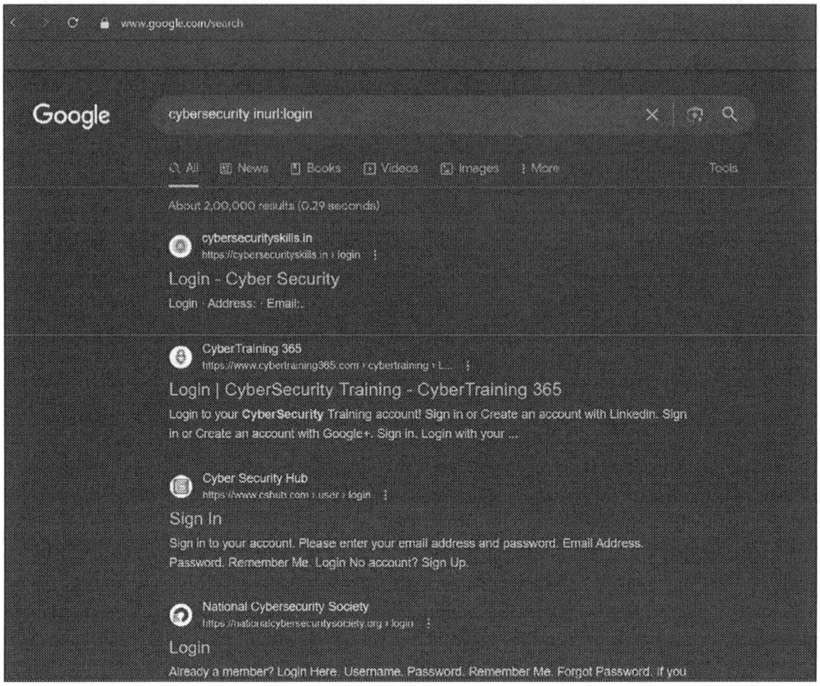

Figure 6.7: *inurl Command Search Result*

- **`filetype`:** Searches for distinct file types. For instance, **`filetype:pdf`** would retrieve PDF files.

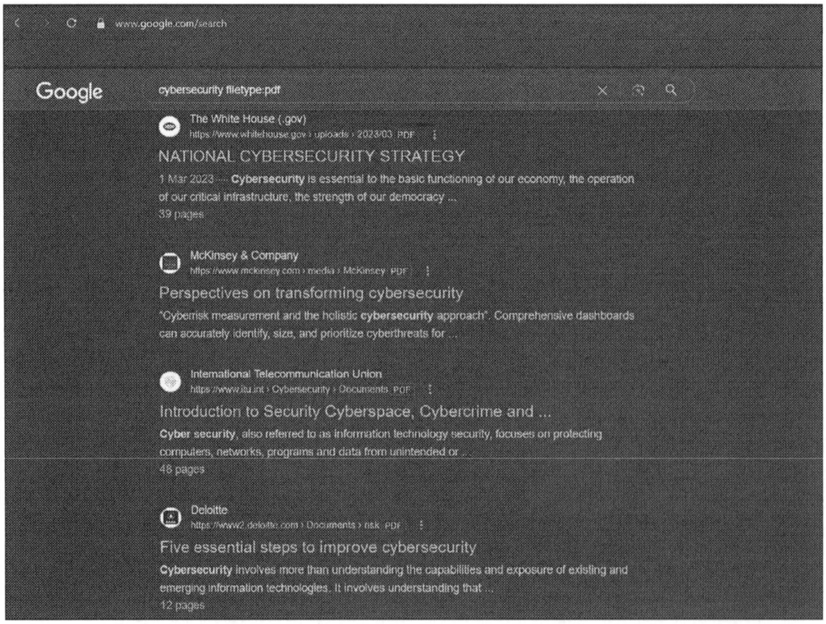

Figure 6.8: *filetype Command Search Result*

- **`site`**: Restricts the search to a specific website. For example, **`site:amazon.com`** would exclusively search within the amazon.com domain.

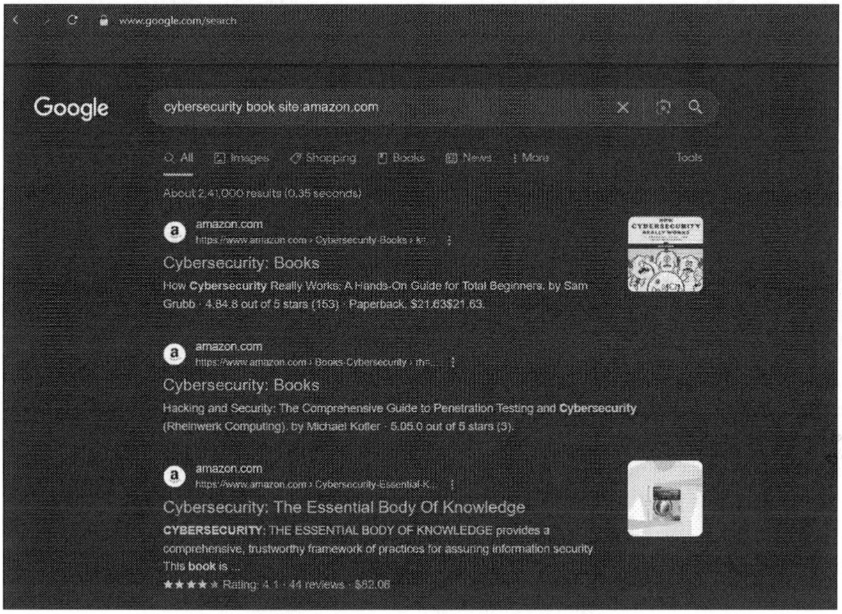

***Figure 6.9**: site Command Search Result*

- **`link`**: Discovers pages that link to a particular URL. For example, **`link:example.com`** would find pages linking to example.com.

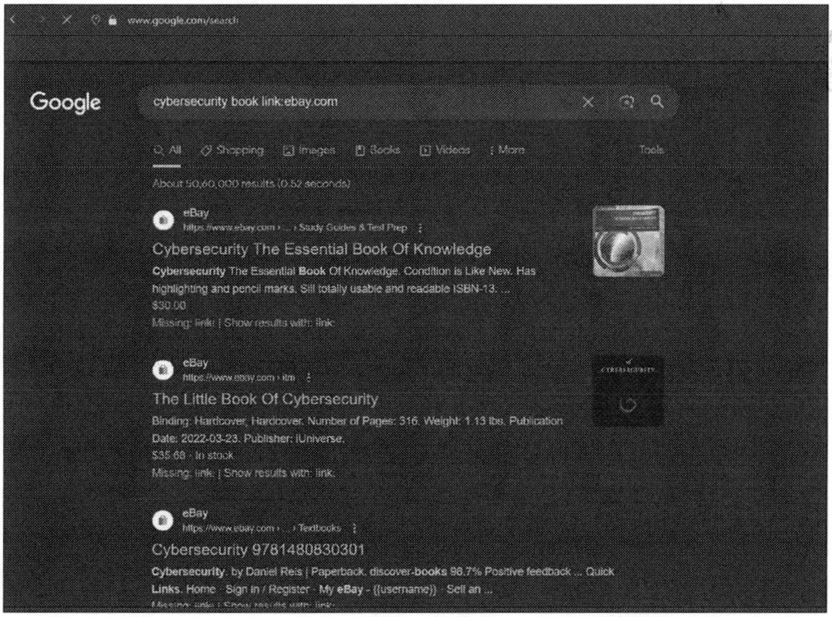

***Figure 6.10**: link Command Search Result*

Hands-on Exercise: Uncovering Hidden Information

To apply your Google Dorking skills, try the following exercise:

1. Identify a specific type of information you want to uncover, such as misconfigured websites or vulnerable web applications.
2. Formulate a Google Dork query using the relevant operators and keywords.
3. Run your Google Dork query and analyze the results. Look for patterns, anomalies, or unexpected information.
4. Refine your Google searches based on your findings to narrow down your search and uncover more specific information.

Remember, Google Dorking is a powerful tool, but it should be used responsibly and ethically. Avoid targeting individuals or organizations without their consent, and respect the privacy of others.

Ensuring Privacy and Ethical Considerations in Google Dorking

Here is a breakdown of crucial considerations to ensure your Google Dorking practices align with ethical principles:

- **Respecting Privacy:**
    - ***Target with Consent:*** Steer clear of targeting individuals or organizations without explicit consent. Avoid using Google Dorking to intrude on someone's privacy or collect personal information without their knowledge or permission.
    - ***Respect Sensitive Data:*** Exercise prudence when dealing with sensitive data like financial information, medical records, or personal details. Refrain from collecting or sharing such data unless duly authorized.
    - ***Minimize Data Collection:*** Gather only the information necessary for your intended purpose. Avoid accumulating excessive data that may not be relevant or could compromise someone's privacy.
- **Respecting Legal Limits:**
    - ***Mind Copyright Laws:*** Steer clear of employing Google Dorking to obtain or distribute copyrighted material without proper authorization. Show regard for intellectual property rights and abstain from activities that infringe on copyright laws.

  - ***Stay Clear of Unlawful Actions:*** Refrain from using Google Dorking for illegal endeavors, such as accessing unauthorized data, breaching network security, or causing disruptions to websites or networks. Adhere strictly to cybersecurity laws and regulations.
  - ***Validate Findings Legitimacy:*** Prior to acting upon information gathered through Google Dorking, ensure its legitimacy and accuracy. Avoid making assumptions or reaching conclusions based on incomplete or unverified information. It is a matter of staying informed responsibly and ethically.

- **Using Findings Responsibly:**
  - ***Avoid Malicious Purposes:*** Do not use the information gathered through Google Dorking for malicious purposes, such as spreading misinformation, damaging reputations, or causing harm to individuals or organizations.
  - ***Maintain Transparency:*** Be transparent about your Google Dorking activities and the purpose behind them. Avoid concealing your intentions or using the technique for deceptive or misleading purposes.

Case Studies: Real-world Scenarios Showcasing the Power of Google Dorking

Case Study 1: Uncovering Social Engineering Opportunities

In one instance, a security analyst used the query **`name "John Doe" intitle:"LinkedIn"`** to find LinkedIn profiles of a specific individual. The analyst gathered information about the individual's professional background, interests, and connections, which could be used for social engineering attacks.

Case Study 2: The 2013 LinkedIn Data Breach

In 2013, a massive data breach exposed the personal information of over 167 million LinkedIn users. The attackers were able to gain access to LinkedIn's systems by exploiting a vulnerability in an open-source software library used by the company.

Prior to the breach, the attackers conducted extensive reconnaissance using Google Dorking techniques to identify vulnerable endpoints and gather information about LinkedIn's network infrastructure. They used the query **`inurl:"admin"`** to find pages with the **`'admin'`** directory accessible, which revealed a misconfigured page containing sensitive data.

By effectively utilizing Google Dorking, the attackers were able to identify a critical vulnerability and gain unauthorized access to LinkedIn's systems, leading to a significant data breach.

Case Study 3: The 2016 Yahoo Data Breach

In 2016, Yahoo experienced a massive data breach that affected over 500 million user accounts. The attackers were able to steal user credentials, including email addresses, passwords, and security questions, allowing them to access user accounts and steal sensitive information.

The attackers used Google Dorking to identify vulnerable web applications on Yahoo's systems. They used a combination of queries, such as **`filetype:xml inurl:sitemap`** and **`filetype:doc inurl:login`**, to find XML sitemaps and Microsoft Word documents containing sensitive information, including login credentials and API keys.

These case studies demonstrate the real-world applications of Google Dorking in various cybersecurity scenarios.

Shodan: The Search Engine for Devices

In the vast domain of the internet, Shodan stands out as a unique and powerful tool for cybersecurity professionals and researchers. Known as the "search engine for devices," Shodan enables users to discover and explore billions of devices connected to the internet, providing a comprehensive view of the ever-expanding digital landscape.

Unlike traditional search engines that focus on websites and text content, Shodan indexes a wide range of internet-connected devices, including routers, web servers, industrial control systems, and even home appliances. By scanning the internet and collecting information from these devices, Shodan creates a massive database of device profiles, offering valuable insights into their vulnerabilities, protocols, and potential security risks.

Understanding Shodan's Capabilities and Limitations

Shodan's capabilities are as diverse as the devices it indexes. It can be used for a variety of purposes, including:

- ***Identifying vulnerable devices:*** Shodan can be used to scan for devices with known vulnerabilities, enabling security professionals to prioritize remediation efforts and mitigate potential attacks.
- ***Gathering threat intelligence:*** Shodan can reveal the distribution and usage patterns of various malware and hacking tools, providing valuable insights into evolving cyber threats.
- ***Conducting security assessments:*** Shodan can be used to assess the security posture of an organization's network by identifying exposed devices and potential misconfigurations.

- ***Researching emerging technologies:*** Shodan can be used to track the adoption and usage of new technologies, providing researchers with valuable data for their studies.

However, it is important to recognize Shodan's limitations. As a search engine, it only provides information about devices that are publicly accessible and actively communicating on the internet. Devices that are hidden behind firewalls or are not actively communicating may not be visible to Shodan. Additionally, Shodan relies on the information provided by the devices themselves, which may not always be accurate or complete.

Responsible Shodan Usage

Harnessing Shodan's potent capabilities demands ethical and responsible use. Users should observe the following guidelines:

- ***Respect privacy:*** Steer clear of targeting individuals or organizations without their explicit consent. Refrain from using Shodan to amass personal information or intrude on someone's privacy.
- ***Adhere to legal boundaries:*** Avoid leveraging Shodan for illicit activities, such as accessing unauthorized data or disrupting the operations of devices or networks.
- ***Use findings responsibly:*** Employ the information obtained through Shodan judiciously and ethically. Refrain from using it for malicious purposes or inflicting harm on individuals or organizations.

Shodan, when used responsibly, can be a valuable tool for cybersecurity professionals, researchers, and individuals alike. It provides a unique perspective on the interconnected world of devices, enabling users to identify vulnerabilities, gather threat intelligence, and conduct security assessments. By understanding its capabilities and limitations and adhering to ethical considerations, Shodan can be a powerful force for enhancing cybersecurity.

Harnessing Shodan: Real-world Case Studies in Penetration Testing

Shodan, renowned as the search engine for connected devices, plays a pivotal role in penetration testing scenarios. Real-world case studies vividly illustrate the tool's significance in uncovering vulnerabilities and enhancing cybersecurity measures:

- **Critical Infrastructure Vulnerability Assessment**
    - ***Scenario:*** A cybersecurity team engaged in assessing the security posture of a critical infrastructure facility utilized Shodan.

- *Application:* Shodan enabled the identification of internet-facing devices associated with the facility's operational technology (OT) systems.
- *Outcome:* The team uncovered exposed services and potential vulnerabilities, allowing for pre-emptive remediation to safeguard critical infrastructure.

- **Cloud Service Misconfigurations**
  - *Scenario:* A cloud security audit incorporated Shodan to examine the exposure of cloud-based services.
  - *Application:* Shodan scans revealed misconfigured cloud instances, exposed storage buckets, and unintentionally public-facing APIs.
  - *Outcome:* By addressing these misconfigurations, the organization fortified its cloud infrastructure against unauthorized access and data leaks.
- **Internet of Things (IoT) Device Discovery**
  - *Scenario:* A penetration tester engaged in an IoT security assessment leveraged Shodan's capabilities.
  - *Application:* Shodan scans targeted specific IoT device manufacturers to identify devices with known vulnerabilities.
  - *Outcome:* The penetration tester identified and reported vulnerable IoT devices, facilitating timely patches and reducing the risk of exploitation.
- **Exposure of Industrial Control Systems (ICS)**
  - *Scenario:* In a simulation of an industrial network penetration test, Shodan played a crucial role.
  - *Application:* Shodan scans pinpointed internet-exposed industrial control systems, including Human Machine Interfaces (HMIs) and Programmable Logic Controllers (PLCs).
  - *Outcome*: The findings prompted the implementation of network segmentation and additional security controls to mitigate the risk of unauthorized access to critical ICS components.

These real-world case studies underscore Shodan's versatility and effectiveness in identifying, assessing, and addressing vulnerabilities across diverse technological landscapes. As a foundational tool in OSINT and reconnaissance, Shodan empowers cybersecurity professionals with actionable insights to fortify digital environments against potential threats.

Practical Exercises on Finding Devices with Potential Vulnerabilities

Shodan is a powerful tool for cybersecurity professionals, researchers, and individuals alike. However, to effectively utilize Shodan, it is important to understand how to access it and perform searches. Here is a step-by-step guide on how to access Shodan and use the above queries to find devices with potential vulnerabilities:

- **Step 1: Create a Shodan Account**

  Before you can start using Shodan, you need to create an account. Visit the Shodan website (https://www.shodan.io/) and click the **`"Sign Up"`** button. You can create a free account, but it has limited access to Shodan's features. To access the full range of Shodan's capabilities, you will need to upgrade to a paid plan.

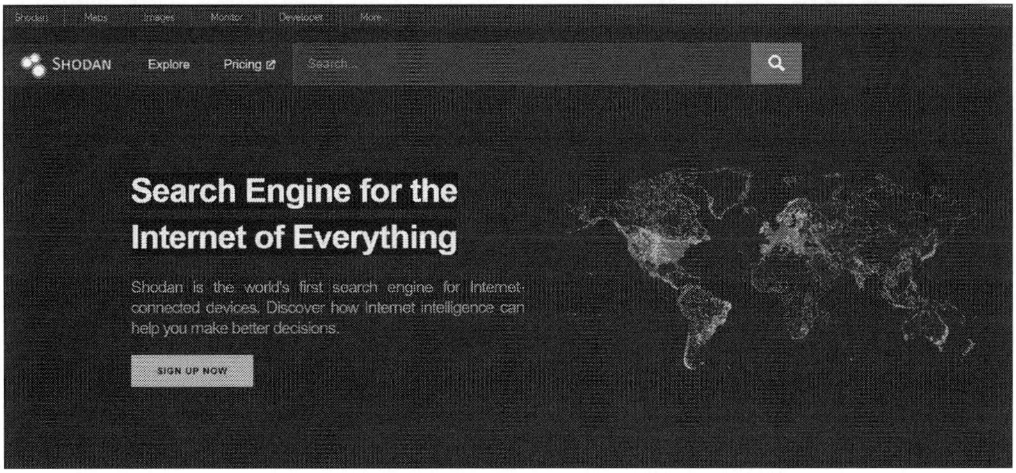

Figure 6.11: *Shodan Interface*

- **Step 2: Familiarize Yourself with Shodan's Search Interface**

  Once you have an account, log in to Shodan and navigate to the search bar. Shodan's search interface allows you to construct queries using various filters and keywords.

- **Step 3: Identify Open Ports (Exercise 1)**

  To find devices with open ports, use the following query in the Shodan search bar:

  ```
  Port:22
  ```

This query will find devices with the SSH port (port 22) open.

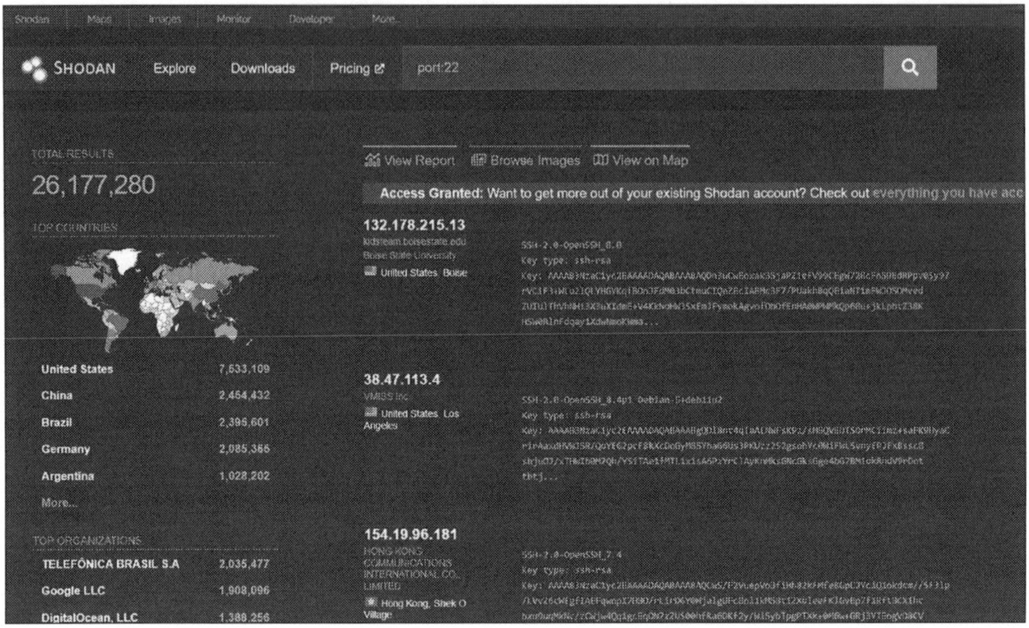

Figure 6.12: *"port:22" Command in Shodan Search*

- **Step 4: Locate Devices Running Vulnerable Software (Exercise 2)**

  To identify devices running vulnerable software, use the following query in the Shodan search bar:

  ```
  software:vuln
  ```

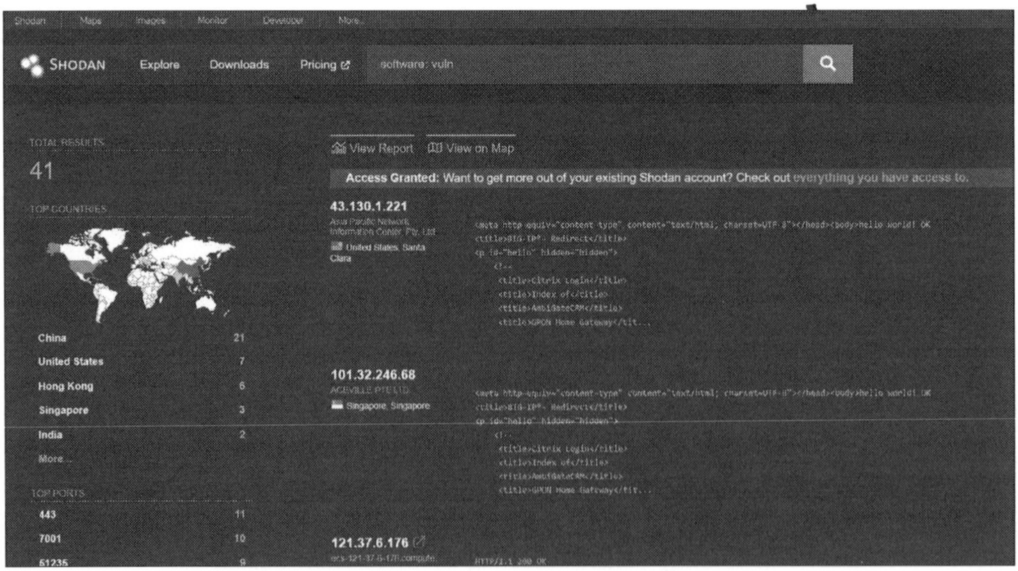

Figure 6.13: *"software:vuln" command in Shodan search*

This query will return a list of devices that are known to be running software with documented vulnerabilities. You can also specify a particular software product to narrow down the search, for example:

```
software:apache
```

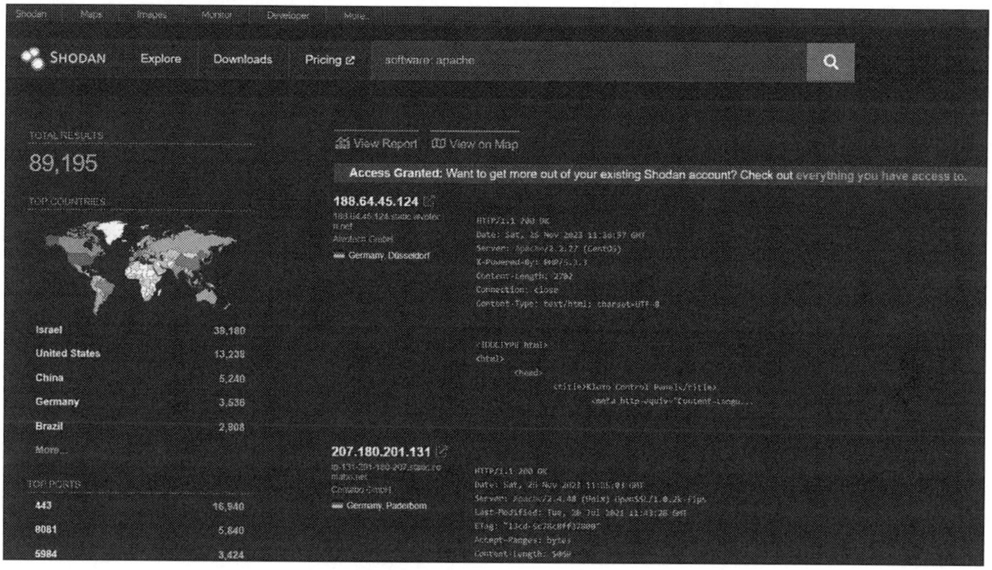

Figure 6.14: *"software:apache" Command in Shodan Search*

- **Step 5: Analyze the Search Results**

  Once you have executed your queries, Shodan will display a list of matching devices. Analyze the results to identify devices with potential vulnerabilities. You can click the individual devices to view more detailed information, including their location, software versions, and open ports.

Safeguarding Personal and Organizational Assets against Shodan Exploration

In our modern, interconnected reality, everything from household gadgets to industrial control systems is becoming internet-connected, creating potential entry points for cyber threats. Shodan, the device-centric search engine, empowers users to explore the internet, uncovering these devices–a boon for cybersecurity experts. However, this convenience comes with a caveat: it implies that your own devices might be susceptible to Shodan searches. It is a reminder to stay vigilant and protective in the digital landscape.

Here are some tips on protecting your personal and organizational assets from Shodan searches:

- **Minimize Device Exposure:**
  - ***Disable unnecessary services and ports:*** Only enable the services and ports that are absolutely necessary for your devices to function. Disabling

unused ports reduces the attack surface and makes it less likely that your devices will be discovered by Shodan.

  - ***Configure firewalls:*** Implement firewalls to restrict access to your devices from unauthorized sources. Firewalls can block Shodan scans and prevent attackers from reaching your devices.
  - ***Use strong passwords and security protocols:*** Employ strong passwords for device access and enable robust security protocols like encryption to protect against unauthorized access.

- **Maintain Software Updates:**
  - ***Regularly update software:*** Regularly apply software updates, including operating system patches and firmware updates, to address known vulnerabilities that could be exploited by attackers.
  - ***Enable automatic updates:*** Configure automatic updates whenever possible to ensure that your devices are always running the latest secure software versions.
  - ***Stay informed about vulnerabilities:*** Keep yourself updated about newly discovered vulnerabilities and prioritize patching those that affect your devices.
- **Strengthen Network Security:**
  - ***Partition your network:*** Break down your network into smaller, distinct subnets to create barriers, keeping sensitive devices separate and thwarting any unauthorized entry to vital systems.
  - ***Install intrusion detection and prevention systems (IDS/IPS):*** Set up IDS/IPS systems to keep a vigilant eye on network traffic, identify any suspicious patterns, and actively block potential attacks.

By putting these measures into action, you can substantially diminish the likelihood of your devices becoming vulnerable to Shodan searches. This, in turn, safeguards your personal and organizational assets from potential cyber threats.

Asset Discovery: WHOIS, ASN Lookup

In this segment, we delve into the powerful tools of WHOIS and ASN Lookup, uncovering the hidden details of domain ownership and network infrastructure. We will learn how these techniques form the backbone of cybersecurity intelligence, providing crucial insights for securing digital assets and fortifying defenses against potential threats.

WHOIS Basics: Understanding WHOIS and Its Role in Reconnaissance

In the vast kingdom of the internet, every website, domain name, and IP address has a unique identifier. WHOIS, an acronym for "Who Is," is an internet directory that provides publicly accessible information about these identifiers. It serves as a valuable tool for cybersecurity professionals, researchers, and individuals seeking to gather information about websites, domain owners, and IP addresses.

Understanding WHOIS

WHOIS stands as both a protocol and a database tasked with preserving registration details for domain names, IP addresses, and autonomous system numbers (ASNs). The usual contents encompass the domain name, the registrant's name, contact information, and technical specifics relating to the domain or IP address. It is essentially the digital directory for who's who and what's what in the vast space of the internet.

Working of WHOIS

WHOIS information is stored in distributed databases maintained by various domain registrars and internet organizations. To access WHOIS information, you can use a WHOIS client or query a WHOIS database directly.

Role of WHOIS in Reconnaissance

WHOIS plays a crucial role in reconnaissance, providing valuable insights for various purposes:

- ***Identifying website owners and contact information:*** WHOIS can reveal the owner of a website, their contact details, and their physical location, which can be useful for tracking down copyright infringements, phishing scams, or other malicious activities.
- ***Gathering information about IP addresses:*** WHOIS can provide information about IP addresses, including their location, network provider, and potential abuse history. This can be helpful in identifying the source of cyberattacks or tracking down malicious actors.
- ***Assessing domain reputation:*** WHOIS information can be used to assess the reputation of a domain, such as its creation date, registration history, and any associated abuse reports. This can help identify potentially risky or malicious domains.

Limitations of WHOIS

While WHOIS is a valuable tool, it has limitations, including:

- ***Incomplete or inaccurate information:*** WHOIS data may not always be complete or accurate, as some registrants may provide false or misleading information.

- ***Privacy concerns:*** Gathering WHOIS data may raise privacy concerns, as it can reveal personal information about domain owners.

WHOIS, when used responsibly, can be a powerful tool for cybersecurity professionals, researchers, and individuals seeking to gather information and conduct investigations.

Beyond WHOIS

While WHOIS offers a valuable glimpse into domain ownership, its limitations necessitate additional investigative tools for robust asset discovery. Let us explore alternative methods, empowering you to peel back the digital layers and unveil hidden assets:

- **Domain/IP/ASN Lookups**
  - ***Domain Lookups:*** Deepen your WHOIS investigation with specialized services like DomainTools, WhoIsXY, and MXTool. These offer historical data, past IP addresses, and associated nameservers, painting a fuller picture.
  - ***IP Lookups:*** Uncover the physical location, organization, and network associated with an IP address using tools like Geolocation DB, Netcraft, and IPLookup. This can reveal connections between seemingly disparate domains.
  - ***ASN Lookups:*** Trace the network path back to the Autonomous System Number (ASN) responsible for an IP address. Services like AS Lookup and RIPE NCC Network Information System provide details on the network owner, further illuminating the digital landscape.
- **Reverse Lookups**
  - ***DNS Reverse Lookups:*** Reverse DNS translates an IP address back to its potential domain names. Tools like DNSSpy and Online-Tool.net (http://online-tool.net/) reveal potentially hidden domains associated with a single IP address, uncovering broader infrastructure.
  - ***MX Record Lookups:*** Identify the mail servers associated with a domain using a simple MX record lookup. This can expose alternative contact points and potentially related domains hosted on the same mail server.
- **Command Line Tools**
  - ***dig:*** Leverage the dig command-line tool on Linux/macOS for powerful DNS queries. Perform reverse lookups, zone transfers (with permission), and record type discovery, unearthing hidden information within DNS records.
  - ***nslookup:*** Another versatile tool, nslookup allows DNS record lookups, server tracing, and type queries. Combine it with dig for a robust command-line reconnaissance arsenal.

- **Third-Party API Services**
  - ***WhoisXML API:*** Integrate WHOIS data directly into your scripts and applications with APIs like WhoisXML. Access historical records, bulk lookups, and domain availability, automating certain aspects of your asset discovery process.
  - ***Shodan:*** This popular search engine indexes internet-connected devices by scanning open ports and banners. It can reveal exposed assets within a specific IP range or ASN, valuable for vulnerability identification.
- **Browser Extensions**
  - ***Wappalyzer:*** This Chrome extension analyzes websites and identifies the technologies used, including CMS, analytics tools, and frameworks. This can reveal connections between seemingly unrelated websites and hidden dependencies.
  - ***Hunter:*** Identify email addresses associated with a domain or website with this extension. Reach out for further information or uncover hidden contacts associated with your target assets.

Remember

- ***Ethics and legality:*** Adhere to ethical and legal considerations when utilizing these tools. Respect privacy laws and avoid unauthorized access to information.
- ***Data verification:*** Do not jump to conclusions based on single sources. Cross-reference data from multiple tools and critically evaluate your findings.
- ***Adaptability and creativity:*** The digital landscape is ever-evolving. Stay updated on emerging tools and methods, and embrace creative approaches to uncover hidden assets.

By mastering these diverse techniques and cultivating a resourceful mindset, you can transcend the limitations of WHOIS and become a truly adept asset discovery hunter, navigating the complex digital undercurrents with precision and confidence.

Impact of Privacy Regulations on WHOIS Data Availability

In the landscape of web reconnaissance, understanding the profound impact of privacy regulations, particularly the General Data Protection Regulation (GDPR), on WHOIS data availability is crucial. GDPR, implemented in May 2018, has significantly altered the way WHOIS data, a valuable resource for reconnaissance, is handled. Here is an in-depth exploration:

- ***Background on WHOIS Data:***

  - ***Overview:*** WHOIS databases traditionally held comprehensive information about domain registrants, including their contact details, facilitating transparency and accountability.
  - ***Pre-GDPR:*** Prior to GDPR, WHOIS data was largely unrestricted and accessible to the public. Security professionals and researchers extensively utilized this data for various purposes, including reconnaissance.
- **Introduction of GDPR:**
  - ***Overview:*** GDPR was introduced to enhance individuals' privacy rights and control over their personal data.
  - ***Impact on WHOIS Data:*** With the enforcement of GDPR, there was a paradigm shift in WHOIS data management. Registrars and registries became obligated to redact certain personal information from publicly accessible WHOIS records.
- **Redaction of Personal Information:**
  - ***Overview:*** GDPR mandates the redaction of personally identifiable information (PII) from WHOIS records, such as names, addresses, and contact numbers.
  - ***Impact on Web Reconnaissance:*** While GDPR enhances privacy for domain owners, it limits the amount of information available for reconnaissance purposes. Security professionals must adapt their strategies, considering the restricted access to certain WHOIS details.
- **Access via Accredited Entities:**
  - ***Overview:*** GDPR allows accredited entities, such as law enforcement and certain cybersecurity organizations, to access complete WHOIS data for legitimate purposes.
  - ***Impact on Security Professionals:*** Reconnaissance practitioners need to navigate new avenues to access WHOIS data. Collaboration with accredited entities or leveraging specialized tools becomes pivotal for obtaining comprehensive information.
- **Challenges and Adaptations:**
  - ***Overview:*** The shift in WHOIS data availability poses challenges for cybersecurity professionals.
  - ***Adaptation in Practices:*** Security professionals need to adapt by exploring alternative OSINT sources, utilizing accredited channels, and employing creativity in reconnaissance methodologies.

In the post-GDPR era, navigating the WHOIS landscape requires a nuanced understanding of privacy regulations and their impact.

Practical Exercises of WHOIS

To access a WHOIS in Kali Linux, you can use the WHOIS command-line tool. This tool is pre-installed on Kali Linux and can be used to query WHOIS servers for information about domain names, IP addresses, and autonomous system numbers (ASNs).

Here is how to use the **`whois`** command to query WHOIS servers:

- **Step 1:** Open a terminal window in Kali Linux.
- **Step 2:** Type the following command, replacing example.com with the domain name, IP address, or ASN you want to query:

```
whois example.com
```

- **Step 3:** Press *Enter*. The **`whois`** command will display the **`WHOIS`** information for the specified domain name, IP address, or ASN.

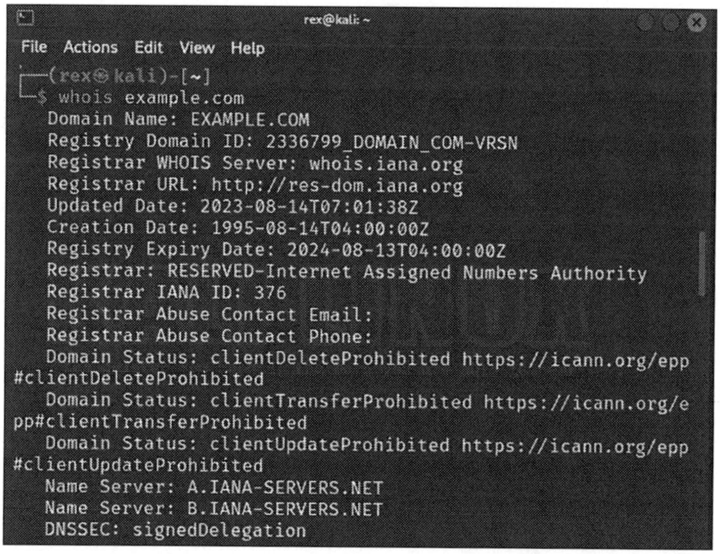

Figure 6.15: *whois Command for example.com*

Here is an example of how to use the `whois` command to query **`WHOIS`** servers for information about the domain name **`google.com`**:

```
whois google.com
```

***Figure 6.16**: whois Command for google.com*

The output of the **`whois`** command will vary depending on the type of information you are querying. For domain names, the output will typically include the domain owner's contact information, the domain's creation date, and the domain's expiration date. For IP addresses, the output will typically include the location of the IP address, the network provider responsible for the IP address, and any associated abuse history. For ASNs, the output will typically include the ASN's owner, the ASN's contact information, and the ASN's routing policy.

Decoding Autonomous System Numbers (ASNs) for Advanced Asset Discovery

In the expansive landscape of the internet, each network is assigned a distinctive identifier known as an Autonomous System Number (ASN). ASNs act as the essential components of internet routing, facilitating smooth communication and data exchange between different networks. For cybersecurity practitioners and researchers, ASNs emerge as pivotal tools in advanced asset discovery, offering valuable insights into network ownership, infrastructure, and potential vulnerabilities.

Unveiling the Autonomous System Number (ASN):

An Autonomous System Number (ASN) is a one-of-a-kind identifier allocated to an organization or entity overseeing a portion of the internet. The management of ASNs falls under regional internet registries (RIRs), such as the American Registry for Internet Numbers (ARIN) and the Réseaux IP Européens (RIPE NCC).

The Mechanism of ASNs:

ASNs function as conduits for directing traffic between diverse networks on the internet. As a data packet journeys from one network to another, it traverses through various ASNs until it reaches its intended endpoint. Each ASN bears the responsibility of steering traffic within its network domain and engaging in the exchange of routing details with other ASNs. It is essentially the internet's way of navigating the highways of digital communication.

Role of ASNs in Asset Discovery

ASNs play a significant role in advanced asset discovery, providing valuable insights into network ownership, infrastructure, and potential vulnerabilities:

- ***Identifying Network Ownership*:** ASNs can be used to identify the organization or entity that owns a particular network. This information can be helpful in tracking down the source of cyberattacks or investigating suspicious network activity.
- ***Mapping Network Infrastructure*:** By analyzing ASNs associated with different IP addresses, you can map the structure and topology of a network, identifying potential subnets, gateways, and firewall locations.
- ***Uncovering Potential Vulnerabilities*:** ASNs can be used to identify networks that are known to have specific vulnerabilities or that are using outdated software versions. This information can be used to prioritize security assessments and remediation efforts.

Methods for ASN Lookup

Several methods are available for performing ASN lookups:

- **`WHOIS`:** **`WHOIS`** records often include information about the ASN associated with a domain name or IP address.
- **ASN *Lookup* Tools:** Specialized ASN lookup tools, such as **`whois.arin.net`** and **`bgpview.io`**, provide detailed information about ASNs, including their ownership, routing policies, and associated IP addresses.
- **API Access:** Some RIRs offer API access for querying ASN information, enabling programmatic access to ASN data.

Practical Exercise of ASN using dig

The dig command in Kali Linux can be used to perform more detailed ASN lookups by querying DNS servers. Here are the steps:

- **Step 1:** Open a terminal window in Kali Linux.
- **Step 2:** Type the following command, replacing 8.8.8.8 with the IP address you want to query:

```
dig +trace 8.8.8.8
```

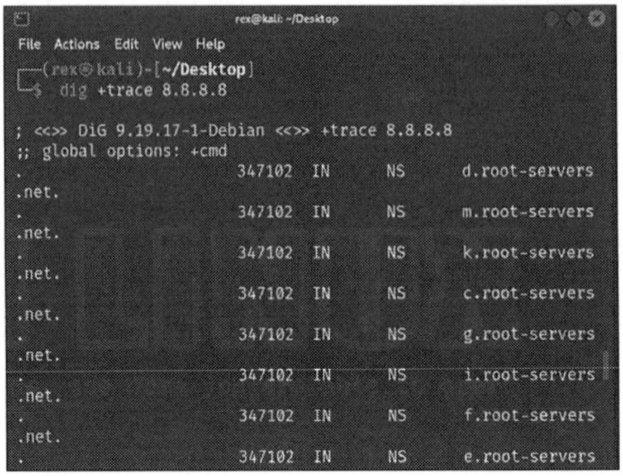

Figure 6.17: *dig Command for ASN Lookup*

Analyze the DNSSEC delegation chain in the output of the **`dig`** command. The ASN for the IP address will be associated with the Autonomous System Number Resource Record (ASNRR) in the delegation chain.

Additional Tools (Try it yourself)

Kali Linux also comes pre-installed with specialized ASN lookup tools, such as **`whois.arin.net`** and **`bgpview.io`**. These tools provide more comprehensive information about ASNs, including their ownership, routing policies, and associated IP addresses.

By following these steps and adhering to ethical considerations, you can effectively utilize the ASN lookup in Kali Linux to gain valuable insights into network ownership, infrastructure, and potential vulnerabilities.

Decoding SSL/TLS Certificates: Understanding Their Importance in Reconnaissance

In today's interconnected world, security is paramount, especially when transmitting sensitive information over the internet. This is where SSL/TLS certificates come into play. SSL (Secure Sockets Layer) and its successor, TLS (Transport Layer Security), are cryptographic protocols that ensure secure communication between a client (for example, a web browser) and a server (for example, a website).

Demystifying SSL/TLS Certificates

Think of an SSL/TLS certificate as a digital identification card for a server. It is a virtual document packed with details about who owns the server, its domain name, and the magic of public key cryptography. This collection of information acts as the secret handshake between your device and the server, guaranteeing that everything you share stays private and untouched. It is like the digital bouncer, making sure only the right folks get access to the exclusive party.

Significance of SSL/TLS Certificates in the World of Reconnaissance

SSL/TLS certificates step into the spotlight during reconnaissance, offering a treasure trove of insights for cybersecurity pros and researchers:

- ***Spotting the Real Deal Websites:*** SSL/TLS certificates act as digital badges, assuring you that a website is a real deal and not a sneaky imposter out to trick you. It is like a virtual security guard, protecting you from phishing and other online dangers.
- ***Unveiling Domain Ownership Details:*** Peek into the SSL/TLS certificate, and you might find the secrets of a website's owner–their name, their organization. It is a valuable clue when you are trying to unmask the mysterious entities behind suspicious websites or cyberattacks.
- ***Judging a Website's Security Game:*** A valid SSL/TLS certificate is like a neon sign saying, **`"This website takes security seriously"`**. It is a green flag that the website is doing its part to keep your data safe. For cybersecurity folks, it is a roadmap for where to focus their efforts in finding and fixing vulnerabilities.

Now, why is this important in the reconnaissance phase of web application testing?

- ***Identifying Secure Communication Channels:*** During reconnaissance, you are like a detective checking the doors and windows of a house. Analyzing SSL certificates helps you identify which websites have secure communication channels. It is like knowing which houses have robust locks and security systems.
- ***Spotting Potential Vulnerabilities:*** SSL certificates also provide clues about the health of a website's security. For example, if a website is using an outdated or weak encryption algorithm, it is like discovering a house with a rusty lock–a potential vulnerability that needs attention.

Basics of SSL/TLS: Understanding the Encryption Process

SSL/TLS employs a combination of symmetric and asymmetric cryptography to achieve secure communication:

- ***Symmetric Key Exchange:*** During the initial connection establishment, the client and server exchange a temporary symmetric key using the Diffie-

Hellman key exchange algorithm. This key is used to encrypt and decrypt all subsequent data exchanged during the session.

- ***Public Key Encryption:*** SSL/TLS certificates also contain a public key, which is used to encrypt a symmetric key that is sent to the server. Only the server, with its corresponding private key, can decrypt this symmetric key, ensuring that only authorized parties can establish a secure connection.
- ***Certificate Validation:*** Before establishing a secure connection, the client verifies the authenticity of the server's SSL/TLS certificate. This involves checking the certificate's signature, ensuring it is issued by a trusted Certificate Authority (CA), and verifying that the certificate is valid for the server's domain name.

Recent Changes in SSL/TLS Protocols and Certificate Standards

In the ever-evolving landscape of cybersecurity, staying abreast of changes in SSL/TLS protocols and certificate standards is paramount for effective web reconnaissance. Recent developments have aimed at bolstering security, addressing vulnerabilities, and adapting to emerging threats. Here are key updates:

- **TLS 1.3 Adoption**
    - ***Overview:*** TLS 1.3 represents a significant advancement, focusing on streamlining the handshake process and enhancing overall security.
    - ***Impact on Web Reconnaissance:*** With faster handshakes and improved encryption algorithms, reconnaissance tools need to support TLS 1.3 for comprehensive analysis. The protocol's widespread adoption mandates that security professionals stay updated on its intricacies for accurate assessments.
- **Deprecation of Older Protocols and Cipher Suites**
    - ***Overview:*** Deprecated protocols like TLS 1.0 and TLS 1.1, along with weak cipher suites, have faced phased removal due to inherent vulnerabilities.
    - ***Impact on Web Reconnaissance:*** Reconnaissance tools must align with the latest industry standards, as websites increasingly disable support for outdated protocols. Adjusting scanning methodologies to account for the deprecation ensures thorough assessments.
- **Certificate Transparency (CT)**
    - ***Overview:*** CT has become a standard practice to enhance transparency in certificate issuance and detect potentially malicious certificates.
    - ***Impact on Web Reconnaissance:*** Security professionals engaging in reconnaissance should leverage CT logs to verify the authenticity of SSL/

TLS certificates. This ensures a more comprehensive understanding of a website's certificate landscape.

- **Wildcard Certificate Changes**
    - ***Overview:*** Changes in how wildcard certificates are validated aim to address potential abuse and ensure stricter controls.
    - ***Impact on Web Reconnaissance:*** Recognition of new wildcard certificate validation practices is vital. Proper validation and interpretation of wildcard certificates play a crucial role in accurately assessing the security posture of web applications.
- **Extended Validation (EV) Certificate Trends**
    - ***Overview:*** EV certificates, once a hallmark of enhanced verification, have seen diminished prominence in favor of simpler certificate types.
    - ***Impact on Web Reconnaissance:*** Security analysts need to adapt their understanding of certificate types, acknowledging that EV certificates might not be as prevalent. This adjustment ensures a realistic interpretation of a website's security measures.

As SSL/TLS protocols and certificate standards undergo refinements, the field of web reconnaissance necessitates continuous learning and adaptation. Security professionals embarking on the journey of OSINT and web reconnaissance must integrate these updates into their skill set to ensure accurate assessments and robust security practices.

Delving into SSL/TLS Certificate Analysis

Embark on a practical journey to analyze SSL/TLS certificates:

Method 1: Manual Inspection with Web Browsers

- **Step 1:** Open your web browser and navigate to the website you wish to scrutinize.
- **Step 2:** Click the padlock icon found in the address bar.
- **Step 3:** Within the certificate details, meticulously examine the following information:
    - `Common Name (CN)`: This reveals the domain name associated with the certificate.
    - `Issuer`: This identifies the Certificate Authority (CA) that bestowed the certificate.
    - `Validity Period`: This outlines the time frame during which the certificate is deemed valid.
    - `Fingerprint`: This serves as a distinctive identifier for the certificate.

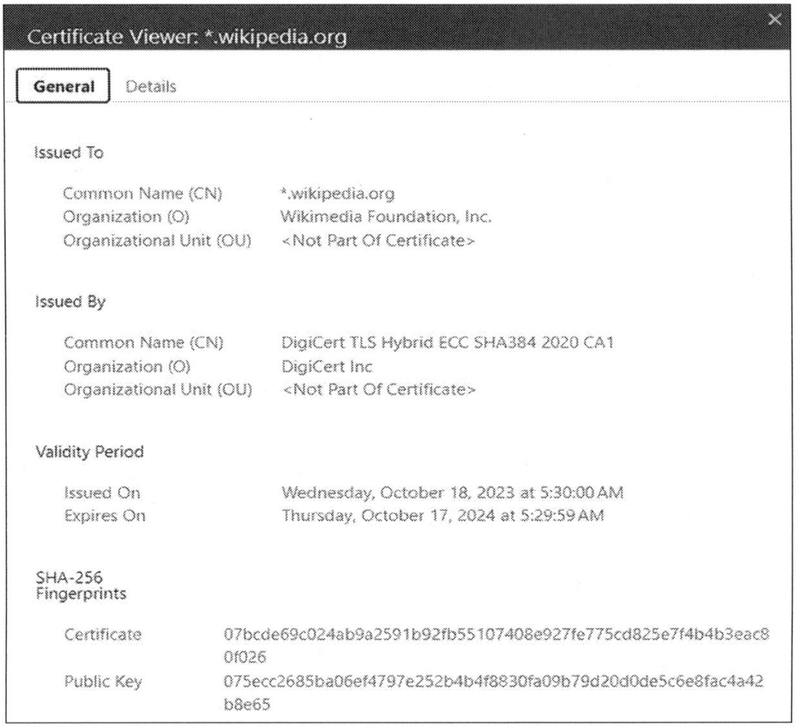

Figure 6.18: *Inspecting Wikipedia's SSL/TLS Certificate*

Method 2: Utilizing Specialized Tools (Try it yourself)

- **Step 1:** Install a dedicated SSL/TLS certificate analysis tool, such as OpenSSL or Mozilla NSS.
- **Step 2:** Use the tool to scan the website's SSL/TLS certificate and extract relevant information.
- **Step 3:** Analyze the extracted information, including certificate details, cipher suites, and potential vulnerabilities.

```
openssl s_client -connect linkedin.com:443
```

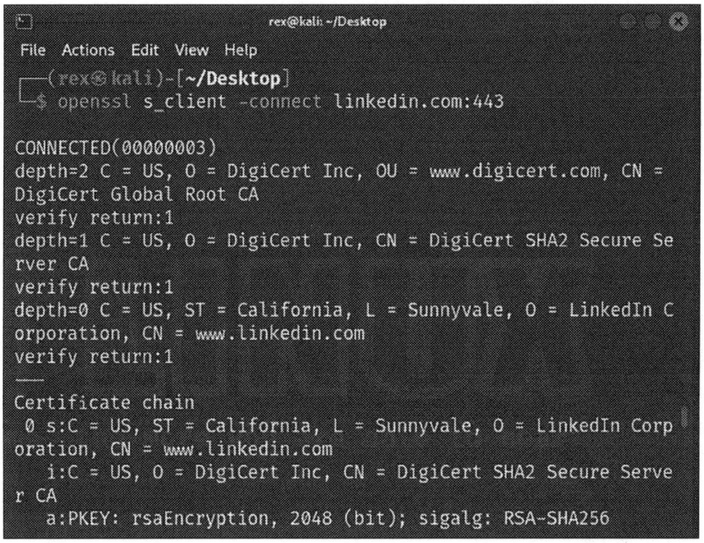

***Figure 6.19**: Analyzing SSL/TLS Certificate using OpenSSL*

Additional Tools

Several online tools provide SSL/TLS certificate analysis capabilities. Examples include:

- ***SSL Labs***: https://www.ssllabs.com/ssltest
- ***Qualys SSL Server Test***: https://www.ssllabs.com/ssltest/
- ***DigiCert's SSL/TLS Certificate Analyzer***: https://www.digicert.com/help/

Content Discovery Basics: Unveiling the Hidden Gems of the Web

In the vast expanse of the internet, websites often harbor hidden directories and files that are not readily accessible through standard navigation. These hidden elements can hold valuable information, ranging from sensitive data to unpublished content. Uncovering these hidden gems through content discovery techniques is crucial for cybersecurity professionals, researchers, and anyone seeking a deeper understanding of a website's structure and potential vulnerabilities.

Importance of Revealing Concealed Directories and Files

Content discovery, the process of pinpointing and accessing concealed directories and files, brings forth various advantages:

- ***Spotting Vulnerabilities:*** Unearthed hidden directories and files might harbor unpatched vulnerabilities or improperly configured security settings, rendering them susceptible to cyber threats. Identifying these covert elements is instrumental in thwarting potential attacks and fortifying website security.
- ***Exposing Sensitive Data:*** Concealed directories may house sensitive information like user credentials, financial data, or confidential documents. The revelation of such data is pivotal in averting data breaches and upholding user privacy.
- ***Understanding Website Architecture:*** Content discovery lays bare the comprehensive structure and organization of a website, offering insights into its functionality and resource repository.
- ***Identifying Unreleased Content:*** Hidden directories may encompass unreleased content, such as beta software versions, developer guides, or internal resources. The discovery of such content contributes valuable intelligence for competitive analysis or research endeavors.

Techniques for Content Discovery

Several techniques are employed for content discovery:

- ***Manual Exploration:*** Manually browsing a website's directory structure can reveal hidden directories and files.
- ***Fuzzing Tools:*** Automated fuzzing tools generate random or invalid URL paths to discover hidden resources.
- ***Web Crawlers:*** Web crawlers systematically scan a website's links and can uncover hidden directories and files.

Advanced Techniques in Content Discovery:

- ***Machine Learning-Based Approaches:***
  - ***Overview:*** Machine learning (ML) techniques can be employed to predict and discover hidden content based on patterns in existing data.
  - ***Practical Implementation:*** Utilizing ML algorithms, a model can be trained on historical data to identify common patterns associated with hidden directories or files. The trained model can then predict potential locations for content discovery on new websites.
- ***Automated Command Line Tools:***
  - ***Overview:*** Command-line enthusiasts can leverage powerful tools for automated content discovery.
  - ***Practical Implementation:*** Tools like Gobuster or FFuF (Fuzz Faster, U Fool) can be used to automate the process. For instance, running a command like `gobuster dir -u <target_url> -w <wordlist>` can systematically

scan for hidden directories. This approach significantly speeds up the content discovery process.

- ***Integration with APIs:***
  - ***Overview:*** Many platforms and services offer APIs that can be integrated for more targeted content discovery.
  - ***Practical Implementation:*** Services like Shodan provide APIs that allow users to programmatically search for specific information, including hidden services or directories. By incorporating API calls into the reconnaissance process, users can efficiently fetch relevant data.
- ***Custom Scripting:***
  - ***Overview:*** Tailoring scripts to the specific needs of content discovery can provide a flexible and personalized approach.
  - ***Practical Implementation:*** Using scripting languages like Python or Bash, security professionals can create custom scripts that mimic the behavior of web crawlers but with added intelligence. These scripts can adapt to unique scenarios and uncover hidden content more effectively.

Benefits of Advanced Techniques:

- ***Precision and Accuracy:*** Advanced techniques, especially machine learning, enhance the precision of content discovery by recognizing nuanced patterns that might elude traditional methods.
- ***Efficiency in Large-scale Scans:*** Automated command-line tools and API integrations significantly boost efficiency, allowing for rapid and thorough scans of large websites or networks.
- ***Adaptability to Evolving Threats:*** Custom scripting empowers security professionals to adapt content discovery methods in response to emerging threats or unique website structures.

In conclusion, while fundamental techniques lay the groundwork, integrating advanced approaches elevates content discovery in web reconnaissance, making it a more robust and adaptive process for cybersecurity professionals.

Ethical Considerations

When engaging in content discovery, it is crucial to adhere to ethical considerations:

- ***Respect Privacy:*** Avoid accessing personal information without consent or for malicious purposes.
- ***Adhere to Legal Boundaries:*** Do not engage in illegal activities, such as accessing unauthorized data or disrupting the operations of websites.
- ***Use Findings Responsibly:*** Use the information gathered through content

discovery responsibly and ethically. Avoid using it for malicious purposes or causing harm to individuals or organizations.

Content discovery, when practiced responsibly, can provide valuable insights into the hidden depths of websites, offering security benefits, uncovering sensitive data, and enhancing understanding of website structure and content. By employing ethical practices and utilizing appropriate techniques, content discovery can be a powerful tool for cybersecurity professionals, researchers, and anyone seeking a comprehensive view of the web.

Leveraging Historic Datasets

In the field of cybersecurity and intelligence gathering, historic data often holds untapped potential, providing valuable insights that can inform and enhance reconnaissance efforts. By carefully examining historical datasets, researchers and security professionals can gain a deeper understanding of past events, identify trends, and uncover hidden patterns that may have otherwise remained unnoticed.

Understanding the Value of Historical Information in Reconnaissance

Historic data plays a crucial role in reconnaissance for several reasons, including:

- ***Unveiling Past Vulnerabilities***: Historical data can reveal previously exploited vulnerabilities, providing valuable context for assessing current security posture and identifying potential weaknesses.
- ***Tracing Attacker Tactics, Techniques, and Procedures* (TTPs):** Analyzing historical data can help identify recurring patterns in attacker behavior, enabling security personnel to anticipate future attacks and implement effective countermeasures.
- ***Identifying Compromised Systems:*** Historical data can be used to identify systems that may have been previously compromised, allowing for remediation efforts and preventing further attacks.
- ***Understanding Domain Activity:*** Historical data can provide insights into the evolution of a domain, its ownership, and its past activities, potentially revealing suspicious or malicious behavior.

Unearthing the Past: Historical Data Sources

When it comes to reconnaissance, a treasure trove of historical data awaits exploration:

- ***Dive into Web Archives:*** Platforms like the Wayback Machine keep a museum of past website versions. It is like time travel for websites, revealing their content and structure evolution.
- ***Unlock the Secrets of DNS Records:*** Delve into DNS records, the archives of

domain ownership, and changes over time. Uncover the connections between domains and trace their journey through the digital landscape.

- ***Tap into Vulnerability Databases:*** Places like the National Vulnerability Database (NVD) hold a historical record of vulnerabilities and how exploitable they have been. It is a goldmine for understanding the weaknesses of systems over time.
- ***Harness Threat Intelligence Feeds:*** Gather insights from threat intelligence feeds that aggregate information on threats, vulnerabilities, and the villains behind them. It's like having a spy network for historical context.
- ***Social Media:*** Social media is not just about the present; it is a rich source for historical insights. Dive into user behaviors, organizational activities, and potential security incidents. It is the storyteller of digital histories waiting to be deciphered.

Understanding Historic Datasets:

- ***Scope of Historic Datasets:*** Historic datasets encompass a wealth of information, ranging from past security incidents to changes in website content and domain ownership.
- ***Challenges in Manual Analysis:*** The sheer volume and complexity of historic data make manual analysis impractical. Big data analytics becomes essential to process, correlate, and extract meaningful patterns.

Leveraging Big Data Analytics:

- ***Data Processing and Cleaning:*** Big data analytics tools excel in handling large volumes of diverse data. The initial step involves processing and cleaning raw datasets to ensure accuracy.
- ***Correlation and Pattern Recognition:*** Through advanced analytics algorithms, these tools correlate data points to identify patterns and trends. This is crucial for recognizing historical attack patterns or changes in web structures.
- ***Temporal Analysis:*** Big data analytics allows for temporal analysis, revealing how certain aspects, such as vulnerabilities or website content, have evolved over time.

Case Study: Extracting Threat Intelligence

Scenario: Analyzing historic security incident reports to extract threat intelligence.

- ***Data Collection:*** Gather historical incident reports, possibly from security databases or past logs.
- ***Data Processing:*** Employ big data analytics to process and clean the incident data, ensuring consistency.
- ***Correlation and Classification:*** Utilize analytics algorithms to correlate

incidents based on attributes. Classify incidents by type, severity, and affected systems.

- ***Identifying Trends:*** Extract insights into recurring patterns, tactics, or vulnerabilities exploited in past incidents.

Benefits of Big Data Analytics in OSINT:

- ***Efficiency and Scale:*** Big data analytics efficiently processes vast datasets, making it feasible to analyze years' worth of information.
- ***Proactive Threat Detection:*** By identifying historical attack patterns, organizations can proactively detect and mitigate potential threats.
- ***Strategic Decision-Making:*** Insights derived from big data analytics inform strategic cybersecurity decisions, guiding resource allocation and security measures.

In conclusion, the integration of big data analytics into web reconnaissance empowers cybersecurity professionals to extract actionable intelligence from historic datasets. This chapter not only introduces beginners to the fundamentals of web reconnaissance but also emphasizes the importance of advanced tools in navigating the ever-evolving landscape of OSINT.

Other OSINT Resources

Welcome to the world of intelligence gathering, where the web is just one piece of the puzzle. Our journey extends beyond websites, and it is like opening doors to a vast universe of information. Let us dive into non-web-based open-source intelligence sources, expanding our toolkit and unlocking new dimensions of knowledge.

- **Exploring Non-Web-Based Open-Source Intelligence Sources**: Delve into non-web sources for a comprehensive understanding of cybersecurity.
    - ***Social Media Platforms:*** Social media is like a virtual town square where people share thoughts, experiences, and information. Analyzing social media platforms provides insights into individuals, organizations, and trends. It is like overhearing conversations in a bustling marketplace, offering a wealth of publicly available information.
    - ***Public Records and Government Databases:*** Government records are a goldmine of information, and accessing public records provides a window into legal documents, permits, licenses, and more. It is like exploring an extensive archive of official documents, shedding light on the activities and histories of individuals and businesses.
    - ***Company Filings and Financial Reports:*** Companies, like characters in a financial story, reveal their narratives through filings and reports. Analyzing financial documents reveals details about a company's health,

strategies, and potential risks. It is like reading a book on a company's financial journey, providing a comprehensive understanding beyond what a website might disclose.

- ***Human Intelligence (HUMINT):*** People are living repositories of information, and engaging in conversations or interviews (ethically and legally) is a form of human intelligence gathering. It is like having conversations with witnesses to gather firsthand accounts, adding a personal touch to the data collected.
- ***Network Traffic and Infrastructure Analysis:*** The digital world is a network of interconnected systems. Analyzing network traffic and infrastructure provides insights into communication patterns, potential vulnerabilities, and technological dependencies. It is like studying the roads and bridges of a city to understand how traffic flows and where potential bottlenecks might occur.
- ***Geospatial Intelligence (GEOINT):*** Geospatial data adds a spatial dimension to intelligence. Mapping locations, movement patterns, and geographical features enhance situational awareness. It is like having a map that visualizes the physical aspects of the intelligence landscape, providing a holistic view.

- **Practical Analogies:** Unlock the power of OSINT with practical analogies, making complex concepts easy to grasp and apply.
  - ***OSINT Map of the World:*** Envision the OSINT landscape as a vast map where web-based sources are just one region. Non-web-based OSINT is like exploring uncharted territories on this map, discovering new landscapes, and uncovering hidden treasures.
  - ***Intelligence Art Gallery***: Think of web-based OSINT as the paintings on the walls of a gallery and non-web-based OSINT as the hidden art in storage. Each piece contributes to a richer, more nuanced understanding of the intelligence canvas.
  - ***OSINT Symphony:*** Consider OSINT as a symphony where web-based and non-web-based sources are different instruments. Each plays a unique role, creating a harmonious composition that resonates with valuable insights.

In essence, non-web-based OSINT is like having a backstage pass to the broader intelligence arena. It is about recognizing that the web is just one facet of a multi-dimensional landscape. By exploring diverse sources, we can enhance our understanding, refine our analyses, and truly unveil the depth of open-source intelligence. So, let us step beyond the web and embrace the richness of information that awaits us in the broader OSINT universe.

Conclusion

As we conclude the fascinating journey through **Reconnaissance and OSINT,** you have delved into the intricacies of web reconnaissance, mastered the art of Google Dorking, harnessed the capabilities of Shodan, and unraveled the secrets of asset discovery using WHOIS and ASN Lookup. By decoding SSL/TLS certificates, understanding content discovery basics, and exploring historic datasets, you have equipped yourself with indispensable OSINT skills.

Congratulations on reaching this milestone! In the next chapter, brace yourself for an exploration of Security Testing and Proxy Tools, where we will dive into the dynamic realm of safeguarding digital landscapes. Get ready for another exciting adventure!

CHAPTER 7
Security Testing and Proxy Tools

Introduction

In our exploration of cybersecurity, we have laid the groundwork for the previous chapter, uncovering the nuances of Reconnaissance and OSINT. Now, buckle up for a journey through **Security Testing and Proxy Tools.** This chapter is a roadmap to fortify web applications, covering essentials from the fundamentals of security testing to wielding powerful tools like Burp Suite and ZAP Proxy. We will demystify web traffic using Fiddler and Charles Proxy, seamlessly integrate proxy tools with browsers, and analyze real-world security breaches. Get ready to empower yourself with practical insights and tools that serve as digital guardians against evolving threats. Welcome to a chapter where simplicity meets robust defense in the vast landscape of cybersecurity.

Structure

In this chapter, we will cover the following topics:

- Introduction to Security Testing in Web Applications
- Burp Suite – A Swiss Army Knife for Web App Testing
- ZAP Proxy – Open-Source Testing with ZAP
- Fiddler – Unraveling the Mysteries of Web Traffic
- Charles Proxy – Debugging Web Applications
- Integration of Proxy Tools with Web Browsers
- Case Studies: Analyzing Security Breaches and the Role of Proxy Tools in Prevention
- Reporting and Documentation

Introduction to Security Testing in Web Applications

In our interconnected global landscape, the internet is an indispensable asset for individuals and businesses. However, this reliance introduces an elevated risk of cyber threats, especially targeting web applications. These digital entities become attractive targets for malicious entities aiming to exploit vulnerabilities and gain unauthorized access to sensitive information.

Enter security testing–a pivotal defense against these digital onslaughts. It is a systematic process meticulously designed to pinpoint and address vulnerabilities before they transform into potential gateways for exploitation. Whether conducted manually or with the assistance of automated tools, this testing seamlessly integrates into the lifecycle of web application development, ensuring a robust shield against cyber threats.

The Crucial Role of Security Testing Amidst Cyber Challenges

In the dynamic world of cybersecurity, the importance of security testing cannot be overstated. With ever-evolving cyber landscapes, malicious actors are consistently devising new strategies, exploiting vulnerabilities to infiltrate web applications and extract valuable data.

The aftermath of a successful cyberattack can be severe, resulting in financial setbacks, damage to reputation, and potential legal ramifications. These attacks disrupt business processes, compromise sensitive customer data, and erode public confidence.

Security testing emerges as the vigilant protector, proactively identifying and resolving vulnerabilities before they become points of exploitation. It provides organizations with assurance–ensuring that their web applications are fortified against both established and emerging threats, safeguarding valuable data, and preserving their reputation.

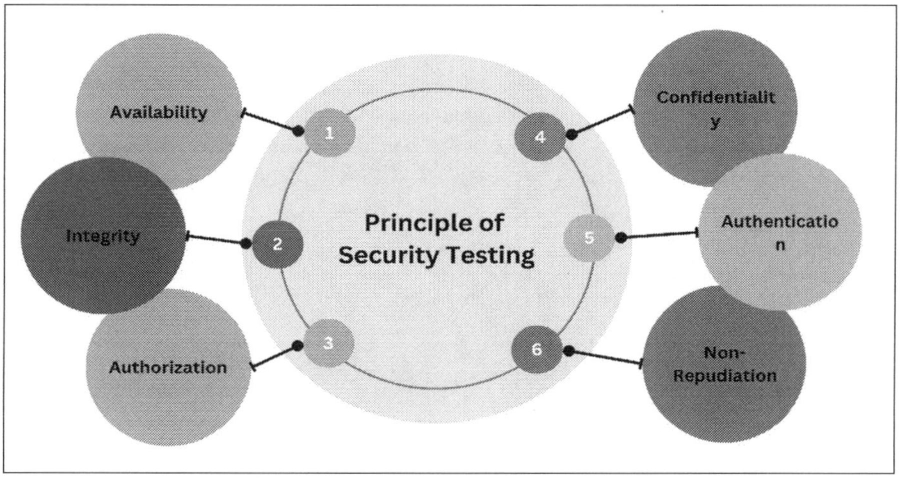

Figure 7.1: *Principle of Security Testing*

Imagine a web application as a fortress, with security testing akin to a meticulous inspection of its walls and gates. Much like a castle undergoes routine scrutiny to prevent breaches, web applications undergo security testing to shield against cyber threats.

This testing employs diverse strategies, including code scanning for errors, attempts to inject malicious code, and evaluations of how the application manages sensitive data. By pinpointing and rectifying vulnerabilities, organizations enhance the resilience of their web applications, minimizing susceptibility to cyber threats.

Crucially, security testing is not a one-time endeavor; it requires ongoing commitment throughout the web application's lifecycle. As new threats emerge and vulnerabilities are uncovered, regular security testing becomes the linchpin, ensuring the enduring strength of web applications against the ever-shifting landscape of cyber challenges.

Types of Security Testing Tools

Security testing tools encompass diverse categories, each serving a unique purpose:

- ***Vulnerability scanning tools:*** These instruments swiftly scour web applications for recognized vulnerabilities like SQL injection and cross-site scripting (XSS), rapidly pinpointing potential weaknesses.
- ***Penetration testing tools:*** Employed by security experts, these tools simulate real-world attacks on web applications, uncovering vulnerabilities that may elude detection by vulnerability scanning tools.
- ***Web Application Firewalls (WAFs):*** Positioned in front of web applications, these tools intercept and block malicious traffic, providing a robust defense against a broad spectrum of attacks.

- ***Static Application Security Testing* (SAST) *tools*:** Delving into the source code of web applications, these tools spotlight potential vulnerabilities not easily discernible during runtime.
- ***Dynamic Application Security Testing* (DAST) *tools*:** Operating while web applications are live, these tools identify vulnerabilities that only surface when the application is running.
- ***Application security testing* (AST) *tools*:** Combining the strengths of SAST and DAST techniques, these tools offer a holistic perspective on the security landscape of web applications.

Beyond these general classes, specialized security testing tools are tailored for specific applications, such as mobile apps and API-driven systems.

Selecting Appropriate Security Testing Solutions

The optimal choice of security testing tools hinges on various factors unique to each organization, such as the scale and intricacy of their web applications, budget constraints, and risk tolerance levels.

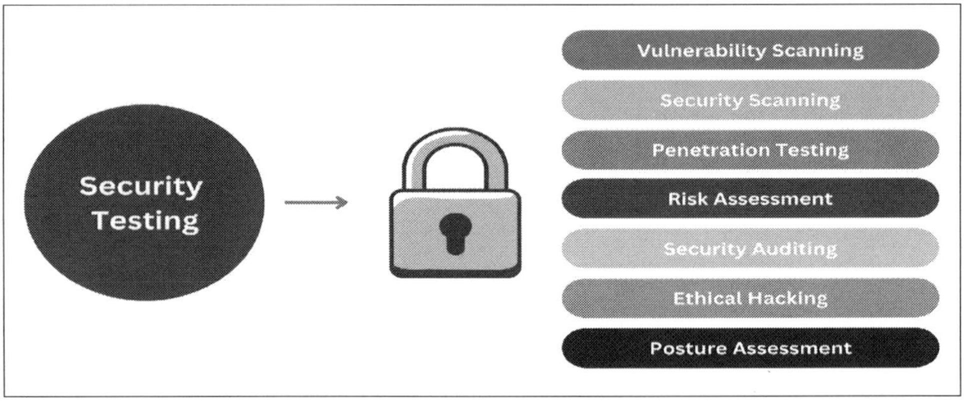

Figure 7.2: *Security Testing Solutions*

A holistic evaluation of web application security necessitates the use of diverse testing tools. Achieving a comprehensive understanding of security requires the utilization of a variety of tools since no single tool can uncover all potential vulnerabilities. Each organization must tailor its selection based on specific needs, ensuring a well-rounded approach to fortifying web applications against potential threats.

Optimizing the Use of Security Testing Tools

Effectively leveraging security testing tools is paramount in the battle against cyber threats. Here are key strategies to maximize their impact:

- ***Clearly define objectives*:** Before employing security testing tools, articulate specific testing goals. What outcomes are you aiming for? Which vulnerabilities are the focus of your identification efforts?

- ***Embrace tool diversity:*** Recognize that no single security testing tool is all-encompassing. Harness the power of various tools to obtain a comprehensive evaluation of your web applications' security.
- ***Carefully interpret results:*** The wealth of data generated by security testing tools demands careful interpretation. Distinguish genuine vulnerabilities from noise to prioritize remediation efforts effectively.
- ***Swiftly address vulnerabilities:*** Identifying vulnerabilities is only half the battle; prompt remediation is crucial. Swift action fortifies web applications, erecting a robust defense against potential cyberattacks.

Burp Suite –A Swiss Army Knife for Web App Testing

In the domain of web application security, Burp Suite stands out as an epitome of robust testing tools. Crafted by PortSwigger, this versatile software has rightfully earned its moniker as the Swiss army knife of web security testing. Burp Suite empowers security professionals with a rich array of capabilities, allowing them to pinpoint, analyze, and address vulnerabilities in web applications.

What began as a modest proxy tool has evolved into a sophisticated toolkit, addressing the diverse needs of security testers. Whether you are a seasoned expert or a novice venturing into web security, Burp Suite emerges as an indispensable ally, offering a holistic approach to shield web applications from potential threats posed by malicious actors.

Delving into the Burp Suite Arsenal

At the heart of Burp Suite's process lies its ability to intercept and manipulate HTTP traffic, enabling testers to scrutinize every request and response exchanged between a web application and its users. This invaluable capability empowers testers to uncover hidden vulnerabilities, dissect the application's behavior, and even manipulate requests to simulate real-world attacks.

Burp Suite's arsenal extends far beyond mere interception, encompassing a suite of powerful tools that cater to every stage of the web security testing lifecycle. From scanning for known vulnerabilities to manually probing for hidden flaws, Burp Suite provides a comprehensive solution for identifying and remediating weaknesses in web applications.

To ensure that web applications remain resilient against evolving threats, Burp Suite offers a dynamic web scanner that continuously monitors applications for emerging vulnerabilities. This proactive approach ensures that security teams stay ahead of the curve, preventing attackers from exploiting newly discovered flaws.

Unlocking Burp Suite's Potential

Burp Suite's versatility extends beyond its core functionality, offering a plethora of extensions and plugins that further enhance its capabilities. These extensions provide access to specialized features, such as advanced vulnerability scanning, application profiling, and even integration with third-party security tools.

Whether you are a security professional seeking to expand your toolkit or a developer aiming to secure your web applications, Burp Suite stands as an invaluable resource. Its comprehensive features, coupled with its extensibility and ease of use, make it an indispensable tool for anyone serious about web security.

Proxy Features: Unveiling Burp Suite's Interception Process

At the heart of Burp Suite's capabilities lies its robust proxy functionality, enabling testers to intercept, analyze, and manipulate traffic flowing between web applications and their users. This powerful feature transforms Burp Suite into a versatile tool for web security testing, providing a comprehensive view of web application communication.

The Essence of Proxying

Imagine a web application as a castle and Burp Suite's proxy as a gatekeeper. Just as a gatekeeper monitors all incoming and outgoing traffic at the castle gates, Burp Suite's proxy intercepts and scrutinizes all HTTP requests and responses exchanged between the web application and its users.

When you configure your browser to use Burp Suite as its proxy, all web traffic is routed through Burp Suite, allowing it to examine and manipulate the data before it reaches its destination. This enables testers to:

- ***Inspect Request and Response Headers:*** Burp Suite captures and displays the headers of HTTP requests and responses, providing valuable insights into the communication between the web application and the browser.
- ***Analyze Request and Response Bodies:*** Burp Suite can decode and display the contents of HTTP request and response bodies, revealing the data being exchanged between the web application and the user.
- ***Modify Request and Response Headers and Bodies:*** Burp Suite allows testers to modify the headers and bodies of HTTP requests and responses. This enables testers to simulate malicious attacks or test the application's behavior under different conditions.

Unlocking Proxy Potential

Burp Suite's proxy features are not limited to basic interception and analysis. It offers a range of advanced capabilities to enhance its effectiveness in web security testing:

- ***HTTPS Interception***: Burp Suite can decrypt and intercept HTTPS traffic, allowing testers to analyze secure web application communication.
- ***Session Handling***: Burp Suite maintains sessions with web applications, enabling testers to capture and analyze multi-step interactions.
- ***Request Replay***: Burp Suite allows testers to replay captured requests, facilitating vulnerability retesting and attack simulations.

Spider and Scanner Tools: Unraveling Web Application Vulnerabilities

Burp Suite's comprehensive arsenal of tools extends beyond proxy functionality, encompassing a suite of powerful spider and scanner tools that automate the process of identifying vulnerabilities in web applications. These tools work in tandem to efficiently scan web applications for known weaknesses, providing testers with a solid foundation for further testing and remediation.

The Spider's Web-Crawling Process

Imagine a web application as a vast network of interconnected pages. Burp Suite's spider acts like a diligent web crawler, systematically traversing the application's links to discover all accessible URLs and resources. This automated exploration provides testers with a comprehensive map of the web application's structure, revealing hidden pages, potential entry points, and areas that may require further scrutiny.

The Scanner's Vigilant Vulnerability Detection

Once the spider has mapped the web application's terrain, Burp Suite's scanner takes center stage, embarking on a meticulous search for vulnerabilities. Armed with a database of known security flaws, the scanner meticulously examines each discovered URL, scrutinizing request parameters, response headers, and form inputs for signs of exploitable weaknesses.

Intruder and Repeater: Unleashing Advanced Techniques for Web App Security

In the arsenal of Burp Suite, two potent weapons stand out—the Intruder and the Repeater. Picture them as your digital ninja and precision marksman, each equipped with unique abilities to uncover vulnerabilities in web applications. Let us delve into practical examples of how to wield these features, demystifying their power for even budding cybersecurity enthusiasts.

Intruder: Your Digital Ninja

Scenario: Imagine you are on a secret mission to test the defenses of a web application. The Intruder tool in Burp Suite is your trusted digital ninja, automating attacks and relentlessly probing for weaknesses.

Example: Brute Force Attack on Login Page

- ***Target:*** A login page with a username and password field.
- ***Objective:*** Test the strength of passwords.
    1. Open Burp Suite and navigate to the `Proxy` tab.
    2. Intercept a login request using the Intercept feature.
    3. Send the intercepted request to the Intruder tool.
    4. In Intruder, go to the `Positions` tab, identify the password parameter, and set it as the payload.
    5. In the `Payloads` tab, load a list of potential passwords or configure settings for a brute force attack.
    6. Launch the attack and observe how the Intruder systematically tests different passwords.

Repeater: Your Precision Marksman

Scenario: You have identified a potential vulnerability, and now it is time for surgical precision. The Repeater tool in Burp Suite is your marksman, allowing you to manually repeat and modify requests for intricate testing.

Example: Cookie Tampering

- ***Target:*** User authentication using cookies.
- ***Objective:*** Test for insecure session management.
    1. Intercept a request containing the authentication cookie.
    2. Send the request to Repeater.
    3. Manually modify the cookie value to impersonate another user or test for session fixation.
    4. Observe the application's response to understand the impact of cookie tampering.

Intruder and Repeater are not just tools; they are precision instruments for uncovering the hidden vulnerabilities within web applications. By mastering these features in Burp Suite, you elevate your web app testing game from basic exploration to surgical precision. Whether you are a cybersecurity professional or an enthusiast, these practical examples empower you to navigate the intricate landscape of web application security with confidence. As we venture deeper into the capabilities of Burp Suite, remember that Intruder and Repeater are your trusted allies in the relentless pursuit of a secure digital space. May your tests be thorough, and may your discoveries be enlightening!

Practical Hands-On: Intercepting Web Traffic with Burp Suite

Objective: Gain practical insights into utilizing Burp Suite for intercepting and analyzing HTTP traffic between a web browser and a target website.

Prerequisites:

- Kali Linux is up and running.
- Burp Suite Community Edition is installed.

Steps:

Step 1: Start Burp Suite

a. Open a terminal in Kali Linux and type:

```
burpsuite
```

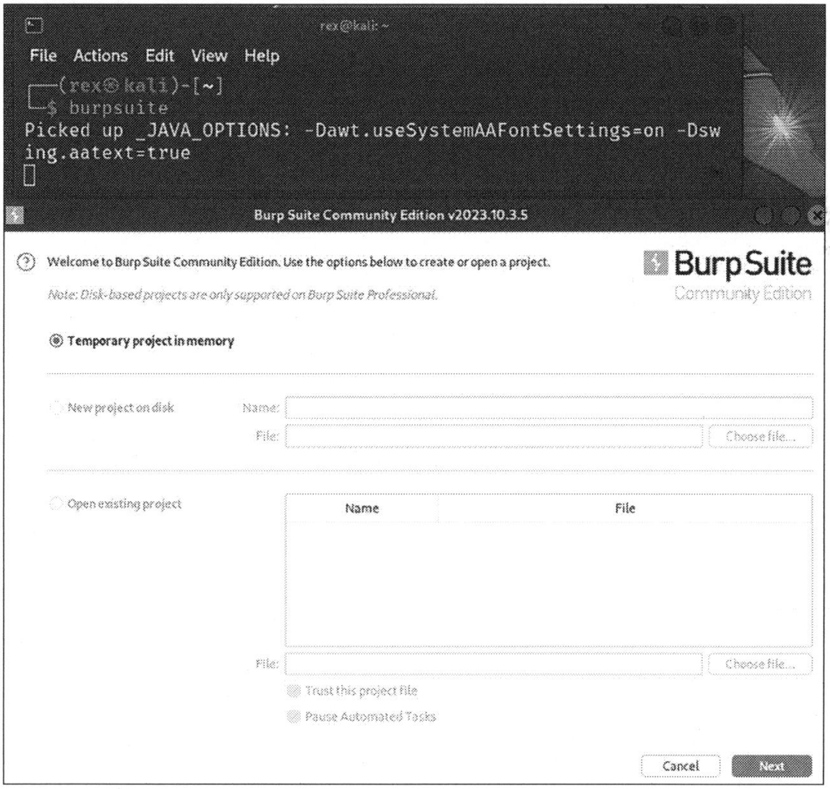

Figure 7.3: *Launching Burp Suite*

Step 2: Configure Browser Proxy Settings

a. Open your web browser (for example, Firefox) in Kali Linux.

b. Go to the browser's settings or preferences and navigate to the proxy settings.

c. Set the proxy to manual and configure it to use Burp Suite. Set the HTTP Proxy to **`127.0.0.1`** and the port to **`8080`** (or the port you configured in Burp Suite).

- **Alternate Approach: Using FoxyProxy Extension in Firefox**

  a. Launch Firefox on your Kali Linux system.

  b. Navigate to the **`Firefox Add-ons`** page and search for **`FoxyProxy Standard`**, an extension that simplifies proxy management.

  c. Install the **`FoxyProxy Standard`** extension.

  d. Once installed, you will find the FoxyProxy icon in the Firefox toolbar. Click the icon.

  e. In the FoxyProxy popup, click **`Options`** to open the configuration settings.

  f. In the FoxyProxy options, click **`Add New Proxy`**.

- **Configure the proxy settings:**

  a. **Proxy Type**: HTTP IP Address: 127.0.0.1 Port: 8080 (or the port configured in Burp Suite) Save the new proxy configuration.

  b. Back in the FoxyProxy popup, select the newly added proxy from the list.

  c. Enable the FoxyProxy extension by clicking the icon again. The selected proxy should now be active.

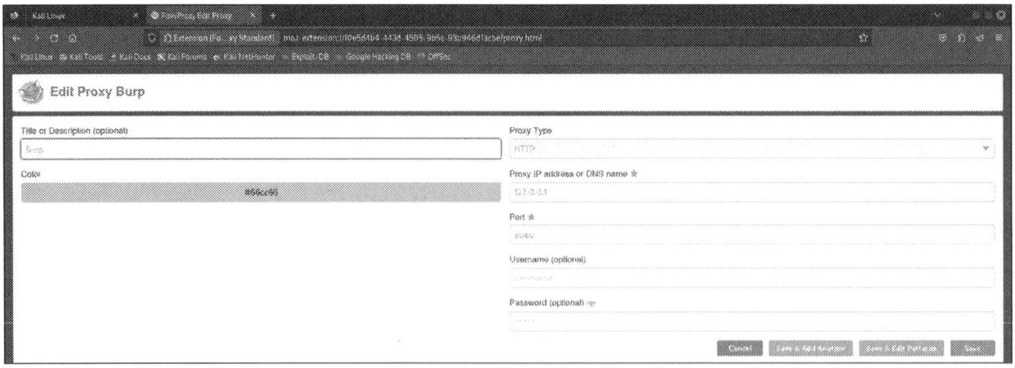

***Figure 7.4**: Configuring Proxy Settings Using FoxyProxy*

Step 3: Navigate to the Test Website

Now that Burp Suite is in action and your browser is attuned to its proxy vibes, let us embark on an adventurous journey by visiting the sacred grounds of the Testfire website (testfire.net). Testfire.net serves as a haven, carefully crafted for honing your web security testing prowess without venturing into the realms of real-world applications.

a. Launch your trusted browser (for example, Firefox) on your Kali Linux domain.

b. Enter the sacred URL testfire.net into the address bar and invoke it with a press of Enter.

c. As the digital tapestry unfolds, witness Burp Suite, with its proxy mastery, capturing the dance of requests. To witness this spectacle, traverse to the **`Proxy`** tab within Burp Suite and enter the realm of the **`Intercept`** sub-tab.

By navigating **`Testfire`**.net, you can safely experiment with Burp Suite's capabilities and sharpen your security testing skills in a sheltered environment. This ensures your endeavors are channeled towards a realm crafted for educational exploits.

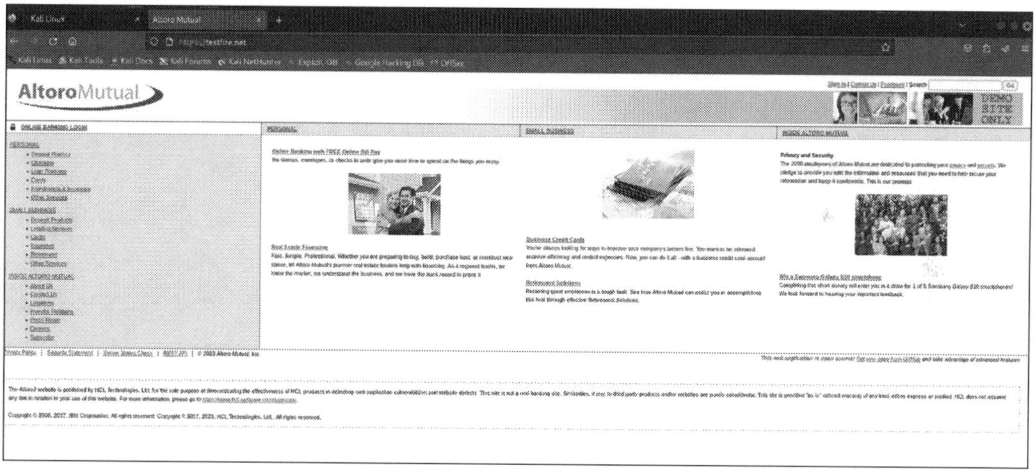

***Figure** 7.5: Testfire.net Interface*

Step 4: Capturing Requests

a. Within Burp Suite, navigate to the **`Proxy`** tab and select the **`Intercept`** sub-tab.

b. Switch on the intercept button, pausing requests from the browser to the website.

c. Return to your web browser and reload the page. Observe as Burp Suite captures and intercepts the request.

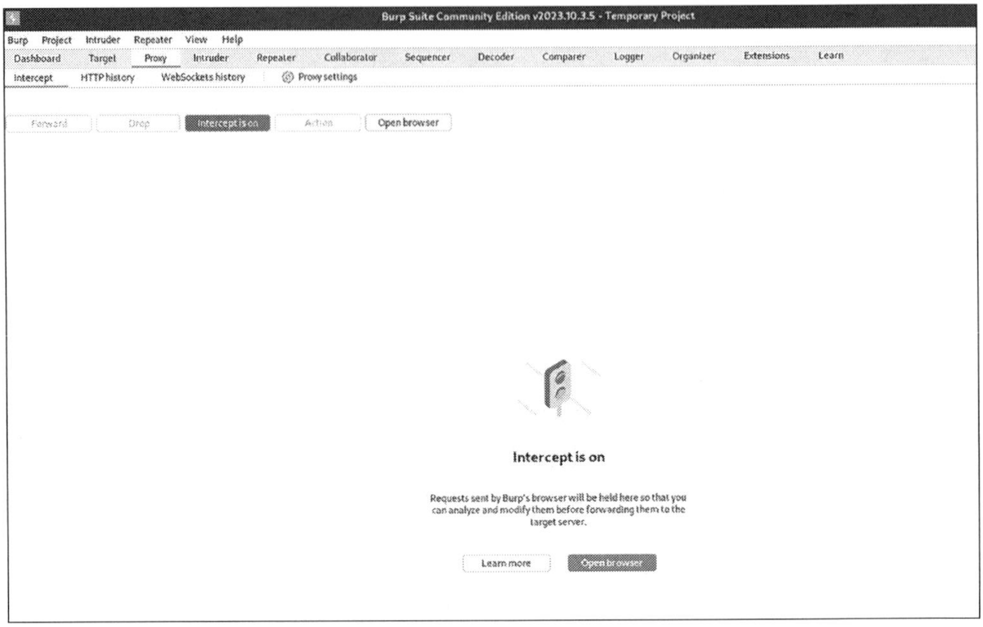

Figure 7.6: *Turning on the Intercept in Burp Suite*

Step 5: Inspect and Forward Requests

a. In Burp Suite, you will see the intercepted request in the intercept tab. Click the **`Request`** to open it in the request editor.

b. Explore the various tabs in the request editor, such as Params and Headers, to inspect the details of the request.

c. If the request looks legitimate, click the **`Forward`** button to send it to the server.

Step 6: Inspect Responses

a. Similarly, you can intercept and inspect the responses from the server. Navigate to the intercept tab, and this time, intercept the response.

b. Explore the tabs in the response editor to understand the structure and content of the response.

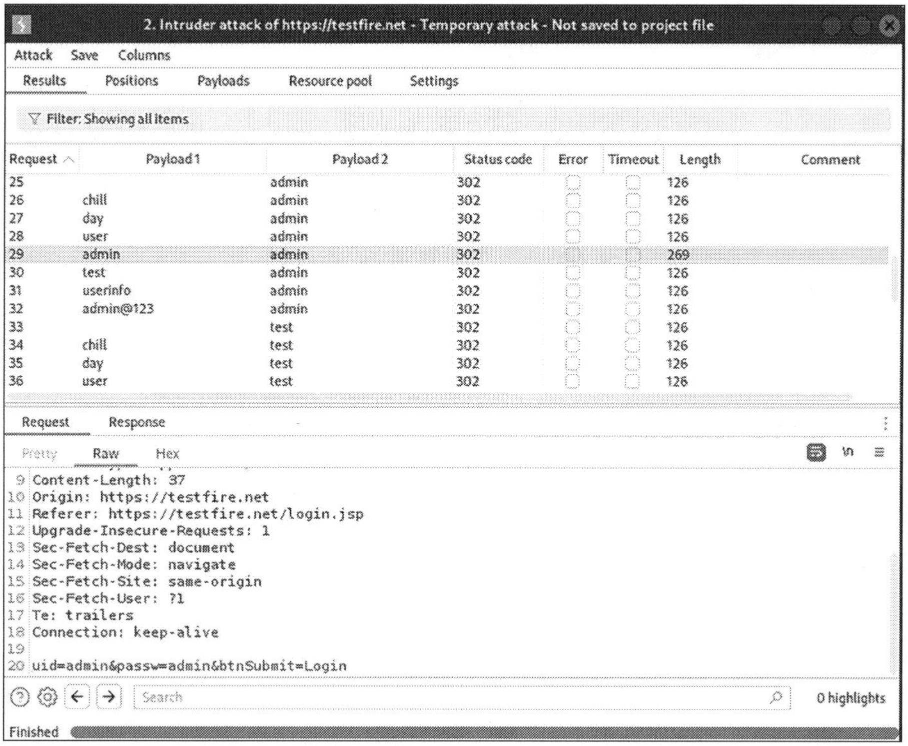

***Figure** 7.7: Inspecting and Modifying Responses*

Step 7: Turn Off Intercept

a. Once you are done inspecting requests and responses, go back to the intercept sub-tab in Burp Suite and toggle the intercept button to **`Intercept is off`**.

Congratulations! You have completed a basic hands-on exercise using Burp Suite in Kali Linux. This exercise introduced you to intercepting and inspecting web traffic, a crucial skill in web application security testing.

ZAP Proxy – Open-Source Testing with ZAP

In the vast domain of web application security testing, Burp Suite has rightfully earned its place as a prominent and extensively utilized tool. However, the cybersecurity arena presents a myriad of choices, and ZAP Proxy stands out as a compelling open-source alternative to Burp Suite. Crafted by the Open Web Application Security Project (OWASP), ZAP Proxy delivers a comprehensive array of features designed to uncover and address vulnerabilities in web applications.

ZAP Proxy: A Versatile Arsenal for Web Security

ZAP Proxy's versatility extends beyond its open-source nature, encompassing a range of features that cater to the diverse needs of security professionals. Whether you are a seasoned veteran or a novice embarking on your web security journey, ZAP Proxy proves to be an invaluable companion, providing a holistic approach to safeguarding web applications from malicious actors.

At the heart of ZAP Proxy's capabilities lies its ability to intercept and analyze HTTP traffic, enabling testers to scrutinize every request and response exchanged between a web application and its users. This powerful capability empowers testers to uncover hidden vulnerabilities, dissect the application's behavior, and even manipulate requests to simulate real-world attacks.

ZAP Proxy's Unparalleled Features

ZAP Proxy's arsenal extends far beyond mere interception, encompassing a suite of powerful tools that cater to every stage of the web security testing lifecycle. From scanning for known vulnerabilities to manually probing for hidden flaws, ZAP Proxy provides a comprehensive solution for identifying and remediating weaknesses in web applications.

- ***Vulnerability Scanning***: ZAP Proxy's Active Scanner and Passive Scanner work in tandem to identify a wide range of vulnerabilities, including SQL injection, cross-site scripting (XSS), and other common web application flaws.
- ***Penetration Testing***: ZAP Proxy's manual tools, such as Intruder and Repeater, empower testers to conduct in-depth penetration testing, simulating real-world attacks and uncovering hidden vulnerabilities.
- ***API Security Testing***: ZAP Proxy's API Scanner specifically targets RESTful APIs, identifying vulnerabilities, and validating API security posture.
- ***Dynamic Application Security Testing* (DAST)**: ZAP Proxy's DAST capabilities enable testers to identify vulnerabilities during runtime, providing a more realistic assessment of application security.

Unlocking ZAP Proxy's Full Potential

ZAP Proxy's comprehensive features are further enhanced by its extensibility, allowing users to add custom plugins and extensions to cater to specific needs and integrate with third-party security tools. This flexibility empowers testers to tailor ZAP Proxy to their unique workflows and testing requirements.

Whether you are seeking an open-source alternative to Burp Suite or simply expanding your web security testing toolkit, ZAP Proxy stands as a powerful and versatile tool. Its comprehensive features, coupled with its extensibility and ease of use, make it an indispensable resource for anyone serious about web application security.

Installation and Configuration

So, you have decided to embrace the power of ZAP Proxy to secure your digital domains. Fear not, for the installation and configuration of this open-source defender are as straightforward as setting up a trusted guardian at the gates. Let us embark on a step-by-step journey to unleash the capabilities of ZAP Proxy and fortify your web applications against potential threats.

Step 1: Update and Upgrade: Open a terminal in your Kali Linux environment and perform a quick update to ensure you are armed with the latest information.

```
sudo apt-get update && sudo apt-get upgrade
```

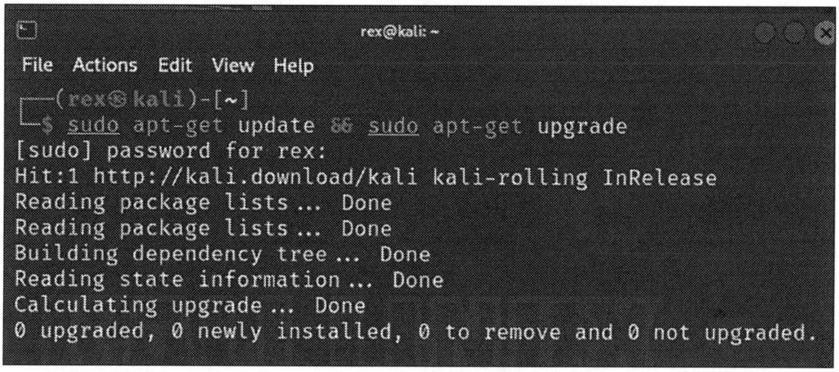

***Figure 7.8**: Update and Upgrade Command*

Step 2: Install ZAP Proxy: Execute the following command to install ZAP Proxy on your Kali Linux system.

```
sudo apt-get install zaproxy
```

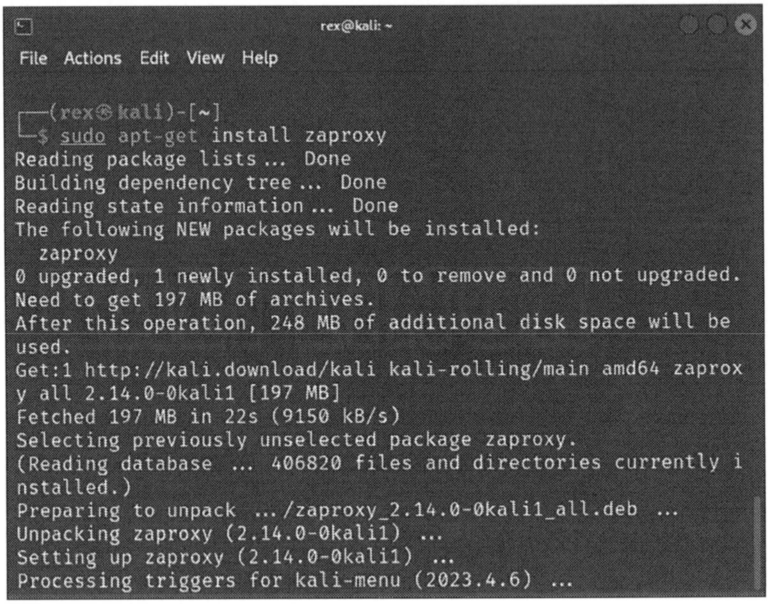

Figure 7.9: *Installing ZAP Proxy*

Setting up ZAP Proxy:

Step 1: Invoke ZAP Proxy: After the installation ritual, conjure ZAP Proxy into existence through the terminal.

```
zaproxy
```

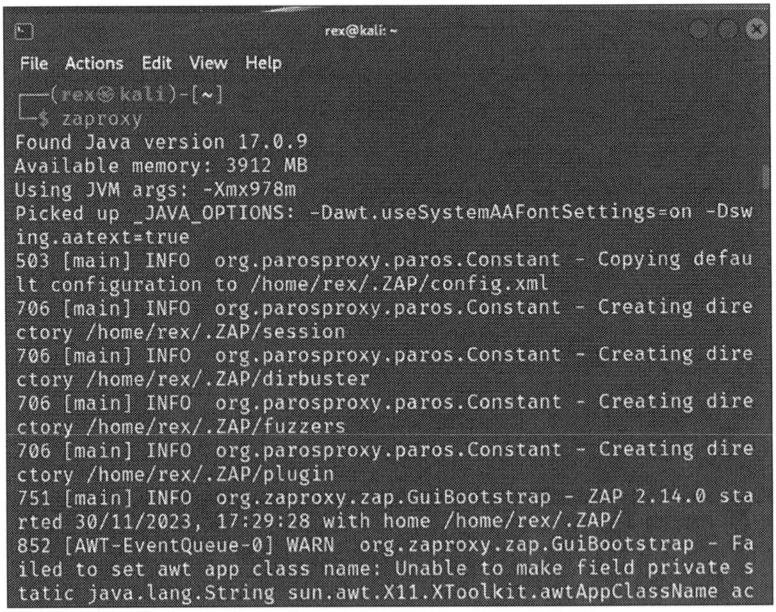

Figure 7.10: *Launching ZAP Proxy*

Step 2: Configure Local Proxy Settings: Embark on a mystical journey to your web browser's settings and weave the proxy enchantment. Channel the proxy's essence to 127.0.0.1 and infuse the default ZAP Proxy port, a magical number known as 8080.

Step 3: Explore the Interface: As ZAP Proxy unfurls its interface, explore the various tabs and functionalities. Familiarize yourself with the dashboard, Sites tab, and Alerts section.

Step 4: SSL Configuration (Optional): For inspecting HTTPS traffic, ZAP Proxy generates a unique SSL certificate. To configure your browser to trust ZAP's SSL certificate, follow these steps:

a. In ZAP Proxy, go to **`Tools`** > **`Options`** > **`Dynamic SSL Certificates`**.

b. Click Save to **`save`** the Root CA Certificate.

c. Import this certificate into your browser's certificate store.

Step 5: Start Testing: With ZAP Proxy configured and ready, navigate to a website in your browser. Observe ZAP Proxy intercepting and analyzing the traffic.

Step 6: Explore Features: Delve into ZAP Proxy's features, such as the Active Scan for automated vulnerability scanning and the Spider for mapping the structure of web applications.

ZAP Proxy, with its open-source spirit, empowers you to take control of your web security testing. By mastering its installation and configuration, you unlock a world of possibilities for securing your digital domains. Whether you are a cybersecurity novice or an experienced guardian, the simplicity of ZAP Proxy's setup ensures that everyone can contribute to the collective effort of making the web a safer place.

Automated Scanning: Unleashing ZAP Proxy's Automation Process

In today's fast-paced web development environment, manual security testing can be a daunting task. ZAP Proxy, the open-source web application security testing tool, offers a powerful solution to this challenge– automated scanning. With ZAP Proxy's automation capabilities, you can streamline the vulnerability discovery process, ensuring that your web applications remain secure without sacrificing efficiency.

Automated Scanning Excellence with ZAP Proxy

Within the arsenal of ZAP Proxy lies a suite of automated scanning tools catering to diverse testing needs. These tools provide varying levels of precision and thoroughness, allowing you to customize your scans according to the unique requirements of your web application.

- ***Dynamic Analysis with Active Scanner***: ZAP Proxy's Active Scanner delves deep into your web application, actively seeking out a spectrum of vulnerabilities such as SQL injection, cross-site scripting (XSS), and insecure direct object references (IDOR).
- ***Effortless Monitoring with Passive Scanner***: ZAP Proxy's Passive Scanner discreetly observes the traffic between your browser and the web application, identifying vulnerabilities that may surface during routine usage.
- ***Targeted API Security with API Scanner***: ZAP Proxy's API Scanner specifically addresses RESTful APIs, adept at uncovering vulnerabilities and validating the security posture of your APIs.

Benefits of Automated Scanning

Automated scanning offers several compelling benefits for web application security testing, such as:

- ***Efficiency***: Automated scans significantly reduce the time and effort required for vulnerability discovery, enabling testers to focus on more complex tasks.
- ***Consistency***: Automated scans provide repeatable and consistent results, ensuring that the same vulnerabilities are identified each time a scan is conducted.
- ***Early Detection***: Automated scans can detect vulnerabilities early in the development process, allowing for timely remediation before deployment.

Automating Scanning with ZAP

ZAP Proxy provides two primary methods for automating scans:

- ***Command-Line Interface (CLI)***: ZAP Proxy's CLI allows you to automate scans through scripting, enabling integration with continuous integration (CI) and continuous delivery (CD) pipelines.
- **ZAP API**: ZAP Proxy's RESTful API provides programmatic access to its scanning capabilities, enabling you to integrate scans into your custom testing frameworks.

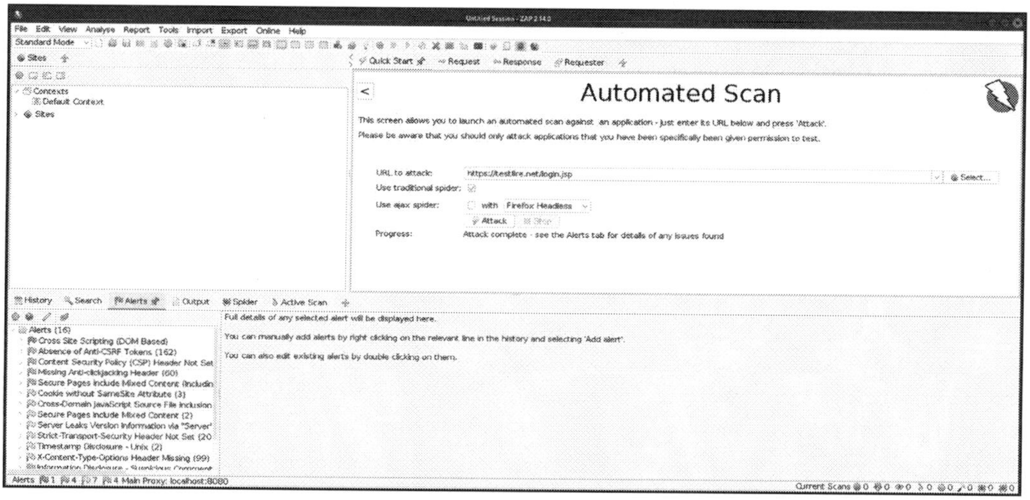

Figure 7.11: *Automated Scanning with ZAP*

Fiddler – Unraveling the Mysteries of Web Traffic

In the domain of web security testing, Fiddler emerges as a potent instrument for capturing, examining, and influencing web traffic. Serving as a mediator between your browser and the internet, Fiddler diligently logs every interaction, meticulously documenting each request and response in the web exchange. This treasure trove of data offers priceless insights into the communication dynamics of web applications, unveiling potential vulnerabilities that may be lurking beneath the surface.

Fiddler's Role in Web Traffic Analysis

Imagine a web application as a vast network of interconnected pages, and Fiddler as a diligent traffic analyst. Just as a traffic analyst monitors the flow of vehicles on a road, Fiddler scrutinizes the flow of data between your browser and the web application. It captures every HTTP request and response, providing a comprehensive view of the application's communication patterns.

Benefits of Fiddler for Web Traffic Analysis

Fiddler's capabilities extend beyond mere traffic capture; it offers a range of features that empower testers to analyze web traffic effectively:

- ***Inspect Request and Response Headers:*** Fiddler allows testers to examine the headers of HTTP requests and responses, revealing valuable information about the communication between the browser and the server.

- ***Analyze Request and Response Bodies*:** Fiddler enables testers to decode and display the contents of HTTP request and response bodies, providing insights into the data being exchanged.
- ***Filter and Search Traffic*:** Fiddler provides powerful filtering and search capabilities, allowing testers to focus on specific types of traffic or quickly locate relevant data.
- ***Modify Request and Response Headers and Bodies*:** Fiddler empowers testers to modify the headers and bodies of HTTP requests and responses, enabling them to simulate malicious attacks or test the application's behavior under different conditions.

Practical Applications of Fiddler

Fiddler's versatility extends to a wide range of web security testing scenarios:

- ***Vulnerability Scanning*:** Fiddler can be used to detect vulnerabilities in web applications by identifying patterns or anomalies in web traffic.
- ***Debugging Web Applications*:** Fiddler can aid in debugging web applications by providing detailed insights into the communication between the browser and the server.
- ***Performance Profiling*:** Fiddler can be used to profile web applications, capturing and analyzing traffic patterns to understand the application's behavior and identify potential bottlenecks.

Fiddler's ability to capture, inspect, and manipulate web traffic makes it an indispensable tool for web security testing. By leveraging its comprehensive features, testers can effectively analyze web traffic, identify vulnerabilities, debug applications, and optimize performance, ensuring the security and efficiency of web applications. Embrace Fiddler's power to unravel the mysteries of web traffic and safeguard your digital assets.

Installation and Configuration of Fiddler

Here is a step-by-step enchantment to bring Fiddler into the mystical realms of Kali Linux:

- **Install Mono:**

Fiddler beckons Mono, the mystical key to unlock Microsoft's .NET Framework secrets. Utter the sacred commands in the terminal to invoke Mono's presence:

```
sudo apt update
sudo apt install mono-complete
```

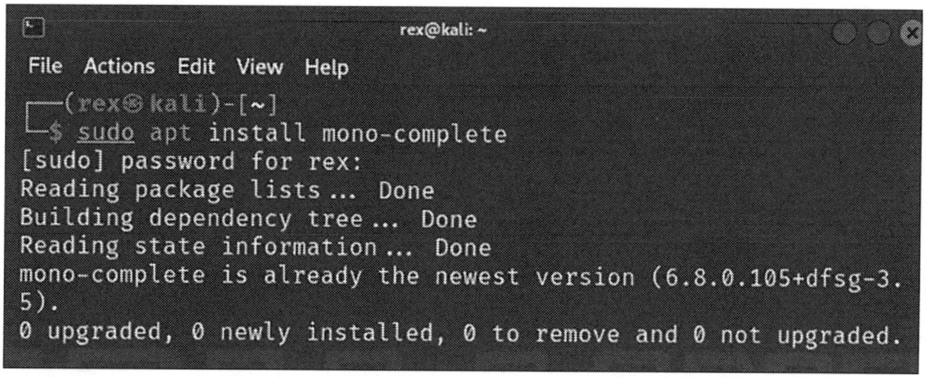

Figure 7.12: *Installing Mono*

- **Download Fiddler:**
    - Embark on a pilgrimage to the official Fiddler sanctuary at www.telerik.com/fiddler.
    - Download the Linux incarnation of Fiddler to your sacred space.
- **Extract the Archive:**

  Navigate to the cryptic location where the downloaded essence resides and unveil its secrets using the incantation:

  ```
  tar -xvf fiddler-linux.zip
  ```
- **Launching Fiddler on Kali Linux:**
    - Navigate to the Fiddler Directory:

      Open a terminal and go to the directory where Fiddler is extracted.

      ```
      cd path/to/fiddler-directory
      ```
- **Run Fiddler:**

  Execute the following command to start Fiddler:

  ```
  mono Fiddler.exe
  ```

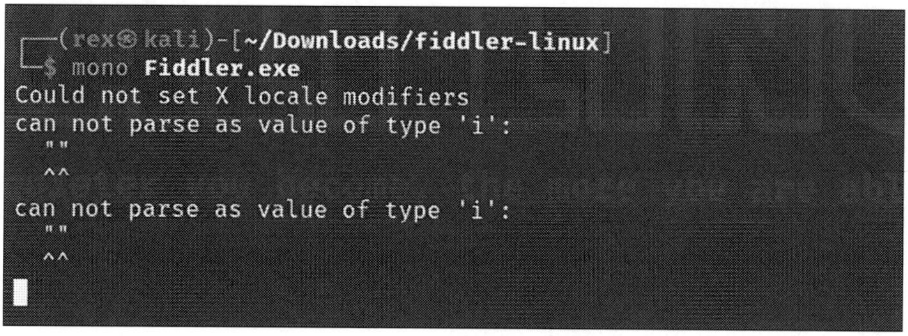

Figure 7.13: *Running Fiddler*

This command launches Fiddler using the Mono runtime.

Configuring Browser Proxy:

- Dive into your web browser and find your way to the network settings.
- Opt for Manual proxy setup in the proxy settings.
- Plug in `127.0.0.1` as the host and `8080` as the port–Fiddler's default magic numbers.
- Lock in the changes, and voila! Your browser is now rocking the proxy setup.

Your First Investigation:

- ***Capture Web Traffic*:**
  - With Fiddler running, open your web browser and start interacting with websites. Fiddler will capture the web traffic.
- ***Inspect Requests and Responses*:**
  - In the Fiddler interface, you will see a list of recorded sessions. Click any session to inspect the details.
  - Explore the various tabs in the Inspectors section to view headers, parameters, and content.
- ***Filtering and Search*:**
  - Use the search bar or filters in Fiddler to narrow down specific requests or responses.
- **HTTPS *Decryption (Optional)*:**
  - If you want to inspect HTTPS traffic, configure HTTPS decryption by going to `Tools` > `Options` > `HTTPS` and enabling options for HTTPS decryption.

Notes:

- Ensure that your Kali Linux system is connected to the internet to capture web traffic effectively.
- Fiddler may prompt you to configure proxy settings in your browser. Follow the instructions provided by Fiddler to set up the proxy.

By following these steps, you have successfully installed and configured Fiddler on your Kali Linux system and are ready to analyze web traffic for security testing, debugging, and performance optimization.

Inspecting HTTP/HTTPS Traffic: Unraveling the Web's Digital Conversations

In the intricate ballet of the internet, web traffic is the language spoken between your browser and the vast digital world. Fiddler, your digital detective, excels at deciphering this language, allowing you to inspect and understand the conversations within HTTP and HTTPS traffic. Let us embark on a journey to demystify the art of inspecting web requests, and uncovering the secrets of the digital kingdom.

Decoding Web Conversations:

- ***Capturing Web Traffic:***
  - Launch Fiddler and let it stand sentinel between your browser and the internet.
  - As you browse, Fiddler captures the dance of requests and responses.
- ***Session List Overview:***
  - In Fiddler's interface, the Session List on the left displays captured interactions. Click any session to dive into its details.
- ***Inspecting Request Headers:***
  - Select a session, and in the Inspectors tab, navigate to the Headers sub-tab.
  - Here, you will find details about the request, including the requested URL, method (GET, POST), and headers.
- ***Exploring Request Content:***
  - Move to the Raw sub-tab to see the raw content of the request. This includes parameters sent to the server.
- ***Understanding Response Headers:***
  - Switch to the Response tab to explore the headers sent back by the server. This includes information like content type and status codes.
- ***Analyzing Response Content:***
  - Move to the Raw sub-tab under Response to see the raw content sent by the server.

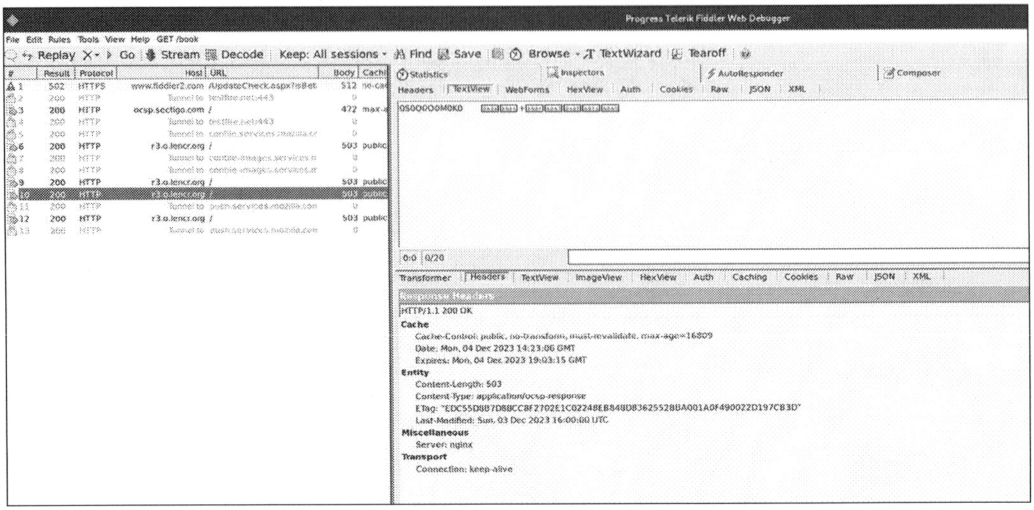

Figure 7.14: *Inspecting Traffic Using Fiddler*

Practical Examples:

- ***Debugging and Troubleshooting*:**
  - ***Scenario:*** You encounter a webpage error. By inspecting the response headers and content, you can identify the error code and understand the issue.
- ***Security Analysis*:**
  - ***Scenario:*** You suspect a security vulnerability. By inspecting requests, you can identify potential issues, like exposed sensitive information in parameters.
- ***Performance Optimization*:**
  - ***Scenario:*** A web page is slow to load. By analyzing the timing information in request headers, you can identify bottlenecks and optimize resource loading.
- ***API Testing*:**
  - ***Scenario:*** You are testing an API. By inspecting API requests and responses, you ensure proper communication and data exchange.

As you venture into inspecting web traffic with Fiddler, remember that each session is a story waiting to be told. May your inspections be insightful, your troubleshooting precise, and may Fiddler be your guiding light in the exploration of digital conversations!

Charles Proxy – Debugging Web Applications

In the field of web development, debugging often presents a daunting task, requiring testers to delve into intricate code and decipher cryptic error messages. However, Charles Proxy, a powerful web debugging proxy tool, emerges as a beacon of hope, illuminating the path toward efficient and effective web application debugging.

Charles Proxy: A Debugging Companion

Charles Proxy acts as a man-in-the-middle between your browser and the web server, intercepting and analyzing all HTTP traffic. This comprehensive view of web interactions empowers developers and testers to pinpoint the root cause of bugs and identify performance bottlenecks with greater precision.

Charles Proxy's Debugging Prowess

Charles Proxy's debugging capabilities extend far beyond mere traffic interception; it offers a suite of tools that cater to the diverse needs of web debugging:

- ***Inspecting HTTP Requests and Responses:*** Charles Proxy allows developers to scrutinize every HTTP request and response exchanged between the browser and the server, providing insights into the flow of data and potential errors.
- ***Modifying HTTP Requests and Responses:*** Charles Proxy empowers developers to manipulate HTTP requests and responses, simulating real-world scenarios and testing the application's behavior under different conditions.
- ***Debugging JavaScript and AJAX:*** Charles Proxy's JavaScript debugger enables developers to step through JavaScript code, set breakpoints, and examine variables, facilitating efficient debugging of client-side code.
- ***Analyzing HTTP Timings:*** Charles Proxy provides detailed timing information for each HTTP request and response, helping developers identify performance bottlenecks and optimize application responsiveness.

Practical Debugging Scenarios

Charles Proxy's adaptability shines through in a myriad of practical web debugging scenarios:

- ***Uncovering HTTP Errors:*** Charles Proxy excels at capturing and analyzing HTTP error codes like 404 Not Found or 500 Internal Server Error, offering valuable insights into the root causes of these errors.
- ***Solving AJAX Puzzles:*** For developers, Charles Proxy's AJAX debugger is a

boon, allowing inspection and modification of AJAX requests to ensure flawless asynchronous data retrieval.

- ***Validating Cross-Domain Communication:*** Charles Proxy proves invaluable in testing cross-domain communication, particularly interactions with APIs or third-party services. This ensures secure and reliable data exchange.
- ***Streamlining CSS and JavaScript Loading:*** Leveraging Charles Proxy's timing information, developers can pinpoint performance bottlenecks related to CSS and JavaScript loading. This insight empowers them to optimize resource loading, subsequently enhancing page load times for an improved user experience.

Charles Proxy's debugging capabilities prove invaluable for web developers and testers, providing a comprehensive toolkit for identifying and resolving bugs, optimizing performance, and ensuring the overall quality and stability of web applications. By embracing Charles Proxy as a debugging companion, developers can navigate the intricate world of web debugging with greater confidence and efficiency.

Advantages of Charles Proxy in Mobile Application Testing:

- **Mobile Traffic Inspection**
  - ***Scenario:*** Charles Proxy excels in inspecting and analyzing HTTP/HTTPS traffic between mobile applications and servers.
  - ***Advantage:*** It provides detailed insights into the communication, allowing testers to identify potential security issues and vulnerabilities.
- **SSL/TLS Decryption**
  - ***Scenario:*** Charles Proxy can decrypt SSL/TLS traffic, providing clear visibility into encrypted data.
  - ***Advantage:*** This feature is valuable for uncovering security flaws in the communication between mobile apps and servers, enhancing overall testing efficacy.
- **Request and Response Manipulation**
  - ***Scenario:*** Charles Proxy allows testers to modify requests and responses on-the-fly.
  - ***Advantage:*** Testers can simulate various scenarios by manipulating traffic, aiding in the identification of potential weaknesses in mobile app behavior.
- **Comprehensive Debugging**
  - ***Scenario:*** Charles Proxy's debugging capabilities extend to mobile app scenarios, assisting in identifying and resolving issues.
  - ***Advantage:*** Testers can trace the flow of data, inspect headers, and debug mobile app communication effectively for enhanced testing outcomes.

- **Efficient Cross-Origin Resource Sharing (CORS) Testing**
  - ***Scenario:*** Charles Proxy facilitates CORS testing for mobile applications.
  - ***Advantage:*** It helps ensure secure cross-origin data exchange, a critical aspect of mobile app security.

In these specific use cases, Charles Proxy stands out by offering unique features and capabilities that enhance the testing process for mobile applications, providing a comprehensive and detailed view of their interactions with servers.

Installation and Configuration of Charles Proxy

Installing and setting up Charles Proxy on Kali Linux involves downloading the Charles Proxy executable file and configuring your browser to use Charles Proxy as its proxy. Here is a step-by-step guide:

Step 1: Prerequisites

Ensure you have a web browser installed on your Kali Linux system.

Step 2: Download Charles Proxy

Open your web browser and go to the Charles Proxy website: (https://www.charlesproxy.com/download/latest-release/).

Download the latest version compatible with your operating system.

Step 3: Extract Charles Proxy

Open a terminal window and navigate to the directory where the Charles Proxy package is downloaded.

```
cd /Downloads
```

Extract the downloaded file.

```
tar -xzf charles-proxy-linux-*.tar.gz
```

Step 4: Run Charles Proxy

Navigate to the bin folder.

```
cd charles-proxy-linux-*/bin
```

Execute the Charles Proxy binary.

```
./charles
```

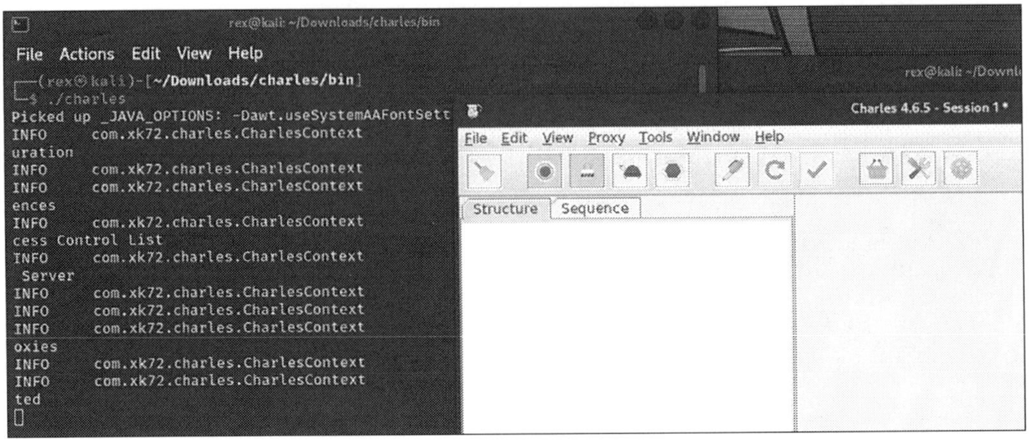

Figure 7.15: *Running Charles Proxy*

Charles Proxy will start, and you will see its graphical user interface.

Configuring Browser Proxy:

a. Open your web browser and navigate to its network settings.

b. Under proxy settings, select **`Manual`** proxy setup.

c. Enter **`127.0.0.1`** as the host and **`8888`** as the port. These are the default settings for Charles Proxy.

d. Save the proxy settings.

Using Charles Proxy:

- Launch Charles Proxy.

  a. Click **`Start Charles`** to begin capturing web activity.

  b. Surf a website in your browser–watch as Charles Proxy grabs and logs the back-and-forth of data between your browser and the site.

  c. Dive into the Charles Proxy Inspectors tab to explore details. Double-click a captured piece to uncover headers, content, and timing.

  d. End the capture by clicking **`Start Charles`** again. Your journey through Web Secrets is complete.

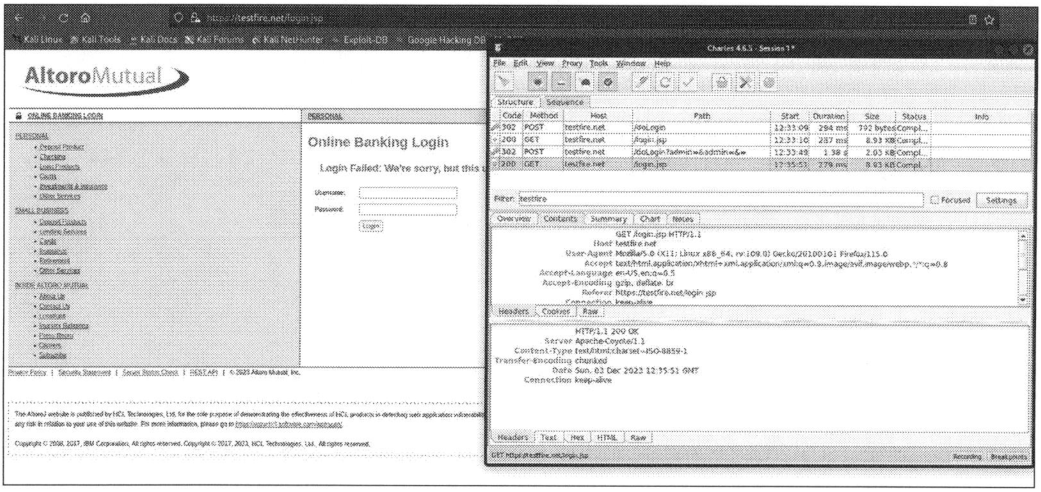

***Figure 7.16**: Capturing Traffic Using Charles Proxy*

Integration of Proxy Tools with Web Browsers

Proxy tools, exemplified by ZAP Proxy and Fiddler, have transformed the landscape of web development and security testing by intercepting and scrutinizing web traffic. To unlock their full potential, the key lies in integrating these tools seamlessly with popular web browsers. This guide serves as your companion, providing the knowledge needed to effortlessly amalgamate proxy tools with a variety of browsers. Empowering you to harness their capabilities, this integration ensures a powerful toolkit for efficient web debugging and security testing.

Getting Ready for Proxy Magic: Easy Setup Guide

- **Fire up your chosen proxy tool (ZAP Proxy or Fiddler) hassle-free.** Just follow the setup guides, and you are ready to roll.
- **Make sure your proxy tool is on and catching web traffic.**

Adjusting Proxy Preferences in Common Web Browsers:

For Google Chrome (Windows/macOS/Linux):

1. Open Chrome and go to **`Settings > Advanced > Open proxy settings`**.
2. Choose **`Manual proxy setup`** and turn on **`Use a proxy server`**.
3. Enter the important details:
    a. **`HTTP proxy`**: Your proxy tool's home IP (usually 127.0.0.1)
    b. **`Port`**: Your proxy tool's hub (usually 8080 for ZAP Proxy, 8888 for Fiddler)

4. Click **`Apply`**, then hit **`OK`** to lock in your settings. Now you are all set for the proxy magic!

Mozilla Firefox (Windows/macOS/Linux):

1. Open Firefox and navigate to **`Options > Preferences`**.
2. Select the **`Network`** tab.
3. **`Under Connection Settings`**, click the **`Settings`** button next to **`Use a proxy server for all protocols`**.
4. Select **`Manual proxy setup`**.
5. Enter the following information:
    a. **`HTTP Proxy`**: Your proxy tool's host IP address (usually 127.0.0.1)
    b. **`Port`**: Your proxy tool's port (usually 8080 for ZAP Proxy, 8888 for Fiddler)
6. Click **`OK`** and then **`Close`** to save the settings.

Safari (macOS):

1. Open Safari and navigate to **`Preferences > Advanced`**.
2. Click the **`Proxies`** tab.
3. Select **`Manual proxy configuration`**.
4. Enter the following information:
    a. **`Web Proxy Server`**: Your proxy tool's host IP address (usually 127.0.0.1)
    b. **`Web Proxy Port`**: Your proxy tool's port (usually 8080 for ZAP Proxy, 8888 for Fiddler)
5. Click **`OK`** to save the settings.

By successfully integrating proxy tools with your preferred web browser, you have unlocked a world of possibilities for web debugging and security testing. These tools empower you to intercept, analyze, and manipulate web traffic, providing valuable insights into application behavior and potential vulnerabilities. Embrace the power of proxy tools and elevate your web development and security testing practices to new heights.

Case Studies: Analyzing Security Breaches and the Role of Proxy Tools in Prevention

Proxy tools, such as ZAP Proxy and Fiddler, have emerged as indispensable assets in web security testing, empowering developers and security professionals to identify and address vulnerabilities before they are exploited. By analyzing real-world security breaches, we can gain valuable insights into the potential preventive measures that proxy tools could have offered.

Case Study 1: Equifax Data Breach (2017)

In the year 2017, Equifax, a prominent credit reporting agency, faced a colossal data breach exposing the personal details of more than 147 million individuals. This breach was linked to a vulnerability in Apache Struts, a widely used Java web framework.

Imagine if tools like ZAP Proxy had been employed to uncover this vulnerability during the development and testing stages, thwarting the breach. ZAP Proxy's prowess in scanning for vulnerabilities could have pinpointed the insecure coding practices that paved the way for the vulnerability. Such early detection would have empowered developers to rectify the issue before deploying the system, averting the catastrophic consequences of the breach.

Lessons Learned:

- Swift detection of vulnerabilities during the development phase is critical.
- Insecure coding practices can lead to catastrophic breaches.

Proxy Tool Use:

- ZAP Proxy could have been deployed for early vulnerability scanning.
- Regular scans during development could identify and rectify coding vulnerabilities.

Case Study 2: Yahoo's Data Breaches (2013-2016)

Between 2013 and 2016, Yahoo grappled with a series of data breaches affecting over three billion user accounts. These breaches, involving stolen passwords and forged cookies, provided unauthorized access to user accounts, leading to the illicit acquisition of sensitive information.

Imagine the impact if tools like Fiddler had been utilized to scrutinize network traffic, identifying suspicious activities such as unauthorized access attempts and unusual data exfiltration. Fiddler's capacity to capture and analyze HTTP requests and responses could have provided vital insights into the methods employed by the attackers. Such insights would have empowered Yahoo to respond swiftly, mitigating the breaches and preventing the compromise of sensitive user data.

Lessons Learned:

- Consistent surveillance of network traffic plays a pivotal role in identifying potential threats.
- Responding promptly to abnormal data exfiltration is of utmost importance.

Proxy Tool Use:

- Fiddler's meticulous examination of network traffic had the potential to uncover unauthorized access attempts.
- Immediate scrutiny of HTTP requests in real-time could facilitate a rapid response to suspicious activities.

Case Study 3: Marriott Data Breach (2018)

In 2018, Marriott International, a global hotel chain, suffered a massive data breach that affected approximately 500 million guests. The breach involved stealing customer information, including passport numbers and travel itineraries.

Proxy tools like Charles Proxy could have been used to test the security of Marriott's web applications and identify any potential vulnerabilities that could have been exploited by attackers. Charles Proxy's debugging capabilities could have allowed security testers to trace the flow of data and identify any weaknesses in the authentication and authorization mechanisms.

Lessons Learned:

- Robust authentication and authorization mechanisms are paramount.
- Regular testing of web applications can uncover potential vulnerabilities.

Proxy Tool Use:

- Charles Proxy's testing capabilities could assess authentication and authorization weaknesses.
- Debugging features could trace data flow, aiding in fortifying security mechanisms.

Case Study 4: Heartbleed Bug (2014)

In 2014, the Heartbleed bug, a serious vulnerability in the OpenSSL encryption library, was discovered. The bug could be exploited to steal sensitive information, such as login credentials and credit card numbers, from websites that use OpenSSL.

Proxy tools like Fiddler could have been used to scan websites for the Heartbleed vulnerability. Fiddler's ability to capture and analyze HTTP requests and responses could have identified websites that were vulnerable to the Heartbleed bug, allowing website owners to patch the vulnerability before it could be exploited.

Lessons Learned:

- Critical vulnerabilities like Heartbleed require prompt identification.
- Proactive scanning for known vulnerabilities is essential.

Proxy Tool Use:

- Fiddler could have conducted scans for the Heartbleed bug.
- Capturing and analyzing HTTP requests could identify vulnerable websites for timely patching.

General Lessons for Proxy Tool Use:

- Integrate proxy tools into the development lifecycle for continuous monitoring.
- Regular scans with tools like ZAP Proxy, Fiddler, and Charles Proxy can prevent and mitigate security breaches.
- Proxy tools contribute to a proactive security stance, identifying vulnerabilities before they are exploited.
- Education and awareness about proxy tools among development and security teams are crucial for effective utilization.

Reporting and Documentation

In the domain of web security testing, comprehensive reports serve as the backbone of effective communication and remediation. They provide a clear and concise narrative of the testing process, detailing the identified vulnerabilities, their potential impact, and recommended mitigation strategies. By following these guidelines, security testers can craft reports that resonate with stakeholders and drive meaningful security improvements.

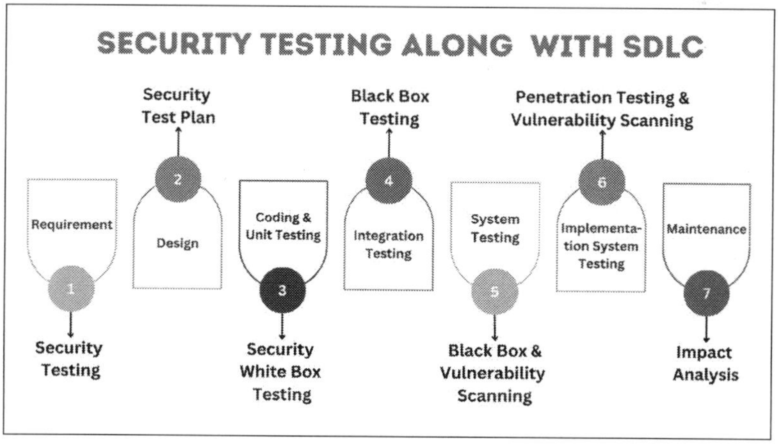

Figure 7.17: *Reporting in Security Testing*

Structure and Organization:

- ***Executive Summary:*** Deliver a brief overview of the testing's scope, goals, and significant discoveries, tailored for those less familiar with technical details.

- ***Introduction:*** Present the testing methodology, tools, and the environment applied during the assessment.
- ***Scope and Objectives:*** Clearly outline the assessment's scope, specifying the tested web applications or systems.
- ***Vulnerability Findings:***
    - ***Vulnerability Details:*** For each vulnerability, furnish a unique identifier, classification, severity level, and an in-depth description of the vulnerability.
    - ***Impact:*** Outline the potential repercussions of the vulnerability, including risks like data breaches, unauthorized access, or system disruptions.
    - ***Exploitation:*** Detail the steps an attacker might employ to exploit the vulnerability and the potential aftermath.
- ***Recommendation and Mitigation Strategies:***
    - ***Recommendations:*** Propose clear and actionable remediation steps for each vulnerability, offering specific measures to address or patch the identified issues.
    - ***Mitigation Strategies:*** Provide broader strategies to enhance overall security, encompassing practices like secure coding, vulnerability scanning, and user awareness training.
- ***Conclusion:*** Summarize the primary discoveries, recommendations, and the overall security status of the tested web applications or systems.

Templates for Reporting and Documentation

- **Basic Report Template:**

    This simple template outlines key sections to ensure all essential information is covered:

    - **Executive Summary:** Briefly summarize the findings, highlighting critical vulnerabilities and recommendations.
    - **Introduction:** State the project scope, methodology used, and limitations.
    - **Findings:** List identified vulnerabilities with detailed descriptions, severity levels, and potential impact. Use tables or screenshots for clarity.
    - **Recommendations:** Provide actionable steps to remediate vulnerabilities, prioritize risks, and suggest additional security measures.
    - **Conclusion:** Summarize key findings and reiterate the importance of addressing vulnerabilities.
- **Advanced Report Template:**

This template expands on the basic structure, incorporating additional sections for a more comprehensive analysis:

- System Overview: Describe the target system, architecture, and components.
- Threat Modeling: Assess potential threats and attack vectors relevant to the system.
- Testing Methodology: Detail the specific tools and techniques used during the assessment.
- Vulnerability Management: Explain the process for classifying and prioritizing vulnerabilities.
- Exploitation Attempts (Optional): If applicable, document attempts to exploit identified vulnerabilities (with proper authorization).
- Appendix: Include supporting evidence like screenshots, logs, and technical documentation.

- **Example Report – Web Application Penetration Test:**

Here is a sample report excerpt showcasing findings from a web application penetration test:

- Vulnerability: SQL Injection (High Severity)
- Description: A parameter in the login form is vulnerable to SQL injection attacks, allowing an attacker to bypass authentication and potentially access sensitive user data.
- Impact: An attacker could gain unauthorized access to user accounts, steal sensitive information, or even modify or delete data.
- Recommendation: Implement proper input validation and sanitization techniques to prevent SQL injection attacks.

- **Visualization Tools:**

Consider using reporting tools like BreachLock or PentestReport to generate professional-looking reports with dynamic charts, graphs, and risk-scoring mechanisms.

Remember, the ideal report format will depend on your specific project, audience, and organizational requirements. Customize these templates and examples to create standardized reports that effectively communicate your security findings and drive proactive mitigation efforts.

By consistently utilizing clear and comprehensive reports, you can ensure that valuable security insights are readily understood and acted upon, leading to a more secure digital landscape for everyone.

Documentation Best Practices

- ***Clarity and Conciseness:*** Use simple and easy-to-understand language, avoiding technical jargon that may alienate non-technical stakeholders.

- ***Evidence and Proofs:*** Provide supporting evidence, such as screenshots, code snippets, or network traffic captures, to substantiate the findings.
- ***Risk Assessment:*** Include a risk assessment matrix, assigning severity and likelihood ratings to each vulnerability, and prioritizing the most critical issues.
- ***Actionable Recommendations:*** Clearly outline the recommended remediation steps, including timelines and resource estimates.
- ***Regular Updates:*** Regularly update the report as the testing process progresses and new vulnerabilities are discovered.
- ***Version Control:*** Maintain version control of the report to track changes and ensure consistency.
- ***Stakeholder Review:*** Share the draft report with key stakeholders for feedback and incorporate their input before finalizing it.
- ***Accessibility:*** Ensure the report is accessible to all stakeholders, including those with visual impairments or color blindness.

By adhering to these guidelines and best practices, security testers can produce comprehensive reports that effectively communicate vulnerabilities, prioritize risks, and drive meaningful security improvements, ultimately safeguarding web applications and the data they protect.

Conclusion

As we wrap up our journey through **Security Testing and Proxy Tools,** kudos to you for delving into the world of web security. From the basics to the hands-on with Burp Suite, ZAP Proxy, Fiddler, and Charles Proxy, you have armed yourself with crucial insights.

Congratulations on reaching this milestone! The tools explored are now your allies in the ongoing battle for digital security. But, our adventure continues. In the next chapter, we will unravel the dance of scripts in Cross-Site Scripting (XSS). Get ready for an exploration into a fascinating threat landscape.

May your cybersecurity endeavors be victorious, your code resilient, and may the journey ahead be filled with discoveries. Onward to the next chapter!

Chapter 8
Cross-Site Scripting

Introduction

Welcome to the enthralling world of **Cross-Site Scripting (XSS),** where we demystify the digital threats lurking in the shadows. In our previous chapter, we delved into the sphere of Security Testing and Proxy Tools, laying the groundwork for your journey into cybersecurity.

Now, buckle up as we explore the multifaceted landscape of XSS. From comprehending the intricacies of XSS types—Stored, Reflected, and DOM-based—to unraveling the techniques of Attack Vectors and Payloads, we are on a mission to empower you with practical insights. We will navigate the domain of Detection and Exploitation, arming you with the skills to safeguard against digital intruders. And fear not, for we will not just leave you with knowledge—we will equip you with Mitigation and Best Practices, showcasing real-world case studies of companies that have triumphed against XSS threats.

Structure

In this chapter, we will cover the following topics:

- Understanding Cross-Site Scripting (XSS)
- Types of XSS: Stored, Reflected, DOM-based
- Attack Vectors and Payloads
- Detection of XSS Vulnerabilities
- Mitigation and Best Practices
- Real-world Case Studies of Notable XSS Attacks

Understanding Cross-Site Scripting

Imagine this: You are browsing the web, reading the news, checking social media–all perfectly normal stuff. But unbeknownst to you, lurking in the shadows is a tiny saboteur, a digital trickster called Cross-Site Scripting (XSS). This mischievous villain can sneak malicious code onto the web pages you visit, turning them into unsuspecting weapons aimed at stealing your data, hijacking your accounts, or even spreading malware.

Overview of XSS

Think of it like this: Websites function as digital platforms, analogous to culinary kitchens, and user input serves as the raw ingredients in this virtual culinary space. In ordinary circumstances, the website processes user input securely, akin to a skilled chef preparing a delightful meal in the kitchen. However, in the context of Cross-Site Scripting (XSS), a malicious actor, akin to a surreptitious chef, can introduce a malevolent spice in the form of code. Once triggered, this code has the potential to execute various harmful actions on the user's device, all while the website owner, analogous to the head chef, remains oblivious to the compromise of the digital culinary environment.

Types of XSS:

- ***The Sneaky Impersonator* (Reflected XSS):** This one hides in plain sight. When you enter data on a vulnerable website (think comments, search bars), the attacker's code gets reflected to you, disguised as part of the webpage. Boom, you are infected!
- ***The Persistent Poisoner* (Stored XSS):** This villain leaves a permanent mark. The attacker's code gets saved on the website (think forum posts, guestbooks), infecting every unsuspecting visitor who views it. It is like a booby trap waiting to explode!
- ***The Man-in-the-Browser Monster* (DOM XSS):** This one plays with the building blocks of the webpage. The attacker manipulates how the browser displays elements, creating hidden phishing forms or stealing your cookies without you even noticing. It is like a puppeteer controlling your browser from within!

Impact of XSS

XSS is a serious threat because it can:

- ***Steal your data*:** Passwords, credit card numbers, personal information–all are at risk.
- ***Hijack your accounts*:** Imagine your email or social media becoming the attacker's playground.

- ***Spread malware:*** One click on a malicious link makes your computer a virus-infected mess.
- ***Damage reputations:*** Websites can be defaced, spreading misinformation and causing chaos.

Working of XSS: Unraveling the Attack Mechanism

Now that we have dipped our toes into the world of Cross-Site Scripting (XSS), let us take a closer look at the mechanics behind this digital trickery. Imagine you are enjoying a movie, and suddenly, the characters start saying things they should not—XSS is a bit like that, injecting unexpected lines into the script of your favorite web pages.

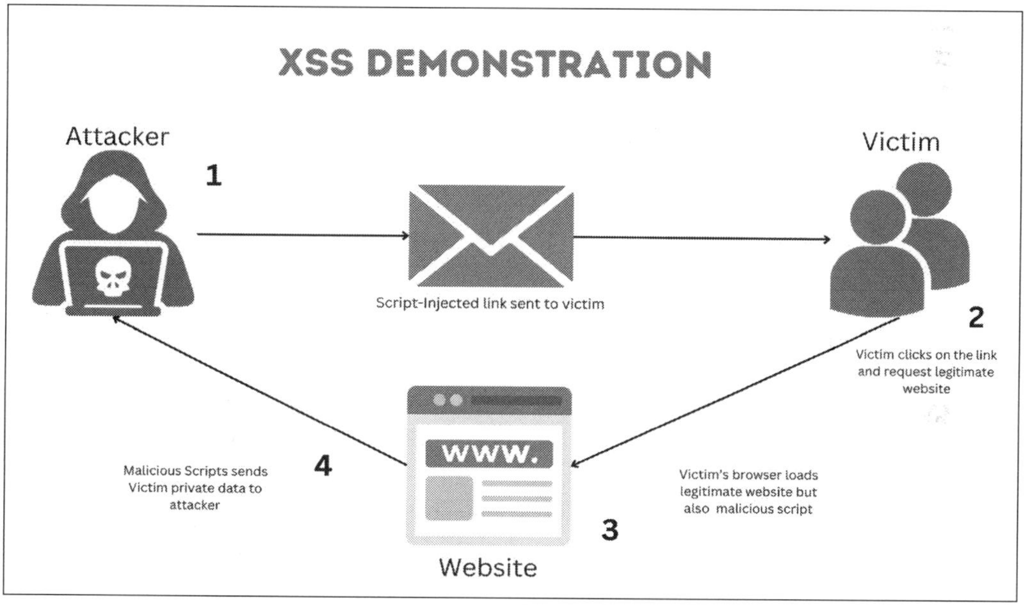

Figure 8.1: *Working of XSS*

Key Concepts:

- ***The Play: Your Browser as the Stage***

  Every time you visit a website, your browser is the stage where the play unfolds. Websites deliver content and scripts to your browser, which then interprets and presents them as the web pages you see.
  Simple Analogy: *Your browser is like a movie screen, and websites are the directors delivering the scenes. You are the audience, enjoying the show.*

- **Enter the Script: Innocent-Looking Code**

  XSS attackers are like mischievous scriptwriters. They sneakily inject their lines into the web page's script. This injected code is often disguised as harmless content, such as a comment, a search query, or a message.
  Everyday Comparison: *It is as if someone slipped a hidden message into a letter you are reading, and when you reach that point, things take an unexpected turn.*

- **The Unexpected Twist: Execution in Your Browser**

  Now comes the plot twist–when you load the compromised web page, your browser unwittingly executes the injected script. It is like the actors in our movie suddenly uttered ad-libbing lines they were not supposed to say.
  Practical Insight: *Think of this as a surprise twist in the story, but instead of entertainment, it is a potential threat to your online safety.*

- **Consequences Unveiled: From Information Theft to Manipulation**

  The executed script can do a variety of things, from stealing your login credentials to altering the content of the page you are viewing. Essentially, it gives the attacker a backstage pass to your digital experience.
  Everyday Scenario: *It is akin to someone altering the text of a letter you are reading or stealing a note you wrote.*

Types of XSS: Reflected, Stored, and DOM-based

In the dynamic sphere of cybersecurity, understanding the nuances of Cross-Site Scripting (XSS) is pivotal. This topic delves into the fascinating world of XSS types: Reflected, Stored, and DOM-based. Brace yourself for an insightful journey as we demystify Stored XSS, unveiling its definition, potential dangers, and offering a hands-on experience. Moving forward, Reflected XSS takes center stage, offering a clear explanation accompanied by practical scenarios, followed by a thoughtful comparison with Stored XSS. Finally, immerse yourself in the unique characteristics of DOM-based XSS, gaining a deep understanding through practical, hands-on exploration. Let us embark on this enlightening voyage through the diverse landscapes of XSS types.

Reflected XSS: The Bait and Switch of Cross-Site Scripting

Imagine a mischievous magician who swaps out your harmless sugar cube with a tiny explosive disguised as candy. That is kind of how Reflected XSS works. It is a sneak attack where the website itself becomes the magician's assistant, reflecting your tricked-out data at you with a bang (or rather, a malicious script execution).

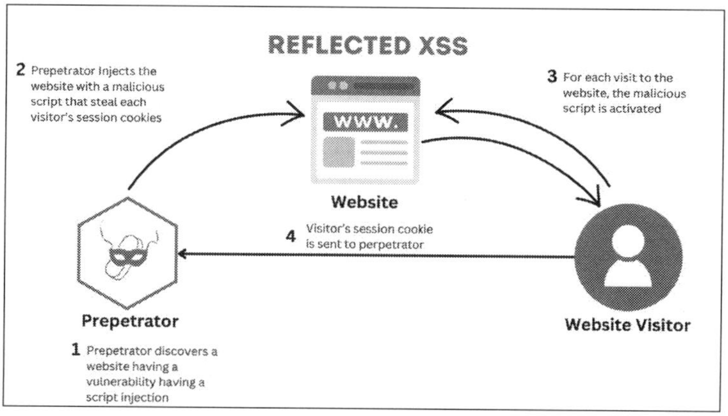

Figure 8.2: *Reflected XSS*

Here is how it plays out:

- **You, the unsuspecting web surfer,** visit a website and see a search bar. You type in a seemingly harmless query, like **`"best cat videos"`.**
- **But wait!** Unbeknownst to you, the search bar is rigged with a vulnerability. The website does not properly sanitize user input.
- **The mischievous hacker lurking in the shadows** has injected a hidden script into another part of the website. It could be anywhere – a comment, an ad banner, even a seemingly innocent image.
- **Your search query gets mixed with the hacker's script** and gets reflected to you in the search results or even the website itself. It is like the magician handing you back your "candy," but now it is primed to explode.
- **Boom!** As your browser renders the page, it unknowingly executes the hidden script. This could mean anything from stealing your cookies to hijacking your session, spreading spam, or even taking control of your computer!

Let us break down some real-life scenarios to understand the different ways Reflected XSS can attack:

- ***Search bar shenanigans:*** Imagine a malicious script injected into a news website's search function. When you search for **`"breaking news",`** it steals your login information. By the time you realize it, the hacker has already accessed your sensitive data.
- ***Phishing with a twist:*** A hacker injects a script into an email's unsubscribe link. When you click it, instead of unsubscribing, the script redirects you to a fake login page that steals your credentials. It is like the unsubscribe button turning into a bait-and-switch trap!
- ***Social media mayhem:*** A script injected into a seemingly innocent comment on a popular celebrity's post. When you click the **`"like"`** button, it activates the

script, which spams your entire network with unwanted messages. It is like the "`like`" button becoming a social media megaphone for the hacker's voice.

Guarding Against the Digital Bait and Switch

- ***Be wary of suspicious links and forms:*** If something seems too good to be true, it probably is. Do not click on shady links or submit sensitive information to untrustworthy websites.
- ***Keep your software updated:*** Outdated browsers and plugins are often riddled with vulnerabilities that attackers can exploit for Reflected XSS. Patching up your software is like putting on a protective shield against digital explosives.
- ***Report suspicious activity:*** If you encounter anything that seems off on a website, report it to the website owner or security team. Remember, vigilant netizens are the first line of defense against cyber threats.

By being aware of how Reflected XSS works and taking these precautions, we can turn the tables on the mischievous magicians. We can become savvy web browsers, not unsuspecting victims. Let us keep the internet a safe and secure space for everyone, one click at a time!

Stored XSS: When Innocence Turns into Information Theft

Consider a scenario where a meticulously crafted cake, symbolizing a website, undergoes a nefarious alteration. Instead of benign sprinkles, a malevolent pastry chef discreetly incorporates minuscule, malicious elements that, upon consumption, trigger confetti explosions. This analogy encapsulates the essence of Stored Cross-Site Scripting (XSS) occurrences, where unauthorized code injections compromise the integrity of a website, leading to potential security vulnerabilities and adverse consequences for users.

Stored XSS is where an attacker injects malicious code (like those confetti sprinkles) into a website that gets saved (stored) on the server. This code then explodes (gets executed) whenever someone visits the page, affecting everyone who takes a bite (reads the page).

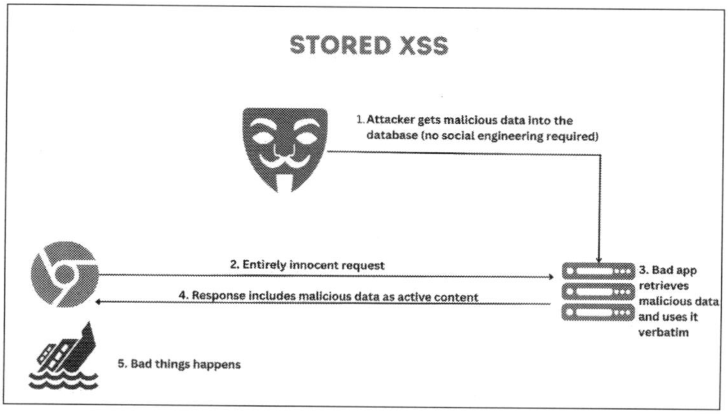

Figure 8.3: *Stored XSS*

Think of it like a forum where anyone can post comments. If someone posts a comment with a hidden script that steals cookies, everyone who reads that comment gets their cookies stolen! Scary, right?

Real-life Instances of Stored XSS:

- ***On a news platform:*** A malevolent actor introduces a script into the comments section of a news article. As users peruse the article, the script discreetly snatches their login credentials.
- ***In an online store:*** A malicious actor embeds a script within a product description. Should a user add this product to their cart, the script cunningly redirects them to a fraudulent checkout page, pilfering their credit card details.
- ***Within a social media network:*** A perpetrator injects a script into their profile's biography. As visitors explore their profiles, the script orchestrates the delivery of spam messages to all of their friends.

The Inherent Danger of Stored XSS

- ***Persistent:*** The attack code stays hidden on the server, poisoning everyone who visits the page, unlike other XSS types that only affect a single user.
- ***Widespread damage:*** It can affect countless users, especially on popular websites.
- ***Hard to detect:*** The malicious code is often hidden within seemingly harmless data like comments or descriptions.

Preventive measures

- ***Sanitize user input:*** Websites should thoroughly check all data entered by users before storing it, removing any suspicious code. Think of it like having a security guard at the bakery who checks every sprinkle before it goes on the cake.

- ***Encode data before output:*** When displaying user-generated content, websites should encode it to prevent the browser from interpreting it as code. Imagine the bakery baking the sprinkles into the cake, making them harmless treats instead of exploding surprises.
- ***Regular security audits:*** Websites should be regularly scanned for vulnerabilities that attackers could exploit for Stored XSS. It is like having a team of bakers taste-testing the cake every day to make sure there are no hidden nasties.

We have seen how Stored XSS works like an evil pastry chef, hiding confetti sprinkles in a cake. Now, let us dive into the real danger lurking inside those tiny bits of code. The damage potential can escalate quickly, depending on the website you are on and the attacker's intentions:

- ***Financial Fraud:*** Imagine a banking website infected with Stored XSS. Hackers could steal account details and drain funds, leaving victims with empty wallets and shattered trust.
- ***Identity Theft:*** On social media platforms, a Stored XSS attack could spread like wildfire, stealing personal information from countless users and enabling the creation of fake profiles for nefarious purposes.
- ***Website Takeover:*** In the worst-case scenario, the attacker could gain complete control of the website, turning it into a platform for malware distribution, spam campaigns, or even political propaganda.

Stored XSS is like a silent thief in the night, lurking in the shadows of seemingly harmless websites, waiting to pounce on unsuspecting visitors. It is a powerful weapon in the hands of malicious actors, capable of causing widespread damage and compromising sensitive data.

Reflected XSS versus Stored XSS: A Side-by-Side Comparison

Let us unravel the mysteries of Cross-Site Scripting by putting Stored XSS and Reflected XSS side by side, like comparing apples to oranges but within the world of web security. Imagine you are at a bakery, choosing between two types of pastries–Stored and Reflected XSS are like two distinct flavors, each with its unique characteristics.

Key Concepts:

Aspect	**Reflected XSS**	**Stored XSS**
Persistence	Momentary encounter; scripts are reflected immediately upon user interaction	Persistent threat; scripts stay on the server until triggered by a user

Injection Point	Injected into URL parameters or input fields that reflect user input directly	Injected into areas where user-generated content is stored (for example, comments, profiles)
Execution	Requires a specific user action, like clicking a manipulated link or interacting with a compromised form	Triggered when any user interacts with the compromised content, not necessarily the user who injected the script
Timeframe for Attack	Typically occurs when the victim interacts with the malicious input; the threat is more transient	Can be triggered by any user over an extended period; persists until the injected content is removed
Example Scenario	Attacker sends a manipulated link to the victim; when the victim clicks it, the script is reflected and executed	Attacker injects a script into a comment on a blog; any user viewing that comment becomes a potential victim
Consequences	Rapid consequences, such as stealing session cookies or redirecting users to malicious sites	Can lead to persistent data theft, site defacement, or reputation damage
Prevention	Emphasizes securing input fields and URL parameters to prevent immediate script execution	Requires robust input validation and content sanitization; emphasis on securing areas with user-generated content

Table 8.1: *Comparison between Reflected XSS and Stored XSS*

In Practice:

Imagine you are choosing between pastries at a bakery:

- ***Reflected XSS is like a cookie:*** It is created on the spot, and handed over to the customer for immediate consumption. The baker must be cautious not to accidentally reflect any unexpected ingredients to the customer.
- ***Stored XSS is like a cake:*** It is prepared in advance, sitting on display for anyone to interact with. The baker needs to ensure the cake is well-guarded to prevent surprises.

Understanding these distinctions is akin to knowing the ingredients in your pastries—it helps you make informed choices and stay one step ahead in securing your web experiences.

DOM-based XSS: Unraveling the Digital Puppeteer

In our exploration of Cross-Site Scripting (XSS), we have encountered the persistence of Stored XSS and the fleeting surprises of Reflected XSS. Now, let us step into the world of DOM-based XSS—a unique flavor that is like a digital puppeteer pulling strings behind the scenes. Imagine you are playing with a marionette, but in this scenario, the puppeteer is invisible, manipulating the show from the shadows.

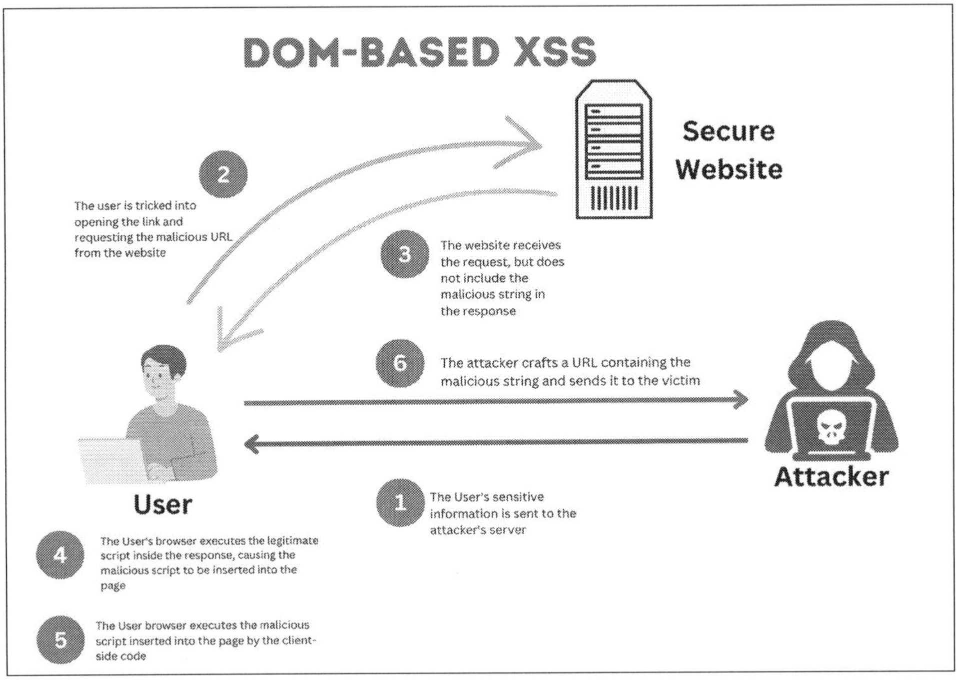

Figure 8.4: *DOM-based XSS*

Key Concepts:

- ***Definition: Scripts on the Move***
  - **DOM (*Document Object Model*):** Think of it as the blueprint of a web page—the structure and elements that browsers use to represent a page.
  - ***DOM-based* XSS:** Involves manipulating the Document Object Model through malicious scripts, leading to unintended consequences.
- ***Everyday Analogy***: It is like someone rearranging the backstage of a play to create unexpected scenes during the performance.

- ***Unique Characteristics: Scripting the Play***
  - ***Location of Manipulation:*** Unlike Stored and Reflected XSS, where the server is the stage, DOM-based XSS focuses on manipulating the client side, directly altering how the browser interprets and presents content.
  - ***Execution Dynamics:*** Instead of relying on the server to reflect or persist the script, the attack occurs on the client side. The manipulated script affects how the browser constructs the page dynamically.
  - ***User Interaction Dependency:*** DOM-based XSS often requires specific user actions or interactions to trigger the manipulated script, making it a more subtle threat.
- ***Simple Explanation:*** Picture it as a hidden director's script that influences how the play unfolds, only revealing its impact when certain actions take place on the stage.
- ***Practical Scenario: The Invisible Strings***
  - ***Scenario:*** Imagine a website that dynamically loads user profiles. The URL contains a parameter indicating the username and the website uses JavaScript to display the profile dynamically.
  - ***Manipulation:*** An attacker crafts a link with a manipulated parameter, injecting a script that alters the user's profile.
  - ***Execution:*** When the targeted user clicks the link, the script executes in their browser, modifying their profile in unexpected ways.
- ***Everyday Scenario:*** It is like someone subtly changing the details in your profile by handing you a specific link, and only when you click it, do the changes become apparent.
- ***Consequences: Subtle yet Potent***
  - ***Information Pilferage:*** Much like Stored XSS, DOM-based XSS can result in the pilferage of critical data. However, it achieves this by manipulating how data is represented on the client side.
  - ***Dynamic Content Alteration:*** Perpetrators possess the capability to dynamically modify content, leading to misinformation or a skewed user experience.
- ***Practical Insight***: Picture it as an unseen force delicately adjusting elements on a webpage, shaping what you perceive and potentially filtering information in the process.

Unique features of DOM-based XSS

- ***No server-side storage:*** The script does not get saved on the server like in Stored XSS. It lives within the user-generated content and activates only when that content is loaded. Think of it like a temporary tattoo that disappears with a wash.

- ***Client-side execution:*** The script runs directly in your browser, not on the server. It is like a ninja attacking you inside your own home, using your tools against you.
- ***Exploiting existing functionality:*** The script does not need to be super complex. It can leverage the website's built-in features, like image loading or event handlers, to wreak havoc. Imagine the ninja using your kitchen knife instead of their weapon.

Understanding Sources and Sinks in DOM-Based XSS

In the sphere of DOM-Based XSS, comprehending the roles of sources and sinks is paramount. Let us simplify:

Sources: These are spots within a webpage where attackers can inject malicious JavaScript code into the Document Object Model (DOM). Examples include user input fields, URLs, third-party content, and cookies.

Sinks: These are elements or functions within the webpage that can execute the injected script, thereby enabling malicious actions. Examples encompass properties like innerHTML, event handlers, and functions like eval.

Practical Demonstration: Understanding Sources and Sinks in DOM-Based XSS

1. ***Set Up a Simple HTML Page:*** Create a basic HTML file and define user input fields.
2. ***Implement JavaScript Functions:*** Write functions to handle user input and interact with the DOM.
3. ***Identify Sources and Sinks:*** Identify where malicious code could be injected (sources) and where it could execute (sinks).
4. ***Inject Malicious Payloads:*** Attempt to inject malicious payloads into identified sources.
5. ***Observe Script Execution:*** Check if the injected script executes and triggers unintended actions.
6. ***Mitigation Strategies:*** Experiment with techniques like input validation and output encoding to prevent script execution.
7. ***Test and Iterate:*** Thoroughly test your implementation and refine mitigation strategies based on results.

By following these steps, beginners can gain hands-on experience in identifying and mitigating DOM-Based XSS vulnerabilities. Remember, practice is key to mastering cybersecurity concepts.

Reflected XSS, DOM-based XSS, and Stored XSS: Hands-on

Embark on an interactive exploration of Reflected XSS, DOM-based XSS, and Stored XSS without delving into the world of malicious activities. These hands-on tutorials aim to demystify these vulnerabilities, offering insights without the need for hacky maneuvers.

To undertake these tutorials, we will be utilizing OWASP WebGoat, a purposefully vulnerable application designed for educational purposes. Before we dive in, a crucial disclaimer– refrain from performing these exercises on live websites without explicit permission.

Our first step is to install OWASP WebGoat, setting the stage for a secure and insightful learning experience. Now, let us venture into the world of XSS vulnerabilities responsibly!

Simple Guide to Install OWASP WebGoat on Kali Linux

Step 1: Get WebGoat

Visit the official OWASP WebGoat website => (https://owasp.org/www-project-webgoat/) to grab the standalone JAR file.

Step 2: Terminal Trek

Pop open a terminal in Kali Linux and navigate to where the downloaded file hangs out. Use the `` `cd` `` command to make your way there.

Step 3: Launch WebGoat

Fire up WebGoat with this command in the terminal:

```
java -jar “filename”
```

Do not forget to swap “filename” with the real name of the JAR file you snagged.

Figure 8.5: *Executing WebGoat*

Step 4: Say Hello to WebGoat

Upon the terminal providing pertinent information, including a hyperlink commencing with **"`localhost`",** proceed to initiate your web browser and navigate to the specified link.

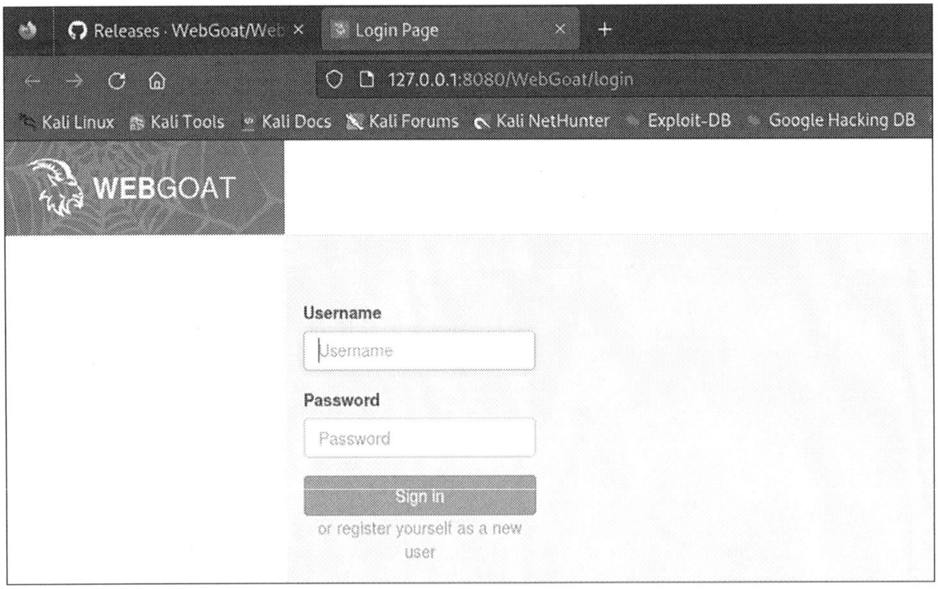

Figure 8.6: *Launching WebGoat*

Step 5: New Kid in Town

On the WebGoat webpage, spot the sign-up option and create a shiny new user account by following the cues.

Pat yourself on the back! You have triumphantly wrangled OWASP WebGoat onto your Kali Linux setup. Time to dive into the world of cybersecurity vulnerabilities in a safe, controlled environment. Always play with WebGoat responsibly, and only on systems where you have the green light for security testing. Happy exploring!

A Beginner's Guide to Learning XSS with OWASP WebGoat

Step 1: Find Your Way to the Injection Lab

Start your journey on the WebGoat homepage by locating and clicking the **"`A3) Injection`"** lab. This special section is your gateway to hands-on exercises that unveil the secrets of injection vulnerabilities.

Step 2: Dive into the XSS Tutorial

Inside the Injection lab, and seek out the **`Cross-Site Scripting (XSS)`** tutorial. Take the plunge by selecting this option to kickstart the tutorial.

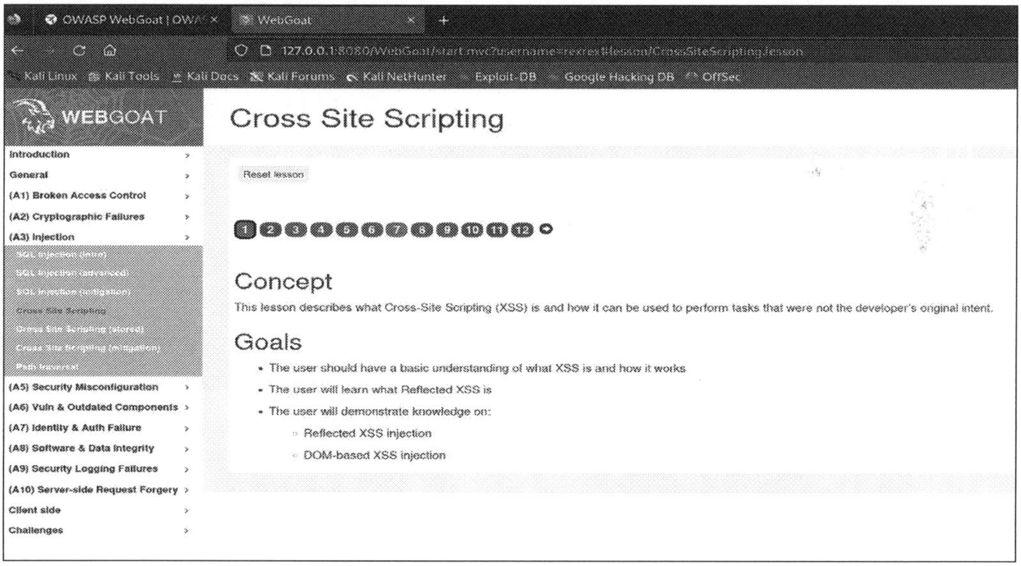

Figure 8.7: *WebGoat XSS Tutorial*

Step 3: Walk Through the Tutorial Steps

Follow the outlined steps in the tutorial with care. Let the tutorial be your guide, leading you through the process of exploiting XSS vulnerabilities within a safe and controlled environment.

Step 4: Unleash Your Skills

As you progress through the tutorial, gain insights into the mechanics of XSS attacks. Experiment with the provided examples and witness firsthand the impact of XSS in a secure space.

Disclaimer: Always keep in mind that this environment is controlled and designed for educational purposes. Avoid attempting these attacks on live websites unless you have explicit permission. This tutorial serves as a tool for learning and practicing security concepts responsibly.

You have completed the necessary steps to delve into XSS within a controlled setting. This hands-on experience will enrich your understanding of XSS vulnerabilities and empower you to explore and learn responsibly on your cybersecurity journey. Happy exploring!

Attack Vectors and Payloads

In our exploration of cybersecurity, this topic thrusts us into the intricate landscape of Attack Vectors and Payloads. Embark on an illuminating journey as we conduct an in-depth analysis of common vectors, dissecting elements like form inputs and URL parameters. Real-life cases will serve as our guiding beacons, shedding light on these attack vectors with practical illustrations. As we dive deeper, unravel the artistry behind crafting malicious payloads, demystifying the process with clear explanations and offering hands-on examples for readers to grasp the intricacies swiftly.

Attack Vectors

In this section, we will delve into the practical aspects of common attack vectors in Cross-Site Scripting (XSS).

- ***Form Inputs:***
    - ***Overview:*** Attackers can sneak malicious scripts into places where users input information, like login or search boxes.
    - ***Example:*** An attacker might enter a harmful script in a username or password field, waiting for the next user to interact with it.
- ***URL Parameters:***
    - ***Overview:*** URLs often carry additional information through parameters. Attackers manipulate these parameters to inject and execute scripts.
    - ***Example:*** A manipulated link, such as

      `example.com/page?parameter=<script>alert('XSS!');</script>`, can inject a script into the URL.

- **Cookies:**
  - ***Overview:*** Cookies store user information. Attackers inject scripts into cookies to potentially steal sensitive data when the cookie is sent to the server.
  - ***Example:*** A malicious script injected into a cookie may attempt to steal a user's session information.
- **DOM *Manipulation:***
  - ***Overview:*** Attackers manipulate the structure of a web page dynamically by injecting scripts that exploit the Document Object Model (DOM).
  - ***Example:*** An attacker injects a script that changes the content of a webpage after it loads, potentially spreading misinformation.
- ***Script-embedded Content:***
  - ***Overview:*** Attackers target user-generated content areas, like comments, by injecting scripts that get displayed to other users.
  - ***Example:*** An attacker leaves a comment containing a script on a blog post, posing a threat to anyone who reads the comment.

Understanding these common attack vectors is essential for securing web applications against XSS threats.

Payloads: Unveiling the Digital Mischief

In this section, we will demystify the process of crafting malicious payloads for Cross-Site Scripting. Think of a payload as the mischievous content attackers sneak into web applications to exploit vulnerabilities.

Understanding Payloads:

- ***Definition of Payload***: A payload is the sneaky content attackers inject into a web application. It is like a secret message they slip in, aiming to trick the application into doing something unintended.
- ***Components of a Payload:***
  - ***Script Tags:*** The basic building blocks. Think of them as the brackets enclosing the mischievous script.
  - ***JavaScript Code:*** The actual mischief-maker. This is where attackers put the commands they want the application to follow.

Types of Payloads:

- ***Stored Payloads:***
  - ***Example:*** An attacker leaves a comment on a blog post containing a payload. When anyone views the comment, the payload executes.

- ***Reflected Payloads:***
    - **Example:** An attacker crafts a manipulated link with a payload. When someone clicks the link, the payload is reflected and executed.
- ***DOM-based Payloads:***
    - **Example:** A payload is injected that manipulates the Document Object Model (DOM), dynamically changing the content of a webpage.

Understanding payloads is crucial because they are the tools attackers use to carry out their mischief. By crafting payloads, attackers can steal user data, spread false information, or even gain unauthorized access to sensitive areas of a web application.

Crafting Payloads: Try It Yourself

In this hands-on section, we will give you a taste of crafting malicious payloads. Do not worry; it is all within the bounds of learning to defend against these tricks. Think of it as a virtual training ground where you get to play both the attacker and the defender.

Creating a Basic Payload:

1. ***Open any Text Editor:*** Whether it is Notepad on Windows, TextEdit on Mac, or any other text editor you are comfortable with.
2. ***Start with Script Tags:*** Type the following to open your script:

    a. `<script>alert('Hello, XSS!');</script>`

3. ***Save as HTML:*** Save this file with an **“.html”** extension, for example, **“mypayload.html.”**
4. ***Open in a Browser:*** Double-click your HTML file and watch what happens when the page loads.

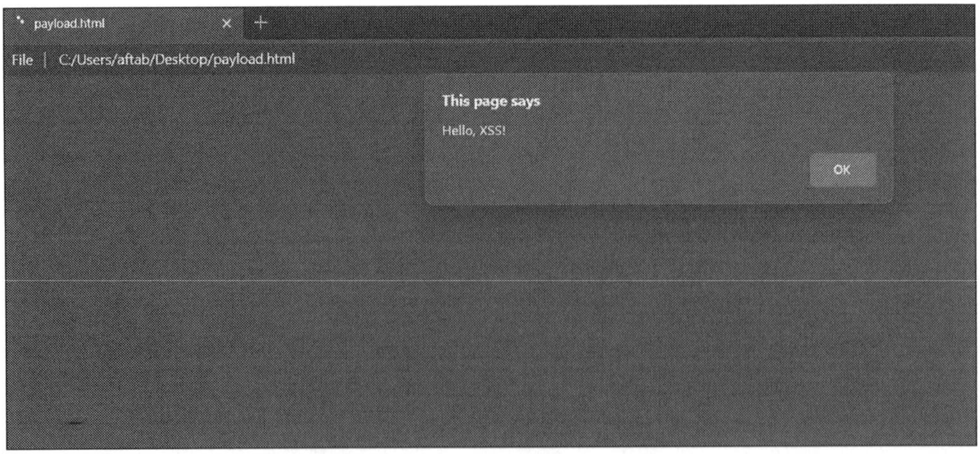

Figure 8.8: *Crafting a Basic Payload*

Crafting a Payload for Redirection:

1. Open your text editor.
2. Enter the following script to redirect users to Hacktify page:
   a. `<script> window.location.href = '<https://hacktify.in>'; </script>`
3. Save the file with a "**`.html`**" extension, such as "**`redirection_payload.html.`**"
4. Double-click the HTML file to open it in a web browser and observe the redirection to the phishing page.

Creating a Payload for Denial of Service (DoS) Attack:

1. Open your preferred text editor.
2. Insert the following script to initiate a DoS attack by continuously reloading the page:
   a. `<script> setInterval(function(){ location.reload(); }, 1000); </script>`
3. Save the file with a "**`.html`**" extension, such as "**`dos_attack.html.`**"
4. Launch the HTML file in a web browser by double-clicking it, and observe how the page continuously reloads, causing denial of service.

Congratulations! You have just completed crafting a basic payload that triggers an alert. Additionally, you have learned how to create payloads for redirection and denial of service (DoS) attacks. Remember, these exercises are for educational purposes only.

Payload Balancing

Payload balancing refers to the practice of crafting malicious payloads in a way that evades detection by security mechanisms while still achieving the intended malicious outcome. In essence, it involves manipulating the payload's structure, format, or content to bypass security filters, such as input validation or intrusion detection systems.

Payload balancing can include techniques like obfuscation, encoding, or fragmenting the payload to disguise its true nature. By carefully balancing the characteristics of the payload, attackers can increase the likelihood of successful exploitation while minimizing the risk of detection.

This technique is commonly employed in various cyber attacks, including Cross-Site Scripting (XSS) and SQL injection, to circumvent security defenses and compromise vulnerable systems.

Practical hands-on

Here is a practical hands-on exercise on payload balancing:

Step 1: Choose a Target. Select a vulnerable web application or create a test environment where you can safely conduct security testing.

Step 2: Identify the Vulnerability. Identify a vulnerability within the target application that can be exploited using Cross-Site Scripting (XSS). This could be a reflected or stored XSS vulnerability.

Step 3: Craft a Basic Payload. Start by crafting a basic payload to exploit the XSS vulnerability. For example, you could create a payload that pops up an alert box with a simple message, such as:

```
<script>alert('XSS');</script>
```

Step 4: Test the Payload. Inject the payload into the vulnerable parameter of the target application and observe its behavior. Verify whether the payload executes successfully and triggers the intended action, such as displaying an alert box.

Step 5: Optimize the Payload. Once you have confirmed that the basic payload works, focus on optimizing it to evade detection by security measures. Experiment with techniques such as obfuscation, encoding, or splitting the payload into smaller fragments.

For example, you could encode the payload using JavaScript functions like **`encodeURIComponent()`** or **`btoa()`**:

```
<script>eval(atob('c3RyaW5nPWZ1bmN0aW9uKCl7Y29uc29sZS5sb2coJ1h-
TUycpO30='));</script>
```

Step 6: Test the Optimized Payload. Inject the optimized payload into the target application and assess whether it still successfully executes the desired action while evading detection by security controls.

Step 7: Refine and Iterate. Continue refining your payload based on the results of your testing. Iterate through different techniques and combinations until you find a balance between effectiveness and stealthiness.

By following these steps, you can gain practical experience in payload balancing and better understand how attackers optimize their payloads to maximize their impact while minimizing the risk of detection.

Detection of XSS Vulnerabilities

In this section, we will explore the world of detecting Cross-Site Scripting (XSS) vulnerabilities–a bit like shining a flashlight to uncover hidden dangers in your web applications.

Understanding XSS Detection:

- ***Manual Inspection:***
  - ***Overview:*** Imagine you are inspecting a house for security vulnerabilities. Similarly, manual inspection involves scrutinizing the source code of a web application to identify potential XSS threats.
  - ***Implementation***: Right-click a webpage, select **`"Inspect"`** (or **`"Inspect Element"`**), and explore the **`"Elements"`** and **`"Console"`** tabs. Look for suspicious script injections in the HTML source code.
- ***Automated Scanning Tools:***
  - ***Overview:*** Think of these tools as digital assistants that help you inspect the entire neighborhood instead of going house by house. Automated scanners like OWASP ZAP or Acunetix can efficiently identify XSS vulnerabilities across a web application.
  - ***Implementation:*** Install an automated scanning tool, provide the target URL, and let the tool analyze the application for potential XSS weaknesses.
- ***Browser Extensions:***
  - ***Overview:*** Picture this like having a security app on your phone that warns you about potential threats. Browser extensions like XSStrike or AlertSite Browser Recorder can highlight XSS vulnerabilities as you browse.
  - ***Implementation***: Install the extension, navigate through web pages, and pay attention to any alerts or warnings regarding potential XSS issues.
- ***Understanding Exploitation:***
  - ***Overview:*** Now that you have identified the weak spots, it is time to fix them. Think of it as patching up holes in your house to prevent burglars from sneaking in.
  - ***Implementation***: If you find an XSS vulnerability, report it to the website owner or developer. They can implement fixes such as input validation or output encoding to secure the application.

Detecting XSS vulnerabilities is akin to being a vigilant security guard, using tools and techniques to identify potential threats. Once you uncover a vulnerability, it is like finding a crack in the wall–you patch it up to ensure the security of your digital space.

Mitigation and Best Practices

In this section, we will explore the importance of secure coding practices and introduce the concept of security frameworks–think of them as the blueprint for building fortified digital fortresses.

Importance of Secure Coding Practices:

- ***Building a Strong Foundation:***
    - ***Overview:*** Imagine constructing a house on solid ground rather than shaky terrain. Secure coding practices provide a robust foundation for web applications, minimizing vulnerabilities like Cross-Site Scripting (XSS).
    - **Example:** Validating user input, using parameterized queries in databases, and escaping output is like using quality building materials to ensure the integrity of your digital structure.
- ***User Input Validation:***
    - ***Overview:*** Think of this as thoroughly inspecting items before allowing them into your house. Validate user input to ensure it meets expected criteria, preventing malicious content from entering.
    - **Example:** If your application expects a numerical input, validate that the user's input is indeed a number and not a script.
- ***Output Encoding:***
    - ***Overview***: Similar to presenting information in a language everyone understands. Encode output to render potentially harmful content harmless, protecting users from script execution.
    - **Example:** Convert special characters like < to their HTML entities (**<**) to prevent them from being interpreted as part of a script.

Overview of Security Frameworks:

- ***Concept of Security Frameworks***
    - ***Overview:*** Picture a comprehensive set of guidelines and tools–a security framework is like having a well-thought-out plan and a set of specialized tools to safeguard your digital space.
- ***Popular Security Frameworks:***
    - **Example:** OWASP (Open Web Application Security Project) is a widely recognized security framework. It provides detailed documentation, tools, and best practices to help developers build secure applications.
- ***Integrated Development Environments (IDEs):***
    - ***Overview:*** Think of IDEs as your assistants–they highlight potential security issues and suggest improvements in real time as you write code.

   - **Example:** Visual Studio Code with security extensions can be compared to having a vigilant assistant pointing out security concerns while you code.

Securing web applications is akin to building a fortress with solid walls and vigilant guards. Adopting secure coding practices and leveraging security frameworks is like implementing the best architectural and defense strategies to protect your digital kingdom.

Input Validation and Sanitization: Fortifying Your Web Defenses

In this section, we will explore the essential practices of input validation and sanitization–imagine them as the gatekeepers that thoroughly inspect and cleanse every item entering your digital fortress. Let us unravel these concepts in simple, everyday language.

Best Practices for Input Handling:

- ***Imagine a Security Checkpoint:***
   - ***Overview:*** Picture a checkpoint at the entrance of your digital kingdom. Input validation is like the meticulous inspection every item undergoes before being allowed in.
- ***Define Strict Input Criteria:***
   - ***Overview:*** Set clear rules for what constitutes acceptable input. It is akin to specifying the types of items permitted through the security checkpoint.
   - **Example:** If your application expects a numerical age, validate that the input consists only of numbers.
- ***Regular Expressions as Guards:***
   - ***Overview:*** Think of regular expressions as the security guards with a keen eye for specific patterns. They help ensure that input adheres to the defined criteria.
   - ***Example:*** Use a regular expression like `\\d{3}-\\d{2}-\\d{4}` to validate a Social Security Number in the format XXX-XX-XXXX.

Examples of Effective Validation and Sanitization Techniques:

- ***Numeric Input Validation:***
   - ***Overview:*** Ensuring only numbers pass through the checkpoint. It is like allowing only passengers and not unauthorized cargo.

- **Example Code (JavaScript):**

```
function validateAge(age) {
      return /^\\\\d+$/.test(age);
}
```

- ***Email Address Validation:***
  - ***Overview:*** Verifying that the input follows the email format. It is similar to allowing only properly labeled packages.
  - **Example Code (Python):**

```
import re
def validate_email(email):
      return bool(re.match(r'^\\S+@\\S+\\.\\S+$', email))
```

- **HTML *Sanitization:***
  - ***Overview:*** Cleansing input to remove potentially harmful HTML content. It is like inspecting packages to ensure they do not contain hidden threats.
  - **Example Code (PHP):**

```
$input = '<script>alert("XSS!");</script>';
$clean_input = filter_var($input, FILTER_SANITIZE_STRING);
```

Implementing input validation and sanitization is akin to having diligent gatekeepers at the entrance of your web application. By defining strict criteria and thoroughly inspecting incoming data, you strengthen the defenses of your digital fortress against potential attacks.

Real-world Case Studies of Notable XSS Attacks

In this section, we will embark on a journey through real-world case studies of Cross-Site Scripting (XSS) attacks—imagine it as exploring the mysteries behind significant digital intrigues. Let us unravel these incidents in simple, everyday language and draw valuable lessons for safeguarding your web applications.

- ***Google Zero-Day Exploited via Zimbra* (2023):**
  - ***Attack type:*** Stored XSS
  - **Impact:** Government organizations compromised, potential data breaches
  - **Details:** Attackers exploited a zero-day vulnerability in Zimbra collaboration software, injecting malicious scripts into user accounts. This enabled them to steal sensitive information and potentially escalate privileges for further

attacks. This case emphasizes the criticality of patching vulnerabilities promptly, especially in critical infrastructure.

- **Lesson:** Patching vulnerabilities promptly, especially in critical infrastructure, is crucial to prevent exploitation. Zero-day vulnerabilities pose a significant risk, and rapid response is essential.

- ***Roundcube Zero-Day Targets European Government Servers* (2023):**
  - ***Attack type:*** Stored XSS
  - ***Impact:*** Compromise of government email servers, potential data leaks
  - **Details:** A zero-day vulnerability was discovered in Roundcube webmail, allowing attackers to inject malicious code into the email accounts of European government officials. This vulnerability posed serious risks, including facilitating phishing attempts, data exfiltration, or further compromise of sensitive information. This incident underscores the critical importance of implementing robust security measures within government systems and the inherent dangers associated with zero-day exploits.
  - **Lesson:** It is imperative to prioritize the implementation of robust security measures within government systems and promptly patch known vulnerabilities to minimize the potential attack surface for zero-day exploits.

- ***WordPress Plugin Flaw Exposes Millions to Takeover* (2023):**
  - ***Attack type:*** Reflected XSS
  - ***Impact:*** Millions of WordPress websites vulnerable, potential account hijacking
  - **Details:** A critical vulnerability in the popular **"`Ninja Forms`"** plugin allowed attackers to inject malicious scripts into contact forms. This could be used to steal user information, redirect visitors to phishing sites, or even take over entire websites. This case emphasizes the importance of using secure and updated plugins, especially for content management systems like WordPress.
  - **Lesson:** Use secure and updated plugins, especially for popular content management systems like WordPress. Regularly scan and update plugins to address potential vulnerabilities.

- ***Microsoft Teams Bug Enables Data Theft* (2023):**
  - ***Attack type:*** Reflected XSS
  - ***Impact:*** Potential unauthorized access to user data, including conversations and files
  - **Details:** An XSS vulnerability affecting Microsoft Teams' whiteboard

feature was exploited by attackers to inject malicious scripts when users engaged with the whiteboard. This exploitation could have facilitated the theft of sensitive information such as chat logs and files. This incident underscores the critical importance of deploying secure collaboration tools and promoting vigilant user practices when interacting with external content.

- **Lesson:** It is essential to deploy and maintain secure collaboration tools like Microsoft Teams and to educate users on the importance of exercising caution when interacting with external content. Users should be encouraged to refrain from clicking on suspicious links or engaging with untrusted elements to mitigate the risk of similar vulnerabilities being exploited in the future.

- ***Hackers Steal Data From Millions Using SQL Injection and XSS (2023):***
  - ***Attack type:*** Combined SQL injection and XSS
  - ***Impact:*** Over 2 million users affected, data breaches across multiple platforms
  - **Details:** Attackers used a combination of SQL injection and XSS vulnerabilities in various websites to steal user information like usernames, passwords, and email addresses. This demonstrates how attackers can chain multiple vulnerabilities for maximum impact and the importance of layered security measures.
  - **Lesson:** Implement layered security measures to mitigate the combined impact of multiple vulnerabilities. Address both SQL injection and XSS vulnerabilities to reduce the risk of data breaches.

These recent cases showcase the ongoing threat of XSS and the need for continuous vigilance. Remember:

- **Stay updated on vulnerabilities and patch promptly.**
- **Implement secure coding practices and input validation.**
- **Use secure plugins and content management systems.**
- **Educate users about phishing and suspicious links.**
- **Monitor systems for suspicious activity and potential breaches.**

By combining these strategies, organizations can significantly reduce the risk of XSS attacks and protect their users' data.

Conclusion

As we wrap up our journey through the intricacies of **Cross-Site Scripting (XSS),** you have traversed the digital landscape, uncovering the nuances of XSS types, understanding attack vectors, and mastering mitigation strategies. Your journey through stored, reflected, and DOM-based XSS has been a quest for digital resilience.

Hats off to your commitment! Your grasp of XSS intricacies and adoption of best practices showcase a commendable dedication to securing the digital frontier. In our next chapter, **Broken Access Control**, we will delve into the world of ensuring judicious access—a crucial aspect in the dynamic world of cybersecurity.

As the digital odyssey continues, your pursuit of knowledge and vigilance against cyber threats set you on a path of cybersecurity mastery. Stay engaged, stay curious, and anticipate more revelations in the chapters ahead. Bravo on your accomplishments, and let the spirit of digital defense guide you forward!

CHAPTER 9
Broken Access Control

Introduction

Embark on a cybersecurity journey with our chapter, **Broken Access Control,** where we demystify web application security. Let us explore Insecure Direct Object Reference (IDOR), Privilege Escalation, and Access Control Vulnerabilities in simple terms. We will learn to identify and fortify against digital vulnerabilities, understand Secure Access Control Design, and gain insights from real-world case studies in Access Control Failures.

Building on our previous discussion of Cross-Site Scripting (XSS), this chapter offers practical insights to enhance your cybersecurity expertise, making it a must-read for anyone keen on securing the digital frontier.

Structure

In this chapter, we will cover the following topics:

- Broken Access Control
- Insecure Direct Object Reference (IDOR)
- Privilege Escalation: Vertical and Horizontal
- Access Control Vulnerabilities
- Identifying and Exploiting Vulnerabilities
- Secure Access Control Design
- Case Studies in Access Control Failures

Broken Access Control: An Exploitable Vulnerability

Web applications implement access control mechanisms to restrict user access to resources based on their authorized privileges. These mechanisms typically involve verifying user identity and permissions before granting access to specific data, functions, or functionalities.

Broken Access Control (BAC) occurs when the mechanisms designed to enforce access restrictions fail, opening the door for unauthorized users to reach resources beyond their intended permissions. This vulnerability introduces several security risks, including:

- ***Data Breaches:*** Unwanted access to sensitive information, like user records, financial data, or confidential business documents.
- ***Privilege Escalation:*** Exploiting vulnerabilities to gain higher-level access within the application, potentially seizing control of administrative functions.
- ***Resource Manipulation:*** Unauthorized modification or deletion of application data, disrupting functionality and causing service interruptions.
- ***Malicious Code Injection:*** BAC empowers attackers to insert harmful scripts, such as Cross-Site Scripting (XSS) payloads, into the application. This compromises user sessions and facilitates the theft of sensitive information.

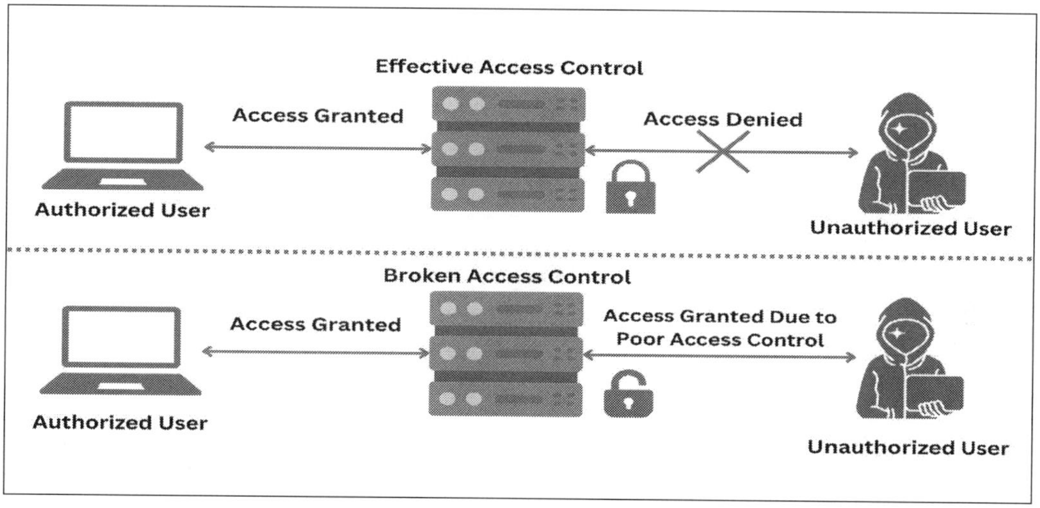

Figure 9.1: *Effective versus Broken Access Control*

Commonly exploited BAC vulnerabilities include:

- ***Insecure direct object references* (IDOR):** Applications relying on user-controlled identifiers to access resources can be vulnerable to tampering, allowing unauthorized access.
- ***Missing authorization checks:*** Applications fail to implement proper authorization checks before granting access to sensitive resources.
- ***Broken session management:*** Weak session management practices can allow attackers to steal or hijack user sessions, gaining unauthorized access.

- ***Insecure API endpoints:*** Publicly accessible API endpoints without proper authorization checks can be exploited by attackers to access internal data and functionalities.

Avoiding Broken Access Control (BAC) Risks:

- ***Embrace the principle of least privilege:*** Provide users with the fewest permissions necessary for their designated tasks.
- ***Deploy robust authentication and authorization methods:*** Utilize secure password hashing algorithms and strong access control frameworks.
- ***Thoroughly validate user input:*** Scrutinize and validate all data provided by users to prevent manipulation of identifiers and other crucial parameters.
- ***Conduct routine security assessments:*** Regularly inspect applications for vulnerabilities, swiftly addressing and remedying any issues.
- ***Fortify API endpoints:*** Implement robust authentication and authorization protocols for all API endpoints.

By comprehending the nuances of BAC vulnerabilities and integrating these best practices, developers can construct web applications with enhanced security, shielding sensitive data and fostering user trust.

Broken Access Control: Unveiling the Myths and Misconceptions

Imagine your website as a treasure chest overflowing with valuable information. Access control acts as the lock, safeguarding your treasures and ensuring only authorized individuals can access them. However, myths and misconceptions often surround this crucial security mechanism. Let us break down some common misconceptions and shed light on the truth:

Myth 1: Access control is only important for large websites.

Reality: Every website, regardless of size, stores valuable information. Whether it is user data, financial records, or even internal documents, all information deserves protection. Broken access control can expose any website, big or small, to serious vulnerabilities.

Myth 2: Implementing access control is complex and expensive.

Reality: While advanced access control solutions exist, basic implementations are accessible and affordable. Open-source tools, secure coding practices, and user education can go a long way in strengthening your website's defenses.

Myth 3: Secure passwords are enough to prevent unauthorized access.

Reality: While strong passwords are essential, they are just one piece of the puzzle. Even the strongest password can become useless if access control mechanisms are flawed. A layered approach combining passwords with secure access controls provides comprehensive protection.

Myth 4: Broken access control only affects sensitive data.

Reality: Attackers often exploit vulnerabilities to gain initial access and then navigate through the website, potentially reaching and manipulating even seemingly harmless data. Comprehensive access control ensures that all information, regardless of perceived sensitivity, is protected.

Myth 5: Access control is a one-time setup.

Reality: Websites evolve, and so should their access controls. Regularly reviewing user permissions, updating security protocols, and adapting to new threats are crucial for maintaining a robust defense.

Remember, broken access control is not just a technical issue; it threatens your website's security and reputation. By understanding these misconceptions and implementing effective access control measures, you can secure your website and safeguard the information entrusted to you.

Insecure Direct Object Reference

In the virtual corridors of web security, Insecure Direct Object Reference (IDOR) acts as a sneaky infiltrator, exploiting loopholes that can compromise sensitive data. Imagine you are in a library, and the librarian steps away, leaving the bookshelves unguarded. IDOR is akin to someone peeking at restricted books on the shelves they should not access. Now, let us break it down:

Definition: IDOR occurs when an attacker can access, modify, or delete objects (like files or database records) directly, bypassing proper authorization processes. It is like having a secret passage in the library that allows unauthorized individuals to grab books they are not supposed to.

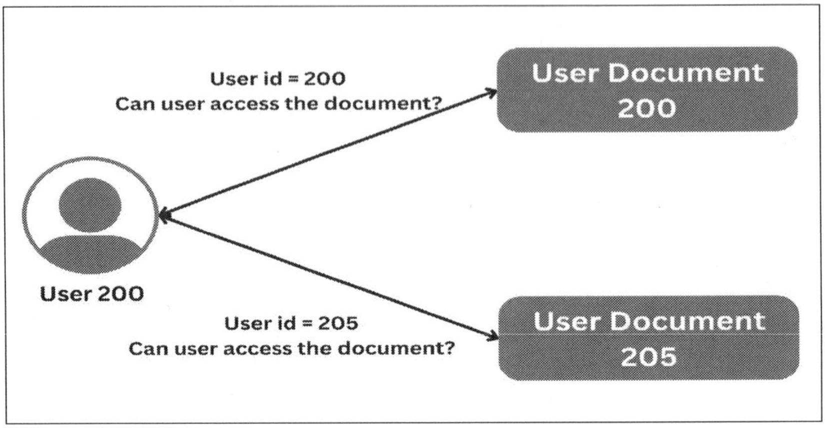

Figure 9.2: *IDOR Vulnerability*

Think of it like this:

- You are a user with limited access, authorized to view only books with IDs 1 to 100.
- The library uses an insecure system where you can access any book by simply typing its ID in the URL.
- By changing the URL from **`book/10`** to **`book/1001`,** you can access a restricted book even though you are not authorized.

Significance: The significance lies in the potential havoc an attacker can wreak. Consider a scenario where a user can change the URL in their browser and access another user's private information—that is IDOR in action. The consequences can range from unauthorized access to critical data to privacy breaches on a significant scale.

Real-world Instances of IDOR Vulnerabilities

- **In 2018, Instagram fell victim to an IDOR vulnerability.** Exploiting manipulated user IDs, attackers accessed private photos and videos.
- **In 2020, a widely used e-commerce platform encountered an IDOR vulnerability.** By altering order IDs, attackers could access and pilfer other customers' purchase details.
- **In 2021, a healthcare provider inadvertently exposed patient records through an IDOR vulnerability.** Manipulating patient IDs in the URL granted attackers access to specific patient data.

Understanding IDOR is akin to discovering hidden passages in a library and ensuring they are securely sealed. This chapter arms you with the tools to detect and thwart these digital infiltrations, ensuring that your web applications stand resilient against the subtle yet potent threat of Insecure Direct Object Reference (IDOR).

Detecting IDOR Vulnerabilities: Tools and Techniques

Now that we have exposed the concept of Insecure Direct Object Reference (IDOR) as a sneak peek into unauthorized territories, let us equip you with the detective tools and techniques to identify and seal these digital cracks.

Tools for Detecting IDOR Vulnerabilities:

- ***Burp Suite:***
  - ***Description:*** Think of Burp Suite as your cybersecurity magnifying glass. This tool intercepts and examines web traffic, helping you spot anomalies that could indicate IDOR vulnerabilities.
  - ***How to Use:*** Set up Burp Suite as a proxy, navigate through your application, and analyze requests and responses for unexpected manipulations.
- **ZAP (*Zed Attack Proxy*):**
  - ***Description:*** ZAP is your digital detective partner, continuously scanning your web application for potential security issues, including IDOR vulnerabilities.
  - ***How to Use:*** Launch ZAP, configure it in your application and let it crawl through the pages, identifying instances where objects might be accessed directly.

Techniques for Detecting IDOR Vulnerabilities:

- ***Change Parameter Values:***
  - ***Description:*** Like turning the dial on a safe, manipulating parameters in URLs or requests can reveal hidden treasures (or vulnerabilities).
  - ***How to Use:*** Try changing numeric or alphanumeric values in URLs to access objects that might not be within your authorized scope.
- ***Horizontal and Vertical Testing:***
  - ***Description:*** This is like systematically searching every shelf in the library. Horizontal testing explores different objects at the same level, while vertical testing digs deeper into specific object hierarchies.
  - ***How to Use:*** Systematically test different IDs across various levels to ensure all possible pathways are secure.
- ***Use of Automated Scanners:***
  - ***Description:*** Think of automated scanners as your tireless assistants. They systematically scan your application for potential vulnerabilities, including IDOR.

 - ***How to Use:*** Deploy reputable automated scanners that incorporate IDOR checks and analyze the results for potential weaknesses.

Let's put these tools into action:

- ***Scenario:*** Imagine a shopping cart application where users can add items by clicking an **"Add to Cart"** button. The button link contains the product ID.
- ***Potential Vulnerability:*** If the application uses the product ID directly to add the item to the cart without verifying user permissions, an attacker could add products belonging to other users.
- ***Detection:*** Using fuzz testing, we could try adding invalid product IDs or IDs belonging to other users. If the application allows this, it indicates an IDOR vulnerability.

Beyond Detection:

Detecting IDOR is only the first step. To truly secure your application, you must:

- ***Implement access control checks:*** Verify user permissions before granting access to any object.
- ***Sanitize and validate user input:*** Ensure that user-provided data does not contain malicious code or manipulation attempts.
- ***Perform regular security assessments:*** Continuously scan your application for vulnerabilities and implement timely remediation measures.

By actively detecting and mitigating IDOR vulnerabilities, you can build a robust defense against unauthorized access and protect your valuable assets. Remember, the responsibility of securing your web application lies in your hands.

Privilege Escalation: Vertical and Horizontal

In the intricate landscape of cybersecurity, the concept of privilege escalation acts as both a labyrinth and a key to fortified gates. Imagine it as a journey where digital explorers seek to ascend, gaining higher levels of access within a system. Join us as we delve into the dynamic spheres of Vertical and Horizontal Privilege Escalation–an exploration that unveils the art of climbing the access ladder and the strategies employed by both defenders and adversaries. Let us ascend together the captivating world of privilege escalation.

Climbing the Ladder: Understanding Vertical Privilege Escalation

Imagine a castle with various levels of access, each requiring specific keys. A regular visitor can only access the ground floor, while guards with higher keys can access specific rooms or even the king's chambers. Similarly, in the world of web applications, access is controlled by privileges. Vertical Privilege Escalation (VPE) is like a sneaky thief stealing a guard's key to gain unauthorized access to higher levels.

Understanding Vertical Privilege Escalation (VPE)

VPE occurs when an attacker, initially possessing limited access, exploits vulnerabilities to gain higher privileges within an application. This can involve accessing restricted data, modifying sensitive information, or even taking complete control of the system.

Instances of VPE:

Attackers may exploit various vulnerabilities to achieve VPE, including:

- ***Insecure Direct Object References (IDOR):*** By manipulating object references, attackers can access resources they should not be able to, potentially leading to higher privileges.
- ***Missing authorization checks:*** Applications that lack proper authorization checks create opportunities for attackers to bypass access controls and gain elevated privileges.
- ***Vulnerable APIs:*** Publicly accessible APIs without proper authentication and authorization can be exploited by attackers to gain unauthorized access to internal resources and escalate their privileges.
- ***Exploiting software vulnerabilities:*** Attackers may exploit vulnerabilities in software libraries or frameworks used by the application to gain code execution and potentially elevate their privileges.

Consequences of VPE:

VPE can have severe consequences, including:

- ***Data breaches:*** Attackers with higher privileges can access sensitive data like user records, financial information, or confidential business documents.
- ***System compromise:*** Gaining administrative access can allow attackers to install malware, manipulate data, or even disable security controls.
- ***Disruptions and outages:*** Attackers can disrupt service delivery, cause outages, and negatively impact user experience.

Guarding Against Vertical Privilege Escalation (VPE):

Here are effective strategies to safeguard against VPE:

- ***Embrace the principle of least privilege:*** Provide users with only the minimum permissions essential for their tasks.
- ***Deploy robust authentication and authorization methods:*** Utilize strong password hashing algorithms and comprehensive access control frameworks.

- ***Conduct routine security assessments:*** Regularly examine applications for vulnerabilities, promptly applying remedial actions.
- ***Fortify* APIs:** Implement robust authentication and authorization protocols for all API endpoints.
- ***Keep software libraries and frameworks up to date:*** Ensure all software components are promptly updated to the latest versions, addressing known vulnerabilities.

By grasping VPE intricacies and integrating suitable security measures, you can thwart attackers attempting to ascend the privilege ladder, thus shielding your web applications from unauthorized access and potential data breaches.

Moving Sideways: Unveiling Horizontal Privilege Escalation

Imagine a bank where employees have access to specific accounts based on their roles. A teller can access basic account information, while a loan officer can modify loan details. In the horizon of web applications, horizontal privilege escalation (HPE) occurs when an attacker gains access to the same level of privileges as another user, but for a different account.

Understanding Horizontal Privilege Escalation (HPE)

In contrast to vertical privilege escalation, where the aim is to elevate privileges, Horizontal Privilege Escalation (HPE) focuses on gaining access at the same privilege level as another user. This typically involves exploiting weaknesses in access control mechanisms.

Instances of HPE:

Attackers may exploit various vulnerabilities to achieve HPE, including:

- Unauthorized access to a user's session cookies, enabling entry into their account.
- Exploiting vulnerabilities in an online forum to access other users' profile information.
- Manipulating user IDs or other identifiers to gain access to accounts beyond the intended scope.

Consequences of HPE:

While HPE may not grant the attacker the same level of power as gaining administrator access, it can still have significant consequences, including:

- ***Identity theft:*** Attackers can use stolen login credentials to access sensitive information, make unauthorized transactions, or damage the victim's reputation.
- ***Data breaches:*** Attackers can access and potentially steal sensitive data belonging to multiple users.
- ***Spam and phishing attacks:*** Gaining access to multiple accounts allows attackers to spread spam messages or launch phishing attacks on a larger scale.

Preventing HPE:

Several measures can help prevent HPE:

- ***Implement strong session management:*** Utilize secure session tokens, enforce session timeouts, and invalidate sessions on logout or inactivity.
- ***Employ secure authentication mechanisms:*** Use multi-factor authentication, strong password hashing algorithms, and secure login protocols.
- ***Validate and sanitize user input:*** Sanitize user-provided data to prevent manipulation of identifiers and other sensitive information.
- ***Perform regular security audits:*** Regularly assess applications for vulnerabilities and implement timely remediation measures.
- ***Educate users:*** Train users to be aware of phishing attacks, create strong passwords, and avoid sharing login credentials.

By understanding HPE and implementing appropriate security measures, you can prevent attackers from moving sideways within your application and protect your users' data and privacy. Remember, a secure web application is one where everyone feels safe and their information remains protected.

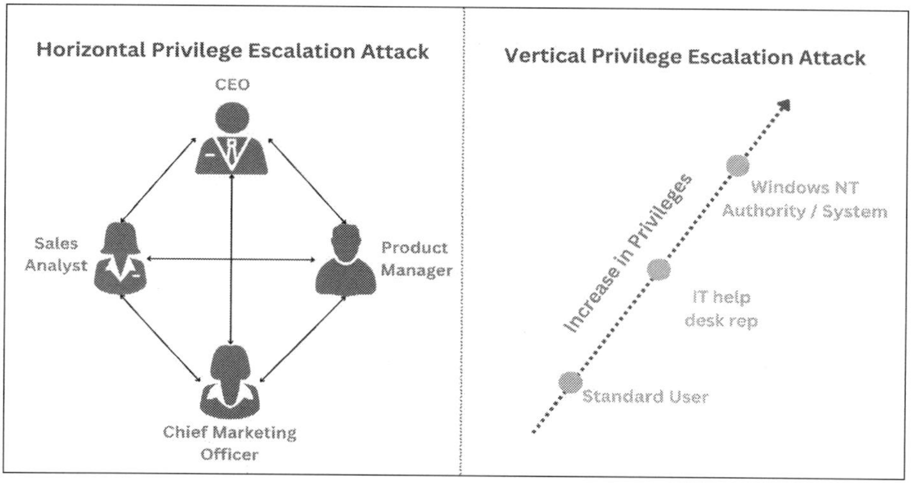

Figure 9.3: *HPE versus VPE Attack*

Access Control Vulnerabilities

Embark on a journey into the field of Access Control Vulnerabilities, where the digital gates and barriers might harbor unseen gaps. Picture your web application's access control like a maze with potential shortcuts that unauthorized individuals can exploit. In simple terms, let us explore the common weaknesses that, if overlooked, could compromise the sanctity of your digital fortress.

Overview of Various Access Control Vulnerabilities:

- ***Insufficient Authentication:***
  - **Description:** Weak or inadequate methods of verifying user identities, akin to a guard accepting any ID without scrutiny.
  - **Risk:** Allows unauthorized individuals to gain access to restricted areas.
  - **Best Practice:** Implement robust authentication methods such as multi-factor authentication (MFA) or strong password policies. Utilize secure authentication protocols like OAuth or OpenID Connect. Regularly audit user accounts and deactivate inactive or suspicious accounts.
- ***Overly Permissive Access Controls:***
  - **Description:** Assigning broader permissions than necessary, like giving every guest a master key to all rooms.
  - **Risk:** Opens the door for users to access functionalities or data beyond their intended scope.
  - **Best Practice:** Adhere to the principle of least privilege (PoLP), providing users with the minimum permissions necessary for their tasks. Implement role-based access control (RBAC) or attribute-based access control (ABAC) to proficiently handle permissions. Consistently assess and revise access control lists to guarantee alignment with organizational needs.
- ***Insecure Direct Object Reference (IDOR):***
  - **Description:** Allowing users to directly access objects, such as files or database records, without proper authorization checks.
  - **Risk:** Enables unauthorized viewing, modification, or deletion of sensitive data.
  - **Best Practice:** Implement proper authorization checks at the object level to validate user access rights before serving data. Utilize indirect object references or obfuscated identifiers to prevent direct object referencing. Conduct thorough security testing, including vulnerability scanning and penetration testing, to identify and remediate IDOR vulnerabilities.

- ***Inadequate Session Management:***
  - **Description:** Poor handling of user sessions, similar to a hotel issuing keys without verifying identities.
  - **Risk:** Facilitates session hijacking, leading to unauthorized access to or manipulation of user sessions.
  - **Best Practice:** Implement secure session management practices, including using unique session identifiers, encrypting session data, and employing session expiration mechanisms. Implement secure cookie attributes such as HTTPOnly, Secure, and SameSite. Regularly review and monitor active sessions to detect and mitigate suspicious activities.
- ***Missing Function-Level Access Controls:***
  - **Description:** Failing to implement proper checks on function-level access, like a concert attendee accessing backstage without proper credentials.
  - **Risk:** Allows users to execute functions or actions they should not have permission to perform.
  - **Best Practice:** Implement access controls at the function level to enforce granular permissions. Utilize authorization frameworks or middleware to enforce access control rules consistently across all application functions. Regularly review and update access control configurations to align with evolving business requirements and security best practices.

Implementing these recommended practices can enhance your web application's access control systems while mitigating the risks associated with typical access control vulnerabilities.

Implications of Weak Access Controls: Unraveling the Domino Effect

Access controls act as the silent guardians of our digital vaults, protecting sensitive data and functionalities. However, just like cracks in a vault's foundation, weaknesses in access control mechanisms can trigger a domino effect, leading to devastating consequences.

Understanding the Potential Consequences:

- ***Data Integrity Compromised:***
  - **Description:** Weak access controls can allow unauthorized individuals to manipulate or tamper with your data, akin to a forger altering the contents of a sealed envelope.
  - **Case Study:** In 2023, a healthcare provider fell victim to a data breach due to misconfigured access controls. Attackers accessed and manipulated

medical records, injecting false diagnoses and altering medication prescriptions. This not only violated patient privacy but also posed serious health risks.

   - ***Impact:*** Compromised data integrity leads to unreliable information, potentially resulting in flawed decisions, financial losses, and reputational damage.

- ***Confidentiality Breaches:***
   - ***Description:*** When access controls fail, sensitive information becomes vulnerable, similar to confidential files left in an unlocked cabinet.
   - ***Case Study:*** In 2022, a social media platform faced regulatory fines due to weak access controls allowing unauthorized employees to access user data, including private messages and location information. This incident sparked user outrage and raised concerns about data privacy violations.
   - ***Impact:*** Confidentiality breaches expose individuals to identity theft, financial fraud, and reputational harm. Companies face regulatory fines, lawsuits, and loss of customer trust.
- ***Availability Undermined:***
   - ***Description:*** Access control weaknesses can lead to service disruptions, akin to letting vandals into a museum to wreak havoc on exhibits.
   - ***Case Study:*** In 2021, a ransomware attack targeted a critical infrastructure provider, exploiting weak access controls in their systems. Attackers encrypted crucial data, disrupting operations and causing widespread power outages.
   - ***Impact:*** Availability disruptions can bring businesses to a standstill, impacting productivity, financial losses, and public safety concerns.

The Domino Effect:

Weak access control can have a domino effect, jeopardizing various aspects of your web application:

- ***Loss of trust:*** When users' data is compromised or exposed, it erodes trust in your application and can damage your reputation.
- ***Regulatory compliance issues:*** Failure to comply with data privacy regulations, like GDPR, can lead to hefty fines and legal repercussions.
- ***Business disruptions:*** Data breaches, service outages, and system disruptions can lead to financial losses and impact your business operations.

Crafting a Secure Path Forward:

To counter these threats and safeguard your web application, consider the following measures:

- ***Establish a strong access control framework:*** Implement proven frameworks like RBAC (Role-Based Access Control) to efficiently manage user permissions.
- ***Regularly evaluate your access control system:*** Perform security audits, penetration testing, and code reviews to detect and rectify potential vulnerabilities.
- ***Stay aware of emerging threats:*** Keep yourself updated on the latest security risks and vulnerabilities associated with access control, ensuring your defenses are always current.
- ***Educate your team:*** Provide training for developers, administrators, and users on secure coding practices, access control best practices, and fostering cybersecurity awareness.

Organizations may reduce the risk of catastrophic repercussions and protect their precious digital assets by emphasizing strong access restrictions and fostering a security-conscious culture.

Identifying and Exploiting Vulnerabilities

Embark on a journey where we demystify the art of identifying and exploiting common access control vulnerabilities. Think of it as unraveling the secrets of a puzzle—understanding the weak points and learning how adversaries might exploit them. In simple steps, we will walk you through scenarios resembling a digital treasure hunt, revealing potential exploits that could compromise your web application's security.

Interactive Learning: Exposing the Mysteries of Broken Access Control

Are you prepared to challenge your investigative prowess and grasp the art of identifying and exploiting access control vulnerabilities? Get ready for an engaging journey as we dive into a hands-on training session, providing practical experience within a secure and supervised environment.

Note: *This training module is designed for educational purposes exclusively and must never be executed on live systems without appropriate authorization. Always uphold ethical hacking principles and prioritize the responsible disclosure of any vulnerabilities discovered.*

Tools of the Trade: For our exercises, we will utilize some basic tools commonly used by security researchers:

- ***Web browser with developer tools:*** Inspect network requests, analyze responses, and manipulate parameters to test for vulnerabilities.

- ***Proxy tool:*** Intercept and modify network traffic to gain deeper insights into application behavior.
- ***Fuzzing tools:*** Automatically generate and inject various inputs into web applications to explore potential attack vectors.

Exercise 1: Insecure Direct Object References (IDOR):

- ***Scenario:*** Imagine a shopping cart application where users add items by clicking an **"`Add to Cart`"** button. The button link includes the product ID.
- ***Potential vulnerability:*** If the application uses the product ID directly to add the item to the cart without verifying user permissions, an attacker could exploit this by manipulating the ID and adding products to other users' carts or accessing their shopping history.
- ***Steps:***
    1. Open the application and add a product to your cart.
    2. Inspect the network request generated when clicking the **"`Add to Cart`"** button in your browser's developer tools.
    3. Identify the parameter containing the product ID.
    4. Try modifying the product ID in the URL and adding it to your cart.
    5. Observe the application's behavior. Can you add products belonging to other users?

Exercise 2: Flawed Session Management:

- ***Scenario:*** A social media platform relies on cookies for managing user sessions.
- ***Potential vulnerability:*** If the application employs vulnerable cookies or lacks secure cookie management practices, attackers may exploit this to pilfer or take control of user sessions, gaining unauthorized access to their accounts and personal data.
- ***Steps:***
    - Log in to your social media platform account.
    - Utilize your browser's developer tools to investigate the cookies set by the application.
    - Scrutinize the cookie properties, including name, value, and security settings.
    - Explore online resources to grasp potential vulnerabilities associated with the specific type of cookie used.
    - Contemplate using a proxy tool to intercept and analyze the cookie data transmitted between your browser and the server.

Exercise 3: Missing Authorization Checks:

- ***Scenario***: An online forum allows users to post comments and view others' posts.
- ***Potential vulnerability***: If the application lacks proper authorization checks, any user could potentially delete or modify any comment, regardless of who posted it.
- ***Steps***:
  - Open the application and find a comment you want to investigate.
  - In your browser's developer tools, inspect the network request generated when interacting with the comment (for example, viewing, editing, or deleting).
  - Analyze the request body and headers to identify parameters related to the comment's ID and user information.
  - Try manipulating these parameters. Can you access or modify comments you should not be able to?

Keep in Mind: These activities serve as a jumping-off point. As you accumulate experience, your knack for recognizing and exploiting diverse access control vulnerabilities will flourish. Upholding ethical standards and honoring responsible disclosure principles is paramount.

Through active engagement in these practical exercises, you will glean invaluable insights into the exploitation of access control vulnerabilities and how to spot them within your applications. Armed with this knowledge, you will be empowered to construct web applications that are not only more secure but also resilient—safeguarding user data and upholding the integrity of your online services.

Ethical Hacking Techniques: Safeguarding by Breaking Safely

Welcome to the world of ethical hacking, where the goal is to strengthen the fortress by breaking in—but all in the name of security. Imagine hiring a friendly burglar to find the weak spots in your house and tell you how to reinforce them. Let us delve into the fundamentals of ethical hacking, the art of identifying vulnerabilities, and the responsible disclosure guidelines that ensure the safety of the digital kingdom.

Ethical hacking is like having a white-hat superhero on your side. These cybersecurity experts use their skills to identify and exploit vulnerabilities, just as malicious hackers might, but with the noble intention of fortifying digital defenses. Think of them as the cybersecurity detectives, ensuring that your web applications stand resilient against potential threats.

Guidelines for Responsible Disclosure: Responsible disclosure is the ethical compass of ethical hacking. It is akin to discovering a hidden passage in a castle and discreetly informing the king, rather than exploiting it for personal gain. Let us break down the key elements:

- ***Identifying Vulnerabilities:***
  - ***Description:*** Ethical hackers meticulously search for weaknesses, scrutinizing every nook and cranny of a web application.
  - ***Analogy:*** Imagine a locksmith examining a door, looking for any vulnerabilities that could be exploited by someone with malicious intent.
- ***Exploiting with Purpose:***
  - ***Description:*** Ethical hackers exploit vulnerabilities, showcasing how an attacker could breach security.
  - ***Analogy:*** Picture a magician revealing their tricks—it is not to deceive but to educate and ensure the magic remains secure.
- ***Documentation and Reporting:***
  - ***Description:*** Ethical hackers document every step of their journey and create detailed reports.
  - ***Analogy:*** Think of it as leaving a map behind, showing exactly where potential weaknesses were discovered and how to strengthen them.
- ***Responsible Disclosure Channels:***
  - ***Description:*** Ethical hackers share their findings responsibly, usually through established channels with the organization or developer.
  - ***Analogy:*** It is like discreetly handing over the map to the castle owner rather than broadcasting it to potential invaders.
- ***Collaboration with Stakeholders:***
  - ***Description:*** Ethical hackers work collaboratively with organizations, developers, or system owners to address and fix vulnerabilities.
  - ***Analogy:*** Consider it as teaming up with architects to fortify the castle, ensuring it is impervious to future attacks.

Ethical hacking is not just a proactive defense strategy; it is a necessity in the ever-evolving landscape of cyber threats. It is like having a preventive health check for your digital infrastructure—addressing vulnerabilities before they can be exploited maliciously.

As we journey into the domain of ethical hacking, remember that these modern-day knights are not adversaries but guardians, ensuring the digital kingdom remains secure. By understanding their techniques and the principles of responsible disclosure, you are not just fortifying your web applications; you are contributing to a safer and more resilient online world. Let the ethical hacking crusade begin!

Secure Access Control Design

In the field of Secure Access Control Design, it is not just about knowing the blueprints; it is about wielding the tools to construct robust digital fortifications. Imagine it as crafting a state-of-the-art lock for every door in your castle, ensuring that only the right keys can unlock them. Let us dive into practical tips – the implementation best practices–to empower you with the skills needed to fortify your web applications against potential breaches.

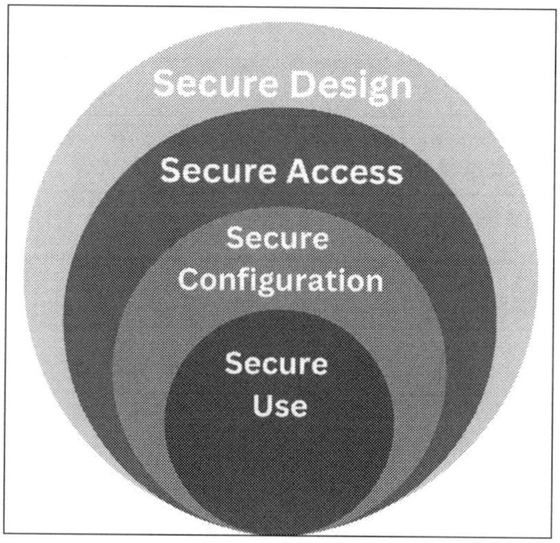

Figure 9.4: *Secure Access Control Design*

- **Embrace the Principle of Least Privilege:**
  - ***Tip:*** Assign the minimum level of access necessary for users to perform their tasks. Do not hand out master keys when a room key will suffice.
  - ***Analogy:*** Think of it as ensuring that every user has precisely the access they need and nothing more.
- **Implement Role-Based Access Control (RBAC):**
  - ***Tip:*** Organize users into roles and assign permissions based on these roles. It streamlines access management and avoids permission chaos.
  - ***Analogy:*** Picture it as giving different badges to employees based on their roles, each granting access to specific areas.
- **Regularly Review and Update Access Rights:**
  - ***Tip:*** Conduct periodic reviews of user access rights, especially during organizational changes. Update permissions to reflect evolving needs.

  - ***Analogy:*** Just like updating your contact list, ensure that users have access to the right resources based on their current roles.

- **Incorporate Multi-Factor Authentication (MFA):**
  - ***Tip:*** Strengthen authentication by integrating MFA. It introduces an additional security layer, demanding that users present various forms of identification.
  - ***Analogy:*** Envision a scenario where accessing a secure vault requires both a key and a confidential code.

- **Enforce Separation of Duties:**
  - ***Tip:*** Divide access responsibilities among individuals to prevent any single point of compromise. Avoid putting all control in one set of hands.
  - ***Analogy:*** It is like having multiple individuals with different keys needed to access critical systems.

- **Communicate Access Policies Clearly:**
  - ***Tip:*** Communicate access policies to users. Ensure they understand what they can access and the implications of their permissions.
  - ***Analogy:*** Think of it as providing a map that marks the areas guests are allowed to explore.

- **Conduct Usability Testing for Access Interfaces:**
  - ***Tip:*** Regularly test and refine the user interfaces for accessing controls. Ensure they are intuitive, user-friendly, and free of potential loopholes.
  - ***Analogy:*** It is like making sure the key turns smoothly in the lock, allowing authorized users easy access.

- **Implement Adaptive Access Controls:**
  - ***Tip:*** Adopt controls that adapt to user behavior and emerging threats. Be flexible in response to different contexts.
  - ***Analogy:*** Think of it as a security guard who adjusts their level of scrutiny based on the situation.

- **Monitor and Audit User Activities:**
  - ***Tip:*** Implement robust monitoring and auditing mechanisms. Keep a watchful eye on user activities to detect and respond to anomalies.
  - ***Analogy:*** Consider it as having security cameras throughout your castle, ensuring constant vigilance.

- **Regularly Update and Patch Access Controls:**
  - ***Tip:*** Keep access control systems up-to-date. Regularly apply patches and updates to address vulnerabilities and improve overall security.

- ***Analogy:*** Similar to updating your computer's antivirus software, ensure your access controls are fortified against emerging threats.

By incorporating these implementation best practices, you are not just securing access; you are constructing a fortified stronghold for your web applications. It is like equipping every entry point with an unbreakable lock, ensuring that only those with legitimate access can enter. As you navigate through the practical tips, envision yourself as the architect of digital fortresses, weaving a tapestry of security that withstands the tests of time and adversaries.

Case Studies in Access Control Failures

Let us take a trip through the history of cybersecurity, looking at real-life cases where access control went wrong. Think of these cases as stories that help us learn from past mistakes. It is like finding hidden treasures of knowledge that can help us better protect our digital space. Let us analyze real-world case studies:

- **LastPass Data Breach (2023):**
  - ***Security Incident:*** Attackers used stolen employee credentials to access internal systems and compromise user data, including encrypted password vaults.
  - ***Consequences:*** Potential exposure of millions of user passwords and other sensitive information, prompting password resets and increased scrutiny of password management services.
  - ***Lesson:*** Enforce strong password policies, implement multi-factor authentication, and continuously improve security measures to protect user data.
- **Twilio Data Breach Exposes Customer Records (2023):**
  - ***Security Incident:*** A social engineering attack compromised employee credentials, providing unauthorized access to sensitive customer data, including phone numbers and SMS history.
  - ***Consequences:*** The breach poses a risk of unauthorized access to communication records, raising concerns about potential targeted attacks on Twilio clients.
  - ***Lesson:*** To bolster security defenses, it is imperative to maintain vigilance against social engineering attempts. Implementing multi-factor authentication and providing comprehensive training to employees on security best practices are essential measures in preventing similar incidents.

- **Okta Authentication Service Outage (2023):**
    - ***Security Incident:*** Improper access controls within a third-party vendor's network led to a service disruption affecting multiple companies relying on Okta for authentication.
    - ***Consequences:*** Widespread disruptions for businesses and their users, highlighting the risks associated with third-party dependencies.
    - ***Lesson:*** Carefully evaluate the security practices of third-party vendors and implement contingency plans for potential disruptions.
- **Microsoft Exchange Zero-Day Attack (2023):**
    - ***Security Incident:*** Zero-day vulnerabilities discovered in Microsoft Exchange servers enabled attackers to circumvent access controls, leading to unauthorized remote access.
    - ***Consequences:*** The incident has put thousands of organizations at risk, with potential implications including data breaches and deployment of malware.
    - ***Lesson:*** Timely patching of systems, prioritization of zero-day vulnerability mitigation, and the implementation of layered security measures are crucial steps in reducing the attack surface and enhancing overall security posture.

    Magecart Attacks Target Multiple E-commerce Sites (2023):
    - ***Security Incident:*** Misconfigured access controls and exploited vulnerabilities in e-commerce platforms allow attackers to inject malicious scripts, skimming payment information.
    - ***Consequences:*** Ongoing financial losses for e-commerce businesses and potential data breaches for customers.
    - ***Lesson:*** Continuously update and secure e-commerce platforms, implement robust access controls, and monitor systems for suspicious activity.

Additional Notes:

- The Colonial Pipeline ransomware attack, previously mentioned, remains a relevant example with ongoing discussions about critical infrastructure security.
- These cases highlight the diverse nature of BAC vulnerabilities, ranging from human error and social engineering to technical exploits and zero-day attacks.

Key Insights:

- Implement the principle of least privilege and conduct regular reviews of access permissions.
- Ensure secure configurations for all systems and third-party integrations.

- Promptly apply patches to address vulnerabilities, particularly zero-day threats.
- Utilize multi-factor authentication for critical accounts to enhance security.
- Provide comprehensive cybersecurity awareness training to employees.
- Develop robust incident response plans and continuously monitor systems for potential breaches.

By assimilating the insights gleaned from recent cases and integrating their lessons learned, organizations can bolster their security stance and mitigate the risks associated with vulnerabilities in access control. It is vital to remain proactive and maintain constant vigilance in today's ever-evolving threat landscape.

Conclusion

Congratulations, cyber adventurers, on navigating the intricate landscapes of Broken Access Control! From decoding Insecure Direct Object References (IDOR) to unraveling the nuances of Privilege Escalation and scrutinizing real-world Access Control Failures, you have honed your skills in identifying and securing web vulnerabilities.

As we bid farewell to this chapter, gear up for the final leg of our journey. In the next chapter, we will unveil the mysteries of Authentication Bypass Techniques, offering insights into the vulnerabilities that lie beyond the authentication gate.

Your commitment to understanding web security has been commendable. Pat yourselves on the back and get ready for the grand finale—where you will become the guardians of secure digital gateways. Congratulations on successfully completing this chapter. Let us now move forward to the next chapter in our cybersecurity journey.

CHAPTER 10
Authentication Bypass Techniques

Introduction

Step into the core of cybersecurity with **Authentication Bypass Techniques.** From fundamentals to advanced strategies like response and status code manipulation, OTP and 2FA bypass, session fixation, credential reuse, Captcha evasion, cookie manipulation, and token-based authentication bypass, this chapter is your concise guide to mastering web security. Building on Broken Access Control insights from the previous chapter, get ready to fortify the digital gates and become a proficient defender in the dynamic landscape of cybersecurity.

Structure

In this chapter, we will cover the following topics:

- Unlocking the Web
- Authentication Bypass Fundamentals
- Response Manipulation
- Status Code Manipulation
- OTP Bypass Techniques
- Two-Factor Authentication (2FA) Bypass
- Session Fixation Attacks
- Credential Reuse Attacks
- Captcha Bypass Methods
- Cookie Manipulation
- Token-Based Authentication Bypass

Unlocking the Web: Mastering Authentication Bypass Techniques

Have you ever wondered how websites keep your personal information safe? The answer lies in a crucial security measure called authentication. Just like a key unlocks a door, authentication verifies who you are before granting access to online resources and services.

However, as web applications become increasingly complex, so do the techniques used to bypass authentication. Understanding these techniques is not just for security experts; it is crucial for anyone who wants to protect their online privacy and data.

This chapter will take you on a journey through the world of authentication bypass, delving into the depths of this fascinating and ever-evolving field. We will explore the why and how of these techniques, equipping you with the knowledge to navigate the online landscape safely and confidently.

The Significance of Authentication Bypass

Imagine authentication as the guardian of our digital world, ensuring only the right people access sensitive data. Sadly, troublemakers are always hunting for ways to sidestep these safeguards and sneak in.

The fallout from a successful authentication bypass can be grim—think data breaches, identity theft, financial hits, and damage to your good name. So, knowing these tricks is no longer a nice to have; it is a must in today's connected world.

This chapter aims to give you practical insights into authentication bypass, even if you are a newcomer to cybersecurity. No need for tech speak or mind-bending concepts; we are sticking to plain explanations and real-world examples.

By the end of this chapter, you will have a solid grip on common authentication bypass methods and how to keep yourself safe online. Knowledge is your power here, and the more you grasp these techniques, the better shielded you will be against cyber threats.

Ready to unravel the mysteries of authentication bypass? Let's begin!

Authentication Bypass Fundamentals

Imagine a castle filled with treasures, guarded by a strong gatekeeper. This gatekeeper ensures that only authorized individuals can enter and access the valuables within. In the world of the web, this gatekeeper is called **authentication**.

Just like the gatekeeper protects the castle's treasures, authentication protects our online information and resources. It acts as a barrier, verifying our identity before allowing us access. This is crucial for protecting our privacy, data, and financial security.

However, just as skilled thieves can sometimes bypass the castle's gatekeeper, hackers can exploit weaknesses in authentication systems and gain unauthorized access. This is what we call an **authentication bypass**.

Consider it akin to discovering a hidden path past the gatekeeper, allowing entry without notice. The repercussions of such a workaround can be severe, leading to:

- ***Data breaches:*** Unauthorized access to sensitive details such as usernames, passwords, financial information, and even medical records.
- ***Identity theft:*** Malevolent actors can utilize stolen credentials to pose as legitimate users, resulting in financial loss and damage to reputation.
- ***System compromise:*** Intruders can infiltrate entire systems, causing disruptions and widespread damage to operations.

Real-World Impact of Authentication Bypass

Let us bring this down to earth with a story. Meet Jane, an ordinary person navigating the digital landscape. One day, her email gets hacked because someone figured out how to bypass the login barricade. Suddenly, private conversations, pictures, and even sensitive work emails are exposed to a stranger. This is the real impact of the authentication bypass–it is not just a technical glitch; it is a breach of trust and privacy.

Think of it like a bank heist where the criminals found a hidden entrance. In the digital world, a successful authentication bypass can lead to identity theft, financial loss, or even the manipulation of critical information. Remember those news headlines about major data breaches? Behind each one, there is a story of an authentication bypass wreaking havoc. By understanding these real-world scenarios, you will grasp why being savvy about authentication bypass is crucial for protecting yourself and the digital community. This is not just about tech; it is about safeguarding the very fabric of our online lives.

Introduction to Common Authentication Mechanisms

Authentication mechanisms are fundamental components of cybersecurity that validate the identity of users accessing digital resources. These mechanisms ensure that only authorized individuals or entities can gain access to sensitive information or perform privileged actions within a system.

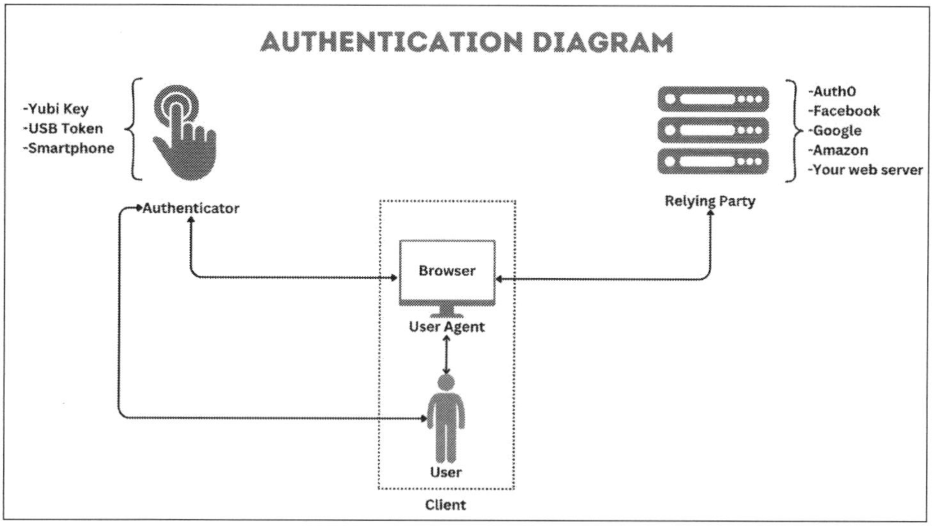

Figure 10.1: *Authentication Mechanism*

Several common authentication methods are widely employed across various digital platforms:

- ***Password-Based Authentication:*** Passwords stand as one of the oldest and most common authentication methods. Users provide a unique combination of characters, usually in the form of a passphrase, to confirm their identity. Although passwords are straightforward to use, they face various security risks, such as brute-force attacks, password guessing, and password reuse.
- ***Multi-Factor Authentication* (MFA):** MFA elevates security by necessitating users to present two or more authentication factors to access a system. These factors typically encompass something the user knows (password), something they possess (smartphone or hardware token), or something they are (biometric data like fingerprints or facial recognition). MFA significantly bolsters security by mitigating risks associated with single-factor authentication methods.
- ***Biometric Authentication:*** Biometric authentication relies on distinct physical characteristics of individuals, such as fingerprints, iris patterns, or facial features, to authenticate their identity. Biometric data is difficult to duplicate or forge, making it a strong authentication method. Nonetheless, concerns about privacy, accuracy, and the possibility of biometric data breaches remain.
- ***Token-Based Authentication:*** Token-based authentication entails using cryptographic tokens or digital certificates to validate user identity. These tokens are typically generated by a trusted third party and exchanged between the user and the authentication system during the login process. Token-based authentication offers high security and resilience against many common attack vectors.

- ***OAuth and OpenID Connect:*** OAuth and OpenID Connect function as open standards for authentication and authorization, particularly in web and mobile applications. OAuth facilitates third-party applications to retrieve user data without revealing credentials, whereas OpenID Connect provides a structure for single sign-on authentication. These protocols are widely embraced by leading tech firms and social media platforms.
- ***Single Sign-On (SSO):*** Single Sign-On (SSO) facilitates users to authenticate just once and gain access to various applications or services without needing to re-enter credentials. This streamlines the authentication process, enriches user experience, and alleviates the hassle of managing numerous passwords. SSO solutions often utilize authentication tokens or centralized identity providers to verify user identity across different domains or applications.

Comprehending these prevalent authentication mechanisms is crucial for devising secure systems and safeguarding sensitive data against unauthorized access.

Recent Advancements and Emerging Trends in Authentication Technology

As technology continues to evolve, new advancements and emerging trends in authentication technology are reshaping the landscape of cybersecurity. These developments aim to address existing security challenges, improve user experience, and adapt to the changing threat landscape. Some recent advancements and emerging trends include:

- ***Passwordless Authentication:*** Passwordless authentication methods eliminate the need for traditional passwords and instead rely on alternative authentication factors such as biometrics, hardware tokens, or cryptographic keys. This approach enhances security by reducing the risk of password-related vulnerabilities such as phishing and credential-stuffing attacks.
- ***Continuous Authentication:*** Continuous authentication systems continually monitor user behavior and interaction patterns to determine the session's continued trustworthiness. Continuous authentication, which continuously adjusts authentication requirements depending on real-time risk indicators, detects and prevents unwanted access more effectively than static authentication techniques.
- ***Zero Trust Architecture:*** Zero Trust Architecture (ZTA) revolutionizes traditional security by abandoning the "trust but verify" approach. Instead, it assumes constant potential threats within and beyond the network perimeter. ZTA enforces granular access controls, granting the least privilege and continuously evaluating user and device identity and trustworthiness before granting access to any resource.

- ***Decentralized Identity:*** Decentralized identity solutions leverage blockchain technology to enable individuals to control and manage their digital identities securely. By decentralizing identity information and eliminating the need for centralized identity providers, decentralized identity systems offer greater privacy, security, and user autonomy.
- ***Behavioral Biometrics:*** Behavioral biometrics analyze unique behavioral patterns such as typing speed, mouse movements, and touchscreen interactions to authenticate users. Unlike traditional biometric methods that rely on static physical characteristics, behavioral biometrics provide continuous authentication without requiring additional hardware or user interaction, making them well-suited for frictionless authentication experiences.

These improvements and developing trends indicate the future direction of authentication technology, promising improved security, usability, and resilience to increasing cyber threats. Incorporating these technologies into authentication procedures can help firms keep ahead of cyber threats while also protecting the integrity and confidentiality of their digital assets.

Response Manipulation – Cracking the Code of Authentication

Imagine a spy trying to decode a secret message. In the world of authentication, that message is hidden within the responses exchanged between your browser and the website you are trying to access. By understanding these responses, we can uncover vulnerabilities and explore how hackers manipulate them to bypass authentication.

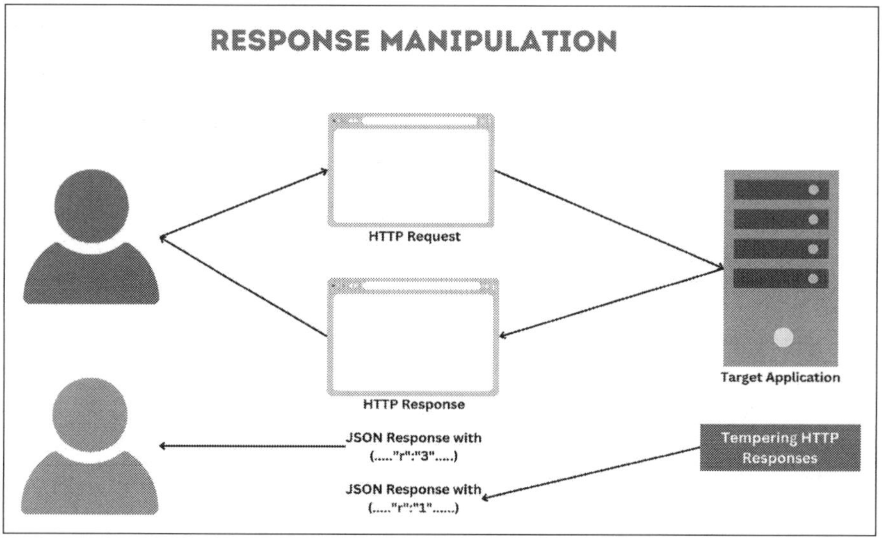

Figure 10.2: *Response Manipulation*

Think of these responses as the website's way of communicating with your browser. They contain information about whether your authentication attempt was successful, along with other details about the requested resources. Let us break down some key aspects of HTTP responses in authentication:

- ***Status codes:*** These codes, like three-digit passwords, tell your browser whether your request was successful or not. Here are some commonly encountered codes:
    - **`200 OK`:** This code means your request was successful and you have access to the requested resource.
    - **`401 Unauthorized`:** This code indicates your login attempt failed, and you need to provide valid credentials.
    - **`403 Forbidden`:** This code means you do not have permission to access the requested resource, even if your login was successful.
- ***Response headers:*** These act like additional notes attached to the response, providing further information. One particularly important header is the WWW-Authenticate header. This header tells your browser what type of authentication the website requires, such as a username and password or a token.
- ***Response body:*** This is the actual content of the requested resource, like the webpage you are trying to access. It may also contain error messages or other information relevant to the request.

To navigate the intricacies of response manipulation, let us explore how hackers exploit website vulnerabilities to bypass authentication. Here are some prevalent techniques:

- ***Tampering with Responses:*** Hackers intercept and modify the responses directed to your browser. By making it seem like your login was successful, they gain unauthorized access without valid credentials.
- ***Exploiting Response Errors***: Certain websites reveal specific error messages in responses, inadvertently leaking sensitive data. Hackers leverage this information to guess passwords or target other vulnerabilities.
- ***Code Injection Tactics:*** Injecting malicious code into a website's response body is another tactic. When executed by your browser, this code can steal your credentials or execute harmful actions.

Understanding these manipulation techniques is pivotal for online protection. Stay vigilant while browsing, armed with the knowledge to mitigate these risks effectively.

Response Manipulation – Bypassing the Gatekeeper with Header Hijinks

Remember those additional notes attached to HTTP responses, called headers? Well, in the world of authentication bypass, these seemingly harmless notes can hold the key to unlocking unauthorized access. Let us explore how hackers can manipulate response headers to fool websites into thinking they are legitimate users.

Think of response headers like the gatekeeper's instructions. They tell the website's internal systems what to do with your request. Hackers can exploit vulnerabilities in these instructions to bypass authentication and gain unauthorized access. Here is how it works:

- ***Intercepting headers:*** Just like a spy intercepting messages, hackers can use specialized tools to intercept the headers being sent between your browser and the website. This allows them to analyze the information and identify potential weaknesses.
- ***Modifying headers:*** Once a vulnerability is found, hackers can modify the intercepted headers before they reach the website. This is like forging a fake ID to fool the gatekeeper. Some common techniques include:
  - ***Changing the "Authorization" header:*** This header usually contains your authentication credentials. Hackers can replace them with fake credentials or even delete them entirely to bypass authentication altogether.
  - ***Exploiting insecure cookies:*** Cookies are small files stored in your browser that can contain session information. Hackers can steal these cookies or manipulate their values to gain unauthorized access.
  - ***Adding malicious headers:*** Hackers can inject malicious headers into the response, tricking the website into granting them access or revealing sensitive information.
- ***Sending the Altered Headers:*** Once the headers undergo modification, the intruder dispatches them back to the website, appearing as if they originated from your browser. If the website lacks robust security measures, it might be duped into treating the forged credentials as genuine, thereby granting unauthorized access.
- ***Attaining Unauthorized Entry:*** With the website deceived, the hacker gains entry to resources and information that should remain off-limits. This encompasses accessing sensitive data, and financial details, or even seizing full control of the website's systems.

Understanding how hackers manipulate response headers empowers us to safeguard ourselves. Here are some practical tips:

- Craft robust passwords and activate multi-factor authentication.
- Exercise caution with links and websites lacking trustworthiness.
- Keep all software up-to-date, including your browser and operating system.
- Employ security tools like firewalls and antivirus software.
- Stay mindful of potential risks and stay updated on the latest security threats.

By familiarizing ourselves with response manipulation and incorporating these security precautions, we can securely lock our digital gates, safeguarding our online identities from unwarranted access. Keep in mind that cybersecurity is an ongoing journey, not a final destination. The more we absorb and adjust, the more confidently we can traverse the ever-changing digital terrain.

It is crucial to emphasize that ethical hacking must strictly adhere to legal and authorized boundaries. Unsanctioned access or attempts to exploit systems without proper approval are against the law and can result in severe consequences. Always ensure explicit permission before engaging in any ethical hacking activities.

Exercise: Understanding Response Manipulation

Assuming you possess proper authorization, here are steps within Kali Linux to ethically delve into authentication bypass techniques:

- ***Leveraging Browser Developer Tools:***
  1. Launch your web browser and visit the designated website.
  2. Right-click the webpage, selecting **`Inspect`** or **`Inspect Element`**.
  3. Explore the Network tab, unveiling HTTP requests, responses, and critical details like headers, status codes, and cookies.
- ***Header Modification Adventure:***
  1. Within the **`Network`** tab, locate the authentication-related request.
  2. Right-click the request and opt for **`Copy`** as cURL to duplicate the request as a cURL command.
  3. Initiate a terminal session and paste the cURL command.
  4. Embark on an exploration by tweaking headers through the manipulation of the cURL command.

     ```
     curl -X POST -H "Content-Type: application/json" -H "Authori-
     zation: Bearer YOUR_TOKEN" -d '{"username": "your_username",
     "password": "your_password"}' <http://example.com/login>
     ```
- ***Status Code Manipulation:***
  - Utilize tools such as Burp Suite or OWASP ZAP to intercept and tweak requests.
  - Play around with altering the status codes in responses and see how the website reacts.
- ***User Agent Spoofing:***
  - Incorporate a browser extension or employ tools like curl with the A flag to alter the User-Agent string.

```
curl -A "Mozilla/5.0 (Windows NT 10.0; Win64; x64) AppleWeb-
Kit/537.36 (KHTML, like Gecko) Chrome/58.0.3029.110 Safari/537.3"
<http://example.com>
```

- ***Cookie Manipulation:***
  - Leverage browser developer tools to examine and modify cookies.
  - Experiment with changing cookie values and observe the effects on authentication.

Remember, these activities should be performed in a controlled environment with explicit permission. If you are practicing ethical hacking as part of your learning process, consider setting up a test environment or using platforms designed for ethical hacking practice. Always adhere to ethical guidelines and respect the privacy and security of others. If you are not sure whether an activity is legal or ethical, seek advice from experienced professionals or legal authorities.

Status Code Manipulation - Decrypting the Guardian's Signals

Visualize a covert agent decoding secret messages. In the cybersecurity domain, HTTP status codes serve as these messages, unveiling vital details about the outcome of an authentication endeavor. Grasping these codes offers valuable insights into how hackers manipulate them to sidestep security controls.

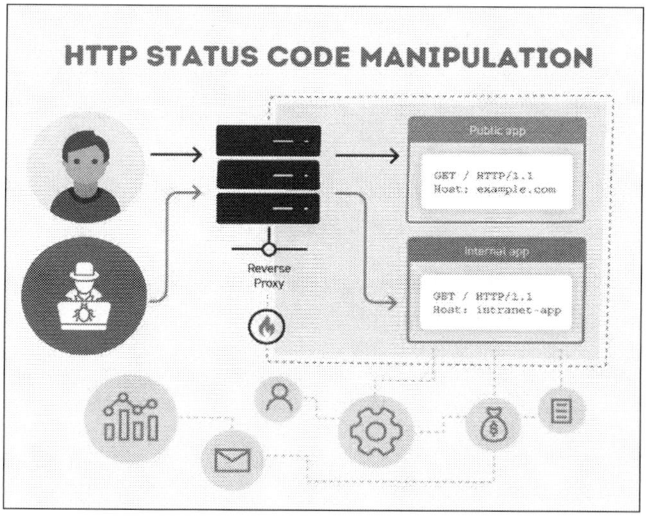

Figure 10.3: *Status Code Manipulation*

Think of HTTP status codes as the gatekeeper's responses to your requests for access. Each code tells you whether your attempt was successful, failed, or requires further information. Here are some key status codes relevant to authentication:

- `200 OK`: This code indicates that your request was successful and you have been granted access. The gatekeeper has recognized you and has opened the door.
- `401 Unauthorized`: This code means your initial attempt to unlock the door failed. The gatekeeper does not recognize you and is requesting valid credentials.
- `403 Forbidden`: This code is different. Even if the gatekeeper recognizes you, you still do not have enough authority to enter this specific area. You lack the necessary permission for this specific action.
- `301 Moved Permanently`: This code tells you that the access point has changed. You need to visit a new location to gain entry.
- `404 Not Found`: This code means the requested resource does not exist. The gatekeeper has no idea what you are asking for.

Now, let us explore how hackers can manipulate these status codes to gain unauthorized access:

- ***Intercepting and Modifying Status Codes:*** Hackers can use specialized tools to intercept and modify the status code sent back to your browser. This is like forging a fake message from the gatekeeper, telling you to have access when you do not.
- ***Exploiting Misconfigurations:*** Sometimes, websites might be improperly configured, causing them to send incorrect status codes. Hackers can exploit these vulnerabilities to bypass authentication or gain access to restricted resources.
- ***Utilizing Open Redirects:*** Some websites allow users to redirect to different pages through specific links. Hackers can trick users into clicking on malicious links that exploit these redirects to bypass authentication and gain access to sensitive information.
- ***Brute-Forcing Status Codes:*** Hackers can use automated tools to send numerous requests with different credentials, hoping to eventually generate a successful status code and gain access. This is like trying every key on the key ring until you find the one that unlocks the door.

Understanding how hackers tinker with status codes empowers us to fortify our defenses:

- Exercise caution when clicking links, especially from unfamiliar sources.
- Craft robust passwords and activate multi-factor authentication.
- Ensure your software, including browsers and operating systems, is up-to-date.
- Employ security tools like firewalls and antivirus software.
- Stay mindful of risks and stay aware of the latest security threats.

Always bear in mind that knowledge is your armor in the digital kingdom. Unraveling the intricacies of status codes and the tactics hackers employ to manipulate them allows you to navigate the web confidently, safeguarding your online identity from unauthorized access. So, remain watchful, stay informed, and keep your digital space secure!

Status Code Manipulation – Deciphering the Cipher for Unrestricted Entry

Picture yourself as a detective unraveling a mystery. In the field of authentication bypass, HTTP status codes serve as vital clues, unveiling concealed vulnerabilities and providing the key to unauthorized access. Grasping how hackers use these codes equips us to reinforce our defenses, ensuring the safety of our online identities.

Think of HTTP status codes as the secret language of websites, conveying information about your requests. Each code, like a cryptic message, tells you whether your attempt to access a resource was successful or not. Let us explore some key status codes and how they can be manipulated for unauthorized access:

- ***Sneaking Through the Back Door: Exploiting 301 Moved Permanently Codes***
    - This code, meant to redirect users to a new location, can be exploited by hackers to bypass authentication. Imagine a scenario where a website has a 301 redirect in place for a forgotten password page. Hackers can manipulate this redirect to send users to a fake password reset page that steals their credentials.
- ***Forging the Gatekeeper's Seal: Modifying Status Codes***
    - Just like forging a signature, hackers can intercept and modify the status code sent back to your browser. This is like tricking the website into thinking you are authorized even if you are not. For example, a hacker might change a 401 Unauthorized code to a 200 OK code, granting them access without valid credentials.
- ***Navigating the Digital Landscape: Open Redirect Challenges***
    - Certain websites allow users to build specific links that lead to different pages. Using this capability, cyber adversaries create false links that cause users to mistakenly overcome authentication and access restricted information. Imagine clicking a link and being sent to a bogus login screen meant to steal your credentials.

To defend against these tactics, take the following steps:

- Be cautious when clicking links, especially those from unknown sources.
- Strengthen your defenses by using strong passwords and enabling multi-factor authentication.

- Report any links or strange website activities to the site owners as soon as possible.
- Keep your software up-to-date, including your browser and operating system.
- Use security measures such as firewalls and antivirus software to improve protection.
- Stay up-to-date on the newest security risks and vulnerabilities.

Remember that information is your primary defense in the digital arena. Understanding the complexities of open redirect attacks enables you to traverse the web with awareness, protecting your data from unauthorized access. So arm yourself with knowledge, keep alert, and protect the integrity of your online identity!

OTP Bypass Techniques

One-Time Passwords (OTPs) have become a crucial layer of defense in multi-factor authentication (MFA), adding an extra hurdle for attackers attempting unauthorized access. However, like any security measure, OTPs are not invincible.

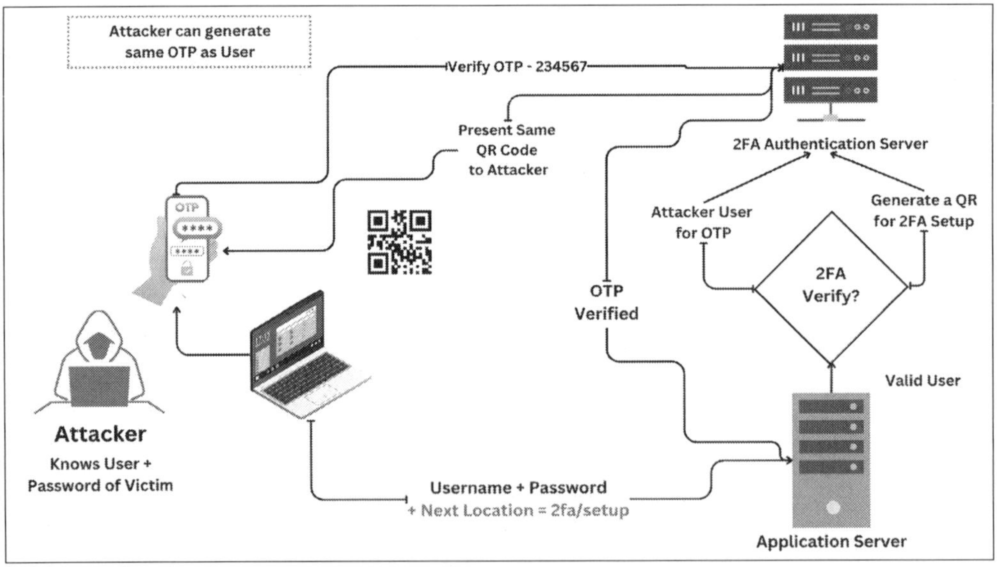

***Figure 10.4**:* *OTP Bypass Mechanism*

Let us delve into common OTP bypass techniques and real-world examples to understand the evolving threat landscape:

- **SIM Swapping**
  - ***Technique:*** Attackers exploit vulnerabilities in mobile carrier processes to transfer a victim's phone number to a SIM card they control, intercepting SMS-based OTPs.

  - **Tools:** Social engineering, compromised employee credentials within mobile providers.
  - ***Real-world example:*** In 2022, attackers bypassed 2FA and stole millions from cryptocurrency exchange Cryptsy by SIM-swapping the CEO's phone.
- **Man-in-the-Middle (MitM) Attacks**
  - ***Technique:*** Attackers intercept communication between the user and service provider, capturing and potentially manipulating OTPs.
  - **Tools:** Public Wi-Fi sniffing tools, malicious network infrastructure.
  - ***Real-world example:*** In 2020, attackers launched MitM attacks against financial institutions, intercepting SMS-based OTPs and stealing funds.
- **Mobile Malware**
  - ***Technique:*** Malicious apps installed on the victim's device steal or manipulate incoming OTPs.
  - **Tools:** Phishing campaigns, fake app stores, infected downloads.
  - ***Real-world example:*** In 2021, the FluBot malware targeted Android devices, capturing SMS messages containing OTPs for various online services.
- **Application Vulnerabilities**
  - ***Technique:*** Exploiting weaknesses in the authentication process or OTP implementation within applications or websites.
  - **Tools:** Penetration testing tools, vulnerability scanners, exploit kits.
  - ***Real-world example:*** In 2021, a vulnerability in Microsoft Azure AD allowed attackers to bypass MFA and access user accounts by manipulating authentication requests.

Staying Ahead of the Curve

- Implement strong password hygiene and enable MFA on all accounts.
- Avoid public Wi-Fi for sensitive transactions and use VPNs for added security.
- Be cautious of unfamiliar apps and download only from trusted sources.
- Remain vigilant against phishing attempts and never reveal OTPs to anyone.
- Stay updated on security patches and vulnerability disclosures for applications and devices.
- Consider alternative OTP methods like push notifications or hardware tokens for enhanced security.

Remember that security is an ongoing activity. By knowing these bypass tactics and implementing strong security measures, you can dramatically limit the danger of OTP breaches while also protecting your sensitive information.

Putting Your Knowledge to the Test: Hands-on Experiments with OTP Bypass Techniques

While understanding the theoretical aspects of OTP bypass techniques is crucial, hands-on experience solidifies knowledge and empowers you to identify and mitigate these threats in real-world scenarios. So, let us delve into practical exercises where we can explore and test these techniques in a controlled environment.

Exercise: Understanding Secure Implementations

- ***Choose a website known for its strong security:*** Select a website with a reputation for implementing robust security measures, such as online banking platforms or government websites.
- ***Review their OTP authentication process:*** Analyze how they handle OTPs for authentication. Do they use secure protocols for communication? Do they offer alternative methods to SMS-based OTPs?
- ***Compare to insecure implementations:*** Compare their OTP implementation to websites with known vulnerabilities. This will help you understand the difference between secure and insecure practices.
- ***Learn from best practices:*** Identify the best practices employed by the website and how they contribute to stronger security. This knowledge can be used to evaluate the security of other websites and services you use.

Important Note: These exercises are intended for educational purposes only. Simulating phishing attacks on real websites or services is illegal and unethical. Always conduct these experiments in a controlled environment and avoid harming yourself or others.

By actively engaging in these practical scenarios, you will gain valuable hands-on experience in identifying and mitigating OTP bypass threats. Remember, cybersecurity is a continuous learning process. The more you experiment and analyze vulnerabilities, the better you are to confidently navigate the digital world and protect your online identity from unauthorized access.

Two-Factor Authentication (2FA) Bypass: Unveiling the Cracks in the Fortress

Imagine a fortress protected by a devoted guardian who confirms your identity before granting entry. In the digital world, this guardian is known as Two-Factor Authentication (2FA), a security measure that adds an extra layer of defense to your online accounts. Nevertheless, even the most robust guardians can be outmaneuvered, and hackers have devised tactics to circumvent 2FA and gain unauthorized access.

Consider 2FA as a twin lock on your digital gateway. It demands two pieces of information for identity verification: your username and password (the first lock) and an additional factor like a code sent to your phone or a fingerprint scan (the second lock). This significantly heightens the difficulty for hackers to gain access, even if they manage to pilfer your password.

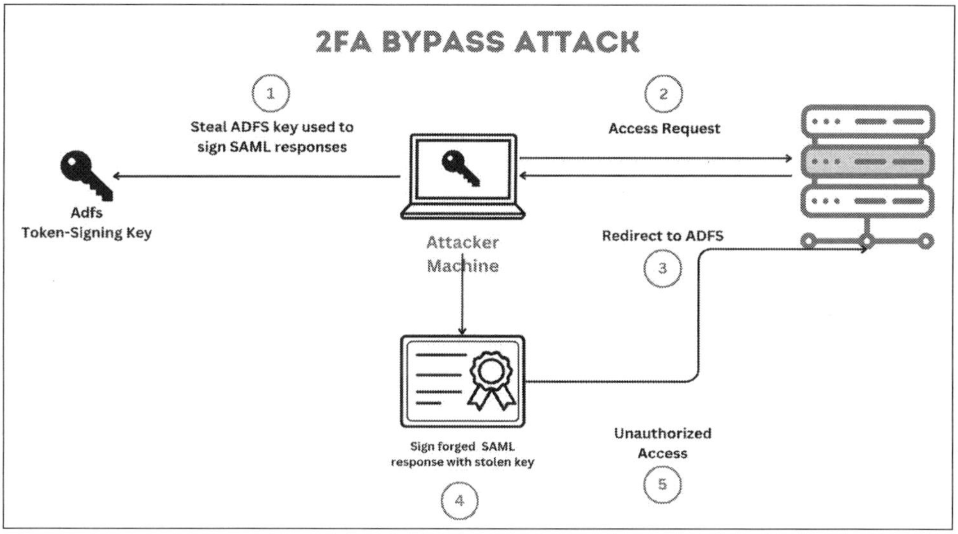

***Figure* 10.5**: *2FA Bypass Attack*

However, akin to any security measure, 2FA is optional. Hackers have devised diverse strategies to exploit vulnerabilities and navigate past this second defense.

Unlocking the Second Door: Methods for Circumventing 2FA

- ***Phishing*:** Deceptive tactics lead users to click on harmful links or open infected attachments, resulting in credential theft or malware installation to intercept 2FA codes.
- **SIM *Swapping*:** Hackers manipulate your mobile carrier to transfer your phone number to a SIM card they control, enabling them to receive your 2FA codes and evade authentication.
- ***Man-in-the-Middle Attacks*:** Hackers intercept communication between your device and the target website or service, allowing them to pilfer 2FA codes or manipulate them for unauthorized access.
- ***Social Engineering*:** Manipulative techniques deceive individuals into divulging 2FA codes or sensitive information. Impersonation as customer service representatives or other manipulation forms are commonly employed.
- ***Exploiting Weak Implementations*:** Vulnerabilities in a website or service's 2FA implementation may be exploited by hackers to circumvent this security measure.

- ***Brute-Forcing Codes:*** Hackers may employ automated tools to guess 2FA codes, particularly if weak or predictable codes are in use.
- ***Hardware Security Key Interception:*** Physical theft or compromise of hardware security keys used for 2FA allows hackers to bypass this additional security layer.

Fortifying Your Digital Citadel: Mitigating 2FA Bypass Risks

While these maneuvers present a risk, there are steps we can take to reinforce the security of our digital strongholds:

- Employ sturdy passwords and choose 2FA with authenticator apps instead of relying on SMS-based codes.
- Exercise caution with questionable links and attachments, refraining from entering 2FA codes on unverified websites or apps.
- Protect your phone number and other confidential details by keeping them confidential.
- Remain wary of unexpected calls or messages from unfamiliar sources claiming connections to your bank, service provider, or other trusted entities.
- Swiftly report any suspicious activities to the relevant authorities or service providers.
- Select services that provide robust 2FA options, such as hardware security keys.
- Regularly update your software and firmware, encompassing your operating system, browser, and mobile apps.

By grasping these approaches and embracing appropriate precautions, we can ensure the resilience of our online strongholds. Remember, vigilance is key in the dynamic world of cybersecurity. The more we comprehend the threats and how to counter them, the better equipped we are to safeguard our online identities and information.

Two-Factor Authentication (2FA) Bypass: Hands-on Training for Security Champions

Now that you have gained theoretical knowledge about 2FA bypass techniques, it is time to put your skills to the test! Buckle up, because this section will guide you through hands-on exercises designed to solidify your understanding and equip you with practical experience in identifying and mitigating these threats.

Activity: Exploring Diverse 2FA Approaches:

- ***Activate 2FA on your social media profiles:*** Pick two or more social media platforms that provide various 2FA alternatives, such as SMS-based codes, authenticator apps, and hardware security keys.

- ***Experiment and compare the methods:*** Engage with each of the 2FA methods offered by the platforms. Assess their user-friendliness, security effectiveness, and overall convenience.
- ***Spot strengths and weaknesses:*** Contrast the diverse 2FA methods and pinpoint their pros and cons. Consider aspects like susceptibility to phishing, the potential for SIM swapping, and the overall user journey.
- ***Opt for the most fitting method:*** Grounded in your evaluation, choose the 2FA method that strikes the optimal balance between security and ease for your specific requirements.

Vital Reminder: These activities are designed solely for educational purposes. Attempting simulated phishing attacks on actual websites or services is both illegal and unethical. It is crucial to carry out these exercises in a controlled environment, ensuring no harm is done to yourself or others.

Through active participation in these practical exercises, you will acquire valuable skills in assessing 2FA implementations, recognizing potential vulnerabilities, and selecting the most secure and user-friendly 2FA methods for your online accounts. Always bear in mind that cybersecurity is an ongoing journey, not a final destination. The more you engage in experimentation and vulnerability analysis, the better prepared you become to confidently navigate the continually evolving digital terrain, safeguarding your online identity against unauthorized access.

Session Fixation Attacks

Let us take a journey into the space of session fixation, a vulnerability that lurks beneath the surface of web authentication. Think of a web session like your passport for a digital journey. Session fixation is like a crafty pickpocket altering your passport, letting them travel in your digital shoes.

In the web world, when you log in, a session is created, and a unique identifier (session ID) is generated. It is like receiving a ticket for the duration of your stay. Now, session fixation occurs when an attacker tricks you into using a session ID they have set. It is akin to someone handing you a doctored passport before your journey begins. You unknowingly carry this compromise throughout your session, and the attacker can later reap the benefits.

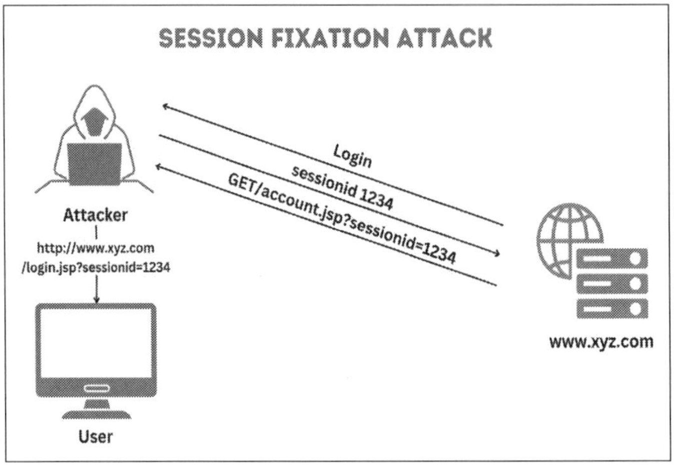

Figure 10.6: *Session Fixation Attack*

Exploiting Session Fixation for Authentication Bypass:

Let us delve into the darker side of this vulnerability, where attackers exploit session fixation to slip past the authentication barriers.

- ***Initial Session Sharing:***
  - Imagine you are innocently sharing a link with a friend, not realizing that it contains a manipulated session ID. Your friend clicks the link, unknowingly adopting the compromised session. This is the inception of the attack, where the session ID is fixed on an unsuspecting user.
- ***User Interaction Hijack:***
  - Once the attacker has tricked someone into using the fixed session, they can wait for that user to authenticate. The attacker is now lurking in the shadows, watching the authentication process unfold. It is like having a spy observe your every move from within your digital persona.
- ***Seizing Control:***
  - The attacker, having witnessed the authentication, can now use the fixed session ID to gain control. It is similar to stealing the keys to a kingdom after observing the royal entry protocol. They exploit the compromised session to bypass authentication checks, gaining unauthorized access as if they were the legitimate user.

Safeguarding Your Digital Identity: Mitigating Session Fixation Risks

Thankfully, there are actions you can take to defend yourself against session fixation attacks:

- Exercise caution when clicking links, particularly those from unfamiliar sources.

- Implement robust passwords and activate multi-factor authentication.
- Ensure your software, encompassing your browser and operating system, remains up-to-date.
- Log out from websites once you have completed your activities.
- Opt for websites employing secure session management practices, such as utilizing HTTPS and unique session IDs.
- Stay mindful of the associated risks and remain updated on the latest security threats.

By grasping the nuances of session fixation and adhering to these safeguards, you can uphold the security of your online sessions, thwarting hackers from seizing control of your digital identity. Remember, knowledge acts as your shield in the digital space. By staying attentive and informed, you can navigate the web with confidence, shielding your online presence from unauthorized access.

Hijacking the Session: Real-World Examples and Preventive Measures

Imagine a thief who steals your house key and uses it to enter your home while you are away. In the digital world, session fixation attacks work similarly, allowing hackers to exploit vulnerabilities in website session management and gain unauthorized access to your online accounts.

Understanding Vulnerability: Real-World Examples

Session fixation attacks have been used in various real-world scenarios to compromise user accounts and steal sensitive information. Here are some notable examples:

- **In 2017, hackers used session fixation to gain access to user accounts on a popular online forum.** They exploited a vulnerability in the forum's software that allowed them to predict and manipulate session IDs.
- **In 2019, attackers used session fixation to steal user data from a government website.** They tricked users into clicking on a malicious link that contained a pre-determined session ID, allowing them to access their accounts without needing passwords.
- **In 2021, hackers used session fixation to target online banking users.** They sent phishing emails containing malicious links that redirected users to fake banking websites with pre-determined session IDs, enabling them to steal financial information.

Safeguarding Your Digital Credentials: Proactive Steps

Learn from real-world scenarios to shield yourself against session fixation attacks. Consider these essential measures:

- ***Stay Watchful:*** Exercise caution when clicking links, especially those from unfamiliar sources or suspicious emails. Scrutinize URLs for errors, typos, or irregularities in sender details.
- ***Strengthen Passwords and Activate Multi-Factor Protection:*** Boost your online defense by utilizing robust passwords and enabling multi-factor authentication. This additional layer of security complicates hackers' attempts, even with knowledge of your password.
- ***Keep Software Up to Date:*** Regularly update your operating system, browser, and other software to their latest versions. These updates often include crucial security patches that address vulnerabilities exploited by hackers.
- ***Secure Logouts:*** Always log out of websites, particularly on public computers or shared devices. This straightforward action prevents unauthorized access if your device falls into the wrong hands.
- ***Select Secure Platforms:*** Select websites with strong session management techniques. Look for sites that use HTTPS and generate unique session IDs each time you log in.
- ***Stay Informed:*** Keep up with the most recent cybersecurity risks and vulnerabilities. This information enables you to understand hazards and take appropriate safeguards.
- ***Use Security Utilities:*** Investigate the use of security solutions such as firewalls and antivirus software. These technologies are critical for detecting and preventing malware and phishing efforts.
- ***Report Abnormal Activity:*** If you suspect your account has been compromised, act quickly. Report any such instances to the website as soon as possible, and strengthen your security by changing your password.

By taking these steps and remaining watchful, you can dramatically lower your risk of falling victim to session fixation assaults and preserve your online identity. Remember, your digital security is in your hands. You can traverse the digital world with confidence and keep your online accounts secure by taking proactive actions and remaining educated.

Credential Reuse Attacks

Let us embark on a journey into the world of credential reuse, a vulnerability that often goes unnoticed in the vast landscape of web authentication. Imagine having a favorite key that you use for various locks. Credential reuse is akin to using the same key for multiple doors, and if an attacker gets hold of it, they can open numerous gates.

In the digital space, users often reuse passwords across different accounts. This practice, while convenient, introduces vulnerabilities. If an attacker successfully acquires login credentials from one platform, they can test those credentials on other websites, exploiting the habit of using the same key for different locks.

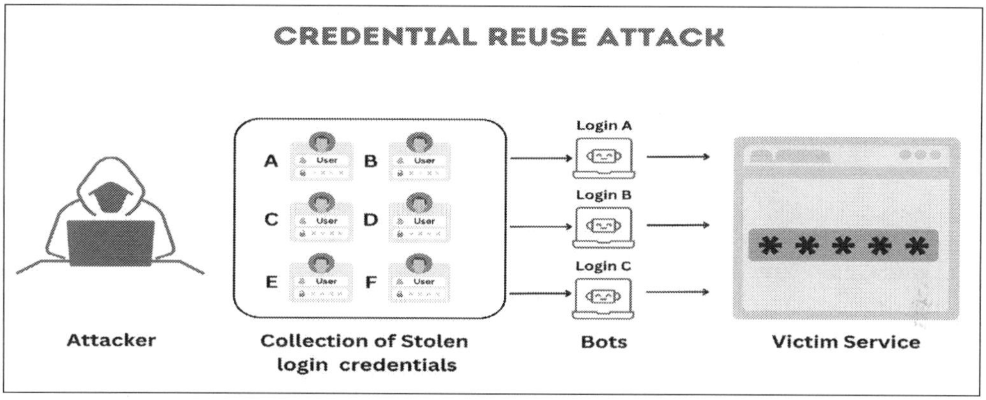

Figure 10.7: *Credential Reuse Attack*

Techniques for Exploiting and Bypassing Authentication using Credential Reuse:

- ***Credential Stuffing:***
    - Credential stuffing is like a relentless burglar trying to steal a key from multiple doors. Attackers leverage automated tools to systematically inject previously compromised username-password pairs across various platforms. If users have reused credentials, this technique becomes a potent means of unauthorized access.
- ***Password Spraying:***
    - Picture password spraying as a subtle, persistent mist. Instead of bombarding a single account with numerous passwords, attackers try a few commonly used passwords across multiple accounts. This method capitalizes on the tendency of users to use easily guessable passwords.
- ***Password Reversal:***
    - Some attackers employ the technique of password reversal, attempting to use the compromised password backward or with slight modifications. It is like trying a mirror image of your key to see if it unlocks the door.
- ***Brute-Force Attacks on Other Accounts:***
    - If an attacker successfully compromises an account with weak credentials, they might launch brute-force attacks on other accounts where the user

has reused the same password. It is like finding a hidden door in a fortress after breaching a weaker section.

Understanding these techniques is crucial, as it empowers both users and administrators to fortify their digital gates against credential reuse attacks. It is akin to advising against using the same key for every door and instead employing unique, robust keys for enhanced security.

Unmasking the Domino Effect: Practical Demonstrations of Credential Reuse Attacks

While understanding the theoretical aspects of credential reuse attacks is crucial, hands-on experience solidifies knowledge and empowers you to identify and mitigate these threats in real-world scenarios. So, let us delve into practical demonstrations where we can explore and experiment with these techniques in a controlled environment.

Exercise: Exploring Credential Stuffing Tools:

- ***Research and download a credential stuffing tool:*** Choose a tool that is used for educational purposes and not intended for malicious activities.
- ***Load the tool with a dataset of leaked credentials:*** This dataset can be obtained from publicly available sources or simulated as in Exercise 1.
- ***Target a specific website or service:*** Choose a website with a known vulnerability or a website you are comfortable experimenting with.
- ***Run the tool and monitor the results:*** Observe how the tool automatically attempts logins with the various stolen credentials.
- ***Analyze the success rate:*** Evaluate the effectiveness of the tool in bypassing authentication and gaining unauthorized access.

Note: These exercises are for educational purposes only. Conducting unauthorized credential-stuffing attacks or simulating phishing attempts on real websites is illegal and unethical. Always conduct these experiments in a controlled environment and avoid harming yourself or others.

By actively engaging in these hands-on demonstrations, you will gain valuable practical experience in identifying and mitigating credential reuse threats. You will also develop a deeper understanding of how hackers exploit this vulnerability and how you can protect yourself from becoming a victim. Remember, cybersecurity is a continuous learning process. The more you experiment and analyze vulnerabilities, the better equipped you are to navigate the digital world with confidence and keep your online identity and information secure.

Captcha Bypass Methods: Cracking the Code

Imagine a gatekeeper guarding a valuable treasure, only allowing entry to those who can decipher a secret code. In the digital world, this gatekeeper is called CAPTCHA, a challenge-response test designed to distinguish humans from bots and prevent automated attacks. However, like any lock, CAPTCHAs can be circumvented, posing a significant threat to online security.

Think of CAPTCHAs as digital puzzles that require human intelligence to solve. They are commonly used on websites and services to prevent automated programs from registering accounts, spamming comments, or engaging in other malicious activities. By requiring users to prove they are human, CAPTCHAs enhance online security and protect against automated threats.

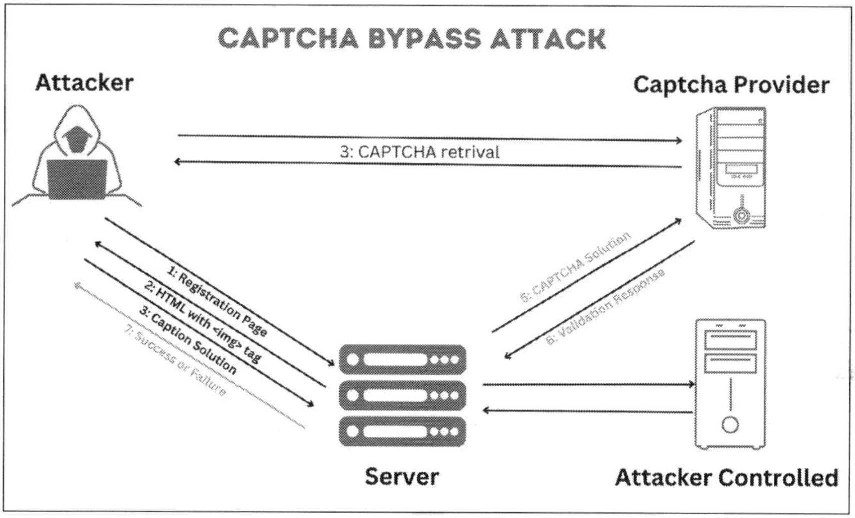

Figure 10.8: *CAPTCHA Bypass Attack*

Methods for Evading Captcha Controls

While CAPTCHAs serve as effective barriers, they are not invulnerable. Cyber attackers have devised various strategies to navigate past these safeguards, gaining entry to protected online content. Here are some common approaches:

- ***Optical Character Recognition (OCR)***: This technology enables machines to decipher and understand text, even when presented in distorted images. Hackers can leverage OCR tools to accurately solve text-based CAPTCHAs.
- ***Machine Learning***: Advanced algorithms can be trained on extensive datasets of CAPTCHA images and their corresponding solutions. This empowers

machines to discern patterns and progressively solve CAPTCHAs with heightened accuracy.

- ***Automation Tools:*** Bots can be programmed to interact with CAPTCHAs, mimicking human behavior. This allows them to surpass challenges relying on basic mouse movements or click patterns.
- ***Exploiting Vulnerabilities:*** CAPTCHA implementations may occasionally harbor vulnerabilities that hackers can exploit for evasion. This could involve pinpointing weaknesses in the code or manipulating the underlying system.
- ***Purchasing Bypass Services:*** In certain instances, hackers can procure access to online services providing CAPTCHA bypass solutions. These services often combine the aforementioned techniques, proving highly effective in outmaneuvering CAPTCHAs.

Advancements in CAPTCHA Technology

The basic CAPTCHA (Completely Automated Public Turing Test to Tell Computers and Humans Apart) has served as a barrier against automated bots, protecting websites from spam and malicious activities. However, its limitations are well-known, and attackers have devised sophisticated tactics to bypass them. CAPTCHA technology evolves alongside the digital landscape, aiming to stay one step ahead. Let us explore recent advancements, featuring both familiar classics and intriguing newcomers:

- ***Traditional Text-Based CAPTCHAs:*** The original and still widely used approach, presenting distorted text or sequences of characters for users to decipher.
  - ***Effectiveness:*** Simple and relatively effective against basic bots relying on simple pattern recognition.
  - ***Limitations:*** Easily bypassed by advanced AI-powered bots, susceptible to dictionary attacks, and accessibility concerns for visually impaired users.
- ***reCAPTCHA v3:*** This Google-developed solution moves beyond simple text recognition. It analyzes user behavior and website interactions, building a risk score based on factors like mouse movements, time spent on pages, and JavaScript execution.
  - ***Effectiveness:*** Highly effective against traditional bot attacks and script-based automation.
  - ***Limitations:*** May be fooled by advanced AI-powered bots mimicking human behavior.
- ***Invisible reCAPTCHA:*** This unobtrusive approach analyzes user interactions in the background, eliminating the need for explicit challenges. Users proceed seamlessly while the system silently assesses their legitimacy.
  - ***Effectiveness:*** Convenient for users and effective against basic bots.

  - ***Limitations:*** Might not be robust enough for high-security applications or against sophisticated attackers.
- ***Honeytrap CAPTCHAs:*** These CAPTCHAs embed hidden elements invisible to normal users but detectable by bots, triggering challenges only for suspicious visitors.
  - ***Effectiveness:*** Effective in identifying and deterring automated attacks.
  - ***Limitations:*** Can be computationally expensive for servers and potentially intrusive for legitimate users.
- ***Image Recognition CAPTCHAs:*** These leverage advanced image recognition technology to present users with challenges like identifying objects, classifying pictures, or selecting specific images.
  - ***Effectiveness:*** More resistant to automated solutions compared to text-based CAPTCHAs.
  - ***Limitations:*** Accessibility concerns for users with visual impairments and potential biases in image selection.
- ***Game-based CAPTCHAs:*** These engaging challenges involve tasks like puzzles, mini-games, or simple animations, adding a playful element to the authentication process.
  - ***Effectiveness:*** User-friendly and potentially more resistant to automated solutions.
  - ***Limitations:*** Can be time-consuming and might not be suitable for all types of websites.

Remember: No single CAPTCHA solution is foolproof. A layered approach combining different techniques and staying vigilant against emerging attack methods is crucial for effective protection. Additionally, consider:

- ***Adaptive Challenges:*** Adjusting the difficulty of CAPTCHAs based on user risk scores.
- ***Continuous Learning:*** Utilizing machine learning to automatically refine detection algorithms.
- ***Human-in-the-Loop Systems:*** Incorporating human review for complex or uncertain cases.

By understanding these advancements and adopting a comprehensive approach, organizations can leverage CAPTCHA technology effectively to mitigate the risks of bot attacks and safeguard their online environments.

Safeguarding the Treasure: Minimizing Captcha Bypass Risks

Thankfully, there are measures both website owners and users can adopt to reduce the dangers associated with CAPTCHA bypass methods:

- ***Opt for robust CAPTCHA solutions:*** Choose providers offering intricate challenges that pose difficulties for automated systems. Look for CAPTCHAs incorporating diverse elements like text, images, and audio to heighten complexity.
- ***Employ supplementary security measures:*** Do not rely solely on CAPTCHAs; enhance security by combining them with multi-factor authentication and stringent password criteria.
- ***Stay vigilant for suspicious behavior:*** Regularly review website logs and analytics to identify potential bot activities and investigate any irregular login attempts.
- ***Regularly update CAPTCHAs:*** Hackers continually devise new bypass methods. Keep your CAPTCHA systems up-to-date with the latest features and versions to stay ahead of evolving threats.
- ***Exercise caution:*** Users should be mindful of CAPTCHA risks and use them judiciously. Avoid using the same CAPTCHA solution across multiple accounts, and promptly report any dubious activities to the website owner.

By comprehending how CAPTCHAs function and the tactics employed to circumvent them, we can fortify our defenses against online threats. This collaborative effort between website owners and users ensures that CAPTCHAs remain potent guardians, protecting online security and thwarting unauthorized access.

Cracking the Code: Hands-on Guide to Bypassing Captchas

While understanding the theoretical aspects of CAPTCHA bypass techniques is crucial, gaining practical experience can solidify your knowledge and empower you to identify and mitigate these threats in real-world scenarios. So, let us delve into a step-by-step guide where we can explore and experiment with these techniques in a controlled environment.

Activity: Exploring Automation Tools for CAPTCHAs

- ***Select a website featuring a straightforward mouse-tracking CAPTCHA:*** Choose a site where users navigate a specific path or solve a puzzle using mouse movements.
- ***Capture your mouse actions during CAPTCHA completion:*** Utilize a screen

recording tool to document your mouse movements while tackling the CAPTCHA.

- ***Reenact the recorded mouse actions:*** Employ a playback tool to automatically recreate the recorded mouse movements on the CAPTCHA challenge.
- ***Evaluate the outcomes:*** Examine whether the automated replay successfully overcomes the CAPTCHA challenge.
- ***Explore diverse CAPTCHAs and recording approaches:*** Assess the effectiveness of automation tools against various CAPTCHA types, experimenting with different recording methods for more intricate challenges.

Note: These exercises are for educational purposes only. Bypassing CAPTCHAs on real websites without authorization is illegal and unethical. Always conduct these experiments in a controlled environment and avoid harming yourself or others.

By actively engaging in these hands-on exercises, you will gain valuable practical experience in identifying and mitigating CAPTCHA bypass threats. You will also develop a deeper understanding of how hackers exploit these vulnerabilities and the limitations of current CAPTCHA technologies.

Remember, cybersecurity is a continuous learning process. As CAPTCHA technology evolves, so too will the techniques used to bypass it. By constantly expanding your knowledge and staying informed about the latest developments, you can better protect yourself and your online resources from malicious actors.

Cookie Manipulation: Crumbling the Cookie Jar

Imagine a bakery that offers delicious treats, but instead of cash, they use special cookies to keep track of who has purchased what. In the digital world, these cookies are known as HTTP cookies, small pieces of data websites store in your browser to remember your login status, preferences, and other information. However, just like any cookie, these digital tokens can be manipulated, posing a significant security risk.

Imagine cookies as the digital keys to your online kingdom. When you log in, the website sends a cookie to your browser, holding critical information like your username and session ID. This clever mechanism keeps you logged in even when you revisit the site. While this convenience adds a layer of ease, it also opens a door to vulnerabilities. If a hacker tampers with or gains access to your cookies, they can pretend to be you, entering your online space without needing your password. This intrusion, known as cookie hijacking, can wreak havoc, leading to data breaches, financial losses, and identity theft.

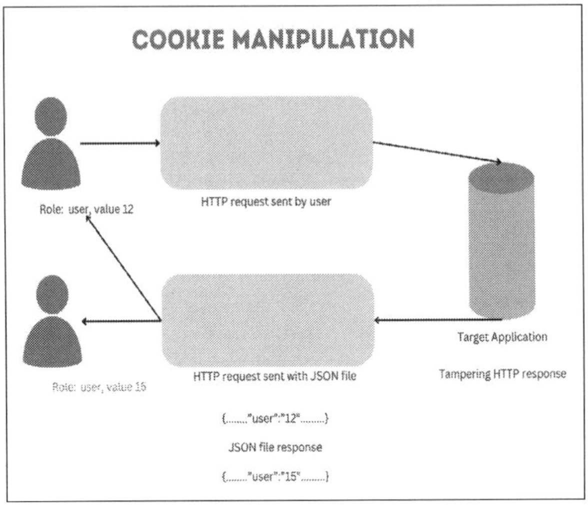

Figure 10.9: *Cookie Manipulation Attack*

Tampering with the Tokens: Techniques for Exploiting Cookie Manipulation

Hackers employ various techniques to exploit cookie vulnerabilities and bypass authentication:

- ***Cross-Site Scripting (XSS) Attacks***: Hackers inject malicious code into a website that steals your cookie data when you visit the page.
- ***Man-in-the-Middle (MitM) Attacks***: Hackers intercept your communication with a website and modify the cookies before they reach your browser.
- ***Session Hijacking***: Hackers steal your session cookie and use it to impersonate you on the website.
- ***Malicious Browser Extensions:*** Hackers trick users into installing extensions that steal their cookies or manipulate their browser settings.
- ***Phishing Attacks***: Hackers deceive users into visiting fake websites that appear legitimate and steal their cookies when they enter their login credentials.

Securing Your Digital Delicacies: Mitigating Risks of Cookie Tampering

The good news is that there are measures you can implement to shield your cookies and thwart manipulation:

- ***Activate HTTP Strict Transport Security (HSTS):*** This security feature encrypts the interaction between your browser and the website, creating a formidable barrier against hackers attempting to intercept your cookies.

- ***Turn Off Third-Party Cookies:*** Disable cookies deposited by websites not directly visited, as they can be exploited for tracking and advertising purposes. This action significantly diminishes the vulnerability to cookie hijacking.
- ***Opt for a Secure Browser:*** Choose a browser fortified with robust security features and ensure it stays up-to-date to the latest version for enhanced protection.
- ***Regularly Purge Your Cookies:*** Routinely cleansing your cookie collection serves as a protective measure, fortifying your data against potential unauthorized access.
- ***Exercise Caution with Unknown Links and Websites:*** Refrain from clicking on links originating from unfamiliar sources, and maintain suspicion towards websites demanding excessive permissions or attempting to mimic legitimate ones.
- ***Deploy a Cookie Oversight Extension:*** Ponder the installation of a browser extension designed for managing cookies, allowing you control over which ones are stored and utilized by various websites.
- ***Fortify with Robust Passwords and Multi-Factor Authentication (MFA):*** Bolster the security of your online accounts by employing formidable passwords and activating multi-factor authentication. This dual-layered approach ensures increased difficulty for hackers attempting to gain access, even if they manage to pilfer your cookies.

Understanding how cookies function and the strategies used to alter them allows you to take proactive efforts to protect your online security and keep hackers at bay. Remember that your internet privacy is entirely in your hands.

Unmasking the Sweet Deception: Practical Examples and Countermeasures against Cookie Manipulation

While understanding the theoretical aspects of cookie manipulation is crucial, gaining practical experience can solidify your knowledge and empower you to identify and mitigate these threats in the real-world scenarios. So, let us delve into practical examples and explore countermeasures to protect your digital cookie jar from unauthorized access.

Case Study 1: Cross-Site Scripting (XSS) Attack

Scenario: Imagine visiting a seemingly legitimate website that embeds malicious code. This code, injected by hackers, steals your cookies when you land on the page.

Impact: Hackers can use your stolen cookies to impersonate you and access your online accounts without needing your password.

Countermeasures:

- ***Use a web browser with robust XSS protection:*** Consider browsers like Firefox or Chrome, known for their advanced XSS protection features.
- ***Enable JavaScript protection extensions:*** Install extensions like NoScript or ScriptSafe to restrict unwanted scripts from running on websites.
- ***Be cautious of user-generated content:*** Avoid interacting with untrusted elements like comments, forums, or chat boxes where malicious scripts might be embedded.

Case Study 2: Encounter with Man-in-the-Middle (MitM) Intrusion

Situation: Picture connecting to a public Wi-Fi network infiltrated by cyber intruders. They intercept your communication with a website, tweaking your cookies before they reach your browser.

Impact: Cybercriminals can insert harmful code into your cookies or modify your session ID, granting them access to your online accounts while connected to the compromised network.

Preventive Measures:

- ***Deploy a VPN:*** Utilize a virtual private network to encrypt your internet traffic, making it challenging for hackers to intercept communication and pilfer cookies.
- ***Exercise caution on public Wi-Fi:*** If feasible, avoid logging in to online accounts or accessing sensitive data while connected to public Wi-Fi networks.
- ***Prioritize HTTPS-enabled websites:*** Ensure the website exhibits a lock icon in the address bar and features HTTPS in the URL, indicating a secure encrypted connection.

Case Study 3: Dealing with Malicious Browser Extensions

Scenario: Envision unwittingly installing a browser extension that inserts malicious code or steals cookies without your awareness.

Impact: The extension can purloin your login credentials, monitor your browsing behavior, and redirect you to phishing sites.

Risk Mitigation:

- ***Source trusted extensions only:*** Steer clear of downloading extensions from unfamiliar developers or websites.

- ***Review reviews and permissions***: Before adding an extension, meticulously assess user reviews and scrutinize the permissions it requests.
- ***Deactivate or uninstall unused extensions***: Regularly assess your installed extensions, deactivating or removing those no longer in use.

Securing Your Digital Treats: Navigating the Cookie Jar Safely

Through these case studies and practical defense strategies, you are not just learning; you are actively building the skills to identify and thwart cookie manipulation threats. This journey goes beyond recognizing vulnerabilities–it is about understanding how hackers exploit cookies and the essential steps to fortify your online security.

In the horizon of cybersecurity, it is crucial to grasp that learning is a continuous journey. As technology advances, so do the tactics of cookie manipulation. Stay watchful, stay informed, and implement the security practices shared above. With these measures, you can confidently traverse the digital landscape, ensuring your online cookie jar remains impervious to unauthorized access.

Token-Based Authentication Bypass

Imagine a secret handshake that grants access to a hidden treasure. In the digital world, this secret handshake is often represented by tokens and digital keys that unlock online resources and services. While convenient and efficient, token-based authentication systems can be vulnerable to exploitation, allowing unauthorized access to your valuable online treasures.

Think of tokens as digital keys that contain information about your identity and permissions. Instead of constantly entering your username and password, websites issue these tokens upon successful login, allowing you to access resources without re-authentication. Tokens can be stored in cookies, browser sessions, or even mobile apps, offering a seamless user experience.

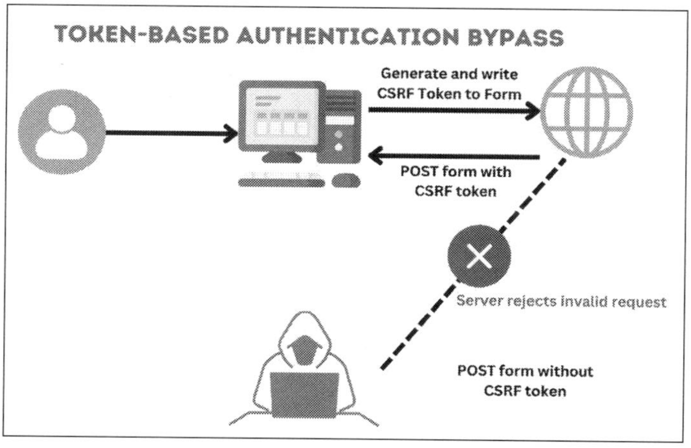

Figure 10.10: *Token-based Authentication Bypass*

Cracking the System: Exploiting Weaknesses in Token-Based Authentication

While token-based authentication systems offer convenience, they are not impervious to threats. Hackers employ diverse tactics to capitalize on vulnerabilities and circumvent these systems:

- ***Intercepting Tokens:*** Hackers can seize tokens during their journey between your device and the server, achieved through man-in-the-middle attacks or snooping on network traffic.
- ***Token Replay:*** Hackers can capture and replay valid tokens multiple times, allowing them unauthorized access to resources.
- ***Forging Tokens:*** Hackers can fabricate counterfeit tokens, complete with falsified information, mimicking legitimate tokens to elude authentication controls.
- ***Token Brute Force:*** Hackers resort to automated tools to systematically test various token combinations until they crack the code and discover a valid one.
- ***Exploiting Token Management Weaknesses:*** Hackers can take advantage of flaws in how tokens are stored or handled on the server or client side, gaining unauthorized access or escalating privileges.

Safeguarding the Treasure: Addressing Risks in Token-Based Authentication

Thankfully, there are various steps you can take to address the vulnerabilities associated with token-based authentication:

- ***Opt for robust token formats:*** Choose formats like JWT (JSON Web Token) with strong encryption and signing algorithms to enhance resistance against forgery or tampering.
- ***Secure token transmission:*** Employ HTTPS encryption to safeguard communication channels, thwarting attempts to intercept tokens during transmission.
- ***Shorten token expiration times:*** Limit the lifespan of tokens to minimize potential damage in case of compromise.
- ***Introduce multi-factor authentication:*** Enhance security by combining token-based authentication with other factors like passwords or biometrics.
- ***Monitor token activity:*** Regularly scrutinize token usage, logging any suspicious activity to detect breaches and unauthorized access attempts.

- ***Maintain updated software:*** Keep your operating system, browser, and other software current to patch vulnerabilities exploited by hackers.
- ***Adhere to secure token management practices:*** Implement secure practices for storing and managing tokens, both on the server and client side. This includes access control measures and encryption.
- ***Stay informed:*** Stay aware of the latest cybersecurity threats and vulnerabilities associated with token-based authentication.

Understanding the weaknesses in token-based authentication and proactively addressing them ensures the safety of your online valuables, preventing unauthorized access. Remember, protecting your digital identity is an ongoing effort.

Breaking the Code: Hands-on Exercises for Token-Based Authentication Bypass

While understanding the theoretical aspects of token-based authentication bypass is crucial, hands-on experience can solidify your knowledge and empower you to identify and mitigate these threats in real-world scenarios. So, let us delve into practical examples and explore exercises to demonstrate how hackers exploit these vulnerabilities.

Exercise: Exploring Token Interception Tools:

- ***Set up a controlled environment:*** Use a virtual machine to isolate the experiment and prevent any harm to your actual device.
- ***Install a network sniffing tool:*** Choose a tool like Wireshark or tcpdump to capture network traffic.
- ***Simulate token exchange:*** Login to a website or service that uses tokens and observe the captured traffic.
- ***Analyze the captured data:*** Identify the tokens used for authentication and understand how they are transmitted.

Crucial Reminder: These exercises serve purely educational purposes. Engaging in malicious attacks on genuine websites or services is both illegal and unethical. Always conduct these experiments within a controlled environment, prioritizing safety and ethical considerations.

Through active participation in these practical scenarios and hands-on exercises, you will amass valuable experience in recognizing and addressing vulnerabilities within token-based authentication systems. This involvement will deepen your comprehension of how hackers exploit these weaknesses and underscore the necessity of deploying robust security measures to safeguard your online identity.

Bear in mind that cybersecurity is an ongoing educational journey. As technology progresses, so do the methods employed to circumvent token-based authentication. By remaining vigilant, well-informed, and actively immersing yourself in ethical exploration, you can confidently traverse the digital landscape and fortify your online treasures against unauthorized access.

Conclusion

In our exploration of Authentication Bypass Techniques, we have unveiled the intricate details that might jeopardize web security. From the basics to manipulating cookies and bypassing with tokens, this journey has been both enlightening and empowering.

As we wrap up our journey within the pages of the ***Ultimate Web Application Pentesting Handbook***, you have traversed a dynamic landscape—from the foundational principles of ethical hacking to the complexities of authentication bypass techniques. We have covered networking essentials, delved into mastering Linux, unraveling the mysteries of cryptography and steganography, and even navigated the human element through social engineering.

With each chapter, you have unlocked new dimensions in the art of securing web applications. From the nuances of broken access control to the challenges of Cross-Site Scripting (XSS), you have become a guardian of digital fortresses.

A sincere congratulations on successfully navigating this handbook. You have not merely gained knowledge; you have earned the esteemed title of a defender against digital threats. Your journey does not conclude here; it is a commencement. May your expertise in web application security pave the way for countless secure online experiences.

As you move forward, armed with this wealth of information, remember you are not just a reader but a protector. Your dedication to understanding and mastering these techniques is a pivotal stride toward a safer digital future. Here's to your success in safeguarding a multitude of web applications with your newfound knowledge! Bravo!

Index

A

Access Control,
case studies 269, 271
Access Control,
vulnerabilities 260, 261
Asymmetric Encryption
about 101
benefits 102
fingerprints,
ensuring 104
limitations 103
private key, utilizing 102
public key,
preventing 102
scenario 103
secure mail,
communicating 102
Attack Vectors
about 238
application,
unveiling 239, 240
aspects 238, 239
payloads,
balancing 241, 242
payloads, crafting 240, 241
Authentication Bypass
about 273
fundamentals 273, 274
mechanisms 274-276
response,
manipulating 277, 278
trends, utilizing 276, 277
Autonomous System Numbers
(ASNs)
about 172
data, unveiling 172
DNS Server,
analyzing 173, 174
mechanism,
utilizing 172, 173
method, optimizing 173
roles, analyzing 173

B

Broken Access Control (BAC)
about 250, 251
Myths, unveiling 252, 253
vulnerability 251, 252
Burp Suite
about 191
functionalities,
utilizing 192
Proxy, unveiling 192
web application,
manipulating 191
Burp Suite, proxy features
application,
unraveling 193-198
essence, proxying 192
HTTPS, intercepting 193
Bus Topology
about 71
advantages 71
disadvantages 71

C

Captcha Bypass
- about 295
- aspects, optimizing 298, 299
- CAPTCHA Technology, utilizing 296, 297
- concepts 295
- strategies, navigating 295, 296

Charles Proxy
- about 211
- capabilities 212, 213
- installing 213, 214
- scenarios 211, 212
- server, debugging 211
- tools, utilizing 211

Charles Proxy with ZAP, integrating 215, 216

Ciphers
- about 106
- Advanced Encryption Standard (AES) 108
- Data Encryption Standard (DES) 108
- real word, applications 107
- types 107

Content Discovery
- about 179
- benefits 181
- datasets, leveraging 182-184
- ethical, considering 181, 182
- importance 179, 180
- OSINT, resources 184, 185
- techniques 180

Cookie Manipulation
- about 299
- aspects, preventing 301-303
- risks, tampering 300, 301
- techniques 300

Credential Reuse 292-294

Cryptography
- about 92
- cybersecurity, unveiling 92, 93
- Encryption 94
- open source, utilizing 112-115
- steganography, concealing 115

Cryptography, concepts
- homomorphic, computations 117, 118
- quantum, harnessing 117

Cryptography, threats
- cloud storage, securing 94
- email, preventing 93
- message app, privacy 93
- online banking, security 93
- website data, protecting 94

Cryptography, tools
- cryptool 111
- GPG 111
- OpenSSL 111

cybersecurity 2

D

Documentation
- about 219
- best practices 221, 222
- strategies 220
- structures, analyzing 219
- template, reporting 220
- tools, utilizing 221
- vulnerabilities 220

DOM-based XSS
- about 232
- characteristics 233
- consequences 233
- features, utilizing 233, 234
- key, concepts 232
- roles, utilizing 234
- scenarios 233

E

Encryption 94
Encryption, types
Asymmetric Encryption 101
Symmetric Encryption 97
Ethical Hackers
about 2-4
cybersecurity, impacting 11, 12
demystifying 13
digital, guardian 23, 24
dynamic, nature 8
importance 8
intellectual, techniques 14
journey, ahead 21, 22
lists, aspiring 23
Myth-busting 10, 11
white hat hackers 5
Ethical Hackers, environment
backup 21
continuous, learning 21
education, resources 21
guidelines 21
isolating 21
network, configuring 20
practices, responsing 21
snapshots 21
software, virtualizing 20
system, operating 20
Ethical Hackers, principles
confidentiality 6
consent 6
continuous, learning 7
legal, compliance 7
non-destructive, testing 6
privacy 7
scope 6
transparency 7
Ethical Hackers, roles
cyber threats, simulating 7
education, empowering 8
penetration, testing 8
principles, hacking 8
step ahead, staying 8
vulnerabilities, unveiling 7
Ethical Hackers, setting up
Aircrack-ng 17
Burp Suite 16
Hashcat 18
Hydra 19, 20
John the Ripper 17
Metasploit, framework 16
NMAP 14
OWASP ZAP 18
Snort 19
Wireshark 15
Ethical Hackers, terminologies
cybersecurity, checking 9
encryption 10
exploits 9
firewalls 10
Intrusion Detection System (IDS) 10
Intrusion Prevention Systems (IPS) 10
patch, managing 10
penetration, testing 9
risk, assessment 9
vulnerabilities 9
Ethical Hackers, vulnerabilities
critical infrastructure, protecting 12
education, promoting 13
financial sector, securing 12
IoT, safeguarding 13

F

Fiddler
  about 205
  benefits, utilizing 205, 206
  HTTP Traffic, unraveiling 208-210
  installing 206-208
  scenarios, analyzing 206
  web traffic, analyzing 205

G

Google Dorking
  about 153
  case, studies 159, 160
  effective keyword, creating 154
  operators, utilizing 155, 157
  principles, utilizing 158
  skills, utilizing 158
Google Dorking, mechanisms
  applications, locating 153
  devices, locating 154
  directories, finding 153
  intelligence, gathering 153
  login page, uncovering 154
  opportunities, uncovering 153
  structures, exploring 154
  website, identifying 153

H

Hash Function
  about 104
  common, functions 104
  scenario 105, 106
  spot, tampering 104
  using 104
Homograph Attacks
  about 133
  illusion, authenticity 133
  techniques, utilizing 133
  vigilance, defending 134, 135
HTTP status codes
  decoding 281-283
  vulnerabilities, unraveling 283, 284
Hybrid Topologies
  about 73
  advantages 74
  architectures 74
  types 74, 75
Hybrid Topologies, applications
  corporate, network 75
  industrial, network 75
  wireless, network 75

I

ID Attacks
  about 132
  Delegation, manipulating 132
  domain, entering 132
  guidelines, verifying 133
ID Attacks, techniques
  fake, documentation 132
  fear, urgency 132
  social proof 132
  trust, exploitating 132
IDOR
  about 253, 254
  techniques 255, 256
  tools, utilizing 255
  vulnerabilities 254
ifconfig command 78
IP Addresses, decoding 60, 61
IPv4, embracing 61
IPv6
  about 61
  best, practices 62
  concepts 61
  Subnetting 63
IPv6, transition ways
  Dual-stack, setup 62
  NAT64 translation 62
  tricks, tunneling 62

K

Kali Linux
  about 27
  community, supporting 28
  cybersecurity, tools 27
  ethical, hacking 28
  installing, steps 28-37

L

Linux
  about 25, 26
  aspect, utilizing 50-52
  Bash, scripting 55-57
  essentials, scripting 54, 55
  file permission, mastering 48-50
  hierarchy system, analyzing 52-54
  SysVinit, utilizing 46-48
Linux, boot process
  BIOS, unraveling 45
  GRUB, utilizing 45
  kernel, loading 45
  system, initializing 46
Linux, commands
  cat 43
  cd 37
  chmod 44
  chown 45
  clear 40
  cp 39
  grep 40
  help 42
  ls 38
  man 43
  mkdir 38
  mv 39
  nano 43
  ps 41
  pwd 41
  rm 40
  rmdir 38
  sudo 41
  top 42
  touch 40
Linux, components
  CentOS 27
  Kali 26, 27
  Parrot OS 27
  Ubuntu 26
Local Area Network, components
  Network Cables 65
  Network Interface Cards 65
  Switches, Hubs 65
  Wireless Access Points 66
Local Area Network (LAN)
  about 64
  connection, configuring 66
  experience, utilizing 65
  resources, optimizing 66

M

Malware, varieties
  ransomware 96
  trojans 96
  viruses 96
  worms 96
Mesh Topology
  about 72
  advantages 73
  disadvantages 73

N

Network
  about 60
  device, decoding 63
  protocols, unveiling 64
  tags, importance 63
Network, commands
  ipconfig/ifconfig 76
  Netstat 76
  Nslookup 76
  Ping 75
  Traceroute 76

Network, function
TCP 64
UDP 64
Networking Protocols 80
Networking Protocols, types
Transmission Control Protocol (TCP) 80
User Datagram Protocol (UDP) 83
Network, role
business, evoluating 60
global, interconnecting 60
smart technological, utilizing 60
Network Topologies
about 69
architectures, navigating 70
connectivity, probing 76
ifconfig, configuring 78-80
traceroute, unveiling 77
Network Topologies, types
Bus Topology 71
Mesh Topology 72
Ring Topology 72
Star Topology 70
Network, types
Local Area Network (LAN) 64
Wide Area Network (WAN) 66
Wi-Fi Essentials 68
NMAP
about 86
commands, utilizing 87
concepts 86
security, auditing 87-89
NMAP, key aspects
Network, discovery 86
OS, fingerprinting 86
port, scanning 87
service, enumerating 86

O

OTP Bypass Techniques 284-286

R

Real-Life Deceptions 130
red flags phishing, concepts
email, checking 128
generic, greetings 128
guidelines, navigating 129
misspelled URL 128
unmasking, phishing 128, 129
unsolicited, attaching 128
urgency, overload 128
Ring Topology
about 72
advantages 72
disadvantages 72

S

Secure Access Control Design
about 267
duties, separating 268
interfaces, analyzing 268
MFA, preventing 268
policies, clearfying 268
principles, embracing 267
RBAC, implementing 267
update, reviewing 267
Security Breaches
about 94
challenges 95
key, security 97
personal, implications 95
professional, implications 95
Security Breaches, threats
cyber, intruders 95
data breaches 96
Malware 96
Security Testing
about 188
case, studies 216-219
factors, utilizing 190
importance 188
roles, utilizing 188, 189
strategies, optimizing 190, 191

Security Testing, tools
AST 190
DAST 190
penetration, testing 189
SAST 190
vulnerability, scanning 189
Web Application Firewalls 189
Session Fixation
about 289-291
preventive, measuring 291
vulnerability 291, 292
Shodan
about 160
assets, analyzing 165, 166
capabilities 160
case, studies 161, 162
guidelines, usage 161
vulnerabilities 162-165
Social Engineering
about 120
case, studies 141
deceptive, unmasking 121
future, trends 140
readers, empowering 120, 121
significance, utilizing 120
Social-Engineer Toolkit, tools 138, 139
Social Engineering, cyber threats
human, factor 125
stealth, decepting 125
wide attack, surface 125
Social Engineering, essential skills
communicating 136
critical, thinking 136
empathy 136
ethical, awareness 136
influence 136
observation 136
Social Engineering, foundations
authority, exploitating 121
Fear Of Missing Out (FOMO) 121
reciprocity, principle 121
Social Engineering, functionalities
Email, crafting 138
media, manipulating 138
vulnerability, exploitating 138
website, cloning 138
Social Engineering, fundamentals
cybersecurity, utilizing 125
deceptive attacks, decrypting 124-125
reciprocity, psychology 122
roots, unveiling 122
Social Engineering, goals
control, accessing 125
data, theft 125
financial gain 125
Social Engineering, roles
cybersecurity 135
development, training 135
marketing 135
sales, nagotiation 135
Social Engineering, tectics
baiting 123
phishing 123
pretexting 123
Quid Pro Quo 124
tailgating 124
Social Engineering, tools
BeFF 137
CredSniper 137
Evilginx2 137
Gophish 137
MailSniper 137
Shellphish 137
Social-Engineer Toolkit 137
social mapper 137
SSL/TLS
about 174
certificates, demystifying 174, 175
components 177-179
concepts, utilizing 175, 176
insights, preventing 175
key, aspects 176, 177

Star Topology
about 70
advantages 70
disadvantages 71
Subnetting
about 63
benefits 63
network, managing 63
Symmetric Encryption
about 97
advantages 101
communication, securing 100
fingerprint, hashing 99
limitations 101
locksmith, creating 98
sender, verifying 99
transit, sealing 98

T

Token-Based Authentication
about 303
aspects, preventing 305, 306
risks, analyzing 304, 305
weakness 304
Transmission Control Protocol (TCP)
about 80
events, utilizing 81
natcat, analyzing 81-83
packages, making 81
Two-Factor Authentication (2FA) 286-288

U

Unlocking Phishing Tactics 126
Unlocking Phishing Tactics, aspects
Email Phishing 126
guidelines, analyzing 127
red flags phishing 128
spear, phishing 126
vishing 126
Unlocking Phishing Tactics, sequence
Bait, harverting 127
first, contract 127
Plea, informing 127
trust, building 127
urgency, unleashing 127
User Datagram Protocol (UDP)
about 83
Kali Linux, using 85
key, characteristics 83, 84
real word, applications 85
use, cases 84

V

Vertical Privilege Escalation (VPE)
about 256
concepts, utlizing 256
consequences 257
HPE, analyzing 258, 259
strategies 257
vulnerabilities 257

W

Web Reconnaissance
about 146, 147
importance 147
penetration, testing 147
real-world, instances 152, 153
Web Reconnaissance, aspects
active information, gathering 150
data analysis, reporting 150
objectives, preventing 150
passive information, gathering 150
Web Reconnaissance, reasons
ahead, staying 151
cybersecurity, crafting 151
incident, response 151
risks, understanding 151
weakness, spotting 151

Web Reconnaissance, steps
analyzing 151
enumerating 151
footprinting 151
identifying 151
mapping 151
scanning 151
Web Reconnaissance, techniques
network traffic, analyzing 149
Passive DNS, analyzing 147
port, scanning 149
social, engineering 148
website, fingerprinting 148
white hat hackers
about 5
concepts, steps 6
white hat hackers, benefits
cyberattacks, minimizing 5
mind, peace 5
security posture, enhancing 5
white hat hackers, goals
penetration, testing 5
security, audits 5
vulnerability, scanning 5
WHOIS
about 167
command-line tool, analyzing 171, 172
domain, preventing 168, 169
limitations 167, 168
privacy, impacts 169, 170
roles 167
Wide Area Network, infrastructure
Backbone Network 67
Internet Exchange Points 67
Internet Service Providers 67
Wide Area Network, technologies
lease lines 67
microwave, links 67
satellite, links 67
telephone, lines 67
Wide Area Network (WAN) 66
Wi-Fi Essentials 68
Wi-Fi Essentials, parts
Network Interface Cards (NICs) 68
Protocols, routing 69
Wireless Access Points 68
Wi-Fi Essentials, vulnerabilities
encrypting 69
firewalls 69
strong, password 69
updating 69

X

XSS, categories
Man-in-the-Browser Monster 224
Persistent Poisoner 224
Sneaky Impersonator 224
XSS (Cross-Site Scripting)
about 224
case, studies 246-248
concepts 224
inspect, handling 245, 246
mechanism, working 225, 226
mitigation, practices 244, 245
threat 224
vulnerabilities 243
XSS, types
DOM-based XSS 232, 233
Reflected XSS 226-228
Stored XSS 228-230

Z

ZAP Proxy
about 199
benefits 204
extension, allowing 200
features, utilizing 200
installings 201, 202, 203
methods, utilizing 204
security, aspects 200
tools, utilizing 203

Made in United States
Orlando, FL
05 November 2026

90229821R00188